Divine Presence and Guidance in Israelite Traditions

THE JOHNS HOPKINS NEAR EASTERN STUDIES
Hans Goedicke, General Editor

Hans Goedicke, *The Report about the Dispute of a Man with His Ba*

J. J. M. Roberts, *The Earliest Semitic Pantheon*

John D. Schmidt, *Ramesses II: A Chronological Structure for His Reign*

David Lorton, *The Juridical Terminology of International Relations in Egyptian Texts through Dyn. XVIII*

Bernard Frank Batto, *Studies on Women at Mari*

Hans Goedicke, *The Report of Wenamun*

Hans Goedicke and J. J. M. Roberts (eds.), *Unity and Diversity: Essays in the History, Literature, and Religion of the Ancient Near East*

Patrick D. Miller, Jr., and J. J. M. Roberts, *The Hand of the Lord: A Reassessment of the "Ark Narrative" of 1 Samuel*

Thomas W. Mann, *Divine Presence and Guidance in Israelite Traditions: The Typology of Exaltation*

Hans Goedicke, *The Protocol of Neferyt*

Divine Presence and Guidance in Israelite Traditions: The Typology of Exaltation

Thomas W. Mann

The Johns Hopkins University Press
Baltimore and London

Manufactured in the United States of America

The Johns Hopkins University Press, Baltimore, Maryland 21218
The Johns Hopkins Press, Ltd., London

Library of Congress Cataloging in Publication Data

Mann, Thomas Wingate.
    Divine presence and guidance in Israelite traditions.

    (The Johns Hopkins Near Eastern studies)
    Bibliography
    1. Presence of God. 2. Assyro-Babylonian religion—
Relations—Judaism. 3. Judaism—Relations—Assyro-Baby-
lonian. I. Title. II. Series: Johns Hopkins Univer-
sity. Near Eastern studies.
BS1192.6.M36   296.3'11   76–49846
ISBN 0–8018–1919–9

For my parents,
Wilton and Dorothy,
and for Constance,
who is well named

CONTENTS

List of Illustrations

Figure

ACKNOWLEDGMENTS

The following study is a revised version of the doctoral dissertation I submitted to Yale University Graduate School in 1975. Its origins, however, can be traced back to seminar papers written for Professor W. Sibley Towner while I was still a student at Yale Divinity School. Further work on the topic was done in a seminar with Professor Brevard S. Childs, to whom I owe much more than the present study could hope to show. For very careful and considerate advice, especially on Part One, I am grateful to Professor William W. Hallo. The influence of his writings will be all too apparent to the reader, although this does not imply that Professor Hallo is responsible for my own interpretive errors. Appreciation is also due to Professors Hans Goedicke and J. J. M. Roberts for accepting this work as part of the Johns Hopkins Near Eastern Studies, and for their counsel and support during the process of revision. I am also grateful to Princeton Theological Seminary for underwriting part of the costs of revision, and to Charles D. Myers, Jr., for help with proofreading and the index.

Above all, I am deeply indebted to my doctoral adviser, Professor S. Dean McBride, Jr. He was always patient, yet thoroughly critical; always encouraging, yet extremely challenging. His knowledge of the field, and his commitment to its explication, have served as a constant model. Without his presence and guidance, I am sure that I would have wandered aimlessly "in a land through which no one can pass."

Aside from my academic mentors, there are those to whom this book is dedicated with warm affection. For many years of financial support from my parents, and for their faithfulness, I shall always be thankful. Finally, there is, of course, one other person without whom this study, and, indeed, my years of graduate work as a whole, would have been far more difficult. That is the person who paid for it all, and, no doubt, paid far more than she had expected. For those years of sacrifice, of unstinting support and continual encouragement, I am deeply grateful to Constance Weigle Mann.

ABBREVIATIONS

In addition to the standard abbreviations within the fields of Old Testament and ancient Near Eastern Studies, the following have also been used. For details, the reader is referred to the bibliography.

ANET   Pritchard, *Ancient Near Eastern Texts*, 3rd ed.

ARAB   Luckenbill, *Ancient Records of Assyria and Babylonia*.

ARI   Grayson, *Assyrian Royal Inscriptions*.

CMHE   Cross, *Canaanite Myth and Hebrew Epic*.

CTCA   Herdner, *Corpus des tablettes en cunéiformes alphabétiques découvertes à Ras Shamra-Ugarit*.

IGL   Falkenstein, *Die Inschriften Gudeas von Lagaš*.

RLA   *Reallexikon der Assyriologie und vorderasiatischen Archäologie* (entries under Hrouda, et al.).

SAHG   Falkenstein and von Soden, *Sumerische und akkadische Hymnen und Gebete*.

SGL I   Falkenstein, *Sumerische Götterlieder*, Teil I.

SM   Kramer, *Sumerian Mythology*.

TCL 3   Thureau-Dangin, *Textes cunéiformes du Louvre*, III.

WM   Haussig, ed., *Wörterbuch der Mythologie*, Band I, Abteilung 1.

INTRODUCTION

Issues and Procedure

The purpose of this study is to investigate the form and function of
motifs of divine presence and guidance in the Old Testament. Most of our
attention will focus on the narratives describing Israel's journey through
the wilderness from Egypt to Canaan, but our interest also will extend to
the period of the Judges (Judges 4-5) and especially to the Davidic-
Solomonic empire. Much of this material is infused with motifs of divine
presence and guidance. In the narratives in Exodus and Numbers, Yahweh
goes before his people in the form of various divine agents (pillar of
cloud and fire, messenger, ark, etc.) in order to guide them out of Egypt,
through the wilderness, on their way to the land of promise. At moments
of crisis, Yahweh also appears in the cloud at the Tent of Meeting, and
the same imagery, of course, is involved in the Sinai theophany. Similarly, the story of the crossing of the Jordan emphasizes the role of the
ark as the symbol of Yahweh's presence and guidance. Finally, the rise
of the Davidic empire is based on Yahweh's presence with David in battle,
and is expressed in the transferral of the ark to Jerusalem. It will be
our purpose to examine the form and function of the various literary
motifs for divine presence and guidance in these narratives. Why did
they become so important in the story of the Reed Sea deliverance, the
wilderness period, the crossing of the Jordan, and the rise of David?
How is the function of these images related to the roles of Moses, Joshua,
and David, as leaders of the people? What is the connection between the
emergence of Israel as a political entity and the fact that such imagery
suddenly blossoms in the book of Exodus? How is the use of these motifs
connected with the recognition of Yahweh's sovereignty over Israel as
well as over her foes?

It is our contention (developed below) that scholarship has largely
ignored the importance and richness of some of these motifs, tending

1

instead to view them only as they reflect other, presumably more important concerns, such as the Sinai theophany or the covenant cult. So, for example, the distinct intensity with which the prose accounts of the wilderness period deal with the mutual problems of divine presence and guidance has been relegated to secondary status. We believe that the significance of these themes for the development of Israelite religion merits greater attention and illumination. A sketch of the widely diverging lines that Old Testament research has taken on the subject of epiphany[1] raises the question of how the results of this work have clarified the use of related motifs within the narratives concerning Israel's Wilderness wanderings.

Following the Introduction, our attention will turn in Part I to a number of major ancient Near Eastern texts, as well as to iconography. Our purpose here will be to investigate the historical, liturgical, and literary context in which motifs of divine presence are found. In doing so, we will be applying a typology developed by William W. Hallo--the "typology of exaltation"--within which we believe motifs of divine presence have an important place.[2]

In Part II, an attempt will be made to apply our conclusions from the Near Eastern material to the Old Testament, and especially to those stories that report the Wilderness March from the Reed Sea to the Jordan River, as well as the rise of the Davidic monarchy. Our purpose here will be to observe both the similarities and the differences between the ancient Near Eastern and the Old Testament understanding of the relationship between divine presence and the typology of divine and human exaltation.

History of Interpretation

In several important respects Hermann Gunkel set the agenda for the contemporary critical discussion of epiphany traditions in the Old Testament. In *Schöpfung und Chaos* (1895), Gunkel compared the accounts of Genesis 1 and Revelation 12 with the Babylonian creation myth, *Enuma eliš*. In the process of interpreting motifs related to this material throughout the Old Testament, he concluded that the biblical descriptions of divine self-manifestation derived from two sources: the Sinai experience and the Babylonian creation myth. According to Gunkel, those epiphanies that portray a conflict between Yahweh and the sea (e.g. Habakkuk 3; Nahum 1; Psalm 18) stem from the Babylonian tradition, while those that either refer to Sinai by name (e.g. Deut 33.2) or make use of volcanic imagery, stem from the experience most fully narrated in Exodus 19.[3] Gunkel emphasized that the conflict motif was borrowed from the Mesopotamian tradition at the earliest period of Israel's existence in Canaan, and was not a late (Exilic) adoption.[4] Moreover, the Old Testament exemplars of this motif are never employed with conscious references to the Babylonian creation myth itself but "exist only as motifs of the poetic tradition."[5] In his literary analysis, Gunkel then suggested that both the Sinai and conflict motifs of epiphany are found in association with various *Gattungen*,[6] but by themselves are part of the general *Gattung* that Gunkel termed the "hymn."[7]

Gunkel's work thus posed several important issues for future research: to what extent were biblical accounts of epiphany rooted in Israel's own experience? If there was significant borrowing, did it consist of isolated literary motifs or was Israel influenced by the substance of a mythic pattern? Was there an original cultic *Sitz im Leben* for epiphany *per se*, or were the motifs primarily used in hymnic literature, appropriate to many different cultic occasions? And, considering the basic outline of Gunkel's reconstruction, can we trace in detail the development of the use of epiphany motifs from Israel's early history to the rise of apocalyptic?

Although the responses to these issues have been complex, reflecting as they do various critical stances, we may discern two major methodological orientations diverging from Gunkel's work. His interest in the Babylonian creation myth led some scholars into an energetic search for ancient Near Eastern myth and ritual patterns by which it was believed many Old Testament texts could be clarified. On the other hand, Gunkel's efforts to recover the "settings in life" of Old Testament texts themselves led others to suggest new configurations in the institutional life of Israel that stand behind her literary heritage.

(1) The Form-critical and Traditio-historical Approaches

Gunkel's methodology and conclusions concerning the Sinai tradition were reflected in the continuing interpretation of epiphany. Gerhard von Rad's epochal study of the Hexateuch in 1938,[8] which itself followed in part Albrecht Alt's form-critical conclusions,[9] sought the source and transmission of the Sinai tradition, which von Rad identified with "the theophany and the making of the covenant."[10] Von Rad suggested that the

3

tradition itself was ancient, but that the literary account of it in J and E was relatively late. He noted that there were "some free, poetical variants of this Sinai tradition" still preserved--Deut 33.2, 4; the introduction to Judges 5; and Habakkuk 3 (we shall call these the "classic epiphany texts").[11] All three show that Sinai and theophany belong together without association to other traditions such as Exodus or Wilderness wanderings.[12] Von Rad then claimed that the "setting in life" of the tradition must lie in the cultic sphere, and he cited Mowinckel's suggestion of the New Year Festival with approval. However, von Rad asserted against Mowinckel that the Sinai narrative is not an *account* of the New Year Festival but "the cult-legend of a particular cultic occasion,"[13] which can only be the autumnal Feast of Tabernacles for covenant renewal, originally practiced at Shechem.[14] Although the place of epiphany within the festival itself is left unclear,[15] its connection to the Sinai covenant renewal tradition appears to be persistent and exclusive.[16]

The interpretation of Old Testament epiphany motifs implicit in von Rad's work was elaborated by Artur Weiser with particular reference to the Psalms. In an article on Psalm 77,[17] Weiser denied that the epiphany passage was a secondary literary unit and refused any modern psychological interpretations of its position. Instead, he asserted, the Psalm reflects an actual cultic event, the epiphany of Yahweh in the sanctuary, coming "on the cloud from Sinai . . . over the cherubs of the ark."[18] Weiser's position was reinforced in his subsequent studies in the Psalter.[19] Epiphanies in the Psalms are seen as reflections of the covenant festival in the cult, and the Sinai narrative itself is the "*Urbild* and *Kanon* for the festival tradition."[20] Weiser's more recent article on Judges 5 similarly posits that a cultic event lies behind hymnic material.[21] Judges 5 is not simply a victory song or an epic poem, but a liturgical composition for the cultic celebration of victory over enemies and of renewed intertribal solidarity as Yahweh's people.[22] Here, as elsewhere, the epiphany (vss. 4-5) is part of the cultic celebration, and its traditional stamp comes from long cultic transmission. Rather than describing Yahweh's advent in a storm during the battle, vss. 4-5 function as a cultic confession to Yahweh.[23]

Walter Beyerlin's study of the Sinai traditions further exhibits the viewpoint of Weiser.[24] For Beyerlin, the epiphany of Yahweh is connected with the covenant cult from the earliest times. During Israel's desert

4

sojourn at Kadesh, Yahweh appeared at the Tent of Meeting, which also served to house the ark from the very beginning. The ark itself was originally a container for the law, and only came to be associated with epiphany after Israel settled in Canaan and concern for Yahweh's presence became troublesome.[25] The classic passages that deal with Yahweh's coming from Sinai or those that deal with the problem of Yahweh's guidance (Exod 33.12-17) reflect this cultic crisis, as does the reinterpretation of the ark by means of the Canaanite 'Cloud-Rider' motif.[26] The motifs that utilize clouds of smoke ($^c nn$, $^c \check{s}n$) to conceal Yahweh himself have been influenced by the incense ritual, but not before the early Canaanite period.[27]

A strong dissenting voice to Weiser's analysis is raised by Claus Westermann, who has also treated the subject of epiphany in connection with the Psalms.[28] Westermann criticizes the cultic school and suggests that the Psalms may best be seen as examples of modes of prayer rather than as cultic or literary units.[29] He distinguishes between "declarative hymns" (to which epiphany belongs) that have their *Sitz im Leben* in "the experience of God's intervention in history," and "descriptive hymns" that are closer to the cult and depict God in "the fullness of his being and activity."[30] In the second part of his book, Westermann reviews the Babylonian and Egyptian hymns and finds the former to be almost purely descriptive, while the latter have many parallels to epiphany Psalms in the Old Testament.[31] However, although the schema of Near Eastern hymns has been borrowed, what were once cosmico-mythological events are now historical ones.[32]

As for epiphany itself, it is never an independent unit but is always originally a part of larger Psalms (probably victory hymns)[33] to which it is naturally linked by the common theme of Yahweh's help to Israel against her enemies.[34] Also, Westermann suggests an original form[35] from which the epiphany descriptions could have developed:

1. God's coming from, or going forth from . . .

2. Cosmic disturbances which accompany this coming of God

3. God's (wrathful) intervention for or against . . .[36]

In opposition to the approach expressed most insistently by Weiser, Westermann (followed by E. Lipiński)[37] asserts that the Sinai epiphany is not the prototype for the epiphanies in the Psalter; these can more reasonably be seen as rooted in the original experience at the Reed Sea.[38] This is partly a result of Westermann's distinction between epiphany and

5

theophany. Epiphany has the purpose of divine aid in the context of historical events; theophany has as its purpose divine communication through a mediator to the cultic community. Epiphany emphasizes the spatial *origin* of God's advent, theophany the *goal*; epiphany is primarily described by meteorological (storm) phenomena, theophany by volcanic phenomena. Thus such passages as Exodus 19 and Judges 5 are understood to present quite different forms of divine appearance.[39]

This distinction has an immediate appeal in its attempt to deal with the ambiguity of our secondary terminology. However, the simplicity that gives it such force may also carry serious weaknesses; therefore the distinction must be tested against the biblical evidence.[40] The emphasis on communication ("theophany") may reflect a more complex development of interpretation of "epiphany," rather than the two being separate types altogether. Thus it is possible that a single tradition or literary source could speak of the intervention of divine presence within a specific historical event, as well as understanding divine presence as a form of communication to an individual or group. Using Westermann's categories, for example, one wonders how to classify the cloud phenomenon, which is used for communication (e.g., Exod 33.7-11) but also for nonverbal guidance (Exod 13.21-22).

Finally, we turn to the recent work of Jörg Jeremias, *Theophanie: Die Geschichte einer Alttestamentlichen Gattung*,[41] which is the first full-length study of a major aspect of the topic and therefore deserves more complete treatment. Jeremias has focused his attention on theophany[42] descriptions in which God himself is not seen, but the phenomena signaling his presence are emphasized. Thus he excludes divine appearances to the patriarchs (cf. J. Kenneth Kuntz[43]), or those texts that portray divine hypostases (1-2). As the subtitle indicates, the method employed is form-criticism, amplified by a section on tradition history (Part II). Jeremias does not directly confront questions concerning the date of literary formulation of the various texts (6).

After separating the "*Gattung* of the theophany descriptions" from its context in numerous psalms, Jeremias proceeds to find "the oldest obtainable form of the *Gattung*" (3-6). Since Judges 5 is commonly acknowledged to be an ancient text, he begins his search here. An analysis of vss. 4-5, along with other texts (especially Ps 68.8-9), leads Jeremias to posit behind this description an older "dual element form" that speaks of "an approach of Yahweh" and of the "upheaval of nature."[44]

6

This is the oldest form of theophany description in the Old Testament, and from it, all others eventually developed (15). The rest of Part I of the book discusses this development, tracing it through virtually all of the Old Testament texts that speak of theophany. In a meticulous form-critical analysis, Jeremias finds various permutations, combinations, and dissolutions of the original form. There are infusions of new material, changes in purpose, specification of cause and effect, expansion of the first and second elements of the form (hereafter designated A and B), expansions of A or B with dissolution of the other, and finally, the "complete dissolution of the form" (16-72).

In Part II, the tradition history section, Jeremias presents a general discussion (followed in III:4 by a more specific one) of storm deities in Near Eastern material and concludes that borrowing by Israel, especially from Syria-Palestine, is implied (73-90). He then turns to seven major tradition-complexes to question whether they influenced the theophanic *Gattung*. The *Chaoskampf* tradition is found to be a mixture of Babylonian and Ugaritic patterns, and, moreover, to be secondary traditio-historically to the Reed Sea traditions (90-96). The Day of Yahweh and theophany descriptions influenced one another, although each originally had its own peculiar motifs (97-100). Surprisingly, the Sinai theophany motifs reveal scant literary parallels with the theophanic form. Sinai is thus not a literary prototype for the *Gattung*, principally because the latter is found in hymnic material, while Sinai accounts are narrative (100-111). Similarly the ark, divine kingship, and the peculiar tradition of 1 Kings 19 (Elijah at Horeb) have influenced the form only in late isolated incidences (111-116). Within the traditions reflecting the "point of departure of Yahweh," Sinai is traditio-historically the oldest (115-117).

In Part III, Jeremias turns to the question of the "*Sitz im Leben* of the *Gattung*." The arguments of Mowinckel, Weiser, Beyerlin, and Kaiser are dismissed as reconstructions: the Jerusalem cult is not the *Sitz*.[45] Jeremias now turns to an examination of the literary context in which the theophanic accounts are found. He determines that the various passages can be divided into four *Gattungen*: "Yahweh hymn;" "prophetic announcement of judgment;" "prophetic announcement of salvation;" and prose accounts (123). The fourth (Exodus 19; 1 Kings 19; Ezekiel 1) arose independently from the theophanic *Gattung* but, in part, adopted concepts from and added to the *Gattung* (136). The field of

Gattungen relevant to the question of the *Sitz* is thus narrowed down to two: hymnic texts and prophetic judgment oracles. Now, since the form AB fits the hymn more closely than the prophetic material, the latter cannot be the provenance of the *Gattung*. Thus the "*Gattung* of the theophany descriptions is attached to the hymn from the outset" (138).

Now, from the hymn, several potential candidates for the "'regular experiences and necessities of life'" that stand behind the *Gattung* are omitted for various reasons.[46] Instead, we must turn to Judges 5, which reveals the original *Sitz im Leben* to be "in the victory song of the wars of Yahweh."[47] This fits with other features of the theophanic texts: Yahweh the warrior, links with *Chaoskampf*, Near Eastern parallels, Reed Sea, and the day of Yahweh (146-148).

This history of the *Gattung* can now be outlined. The origins of A and B are not in the traditions already examined (Part II). Rather, B was adopted from Israel's neighbors.[48] A, on the other hand, has not been borrowed. The parallels are few and weak. Since the *Gattung* could not have been an *ad hoc* creation for the victory song, it must go back to earlier tradition, and that can hardly be anything other than Sinai. Thus, the Sinai *tradition* had a decisive role in the origin of our *Gattung*, although without its *literary* formulations influencing the theophany descriptions (155, emphasis supplied).

Thus A stems from Sinai traditions, B from Israel's neighbors. The two were first combined within the context of victory celebration (157). This setting, however, operated for only a short time in Israel's history. With the rise of the monarchy, the classic institution of holy war was replaced by the professional military, thus dissolving the *Sitz im Leben* for songs like that ascribed to Deborah (144-145, 158). The *Gattung* was now free to follow its rather tortuous journey. While the *Chaoskampf* and Reed Sea traditions may have influenced AB before it was separated from its *Sitz* (151), it is more likely that they and the other traditions (including storm imagery) were assimilated after the break (156-157). Thus originally AB was not connected at all with Reed Sea, Jordan, Wilderness, Conquest, or Election traditions.[49]

Jeremias's study is most impressive in its comprehensive treatment of the theophanic material throughout the Old Testament. At least a descriptive analysis is offered of all the major texts, and the principal traditions commonly associated with theophany are taken into account. Nevertheless, one cannot help being at first puzzled and finally frustrated by his line of argument. He has reconstructed a *Form* that by his own admission is not attested, then has used it as a rigorous standard by which to judge every other occurrence of the *Gattung* as having secondary accretions or deletions. Surely, if the *Gattung* enjoyed such a short life (as Jeremias presumes), it is of little help in interpreting form-critically the later passages that are related to it. Moreover, Jeremias never establishes clearly just what the *Gattung* is. Often, it appears to be identical with the reconstructed short *Form*: ". . . the theophany texts of the *Gattung* in fact speak *per definitionem* of an approach of Yahweh and of the resultant upheaval of nature" (72, cf. 109). Elsewhere, the *Gattung* appears to include the full-blown examples of the genre in general. But if these represent the *Gattung*, they are of the homeless variety, having no longer a *Sitz im Leben* of their own, but depending on the surrounding context for their setting. In the end the theophany passages are found to lie in four *Gattungen*, which are subsequently narrowed down to one—the hymn—which leads us to Judges 5, which is where we began. In short, Jeremias's study is a classic case of overextended form-critical method.

Other problems arise concerning Jeremias's traditio-historical analysis. The conclusion that the Sinai theophany is traditio-historically the provenance of part A of the theophanic *Gattung*, yet has exerted no influence on the *Gattung* literarily, is indeed awkward. Jeremias himself confesses that the problem remains "rätselhaft" (155). Also puzzling is the separation of A and B as being respectively (proto-?) Israelite and foreign in origin. Interestingly, Lipiński (and presumably Westermann) has come to the opposite conclusion concerning A. Furthermore, Jeremias appears to allow for some preparation for B within proto-Israelite traditions, among which he includes Sinai. He also claims that at least two of the Adad hymns have the same "dual element" form as the Old Testament theophany descriptions (79, 81). One can only conclude that the significance and relevance of Near Eastern parallels for the topic has not been precisely determined by Jeremias's method.

One also wonders if Jeremias has done justice to traditions other than Sinai. Why, for example, does Exodus 15 have little or no indication of the *Gattung* as described by Jeremias, yet surely reveals elements of a victory song? Why does the *Gattung*, which ostensibly was linked with holy war motifs early in the Judges period, not have its roots in the Conquest traditions? Finally, are there no connections between the epiphany passages and the traditions of Yahweh's guidance (cloud, ark, tent)[50] in the wilderness, or between the *use* of the epiphany motif and Israel's understanding of herself as "all Israel" and of her election?

In short, a rigid form-critical analysis of the material has produced confusing results, and traditio-historical analysis has reconstructed an awkward line of development. A more convincing treatment will have to deal with the material, at least initially, as literary motifs of remarkable plasticity, and traditio-historical attention must not be fixated on the question of the Sinai theophany alone.

(2) The History of Religions Approach

Gunkel's work on the Babylonian creation myth and his attempts to delineate the individual cultic settings of the Psalms were soon combined and expanded, particularly by Mowinckel and the Scandinavian school. These developments are now generally well-known and need not detain us unduly.[51] As E. Lipiński notes, the trend was already set by P. Volz in 1912 when he posited an autumnal New Year festival (Tabernacles) in pre-exilic Israel that included the epiphany of God in the cult, a ritual combat with his enemies, the reinstatement of his kingship, and the renewal of the covenant—all to be compared to the Babylonian Akitu festival.[52] Thus although this approach (especially as employed by Mowinckel) has also emphasized the role of covenant renewal, as has the form-critical and traditio-historical schools, its basic appeal has been to conformance with a myth and ritual pattern borrowed from Sumero-akkadian culture. Although this "New Year" pattern has not lost its defenders--and we have seen how it was adapted by von Rad-- its immediate relevance has been seriously challenged due to the literary treasures unearthed at Ras Shamra.

With the discovery and progressive translation of the Ugaritic texts since 1929, our understanding of the Old Testament literature (particularly the early poetry) and of Israel's cultural milieu has grown enormously. The result of this vigorous scholarship has opened up new possibilities for the study of epiphany motifs, both from the standpoint of literary analysis and of the use of mythic "patterns." Among those of numerous other scholars,[53] two studies by William F. Albright stand out as indicators. His articles on Habakkuk 3 and Psalm 68[54] demonstrate quite clearly the extent to which Israel's early poetry belongs to the linguistic and conceptual traditions attested in the Ugaritic texts. Moreover, his interpretation of the theophany of Yahweh in Hab 3.8-15 on the basis of "the underlying Canaanite mythology" of the battle of the storm god, Baal, against the Sea[55] illustrates the radical shift in our knowledge of Israel's Near Eastern environment, since Gunkel assigned this same motif to a Babylonian provenance.[56] In short, the effect has been to free Old Testament scholarship from an exclusive search for Sumero-akkadian linguistic and structural parallels, and thus to allow it (albeit with many of the same dangers) to seek out Israel's Northwest Semitic heritage.

The work of H. J. Kraus in some respects can be seen as exemplary of the attempt to reconcile these new discoveries with the traditio-historical and form-critical work that we have sketched above. Following the latter, Kraus presupposes the separation of Sinai traditions (Shechem), Exodus-Conquest traditions (Gilgal) as proposed by von Rad,[57] yet he never mentions epiphany within the context of the covenant ceremonies at Shechem,[58] for, in fact, it is not covenant renewal but the "festival of the installation of the Ark"[59] that is the unifying cultic event in the Psalms. This processional is the central event in the reconstructed Feast of Tabernacles, "the principle feast" of Israel celebrating the election of Zion and of David, which relies heavily on Psalms 132 and 24, as well as on 1 Kings 8.[60] This in turn must be seen as a further development of Kraus's reconstruction of the ark cult of Gilgal as the bearer of the Exodus-Conquest traditions.[61] Indeed, it is only within the context of the ark processional that Kraus discusses epiphany in general,[62] and the ark processional is, for him, the most reasonable explanation of what actually happened in the cult.[63]

It is here that the Ugaritic evidence is introduced. Epiphany accounts generally reveal a rich mixture of Israelite and Canaanite traditions.[64] The ark cult itself soon took on Canaanite-Jebusite traditions inherited from the ancient Jerusalem cult.[65] More particularly, Judges 5 and Psalm 68 reflect elements of the Canaanite Baal myth connected with the cultic center at Mount Tabor. This mythic background has been adapted by a three-tribe Israelite confederacy to refer to Yahweh's historical advent at the defeat of Sisera, thus providing an "advent" concept in contrast to the Jerusalem tradition of Yahweh's presence.[66]

Thus Kraus has shifted the main focus for epiphany away from the Sinai covenant-renewal traditions on to those traditions which are originally associated with Exodus-Conquest and then were expanded by the influx of Canaanite motifs. The classic poetic descriptions of epiphany also (and independently?) reflect this Canaanite milieu.

Although the new study of George E. Mendenhall[67] defies classifica-
tion--perhaps more than any other work treated--we may consider it here
chiefly because of its use of both Sumero-akkadian and Ugaritic materials
as a basis for a comprehensive restructuring of the approach to Israel's
earliest traditions, rivalled only by that of F. M. Cross (see below).
Mendenhall's work is deliberately intended to be a radical challenge to
the traditio-historical and form-critical methodology of biblical scholarship, resulting in a new synthesis of the "formative period" of Israel's
religious traditions in relation to the surrounding world of religio-
political paganism. Mendenhall proposes three stages in the development
of religion in the ancient Near East: (a) "economic-tribal religion,"
where the major religious symbols and deities are projections of a tribal
economy; (b) "political religions" where the major gods and myths guar-
anteed the continuation of the state (both of these "virtually prehistoric
in origin"); (c) the religion of Moses and early Israel, "biblical faith
in which ethical concerns take precedence over all others," including those
of the state, thereby rendering "authentic religion" and "state religion"
incompatible (18). This third stage, which is emphatically revolutionary,
occurred shortly before or, more probably, shortly after "the complete col-
lapse of political organizations" of the late Bronze Age (64).

Mendenhall's understanding of epiphany within this broad scheme takes
its cue from a study by A. Oppenheim on the *melammu* (majesty, glory, etc.)
in Sumero-akkadian texts.[68] A literary and iconographic study of this and
other expressions, especially that of the winged sun disk, reveals an "epi-
phanological polymorphism" in the Bronze Age out of which "what was later
called *epiphany* emerged" (53). The sun disk phenomenon is most closely
associated with the "manifestation of the Divine in the human world" and
with the human counterpart of this in the person of the king. Thus its
basic function is the legitimation of the royal state, "the monopoly of
force which operates through the usual functions of war, law, and economic control" (64-65). On the other hand, the function of the Sinai epiphany and the related motifs in the Exodus-Wilderness narratives makes
it clear that the revolutionary religion of Moses was a flat denial of
this ability of "political power structures to be the 'Ultimate Concern'"
or a manifestation of God (65; cf. 58). Thus for Mendenhall, epiphanies
apparently were only one small aspect of the adoption and adaptation of
old, often barely remembered, forms to serve a new function--to point to

12

the Kingdom of God (or, the "Imperium of Yahweh") rather than the deification of political power.[69] These motifs are concentrated in the Exodus-Wilderness periods because afterwards, with the rise of the monarchy, Israel herself succumbed to the "deification of force" of the old paganism (65). The epiphany motifs (e.g. using the $^c nn$) resume only with the pre-exilic prophets and later material, after the breakdown of Israel's legal and value system. This period points toward the resurgence of divine manifestation as experiential reality (209), culminating in the New Testament formulation of divine manifestion, not in terms of power, but in terms of personality--namely, that of love (213).

By far the most comprehensive and energetic attempt to utilize the fruits of Near Eastern research as the basis for a new approach to Israel's historical traditions is seen in the work of F. M. Cross. Like Mendenhall, he has challenged the methodology that informs the works examined in the previous sections, but not to the point of repudiation. In his new book,[70] Cross expounds on a familiar theme of his former work--the reconciliation of the myth and ritual school and the history of redemption school, now cast in more suggestive terms by the title: *Canaanite Myth and Hebrew Epic*. Although epiphany, of course, is only one link in this process of amalgamation, it is indicative of the whole.

Chapter 7, "Yahweh and Ba^{c}l," bears most directly on our topic, for it includes sections on "The Theophany of Ba^{c}l," "The Storm Theophany in the Bible," and "The Revelation at Sinai." At the outset Cross declares that "any discussion of the language of theophany in early Israel must begin with an examination of the Canaanite lore" (147). The problem with Jeremias's work, for example, is that he did not consider "the Canaanite *Gattung*" of theophany within its mythic cycle (147, n. 1). The first two sections of the chapter investigate both the Ugaritic material and the ancient poetry of Israel, which contain the "same patterns and motifs" of theophany (156). At the conclusion of these sections, Cross reconstructs what he believes to be "an archaic mythic pattern" containing four elements (162-163):

    (a) battle of the divine warrior against a chaos figure

    (b) convulsive reaction of nature to the warrior's wrath

    (c) return of the warrior to his mountain to assume kingship of
        the gods

    (d) utterance of the warrior's voice from his temple and revival
        of nature

This mythic pattern was replaced in Israel by an "epic pattern." Almost all of Israel's old poetry has replaced (a) and (b) by the exodus and conquest wars and the march from Egypt or Sinai, whereas (c) has been replaced by the theophany on Sinai, and both (c) and (d) are reflected in numerous Psalms.[71]

How does this fit with the traditional theories of the history of Israel's traditions? Cross insists that the epic[72] traditions preserve the historical order of events (Exodus, Sinai, Conquest), while the covenant cult preserves the liturgical order (Exodus-Conquest, Sinai) (85). Instead of the fragmentation of festivals and traditions, Cross asserts that "the pattern--Exodus from Egypt, Covenant at Sinai, Conquest of Canaan--is prior, cultically and historically, to the several elements in the pattern or *Gestalt*" (88).

The constitution of the cultic celebrations that preserved these traditions reveals the place and function of those passages dealing with epiphany. The cultic celebrations of the twelve-tribe league consisted of two major segments: the re-enactment of the Exodus-Conquest events, and the renewal of the covenant of Sinai. Cross has thus combined the traditions and cult of Gilgal (following Kraus) and Shechem (von Rad) into one complex (103-105, n. 48). The classic epiphany passages describe the events represented in the first half of the celebration.

> Indeed there is evidence in some early traditions that
> the march of the Divine Warrior from the South or the
> Wars of Yahweh tended to dominate the cultic reenactment
> of the *magnalia Dei* (85). The theophanic language of the
> prose sources of the Sinai revelation is secondary, de-
> rived from the hymns of the Wars of Yahweh, where the
> (Exodus-) Conquest motif is naturally and primitively
> linked with theophany (86).[73]

Before evaluating the contributions and problems of the history of religions approach, we must look briefly at the question of cultic institutions of the wilderness period. It is not surprising that questions surrounding the ark and Tent of Meeting/Tabernacle have engaged biblical scholars for well over a century, for the precise definition of these cultic institutions and their relation to each other from the wilderness period to Shiloh, Jerusalem, and the Priestly formulation is vexed with enormous difficulties.[74] It will not be our purpose to launch a new and

14

and thorough investigation of these problems, but to look at them only as they are related to divine presence and guidance, particularly within the narrative material from Exodus to Conquest.

That the ark and tent are important for our study is clear from the numerous accounts of divine appearance (usually in the cloud or glory) in connection with the latter during Israel's wilderness journey. Quite typically, a survey of interpretation here reveals distinct lines of argument which in general follow those for epiphany. The traditio-historical and form-critical approach is best seen in the work of Beyerlin. Although he rejects von Rad's separation of ark and tent as historical and theological incompatibilities,[75] his interpretation of them is thoroughly imbued with the covenant-renewal setting of theophany. Thus the major passages in question (e.g. Exod 33.7-11) reflect the amphictyonic cult and the Feast of Tabernacles from Shechem to Shiloh.[76]

On the other hand, we can see in Cross the chief proponent of the history of religions approach. Without ignoring the covenant renewal festival, Cross prefers to see the provenance of the tent traditions as directly connected with Canaanite mythology. Thus Yahweh, like the Canaanite El, has his tent dwelling where he meets with others (i.e. with other gods, for El; with Israel and especially Moses, for Yahweh) and from which he delivers oracles and legal edicts. The combination of Tent of Meeting and epiphany motifs therefore corresponds to a very early conflation of Baal and El themes.[77]

While the defenders of each approach hardly disagree completely (e.g. Beyerlin sees a major influx of Canaanite mythological motifs influencing the ark soon after the Conquest; Cross sees the covenant festival as a major cultic institution), the major differences are enough to warrant further clarification. As we have seen, this is also demanded by the position of Westermann, for the use of the same epiphany motif (the cloud) as a means of revelation and as a means of guidance in connection with the tent (P) is not adequately explained by his distinction between epiphany and theophany.

(3) Summary

A large group of scholars has consistently identified epiphany as an element of the covenant renewal festival. Unfortunately, this approach (especially as used by Weiser) often assumes an almost reductionist position that implies that every epiphany motif is ultimately related to this

15

specific cultic context. Moreover, much of the discussion has stemmed from a primary interest in the Psalms, and has been plagued by an awkward use of form-critical method. So, for example, the significance and function of epiphany motifs in the prose accounts of the wilderness journey--not to mention their relation to motifs of guidance--have been handled cavalierly or not at all.

The second group of scholars (including Westermann) understands epiphany as more directly connected with Exodus-Conquest traditions. Although form-critical and traditio-historical methods are still seen as useful (except, possibly by Mendenhall), the basic appeal is to the use of Near Eastern materials as the basis for interpretation. Thus epiphany motifs in the Old Testament are seen as part of a dynamic adaptation of an ancient mythic "pattern" (Cross); or they reflect a more general religio-political ideology, also profoundly revolutionized (Mendenhall); or they simply represent aspects of an iconographic and literary convention that is widespread in the ancient Near East--albeit with distinctive differences (Lipiński, Westermann, et al.).

It is our judgment--which will have to be substantiated below--that the history of religions approach provides the most fruitful ground for further research. Naturally, this does not mean that it is without difficulties. The study of Mendenhall has drawn attention to the important concept of divine sovereignty in the ancient Near East, and to motifs of divine presence (e.g. the ^{c}nn) which express or implement that sovereignty. His basic conclusion is that Israel borrowed the form of these motifs, but that the function was radically altered: in lieu of legitimating the political and militaristic aspirations of ruthless empires, Israel used these motifs to express an irenic Kingdom of God. Unfortunately Mendenhall's conclusions are called into question due to a clearly polemical orientation to ancient Near Eastern religion.[78] The motifs and corresponding iconography deserve a more thorough investigation, clarification, and objective appreciation. Only then can the important question of their relationship to the concept of political and divine sovereignty be answered.

The work of H. J. Kraus and especially F. M. Cross has also made a major contribution to the clarification of motifs of divine presence. The combined attention to both cultic celebrations and historical (or epic) narrative has produced a welcome synthesis which, precisely because it is still highly debatable, provides a model for further study. However, the work of Cross in particular raises the serious hermeneutical problem of "patternism" which, in various forms and degrees, has vexed the history of religions approach from the beginning. Are Israel's early traditions best understood in relation to an ancient Canaanite mythic pattern? The way in which the question is posed in terms of Canaanite *myth* and Hebrew *epic* suggests a crucial gap between Israel and her immediate neighbors. This is due in large measure to Cross's primary focus on the Ugaritic texts as witness to the closest and most logical cultural heritage that influenced Israelite thought.[79] For Cross, as for Mendenhall, Israel has borrowed the form of motifs of divine presence, while the function has been dynamically transformed. But, unlike Mendenhall, this transformation consists of a creative adaptation of a Canaanite mythic pattern, rather than of a repudiation. Instead of expressing mythical reality, the motifs now serve to depict Yahweh's acts in historical events. Such a focus raises the question of whether this myth and epic schematization applies to a comparison between the literatures of Israel and her more distant neighbors in Mesopotamia. Does the function of motifs of divine presence in the Old Testament stand in distinct contrast to their function in other Near Eastern literatures, or are there similarities which are not evident in the Ugaritic corpus?

In short, two of the most recent studies that deal with motifs of divine presence in ancient Near Eastern literature (Cross and Mendenhall) agree that Israel has borrowed the form but radically changed the function. Despite major differences between the presuppositions of the two, both see the function of the motifs as somehow related to the question of divine sovereignty. For Mendenhall, it is pagan despotism in contrast to the Kingdom of God; for Cross, it is the kingship of Baal over the powers of death and disorder in contrast to the kingship of Yahweh over history. With these issues in mind, we propose a fresh study of the form and function of motifs of divine presence and guidance in ancient Near Eastern literature,[80] followed by an attempt to delineate how this material illuminates the story of Israel's Odyssey from the Reed Sea to the Jordan River and the Davidic empire.

[1]There is a serious lack of clarity in our secondary terminology for divine presence. Usually, "theophany," "epiphany," and "appearance" are used interchangeably, along with other terms such as "(self-) manifestation." A significant practical distinction between epiphany and theophany is possible (see below), but it has yet to be thoroughly tested. In the Introduction, we shall limit ourselves as much as possible to the use of "epiphany," inasmuch as this term frequently occurs in the secondary literature. In the rest of this study, however, we shall employ the more general term "divine presence." Admittedly, this is less precise than the other expressions we have mentioned, but it has the benefit of covering a wide range of phenomena without forcing them into rigid categories, which in our judgment are often overly restrictive.

[2]See below, ch. 1, (1).

[3]*Schöpfung und Chaos in Urzeit und Endzeit* (Göttingen: Vandenhoeck und Ruprecht, 1895), 104-107. There is apparently some confusion between this and storm imagery, but this again is an issue which has been debated ever since Gunkel. See his *Die Psalmen* (Göttingen Handkommentar zum A. T. [Göttingen: Vandenhoeck & Ruprecht, 1968] 63-64) on Ps 18.16, where the sea is uncovered but the motif is attributed to volcanic phenomena rather than to the creation myth. Cf. H. Gunkel and Joachim Begrich, *Einleitung in die Psalmen* (Göttingen: Vandenhoeck & Ruprecht, 1933) 73.

[4]*Schöpfung*, 163. The combination of creation myth motifs with the Reed Sea event, however, is late (e.g. Exod 15.7b; Isa 51.9-10), 107-108.

[5]*Ibid.*, 107. Cf. *Einleitung*, 76.

[6]See, for example, *Psalmen*, 67; 215; 410.

[7]*Einleitung*, 86.

[8]"The Form-critical Problem of the Hexateuch," *The Problem of the Hexateuch and Other Essays* (New York: McGraw Hill, 1966), hereafter cited as "Hexateuch."

[9]Albrecht Alt, "The Origins of Israelite Law," *Essays on Old Testament History and Religion* (Oxford: Basil Blackwell, 1966). Applying Gunkel's method for the first time to Old Testament legal material, Alt concluded that Israel's apodictic law pointed to a sacral setting and must have been proclaimed as a renewal of the covenant at the Feast of Tabernacles (also the autumn New Year) every seven years (129). Although Alt did not discuss the place of epiphany in his essay, he did note that his conclusions were generally in accord with Volz, Mowinckel, and Schmidt (128-129, nn. 117 and 120). The agreement between Alt (and von Rad) and the New Year school, however, was actually quite minimal. See below on von Rad.

[10]"Hexateuch," 18.

[11]Von Rad's selectivity for the verses in Deuteronomy 33 is significant. The full texts usually cited are: Deut 33.2-3 (26-29); Judg 5.4-5; Habakkuk 3. Ps 68.8-9 is usually included as a fourth. See Ibid., 19. For convenience, we shall refer throughout to these four as "the classic (epiphany) passages," or the like, to avoid repetitive textual citations. Other texts, of course, are often noted along with these four when epiphany is discussed, but the grouping of the four together recurs with remarkable frequency; for example, see the following: Gunkel, *Schöpfung*,

102, 104; G. H. Davies, "Theophany," *IDB* 4, 260; Edouard Lipiński, *La Royauté de Yahwé dans la poésie et le culte de l'ancien Israël* (Brussels: Paleis der Academiën, 1965) 202, 247, 253; Walther Eichrodt, *Theology of the Old Testament* (2 vols.; Philadelphia: Westminster, 1967) 2:16, nn. 1-2. Martin Noth, *The History of Israel* (New York: Harper & Row, 1960) 132, n. 3; 135; id., *A History of Pentateuchal Traditions* (Englewood Cliffs: Prentice Hall, 1972) 60, n. 186; John Bright, *A History of Israel* (Philadelphia: Westminster, 1959) 115, 117; Gerhard von Rad, *Old Testament Theology* (2 vols.; New York: Harper & Row, 1962) 1:366, n. 23; Otto Eissfeldt, *The Old Testament, an Introduction* (New York: Harper & Row, 1966) 228. Further scholarly references to these four passages are noted in the discussion throughout.

[12]"Hexateuch," 19-20.

[13]*Ibid.*, 22; cf. *Theology* 1: 188-189. For Sigmund Mowinckel's views on epiphany, see below and *Le Décalogue* (Paris: Libraire Felix Alean, 1927) especially 124-129; also id., *The Psalms in Israel's Worship* (New York: Abingdon, 1967) 94 and 141-142.

[14]"Hexateuch," 35-36. Thus he is also opposed to Mowinckel's Jerusalem setting. Cf. *Theology* 1: 192.

[15]See "Hexateuch," 21 and 38 for reconstruction of the New Year festival and Shechem festival, neither of which mention theophany. Cf. *Theology* 1: 192-193.

[16]Curiously enough, in his *Old Testament Theology* (1:366) von Rad takes up the subject of theophany itself under the category of "The Praises of Israel," and sees passages like the classic texts as the clearest examples of an "Old Testament aesthetic" (without mention here of the covenant festival). This is similar to conclusions drawn by E. Pax, *Epiphaneia: Ein religionsgeschichtlicher Beitrag zur biblischen Theologie* (München: Karl Zink, 1955) 126-127. This latter work is marred by a method that approaches Old Testament epiphany by a series of characteristics, as well as by frequent psychologizing and reliance on contrasts between Hebrew and Greek thought. Some helpful criticisms of cultic interpretations (especially those of Weiser, see below) are offered, however.

[17]"Psalm 77: Ein Beitrag zur Frage nach dem Verhältnis von Kult und Heilsgeschichte," *ThLZ* 72 (1947) 133-140.

[18]*Ibid.*, 138.

[19]"Zur Frage nach den Beziehungen der Psalmen zum Kult: Die Darstellung der Theophanie in den Psalmen und im Festkult," *Festschrift Alfred Bertholet*, ed. W. Baumgartner et al. (Tubingen: Mohr, 1950) 513-531, hereafter cited as "Darstellung." See also id., *The Psalms* (Philadelphia: Westminster, 1962). Here Weiser recognizes an "archaic mythological" background to "the canonical point of view" of the Israelite cult (30). On epiphany, see especially 38-40.

[20]"Darstellung," 519, with reference to both Mowinckel and von Rad.

[21]"Das Deboralied: Eine gattungs- und traditionsgeschichtliche Studie," *ZAW* 71 (1959) 67-97. The extent to which Weiser insists on a cultic meaning for such material can be seen in his interpretation of Judges 5.3b where he understands ^{c}*nky lyhwh* not as "*I* will sing to the Lord" but as "I am the Lord's" i.e., as a reference to renewal of covenant relationship, 73.

[22]*Ibid.*, 95-96.

[23]*Ibid.*, 74-75.

[24]*Origins and History of the Oldest Sinaitic Traditions* (Oxford: Basil Blackwell, 1965). Most of the arguments of both are generally affirmed by R. E. Clements, *God and Temple* (Philadelphia: Fortress, 1965) 19-22, 35-38.

[25]See his summary, *Origins and History*, 146-148.

[26]*Ibid.*, 154-155.

[27]*Ibid.*, 156-157.

[28]*The Praise of God in the Psalms* (Richmond: John Knox, 1965), hereafter cited as *Praise*. See 93-101 for the section on epiphany.

[29]*Ibid.*, 30-31.

[30]*Ibid.*, 22.

[31]*Ibid.*, 38, 47-51.

[32]*Ibid.*, 96.

[33]*Ibid.*, 93.

[34]*Ibid.*, 97.

[35]The German is "Form," not "Gattung," in *Das Loben Gottes in den Psalmen* (Berlin: Evangelische Verlagsanstalt, 1953), 69.

[36]*Praise*, 98. The third is curiously most notable in its absence. Interestingly, since this third element is simply what unites the epiphany to the victory song, it may only represent Westermann's attempt to tie the two together more closely form-critically.

[37]*La royauté de Yahwé dans la poésie et le culte de l'ancien Israël* (Brussels: Paleis der Academiën, 1965). Lipiński's work is structured around an exegetical analysis of the "enthronement Psalms," and includes lengthy sections on epiphany in general (219-256). Like Westermann, to whom he continually refers for the following, Lipiński notes the extensive Near Eastern formal parallels for Old Testament epiphany, but also the more significant differences, especially the Old Testament emphasis on redemptive history (187-200). The latter reflects the frequent location of epiphany within victory songs (210). Lipiński also suggests not one, but two, literary patterns. The first is an ancient poetic schema attested in several Sumero-akkadian hymns and echoed in Judg 5.4-5, Ps 68.8-9 (114-116; the latter text especially as reconstructed), where Yahweh departs from his Southern dwelling (202). The second, rather than hymnic, is narrative or epic, and has fewer extrabiblical parallels. Here too, however, the place of divine departure is mentioned (Deut 33.2; Hab 3.3-4; Ps 50.1-3, etc.) (205-209). See below, especially in ch. 9 (4).

Also following Westermann, Lipiński concludes that the lyric examples of epiphany were not intended to refer to Sinai or to covenant renewal (e.g., the use of epiphany in Ps 50.1-3 is a secondary adaptation and thus in direct opposition to the covenant renewal/New Year school). Taken as a whole, they were not influenced by the Pentateuchal Sinai epiphany. Despite the obvious indebtedness to Canaanite storm imagery, the original function of epiphany in the Old Testament supersedes its background in seeing Yahweh as the holy warrior who is victor and lord over the gods of Canaan, and thus over the defeated populations (254-256). At this point, Lipiński differs somewhat from Westermann's emphasis on the Reed Sea event as the original locus of epiphany, but their conclusions are hardly mutually exclusive, as we shall see with F. M. Cross below.

[38]*Praise*, 101. For Weiser's responses, see *Psalms*, 38, n. 2.

[39]*Praise*, 99-101. Other than Exodus 19, the only other examples cited for "theophany" are 1 Kings 19; Isaiah 6; Ezekiel 1, 2.

[40]The distinction between epiphany and theophany in particular has been half-heartedly adopted in a study by Frank Schnutenhaus, "Das Kommen und Erscheinen Gottes im Alten Testament," *ZAW* 76 (1964) 1-21. Although he wants to restate Westermann's distinction in less rigid terms, the effect is to lose the original intent of convenience and to return to ambiguity (see p. 21). Schnutenhaus' claim that the original *Sitz im Leben* of epiphany (although it has several) is in the oracular tent traditions (although it first came from Mesopotamian culture), however problematic, seems to presuppose Westermann's distinction, for Schnutenhaus sees this as explaining why there is an emphasis on divine speech rather than on appearance in the Sinai theophany (13).

[41](Neukirchen-Vluyn: Neukirchener Verlag, 1965). Page references for Jeremias will be cited in the text where space permits.

[42]Jeremias appears to dismiss Westermann's distinction between epiphany and theophany as one not germane to his own work (2, n. 3). He consistently uses the term "theophany."

[43]*The Self-Revelation of God* (Philadelphia: Westminster, 1967) ch. 4. Kuntz does deal with the patriarchal stories, and much more as well. In fact his summary definition is a compendium of numerous characteristics drawn from a variety of theophanic texts, (45). He is heavily indebted to the study of Rolf Rendtorff, "The Concept of Revelation in Ancient Israel," *Revelation as History*, ed. W. Pannenberg et al. (New York: Macmillan, 1968). The coalescence of the terms "revelation" and "theophany" unfortunately has resulted in more confusion than clarity, to the extent that Kuntz would apparently extend what Westermann calls "theophany" to virtually every textual candidate: Exod 24.1-2, 9-11 is "the only Old Testament theophany that is silent from start to finish" (40). This fixation on the "Word" has also marred his form-critical analysis. For example, a passage that describes Yahweh as thundering and one that depicts him as speaking can be grouped together, since both present an audible phenomenon. Kuntz's attempt to establish prototypical texts even rivals that of Jeremias, in that he suggests three: Gen 26.23-25; Exodus 19; Exodus 3. In short, Kuntz's study is another that reveals the contemporary confusion surrounding terminology for theophany and form-critical methodology.

[44]These two elements, of course, are identical to the first two of Westermann's form.

[45]118-122. Jeremias criticizes the identification of the epiphany descriptions as a tradition, made by the latter three scholars.

[46]139; the quotation is from Alt's definition of a *Gattung* (3). The dismissed candidates are Psalms 77, 114; Deuteronomy 33; Psalms 46, 76.

[47]144; the victory song setting is, again, comparable to Westermann.

[48]Some earlier Israelite traditions prepared the way, e.g. those depicting divine power, such as *pḥd yṣḥq 'byr y'qb*. Sinai too appears to be part of this preliminary stage (151-152).

[49]161; here, of course, a major difference from Westermann.

[50]It was not his intent to deal with hypostases (2), but it is our contention that the function of these in the Wilderness March is directly related to passages such as Judg 5.4-5.

[51]Convenient summaries can be found in Westermann, *Praise*, 19-21; Lipiński, *Royauté*, 44-70; Hans-Joachim Kraus, *Worship in Israel* (Richmond: John Knox, 1966) 3-25.

[52]*Royauté*, 47.

[53]See the numerous works by Umberto Cassuto, Theodore H. Gaster, H. L. Ginsberg, Cyrus H. Gordon, Marvin H. Pope, F. A. Schaeffer, and C. Virolleaud, as well as many others, cited in the bibliography provided by Andrée Herdner, *Corpus des tablettes en cuneiformes alphabétiques* (Paris: Imprimerie Nationale, 1963) 294-339, hereafter cited as *CTCA*.

[54]"The Psalm of Habakkuk," in *Studies in Old Testament Prophecy*, ed. H. H. Rowley (Edinburgh: T. & T. Clark, 1950) 1-18; "A Catalogue of Early Hebrew Lyric Poems (Psalm LXVIII)," *HUCA* 23 (1950/51) 1-39.

[55]"Psalm of Habakkuk," 8-9.

[56]Cf. Thorkild Jacobsen, "The Battle between Marduk and Tiamat," *JAOS* 88 (1968) 104-108.

[57]*Worship in Israel*, 156-157.

[58]*Ibid.*, 134-146.

[59]*Ibid.*, 214; note that for Kraus this is not an "enthronement festival."

[60]*Ibid.*, 208-216; cf. 185-186.

[61]*Ibid.*, 152-165.

[62]*Psalmen* (2 vols.; Neukirchener Verlag, 1960) 1:144-145. Also *Worship in Israel*, 216.

[63]Especially in opposition to Weiser and Mowinckel. Kraus also wants to understand theophany accounts as indicative of "prophetic visionary perception," *Worship in Israel*, 168-171.

[64]He sees Old Testament epiphanies as composed of elements from three closely linked strata: the Sinai tradition, $k\bar{a}b\hat{o}d$ concepts, and Canaanite storm-god imagery (*Ibid.*, 216; *Psalmen*, 145), the former two strata relying on von Rad. Kraus seems to assume influence on other Old Testament epiphanies, both from Exodus 19 and from pre- and extra-Israelite sources (*Psalmen*, 145).

[65]*Worship in Israel*, 214. For a critique of the Jebusite hypothesis, see the recent discussion in the study of J. J. M. Roberts, "The Davidic Origin of the Zion Tradition," *JBL* 92 (1973) 329-344.

[66]*Worship in Israel*, 170-171.

[67]*The Tenth Generation: The Origins of the Biblical Tradition* (Baltimore: The Johns Hopkins University Press, 1973); references incorporated in the text where space allows.

[68]"Akkadian *pul(u)ḫ(t)u* and *melammu*," *JAOS* 63 (1943) 31-34. It seems to us that Mendenhall's identification of Ugaritic $^c nn$ with the winged sun-disk is very tenuous (56). However, he has added new dimensions to our understanding of this term both in the Ugaritic texts and in the biblical narrative, which deserve further analysis. Cf. further in ch. 5, (2). For

a more extensive treatment, especially of *melammu*, see Elena Cassin, *La splendeur divine: Introduction à l'étude de la mentalité mésopotamienne* (Ecole pratique des hautes études, Sorbonne; Civilisations et Sociétés, 8; Paris: Mouton, 1968).

[69]203-204, without specific reference to epiphanies.

[70]F. M. Cross, *Canaanite Myth and Hebrew Epic* (Cambridge: Harvard University Press, 1973), hereafter cited as *CMHE*; most references incorporated in the text.

[71]160-164; e.g. Psalms 29; 89B; 96-98; 50.1-6, etc.

[72]i.e., "JE and the epic of which J and E were, in origin, oral variants" (6, n. 9).

[73]It is interesting to note that Cross, like Mendenhall, sees this early period in the emergence of Israel as the bud from which later apocalyptic was to bloom. Although their schematizations of the revolutionary changes in Israel's history are remarkably parallel, their understanding of the causes of these upheavals and their evaluation of them are significantly divergent, revealing the decisive importance of our interpretation of Israel's beginnings. Note the development of Cross's schema for apocalyptic literature by Paul D. Hanson, "Jewish Apocalyptic Against Its Near Eastern Environment," *RB* 78 (1971) 31-58. Also to be consulted by the same author, *The Dawn of Apocalyptic: The Historical and Sociological Roots of Jewish Apocalyptic Eschatology* (Philadelphia: Fortress, 1975).

[74]For an extensive critical review of the research on the ark and tent, here and at the relevant portions of Part II below, the reader is referred to the recent study of Rainer Schmitt, *Zelt und Lade als Thema alttestamentlicher Wissenschaft, Eine kritische forschungsgeschichtliche Darstellung* (Gütersloh: Gerd Mohn, 1972).

[75]"Thus, two completely different 'theologies' are connected with the Tent and with the Ark--with the former it is a theology of manifestation but with the latter one of presence," von Rad, *Theology*, 1:237.

[76]*Origins and History*, 120-121; cf. above, 4-5. Many, though not all, of Beyerlin's conclusions are reflected in Manfred Görg, *Das Zelt der Begegnung: Untersuchungen zur Gestalt der sakralen Zelttraditionen Altisraels* (Bonn: BBB 27; Peter Hanstein, 1967).

[77]*CMHE*, 55, n. 43, and 185-186. Cf. the work of his student, Richard J. Clifford, "The Tent of El and the Israelite Tent of Meeting," *CBQ* 33 (1971) 221-227. For further discussion of Beyerlin's work, see especially our interpretation of *pānîm* in ch. 7.

[78]See the review of Mendenhall's *Tenth Generation* by Jack M. Sasson in *JBL* 93 (1974) 294-296. For further and more detailed discussion of Mendenhall's views, see the section on the Reed Sea narrative in ch. 5.

[79]For further discussion of the work of Cross, see especially our discussion of the North-West Semitic texts in ch. 4, as well as our interpretation of the Song of the Sea and other Old Testament texts in Part II.

[80]It has not proved feasible to include any substantive discussion of religion and literature from cultures other than Mesopotamia and Ugarit (such as Egypt) which may have a bearing on our topic.

PART I

MOTIFS OF DIVINE PRESENCE IN THE ANCIENT NEAR EAST

INTRODUCTION

In the survey of ancient Near Eastern literature that follows, we
have by no means attempted to cover the subject of divine presence in
general. Rather our interest has focused on motifs related by form and
function to those in the biblical narratives. As we have already indicated in the Introduction, those narratives dealing with Israel's march
from Egypt to Canaan use a variety of images to describe Yahweh's presence at the head of his people, a presence that serves both to guide
them through the wilderness and to protect them from enemies along the
way. Some of these images are at times also associated with cultic institutions and, perhaps, with ceremonies. Accordingly, we have sought out
Near Eastern texts in which the gods are depicted as present and active
agents in historical events, but also in settings that reflect the cultic
life of the community. Our attention was initially drawn to motifs that
depict the gods "going in front of" their human constituencies in battle.
We have subsumed the various literary formulations of this idea under the
term "the divine vanguard motif." Our search for the form and function
of this motif disclosed to us, almost at every turn, a concatenation of
closely related literary images and an underlying conceptual framework.
The way in which these factors consistently emerged within individual
texts soon indicated that the motifs of divine presence could not thoroughly be studied in isolation, particularly if we are to understand their
function. Indeed, as one major text suggested similarities to another, we
were increasingly convinced that these motifs of divine presence belong
to a rich and complex literary and conceptual typology developed by William
W. Hallo and J. J. A. van Dijk--the "typology of exaltation."[1] It is our
conclusion (which we establish below) that the common elements of this
typology provide a cogent basis for understanding the close relationship
between what at first seem to be totally unrelated literary genres, both
according to literary form and to institutional setting. The most striking

27

relationship is that between epic and hymnic material, revealing the literary and conceptual reciprocity that determined the ancient Near Eastern understanding of divine presence within the context of history and within the context of the cult. Furthermore, the way in which divine and human sovereignty plays a central role in this typology promises to shed light on the significance of this topic for the biblical sources.

The major portion of this chapter will concentrate on the cuneiform literature of Mesopotamia. As was implied in the Introduction, this material has not been thoroughly explored in relation to the Old Testament understanding of divine presence since the work of Gunkel, but has often been neglected--at times in favor of Ugaritic studies.[2] Within the cuneiform literature, our attention will first turn to major literary texts, with an emphasis on the form and function of motifs of divine presence, especially in the epic tradition. Next we shall explore the possible correspondences between the literary texts and the Assyrian annals, then investigate the connections with cultic iconography and liturgy. Our discussion will conclude with a re-evaluation of the extant Northwest Semitic texts in the light of our topic. Methodologically, an attempt is being made to correlate various types of evidence within the ancient Near Eastern material (e.g. epic, annals, iconography, cult), rather than concentrating on a narrow segment. It is hoped that the breadth of the evidence will prevent an exaggeration of the importance of any one type of material for understanding the Old Testament, either from the standpoint of history of religions or form-criticsm.

NOTES TO INTRODUCTION

[1]William W. Hallo and J. J. A. van Dijk, *The Exaltation of Inanna* (Yale Near Eastern Researches 3; New Haven: Yale University Press, 1968), especially 64-68. See below in ch. 1, (1). It is my understanding that the development of the typology itself is primarily the contribution of Hallo.

[2]One notable exception is the extensive use of cuneiform material to explain the deuteronomistic concept of divine presence expressed by Yahweh's "name," for a discussion of which, see S. Dean McBride, Jr., "The Deuteronomic Name Theology," Ph.D. dissertation, Harvard University, 1969. Of course, Cross also has made use of such materials, but not as a primary focus. The works of Mendenhall and Lipiński, previously discussed, are also notable exceptions.

CHAPTER 1

MESOPOTAMIAN LITERARY TEXTS

(1) The Exaltation of Inanna and the Typology of Exaltation

The first text in our study is a remarkable Sumerian poem translated
by William W. Hallo and J. J. A. van Dijk entitled "The Exaltation of
Inanna" (nin-me-šar-ra). We shall at first attend to portions of the
text itself, and then examine their function within the overall conceptual framework. Our interest is concentrated in the first part of the
poem, which Hallo terms the "Exordium," and near the end, in stanza xv
("The Exaltation of Inanna" proper). Hallo notes that the "Exordium"
produces a climactic movement "worthy of an Amos,"[1] for it progresses
from a stanza praising Inanna as "lady of all the *me's*, resplendent
light" (1. 1), to stanzas concerning her relationship to other deities,
and finally to a stanza describing Inanna's rejection of the city Uruk.[2]
This movement from the heavenly to the earthly realm is highly significant, as we shall see. Although the stanzas should be read in their entirety for the full force of the poem, for conciseness we shall cite only
excerpts here, again following Hallo's translation:

(ii) Inanna and An

9   Like a dragon you have deposited venom on the land

10 When you roar at the earth like Thunder, no vegetation
    can stand up to you.

11 A flood descending from its mountain,

12 Oh foremost one, you are the Inanna of heaven and earth!

13 Raining the fanned fire   down upon the nation,

14 Endowed with m e ' s by An, lady mounted on a beast,

15 Who makes decisions   at the holy command of An.

16 (You) of all the great rites,   who can fathom what is
                                    yours?

30

(iii) Inanna and Enlil

17 Devastratrix of the lands,   you are lent wings by the
                                 storm.

18 Beloved of Enlil   you fly about in the nation.

19 You are at the service   of the decrees of An.

20 Oh my lady, at the sound of you   the lands bow down.
    (ll. 21–25 omitted here)

(iv) Inanna and Iškur

26 In the van of battle   everything is struck down by
                                 you.

27 Oh my lady, (propelled)
      on your own wings,   you peck away (at the land).

28 In the guise of a charging storm   you charge.

29 With a roaring storm   you roar.

30 With Thunder   you continually
                                 thunder.

31 With all the evil winds   you snort.

32 Your feet are filled   with restlessness.

33 To (the accompaniment of) the
      harp of sighs   you give vent to
                                 a dirge.[3]

These vivid lines present a terrifying picture of Inanna the storm-
goddess using literary images that we shall see again and again in other
texts.[4] Inanna roars like Thunder (Iškur); she is both a raging mountain
flood (a-ma-ru = *abūbu*) and a rain of fire; she flies about using the
storm as her wings.[5] At the sound of her approach "the lands bow down,"
and when she assumes the vanguard of battle (igi-me = *panū taḫazi*),
everything is struck down in front of her.

The function of these motifs is clearly to describe the fearsome
military presence in battle that leads Inanna to victory over her enemies.
But what type of battle is this, and who are the enemies? The answer to
these questions comes not only from individual lines of the text, but
also from a consideration of the larger *Tendenz* of the work as a whole.
Inanna is clearly not fighting against a mythical divine being. Her fury
is directed rather at the land (kur = *mātu*, 1.9), or the nation (kalam
= *mātu*, ll. 13, 18). According to Hallo, it is probably launched even
more specifically against the mountain Ebih and finally against the city

Uruk--at least with the latter "the reference is almost certainly to a Sumerian city."[6] The fact that Ebih itself is the subject of another victory of Inanna, the account of which may also come from the stylus of Enheduanna[7] suggests that in the present poem Ebih already functions as the prototypical Enemy.

In short, the poem uses mythical language to point to historical reality, and it is Hallo's interpretation of this point which makes the Exaltation of Inanna such an important part of our study. Hallo suggests that this poem--one of the few cuneiform works of known authorship--in fact reflects an actual historical situation: the Sargonic religio-political program whose purpose was to solidify Sargon's own Akkad to-gether with Sumer into an imperial system. This was effected in part by uniting the primary priestly offices in "the person of his daughter En-heduanna, the devotee of Inanna" and the author of the poem (1. 67), and by representing Inanna "as merely carrying out the commandments of the supreme deity of the Sumerian pantheon, An (1. 15)." The product was essentially a 'Sargonic theology'.[8]

It must be stressed that, except for Enheduanna herself, nowhere in the poem are any of the above historical and political figures named. Yet Hallo's arguments that various stanzas of the poem refer, for example, to Mt. Ebih, Ur, and Uruk, seem to be carefully reasoned conclusions to what are admittedly often difficult lines.[9] Moreover, the name of Luga-lanne, the usurper at Uruk, *is* given in 1. 74, and is known from other sources.[10] Thus it would seem that Hallo's concluding interpretation of stanza x is a convincing explanation of the intention of these lines:

> Translated into historical terms, then, the appeal to
> Nanna is an appeal to his city Ur to aid the Sargonic
> party in the suppression of the revolt of Uruk, or at
> the very least not to support the rebellion.[11]

Hallo also proposes to understand the ambiguous references in 1. 79 of this stanza ["That woman is as exalted (as he)--she will make the city divorce him."] as Inanna, An, Uruk, and Lugalanne respectively.[12] This combination is a pithy expression of Hallo's major thesis concerning the *Tendenz* of this work: the Exaltation of Inanna is perhaps the earliest example of "the close dependence of major 'theogonic' revolutions on his-torical events."[13]

To summarize: we can say that even at an early date, at least during

the latter half of the third millennium, motifs of divine appearance--
especially those utilizing storm imagery--are by no means reserved for
the description of natural phenomena cast into the mold of mythical events.
Inanna here is not simply a goddess of the storm who conquers inimical
divine beings. She is already seen as a goddess who uses her storm-weapons
to shape the course of history in accordance with her will, however thinly
veiled the actual historical connections may be.

(2) The Nur-Adad Letter

Some four and a half centuries after Sargon of Akkad, we find Mesopotamia divided into a number of competing city-states, two of which were
Isin and Larsa. One small segment of this rivalry that lasted some two
hundred years is illustrated by a Sumerian text that provides the first
example of a royal letter addressed to the god(s), perpetuated, among
others, in the "Letter to Assur" of Sargon II.[14] The letter describes
the rise to power over Larsa accomplished by Nur-Adad (c. 1865-1850) and
was apparently commissioned by his son, Sin-iddinam, for the dedication
of a statue of his father, to which the tablet was probably affixed.[15]
The background of the episode involves disputes over water rights which
were becoming increasingly critical, due to the disintegration of unified
control over tidal salinization. The two predecessors of Nur-Adad had
attempted to gain control of Isin's water supply for the benefit of Larsa,
only to have their own supply eventually cut off, evidently through foreign intervention. It was in the midst of this crisis that Nur-Adad im-
posed his coup d'état, reclaimed the city of Larsa from the alien occu-
piers, and restored the water supply.[16]

The text contains an historical section, bracketed by two sections
dealing with the dedication of the work to the sun-god and arbiter, Utu.
An outline of the latter presents the following picture:

Section 1:	lines	1-40:	consecreation of the statue to Utu
Section 2:	lines	41-163:	message to the god entrusted to the statue
a.	lines	48-60:	conquest of Larsa by foreign enemy
b.	lines	61-83:	revolt in the city
c.	lines	84-114:	election of Nur-Adad
d.	lines	115-163:	reconquest and restoration
Section 3:	lines	164-240:	letter of supplication to Utu.[17]

Our interest in the Letter to Utu, in comparison to the Exaltation of
Inanna discussed above, is not only in the obviously political orientation of the work, but in the literary motifs that it utilizes and the
context in which they occur. Most significant is the fact that, precisely
at the climactic point of the historical section where the decisive battle
takes place (2. d above), the text is suddenly flooded with imagery directly related to the vanguard motifs that we have seen in the Exaltation
of Inanna. Thus at the opening of Section 2.d we have the following vivid
description:

	di-nì-gi-na-	According to the just judgment
115	^{d}utu-ta	of Utu;
	en ^{d}nin-gír-su	with the aid
	á-dah̬- a-ta	of lord Ningirsu;
	sún- gal	the grand savage cow,
	^{d}inanna-zabala^{ki}	Inanna of Zabala
120	igi-gin-né-te	going at the front;
	^{d}iškur	Iškur
	dingir-s[i]g$_{14}$-ga-ke$_4$	the god of thunder
	zi-da gin-né-ta	going at (her) right;
	á-dah̬ tab-ba-da [lú?]-	doubling (therefore) the
	kúr-meš	support, he [i.e. Nur-Adad] chased
125	[M]I-ištar?? im-ta-	[the] foreigners (and)
	[an-è?]	[Sill]i ištar??
	ká-gal-larša^{ki}-ma	(and) opened
	gala$_7$ h̬é-bí-in-tag$_4$	the main gate of Larša.[18]

This picture of Inanna taking the vanguard of battle, with Iškur, the god
of thunder, going at her side, is clearly related to the literary tradition that we delineated above.[19] The striking difference, of course, is
that here the text explicitly depicts the gods actively in league with
their human devotee and literally fighting at his side. Moreover, van
Dijk has pointed out the historical implications of these lines by noting that Nur-Adad must have enjoyed the support of the cities of Lagaš,
Zabala, and Ennegi in his revolt, for "Assistance granted by the god implies apparently assistance of the city . . . ."[20] The juxtaposition
here of the action of the gods alongside that of Nur-Adad reminds us of
the complementary relationship between Sargon/Enheduanna and Inanna, and
forms a fitting conclusion for this section of a work which obviously--

34

in part--is intended to legitimate and perpetuate Nur-Adad's (and Sin-iddinam's) hegemony.[21]

It is interesting that just as the vanguard motif is used to *intro-duce* the climactic scene of the historical section, it also occurs near the *end* in 11. 154-160:

154	dingir- gal-gal	The great gods
	ka-mè-šen-šen-na	who had committed themselves
	šà-larsa^{ki}-ma-[šè]	as the vanguard of the battle (and) the attack
	i-in-ku$_4$-re-eš-a	all the way to the heart of Larša,
	nu-úr- ^{d}*adda*	Nur-Addad,
	a-a- ugu-mu	my father who engendered me,
160	ki-bi-šè hé-bi-iu-gi$_4$	restored them to their place.[22]

The language here (especially ka-mè, 1. 155) is similar not only to that in the Exaltation of Inanna, but as van Dijk notes, to three other closely parallel texts that present a "paean of self-glorification of Inanna."[23] These texts present a combination of no less than five expressions for the vanguard (or rear-guard, etc.) motif,[24] and, although they represent a rather mixed literary type, it is interesting that, according to S. N. Kramer's analysis of one, the section that contains the vanguard motif also depicts Inanna as a warrior goddess challenging Utu, Nanna, and Sud.[25]

It is also important for our discussion to observe the reference in these lines to the reinstatement of the gods. Van Dijk surmises that the emphasis in the letter on the homage paid to the gods of the land conquered by Nur-Adad probably indicates that the gods' statues had been carried off by the enemy.[26] At any rate, it is clear from 1.160 that Nur-Adad had them restored "to their place," and the text goes on to list the institution of sacrifices and feast days, as well as the installation of "an *en*-priestess" in the temple of Utu, the emblem (*šunir*) of gold for Nanna, and a golden throne for Inanna.[27] The religio-political action of installing a priest-ess again reminds us of the Exaltation of Inanna and the role of Enheduanna in the empire of Sargon of Akkad. The significance of the divine statues and emblems will become increasingly clear in the texts to which we now turn.

(3) The Tukulti-Ninurta Epic

If Sargon of Akkad was in a very real sense a catalyst for the cuneiform

epic tradition, it must be said that the reign of Tukulti-Ninurta I, more
than a millennium later, had an equally remarkable impact that was recorded in the epic that bears his name. Although this work has been known
for some time,[28] it is yet to be given the complete collation and translation that it deserves.[29] In a recent article, however, W. G. Lambert
has suggested a major reordering of the sequential arrangement of the
known tablets, and a new reading for the crucial line that establishes
the epic as a continuous story celebrating the defeat of the Cassite king,
Kashtiliash, by Tukulti-Ninurta I of Assyria (c. 1244-1208).[30] More than
either of the works we have discussed above, this epic is explicitly historical and ideological (indeed, it has been called a "propaganda poem"),[31]
and it clearly uses many of the motifs and literary expressions that we
have seen in those works, especially that of the divine warrior and his
vanguard. Moreover, the use of the latter motif in the royal annals of
Tukulti-Ninurta presents an interesting case study for the relationship
between epic and annalistic documents.

A brief summary of the epic will prepare us for a closer look at the
text. According to Lambert, the epic in its extant form comprises six
columns.[32] In I, the Babylonian gods are angry with Kashtiliash for breaking the truce, and they forsake their cities. This is followed by a hymn
of praise, apparently to Tukulti-Ninurta. In II, Tukulti-Ninurta acts mer-
cifully to messengers of Kashtiliash but complains to Šamaš[33] about the
Cassite's breaking of the oath between the two kings and their fathers,
and sends a corresponding complaint to Kashtiliash himself. In III,
Tukulti-Ninurta adds to the complaint that Kashtiliash has ravaged his
land while avoiding open warfare. When he learns of Tukulti-Ninurta's
plea to Šamaš and of his threat, Kashtiliash apparently realizes his help-
less position, yet precipitously enters into battle with Tukulti-Ninurta
and just as suddenly retreats. In IV, the land of Kashtiliash is captured,
but the king himself is not. Tukulti-Ninurta now directly challenges the
king to the battle that has just begun when the text breaks off. Column
V contains an impassioned speech by Tukulti-Ninurta's army exhorting him
to seek revenge. What seems to be the decisive encounter begins here. In
VI, the treasures of Babylonia are carried off and the temples of the Assyrian gods are refurbished.

Our discussion will focus on two sections of the epic, one near the
beginning of Column I, and another relating the commencement of the final
battle in Column V. First the text of the former:

1   ....[...] ⌈ú⌉-šar-ri-iḫ ᵍⁱˢkakkīᵐᵉˢ

---

2   šar-ra-ḫat ma-am-lu-su tu-šá-a[q?-tar? la-a] a-di-ri pa-na ù
      ar-ka

3   qa-e-da-at er-ḫu-su tu-ḫa-am-maṭ la-a še-mi-i šu-me-la ù im-na

4   gal-tu me-lam-mu-šu ù-sa-aḫ-ḫa-pu na-gab za-a-a-ri

5   šá kip-pat šár erbetti (TAB.TAB) šá IM.TU i-ta-na-da-ru-uš pu-ḫur
      kâl šarrāni (MAN.MEŠ)

6   ki-ma ᵈad-di a-na ša-gi-im-me-šu it-tar-ra-ru šadû (KUR.MEŠ-ú)

7   ù ki-ma ᵈnin-urta a-na ni-iš ᵍⁱˢkakkīᵐᵉˢ-šu ul-ta-nap-šá-qa
      ka-liš kibrātuᵐᵉˢ

8   ina ši-mat ᵈnu-dim-mud-ma ma-ni it-ti šêr ilāniᵐᵉˢ mi-na-a-šú

9   ina purussî EN.KUR.KUR ina ra-a-aṭ šaturri ilāniᵐᵉˢ ši-pi-ik-šú
      i-te-eš-ra

10   šu-ú-ma ṣa-lam ᵈenlil (BE) da-ru-u še-e-mu pi-i nišīᵐᵉˢ mi-lik
      mâti

11   ki-ma šá-a-šú ana pâni re-de-e EN.KUR.KUR ú-man-du-ú-uš i-ud
      i-na šap-ti

---

12   ú-šar-bi-šu-ma ᵈenlil (BE) ki-ma a-bi a-li-di ar-ki mâri
      bu-uk-ri-šu

13   a-qar ina ši-me-šu a-šar šit-nu-ni ra-ša-aš-šu an-dil-la

14   ul iš-nun ma-ti-ma ina šarrāni (MAN.MEŠ-ni) kúl-la-ti qa-bal-šu
      ma-am-ma

15   ul iz-zi-i[z..........] x ku ga-ba-ra-šu a-šar ta-ḫa-zi

1   ....[...] he exalted the weapons.

---

2   Glorious is his might, it sco[rches] the [ir]reverent in front
      and behind;
    Blazing is his impetuosity, it burns the unsubmissive left and
      right;
    Fearful is his splendour, it overwhelms all his enemies.

5   He who . . . the extremities of the four winds, all kings with-
      out exception live in dread of him:
    As when Addu bellows, the mountains tremble,
    As when Ninurta lifts his weapons, the quarters of the world are
      reduced to continual anguish.

By the fate assigned by Nudimmud his form is reckoned as divine
nature.

By the decree of the Lord of the Lands his forming proceeded
smoothly *inside* the divine womb.

10 He is the eternal image of Enlil, who hears what the peoples
say, the "Counsel" of the land.

Likewise in his utterance he praised the Lord of the Lands *who
designated him to direct the van.*

---

12 Enlil, like a physical father, exalted him second to his first-
born son.

He is precious at his worth, the battlefield offers him protection,

No one among all kings ever vied with him in battle,

15 There did not stan[d.......].. his equal in battle.[34]

This passage is exceedingly rich in expressions related to those we
have already studied in the previous texts and presents some very important
literary and ideological adaptations of those expressions. Although the
opening lines are missing and Tukulti-Ninurta is never mentioned explicitly,
Lambert is certainly correct in describing this pericope as "a hymn of
praise" to that king.[35] Indeed, one of the most significant factors here
is that epithets identical or closely related to those used for deities
in the texts presented above are now used for the king himself. Thus at
first glance the first four lines could easily be understood as referring
to a divine figure, but the reference to "all kings" in 1.5 implies that
we are dealing with a human subject. In fact, this emphasis on the submission of all other kings complements the comparative force of the entire
passage, which praises Tukulti-Ninurta's similarity to the gods.[36] This
is borne out quite clearly in 11. 2-4 by the use of divine epithets to
describe the king's awesome power. Like Inanna, the king is surrounded
by attributes of his military prowess that constitute his vanguard: they
scorch and burn "in front and behind . . . left and right." Tukulti-
Ninurta also possesses a glowing nimbus or splendour (*melammu*, 1. 4) that
"overwhelms (*saḫāpu*) all his enemies."[37]

It is these attributes that cause rival kings to shudder, and the
passage accentuates their cowering submission by drawing a direct comparison to the trembling of the earth at the onslaught of Addu's roar and

Ninurta's weapons (11. 6-7). These two lines, like those preceding, contain highly stereotypical language, which we shall have further occasion to explore. They also form the first of three successive units of bicola that are artfully constructed to begin with a simile for the fear mentioned in 1. 5, move to Tukulti-Ninurta's divine nature, then back to the consequences of this for his earthly rule (cf. the tricola construction in 11. 2-4). Although the text is difficult, Tukulti-Ninurta himself seems to be charged *"to direct the van."*[38] This is immediately followed in the next section[39] by the exaltation of Tukulti-Ninurta. After the second bicolon preceding (11. 8-9) has demonstrated his divine nature, his precise position in the divine hierarchy is now made indubitable: his exaltation makes him second only to Enlil's firstborn! The analogy to the exaltation of Sargon/Enheduanna with Inanna above is clear, for here too we have a double action. Also, this impressive laudation of Tukulti-Ninurta's divine origins can be compared to the well-known legend of Sargon's birth, in that both are attempts to explain--if not legitimate--the heroic rise of these leaders. Our present text presents us with a cogent juxtaposition of the exaltation of both the deity and the epic hero. As Lambert comments:

> Here then is the hierarchy: Enlil, the supreme god,
> has exalted Ninurta his first born as second in com-
> mand, and Tukulti-Ninurta takes third place . . . .
> this explains how the emphasis on one god was achieved
> within the framework of the traditional pantheon.
> Just as the gods has assigned a preeminent position
> to Marduk in the Old Babylonian era, so Ninurta was
> now given the rank of 'high god.'[40]

Our text thus seems to present a graphic illustration for Jacobsen's statement that "Late in the myth-making period, on the verge of that of the epic, interest seems to have shifted to Enlil's son Ninurta."[41]

Thus there are clear indications that this exaltation of Ninurta was not accomplished solely during Tukulti-Ninurta's reign, and there is no indication that it was maintained in conspicuous view among his scribal staff. In fact the exaltation of Ninurta most likely began as early as Old Babylonian times,[42] and this probably influenced Shalmaneser I to name his son after that deity ("My help is Ninurta").[43] Moreover, Ninurta himself does not play a role later on in the epic corresponding to his exaltation referred to at the beginning. While he is called the "leader of the gods" in the next passage quoted below, his role in the battle does not appear more important than Assur, Ishtar, etc. Furthermore, in the corresponding motif in the annals (see below), Ninurta does not appear at all. We may conclude, therefore, that it is not the exaltation of Ninurta, but rather the glorification of Tukulti-Ninurta himself, that is the primary focus of the epic. Nevertheless, the correlation of theogonic and historico-political exaltation is a dominant theme of the "hymn of praise," and near the end of the epic the exaltation of Assur and the king appear together.[44]

The use of the motif of the vanguard in the epic, however, is by no means limited to the hymn of praise to Tukulti-Ninurta. As we have seen above, the motif is at home in contexts of battle, and that is precisely where we find it in Column V. The column opens with a dramatic speech by Tukulti-Ninurta's warriors who again praise his supremacy over all nations and kings, who live in fear of him. The speech ends with a rousing call to arms, and at this crucial juncture in the story the narrator introduces the vanguard motif as a vivid signal for the commencement of battle (V.23-33):

23 tar-ṣa-a-ma ma-za-la-at táq-ru-ub-ti a-šar mit-ḫu-ṣi tuquntu
   ku-un-na-at

24 šá-kín nu-gu-šu-ú dan-nu ina be-ri-šu-nu i-ḫi-il-lu ardâni^m

25 i-me-er ina maḫ-ra ^{d}A-šur ip-pu-uḫ eli nakrûti^m išat na-aš-pan-ti

26 i-šar-rum ^{d}Enlil qa-ab-la-at a-a-[b]i ú-ša-aq-tar! nab-la

27 iš-ku-un ^{d}A-nu me-iṭ-ta la pa-da-a e-lu tar-gi-gi

28 Na-an-na-ru ^{d}Sin ú-kín elu-šu-nu na-mu-un-ga-at qabli

29 ú-šar-di šâru a-bu-ba elu ta-ḫa-zi-šu-nu ^{d}Adad ur-šá-an-nu

30 ú-uṭ-ṭi e-en um-ma-na-at ^{m}âtušu-me-ri ù Akkadî^k ^{d}šá-maš bêl
   di-e-ni

31 ^{d}Ninurta qar-du ašarid (id) ilâni^m iṣukakkê^m-šu-nu ú-še-bi-ir-ma

32 ù im-ḫa-aṣ kip-pa-ša ^{d}Ištar ša qu-ra-di-šu-nu ú-še-eš-ni ṭi-ma

---

33 ar-ki ilâni^m tik-li-šu šar-ru ina pa-ni um-ma-ni ú-šèr-ri qabla

23 The fighting line was spread out on the field of battle; fighting commenced.

24 A great commotion set in among them; the servants trembled.

25 Assur led in the vanguard; he kindled a biting flame against

the foes.

26   Enlil danced (?) in the midst of the enemy; he fanned the burning flame.

27   Anu set a relentless weapon against the evil ones.

28   Nannar Sin forced against them the pressure of battle.

29   Adad the hero sent down a flood-wind against their fighting line.

30   Šamaš, Lord of judgment, dimmed the eyes of the forces of Sumer
and Akkad.

31   Ninurta the warrior, leader of the gods, shattered their weapons.

32   And Ishtar beat her skipping-rope which drove their warriors mad.

---

33   Behind the gods, his helpers, the king in the vanguard of the
army began the fight.[45]

Again the similarity in literary imagery and narrative function
between this passage and the others we have examined--especially the Nur-
Adad Letter--is obvious. The various deities form a devastating vanguard
with fire and flood (*išātu*, *nablu*, and *abūbu*) again part of the divine
weaponry. Behind "the gods his helpers" the king marches into battle,
himself at the head of his human army. Yet despite the glorification of
the king here and in Column I, the text leaves no doubt that it is the
assembly of divine warriors to whom the victory belongs.[46]

To summarize: with this ambitious and artful work we have arrived
at the clearest example of the epic tradition. Throughout the narrative
the focus is continually on the king as hero, and the story is repeatedly
structured around lengthy speeches exchanged between him and his army, as
well as formal pleas to Šamaš as the god of justice and verbal taunts exchanged between Tukulti-Ninurta and his enemy, Kashtiliash. We would see
this use of speeches as characteristic of the epic style of narration.
Moreover, a convergence of factors in the Tukulti-Ninurta Epic strongly
suggests a number of parallels with the texts concerning Enheduanna and
Nur-Adad. Analogous to the former, our epic text contains direct references to the exaltation both of Ninurta (and Assur) and of Tukulti-Ninurta.
As with the latter, we are again dealing with a precise historical event
in which the gods and the hero act as mutual agents--again, expressed by
the intervention of the divine vanguard. It is also quite likely that the
restoration of the cultic statues and/or emblems by Nur-Adad had its
counterpart in the finale of the Tukulti-Ninurta Epic with the capture of

the statue of Marduk and the cultic center erected by the victorious king.[47] Finally, with Sargon and Tukulti-Ninurta, we are dealing with the dramatic rise of empire over Sumer and Akkad, and this is probably similar to Nur-Adad's contributions to the dynasty of Larsa. Thus in an illuminating study, A. K. Grayson has shown that the period of Tukulti-Ninurta in particular demonstrates the "exaltation of the Assyrian ruler's status in relation to his subjects and his gods."[48]

(4) The Erra Epic

For another example of the Mesopotamian epic tradition and its use of the divine vanguard motif, we turn to the Erra Epic. Although this work has been under discussion for almost a century, its definitive interpretation has scarcely been achieved. Only a cursory look at the epic itself reveals the reasons for this consistent ambiguity; it is fraught with literary and historical difficulties that persist despite the recent, thorough, collation and translation by L. Cagni.[49]

The epic consists of five tablets, although II and III remain fragmentary. In Tablet I, we are introduced to the major characters, Erra,[50] Išum,[51] and Marduk, and more importantly, we are presented with a strange interchange between Erra and Marduk in which Marduk is finally persuaded to leave (or perhaps tricked into leaving) his throne and descend to the underworld. In Tablet II, Erra takes advantage of Marduk's absence and wreaks havoc on earth, which prompts a divine assembly to consider the means for the return of Marduk to his lordship. In III, Erra's destruction continues despite the protests of his aide, Išum. In Tablet IV, the violence that heretofore has struck at Babylon's surrounding cities now ignites within Babylon itself, and this, at the instigation of Erra, leads to a bloody rebellion. Erra is finally appeased, however, and in Tablet V, the author (Kabti-ilani-Marduk)[52] points toward a future in which such violence will be forgotten and the land of Akkad will again rise to prominence.

Such an outline would probably find general agreement among most commentators, who would also concur in the estimation that not only the destruction of Babylon and her prophesied renaissance, but also the mention of specific peoples and other cities indicates an historical background to the epic. The delineation of that background entails considerable debate. In his translation of the text, which at the time was the most complete, P. Gössmann emphasized its political orientation, comparing

42

it to the Tukulti-Ninurta epic and other examples of what he termed a
"Gattung von politischen Tendenz-Schriften."[53] Indeed, Gössmann emphasized the nationalistic tone of the epic, which for him did not concern
a city and its temple (as *Enuma eliš*), but a self-conscious concern for
the "Volk" and "Nation" of Akkad that Gössmann likened to Israel's concept of the "chosen people."[54] Moreover, this nationalistic *Tendenz* explains the "outspokenly anti-Assyrian" viewpoint of the epic.[55] As for
the historical background, Gössmann noted that the age and language of
the texts pointed to the Neo-Babylonian period, and that analysis of the
geographical and ethnographical terms used indicated the period of 722-
626 B.C.[56] Even more precisely, Gössmann asserted that the destruction
of Babylon during a revolt and the smashing of the statues of the gods
most likely fit the campaign of Sennacherib against Babylon in 689 as it
is described in the Assyrian annals. Thus the composition of the epic
could be dated to c. 685 B.C.[57]

Not only Gössman's historical conclusions, but also his reconstruction, translation, and general interpretations received serious criticism
from several quarters at almost the same time. Erica Reiner pointed out
that our failure to understand the text "may be due to its difference from
the Babylonian epic tradition," although she too noted the similarity to
the Tukulti-Ninurta epic.[58] More specific criticism and alternatives came
from R. Frankena[59] and, especially, W. G. Lambert.[60] Lambert complained
that Gössman's method of explaining a number of ethnographic terms as
deliberate archaisms did not do justice to the historical background of
the epic, nor, he felt, was it germane to Babylonian literary practice.
Instead, he claimed that names such as Sutû, the Sea country, Subartu,
and Gutium were current in the eleventh century.[61] Thus a *terminus a quo*
is found in the Sutû invasions, c. 1050, and, since the epic ends with a
hope of a Babylonian renaissance that could only have been possible before the rise of Assyria, a *terminus ad quem* is fixed at c.750.[62] More
specifically, Lambert suggested that the epic was written down during the
reign of Nābû-apal-iddina (c. 860), who was the avenger of the Sutû and
the rebuilder of Akkad, and that it reflects the raids of the Sutû that
began during the reign of Adad-apal-iddina (c. 1050). Since the latter
was an Aramaean usurper, the civil war in Babylon could easily be explained as a reaction against his ostensible collusion with the Sutû
invaders against the cities of Akkad.[63] Despite some difference in details,
Cagni has also confirmed an eleventh century background for the epic.[64]

Both views are discussed by Blahoslav Hruška in a review article on Cagni, but Hruška concludes only that the theological and linguistic characteristics of the epic point toward a later date--"surely in the 1st millenium before Christ"--and reserves final judgment until a study promised by W. von Soden appears.[65] In short, the latest critical discussion on the dating of the historical background of the epic by those who have worked most closely with it leaves us with a span of almost four centuries.

While the precise historical circumstances of the epic are, of course, important for a number of interpretive issues, it is our contention that both extremes (from the eleventh to the seventh century) present much the same ideological orientation. Our brief review of the interpretation of the epic already indicates a number of similarities between this orientation and conclusions we have drawn concerning the other major works above. Thus, as in the Exaltation of Inanna, the Tukulti-Ninurta Epic, and the Nur-Adad Letter, the overall concern of the Erra Epic is the vacillations of sovereignty: in this case, "the fall and rise of Akkad," as Lambert puts it.[66] Secondly, the significance of the divine statue, which we have seen with the last three works above, seems to be important here also; indeed Lambert suggests that the "'theology' of the divine statue" is the central religious issue of the Erra Epic. This is a result of Lambert's interpretation of Erra's request to Marduk to relinquish his commanding position as being really a request for him "to separate himself from his statue."[67]

Along with the fluctuations of political victory and defeat, and the way in which this is symbolized in the statue or insignia of the deity, one finds a third element in the Erra Epic that is intimately related to these two and bears further resemblance to our earlier discussion. Each of the works that we have examined above involves a situation in which a revolt against authority must be put down: the revolt of Uruk against the Sargonic party; the revolt in Larsa against an occupying enemy; and the revolt of Kashtiliash against the oath sworn between his and Tukulti-Ninurta's predecessors. Now, in the Erra Epic, Tablet IV reveals a situation possibly very similar to that of the Nur-Adad inscription: the revolt of Babylon against the (perhaps foreign) ruling authority--not to mention Erra's subversion of Marduk's cosmic control.

Finally, there is the fourth element which we have delineated in each of these major works and which is outstanding in the Erra Epic: the use of the divine vanguard motif. We first find this motif almost at the

44

beginning of Tablet I, in the midst of lines that alternate confusingly
between third person and direct address,[68] and it is no simple task to
determine the identity of each speaker. We shall present the text from
Cagni (58, 60) and a translation according to our own interpretation,
followed by an explanation.

4   ^{d}i-šum ṭá-bi-ḫu na-a'-du
       šá ana ⌜*na-*še-*e ^{giš}kakkē^m⌝-šu ez-zu-ti
       qātā^{II}-šu as-ma

5   ù ana šub-ruq ul-me-šú še-ru-ti ^{d}èr-ra qar-rad ilāni^m
       i-nu-*šú ina šub-ti
       i-ris-su-ma lib-ba-šú e-peš ta-ḫa-zi
       i-ta-mi a-na ^{giš}kakkē^m-šú lit-pa-ta i-mat mu-u-ti
       ana ^{d}Sibitti qar-rad la šá-na-an na-an-di-qa kak-⌜ke⌝-ku-un
       i-qab-bi-ma a-na ka-šá lu-ṣi-ma a-na ṣēri

10   a-ta di-pa-ru-um-ma i-na-aṭ-ṭa-lu nu-úr-ka
       at-ta a-lik maḫ-ri-im-ma ilāni^m x̣ [x x x]
       at-ta nam-ṣa-ru-um-ma ṭa-bi-ḫ[u x x x]
       ^{d}èr-ra ti-bi-ma ina sa-pan ma-a-ti
       ki-i nam-rat kab-ta-at-ka ù ḫa-du-u lib-bu-uk

15   ^{d}èr-ra ki-i šá a-me-li dal-pi i-da-a-šú an-[ḫa]
       i-qab-bi a-na lìb-bi-šú lu-ut-bi lu-uṣ-lal-ma
       i-ta-a-ma a-na kak-ke-šú um-me-da tub-qa-a-ti
       ana ^{d}Sibitti qar-rad la šá-na-an a-na šub-te-ku-*nu ⌜tu⌝-ra-ma
       a-di at-ta ta-de-ek-ku-šú ṣa-lil ur-šu-uš-šú

20   it-ti ^{d}ma-mi ḫi-ra-tuš ip-pu-šá ul-sa-am-ma

Išum, the honored slaughterer[69]--
     whose hand is suited for bearing his furious weapons,

5   and, in the flashing of whose mighty sword, Erra,
         the hero of the gods, cowers in his dwelling--
His heart longs for the action of battle.
He declares to his weapons: "Spread venom of death!"
To the Sibitti, peerless heroes: "Put on your weapons!"
He says to you [Erra]: "Let me go out to the field."
[Erra replies:]

10   "You are the torch, they[70] look to you for light;
You are the vanguard, the gods . . . .
You are the sword, the [honored?][71] slaughter[er]."

[Išum persists:]

"Erra, arise and destroy the land!

How splendid your mood is, and how congenial your disposi-
    tion."[72]

15   Erra like a man over-exerted moves his arms painfully,

He says to his heart: "Shall I rise up or lie down?"[73]

He declares to his weapons: "Hide in the corner!"

To the Sibitti, peerless heroes: "Settle back in your abodes."

[the author addresses Išum:]

Until you arouse him, he [Erra] will settle back in his bed;

20   With Mami his spouse he will make love.

While it is by no means certain, we feel that our accounting of the
speakers in the text is preferable. This opening passage is an artfully
constructed piece whose main purpose is to contrast Išum's eagerness for
battle with Erra's lethargic reluctance.[74] As the text now stands,[75]
this is intimated already in 11. 4-5, which picture Išum brandishing his
splendid weapons while Erra (or his statue)[76] cowers in his dwelling
place. The different attitudes of the two are then accentuated by a comparison of 11. 6-8 and 16-18:[77] both are constructed on the same pattern,
but the former depict Išum itching for a fight and inciting his personified weapons[78] to violence, while the latter reveal an ambivalent, almost
irenic Erra.

Perhaps the most troublesome lines are 10-12. Who is speaking and to
whom are the remarks addressed? Is the "you" of line 9 identical to that
in line 10, and how are they related to that in 1. 19? To my knowledge,
only B. Hruška and A. Falkenstein have argued for 11. 10-12 as an address
by Išum to Erra.[80] Although this interpretation may make for smoother
reading, the identification of the vanguard here as Erra is not consonant
with the rest of the epic. Except for IV. 15, the title *alik maḫri* is
consistently used for Išum--at times as the vanguard of the gods in general, but usually as that of Erra.[81] Thus our arrangement would have Erra
responding to Išum's challenge essentially by eschewing the initiative to
battle.

Even more instructive is the occurrence of the motif later in Tablet
I. The passage we have quoted above is followed by a description of the
Sibitti and the functions ascribed to each one by Anu (11. 23-45). They
are then given to Erra to go at his side (*lillikū idaka*) and to be his

furious weapon ($^{giš}kakkū^m$-ka $ezzuti$).[81] The Sibitti, in turn, present a
lengthy exhortation to Erra, attempting to persuade him to overcome his
lethargy (11. 46-91). Their taunts constantly play on the contrast between going to battle ($alak$ $ṣēri$) and staying at home ($ašib$ ina $āli$).
Also, their complaints about the woeful conditions resulting from Erra's
inactivity and their longing for the "festival" of war[82] remind us of
the speech of Tukulti-Ninurta's army before the decisive battle. The
Sibitti's description of the future reaction to Erra's taking the field
are also familiar: the gods above and below will tremble in fear, as
will all kings and lands; the mountains will tumble down, and the depths
of the sea will churn (11. 60-70).

At this point, Erra is goaded into a change of heart, and decides to
muster his forces for destruction. It is at this decisive turn in the
epic that he summons his vanguard, Išum, and addresses him as if he were
the one who had dallied (I. 95-99; Cagni, 66, 68):[83]

min-su še-ma-ta-ma qa-liš tu-u[š-(x)-b]u
ṭu-da pi-*te-ma lu-uṣ-bat ḫar-ra-ni
^{d}Sibitti qar-rad la šá-na-an lu-ʳupˈ-p[it]?   x-[x-(x)]-x
^{giš}kakkē^m-ia ez-zu-tu šu-li-*k[a] i-da-a-a
ù at-ta a-lik maḫ-ri-ia a-lik *ʳarkiˈ-ia

Why are you sitting here listening quietly?
Open the way! Muster the army!
The Sibitti, peerless heroes, . . .
My mighty weapons send at my side,
And you--go before me, go behind me.

In short, this text also reveals unmistakable similarities to those above.
The use of speeches as structural units within the narrative reminds us
of the Tukulti-Ninurta epic, while less explicit reference to actual historical events, and the lack of human agents as major characters, is
reminiscent of the Exaltation of Inanna and stands in contrast to the
Nur-Adad letter and the Tukulti-Ninurta Epic. The interpretation of the
historical situation behind the Erra Epic as involving in part a revolt
in the city of Babylon has clear analogies to several of the above texts,
and the use of the vanguard motif, both in the beginning of the poem and
at the outset of Erra's destructive spree, functions in a way by now familiar to us.

(5) *Enuma eliš*

The preceding discussion has traced the use of the motif of the
divine vanguard through a number of interesting, and, in many ways,
quite different texts. Yet we have found several elements in common
in each that seem to converge around the typology of exaltation. This
is true whether the text itself explicitly narrates historical events
(the Nur-Adad Letter, the Tukulti-Ninurta Epic) or, at least on the sur-
face, appears to be mythological in orientation (the Exaltation of Inanna,
the Erra Epic). We now turn to a text which is by far the best known of
all those discussed--*Enuma eliš*. Our interest in this text centers in
the preparation for, and commencement of, Marduk's battle with Tiamat, as
well as in the most immediate historical background that may lie behind
the epic as a whole.

Our analysis of the text will begin with Tablet IV. After Marduk
is declared king and commissioned to fight Tiamat, a long episode ensues
in which the extensive armory is described. The following lines are the
most important for our discussion:

39 iš-kun birqu i-na pa-ni-šu
40 nab-lu muš-laḫ-mi-ṭu zu-mur-šu um-la-al-la
47 u-še-ṣa-am-ma šârê ša ib-nu-u si-bit-ti-šu-un
48 qer-biš ti-amat šu-ud-lu-ḫu ti-bu-ú arki-šu
49 iš-ši-ma be-lum a-bu-ba (iṣ) kakka-šu raba(a)
50 (iṣ) narkabta u-mu la maḫ-ri gà-lit-ta ir-kab
55 uš-ziz im-nu-uš-šu ta-ḫa-za ra-aš-ba u tu-qu-un-tú
56 šu-me-la a-na-an-ta da-a-a-i-pat ka-la mut-te-ten-di
57 na-aḫ-lap-ti ap-luḫ-ti pul-ḫa-ti ḫa-lip-ma
58 me-lam-mi-šu ra-šub-ba-ti a-pi-ir ra-šu-uš-šu
59 u-te-šer-ma be-lum ur-ḫa-šu ú-šar-di-ma
60 aš-riš ti-amat ša ag-gat pa-nu-uš-šu iš-kun[84]

39 He placed the lightning before him;
40 With a burning flame he filled his body.
    (In the next lines, Marduk constructs a net and organizes
    the various winds which are part of his armament.)
47 The winds which he had made--the Seven--he set loose,
48 To destroy the heart of Tiamat they rose up behind him.
49 The Lord raised up the flood, his mighty weapon,
50 The storm chariot irresistable and terrible he mounted.

55　At his right hand he placed fearsome combat and battle,

56　At his left, Conflict, which shoves aside all conspirators.

57　Muffled in a mantle of fearsome mail,[85]

58　(With) a frightful halo covering his head,

59　The Lord went forth and followed his course,[86]

60　Towards the enraged Tiamat he set his face.

Here once again we have a terrifying picture of the hero and the divine entourage that accompanies him to battle. Marduk is literally surrounded by weapons--in front and behind, and at each flank--most of which are expressions of storm phenomena and personifications of warfare. Thus the vanguard motif that we have seen in various forms above achieves its fullest expansion here.

Despite Marduk's powerful armament, the battle is hardly determined from the outset, for Tiamat, too, has her host of weaponry with precisely the same designation as those of Marduk--"the gods her helpers who march at her side" (*ilū ri-ṣu-ša a-li-ku i-di-ša*, 1. 107, cf. 69). Chief among these is Kingu, whose position is described as follows (I.149-151):

a-li-kut maḫ-ri pa-an um-ma-ni mu-'-ir-ru-tu pu-uḫ-ri

na-še-e ⁱṣkakki ti-iṣ-bu-tu di-ku-u a-na-an-ta

ša! tam-ḫa-ru ra-ab-sik-kát-tu-tu[87]

The vanguard, leader of the army, command of the Assembly,

The raising of weapons for battle, instigator of combat,

In war the commander-in-chief.

Thus among Tiamat's divine retinue, it is preeminently Kingu who "marches before her" into battle (II.56), and his elevation by Tiamat to the "rank of Anu" (I.158) stands in direct challenge to the exaltation of Marduk.

The correspondence between this and the exaltation of Inanna to the rank of An is not simply coincidental. Indeed, *Enuma eliš* provides perhaps the most salient example of the typology of exaltation, especially in the correlation between theogonic and political events. Thus Marduk's kingship of the gods finds its most immediate explanation in the events during the reign of Nebuchadnezzar I (c. 1124-1103), especially the victory over Elam and the celebrated return of the statue of Marduk from its captivity there.[88] As Hallo notes,

> The magnitude of the military triumph, then, may well

> have combined with the dramatic recovery of the statue
>
> to lay the basis for Marduk's exaltation at Babylon . . . .[89]

This, of course, does not mean that *Enuma eliš* or Marduk's exaltation were created *in toto* at this time. Thus, as Lambert has suggested, the promotion of Marduk to a higher rank in the pantheon was already a consequence of Hammurabi's selection of Babylon as the capitol city. Marduk became one of the 'great gods,' although he was not head of the pantheon.[90] Similarly, Thorkild Jacobsen has most recently suggested that the battle between Marduk and Tiamat reflects the political tension between Babylonia and the Sealand that began in the early second millenium. For Jacobsen, the first stage of crystallization was somewhat later than Hammurabi:

> The kingship Marduk achieved by his victory would then
> represent the kingship of the unified Babylonian world,
> such as it existed after the unification under Ulam-
> buriash--but pushed back into mythical times.[91]

This stage, however, was only part of a long development from the Fertility Drama of 'primitive' society to the Battle Drama of the first millenium. In the latter, a

> new form comes to be the preferred vehicle for a new
> *political* drama celebrating and reaffirming the birth
> of the nation as a divine achievement that was from
> the beginning, in mythical time.[92]

At any rate, it is clear that *Enuma eliš* is the product of a long process of development during which the historical events that surrounded its origins were obscured, thereby allowing the cosmic, mythological aspects to play the dominant role.[93] Nevertheless, the exaltation of Marduk that it relates cannot be fully understood apart from those historical events, and the final stage of that exaltation finds its most likely setting at the end of the second millenium, under the reign of Nebuchadnezzar I.

We may conclude that extensive imagery of the divine vanguard, the overthrow of a previously controlling political power, the return of the cultic statue, and the divine authorization of the cultic institutions of Babylon, are all factors we have found to be important in the texts that exemplify the typology of exaltation. *Enuma eliš* could thus rightly be termed "The Exaltation of Marduk" rather than the customary "Epic of Creation."

50

It is difficult to summarize this entire section without succumbing to the danger of distorting the individual integrity of each of the literary works discussed in the attempt to force each one to fit a pattern that is, at best, an artificial construct. As we noted at the outset of this study, the problem of literary and conceptual "patterns" has persistently plagued the discussion of divine presence, both in the ancient Near Eastern material and in the Old Testament. Nevertheless, it is clear that each of the texts we have discussed has a number of features in common with several, if not all, of the others. Our discussion in the remainder of the book will reveal the significance of many of these features, including the roles of cultic objects and institutions. For now we shall only mention two major areas of agreement:

(1) At least three of the texts reflect an historical situation that is intricately involved with the founding and/or renaissance of an empire --in the Exaltation of Inanna and the Tukulti-Ninurti Epic, over Sumer and Akkad; in *Enuma eliš*, that of Nebuchadnezzar I. This historical situation gives rise to and is expressed by the religious dimension of theogonic exaltation--of Inanna and Sargon/Enheduanna; of Ninurta (and Assur) and Tukulti-Ninurta; and of Marduk and Babylon (Nebuchadnezzar). The political aspect of this typology is also implied in the circumstances of the Nur-Adad letter (Larsa) and the Erra Epic (Akkad), although the theological side is absent or less explicit.

(2) All five texts utilize the motif of the divine vanguard, often accompanied by the language of storm phenomena.[94] In the Nur-Adad Letter and the Tukulti-Ninurta Epic this involves a precise historical event, and the divine warriors are portrayed as being actively present alongside the human heroes of the narrative. In the latter especially, the text as a whole has clearly achieved epic proportions. In the Erra Epic, a precise historical event may be in mind; and the vanguard motif also comes at a critical juncture, but the narrative lacks a human character similar to Nur-Adad or Tukulti-Ninurta. Finally, in the Exaltation of Inanna the appearance of the goddess does not come at a climactic battle involving explicit human characters but seems to describe in more general terms the victories that she has already achieved and the potential destruction that her renewed intervention would mean for all those aligned against the Sargonic hegemony.

[1] *Exaltation*, 48.

[2] The specific name of the city is only a probability; see *Ibid.*, 52 on stanza vii.

[3] *Ibid.*, 15-19.

[4] The storm imagery in this passage, as well as that of others discussed below, is treated also by Moshe Weinfeld, "'Rider of the Clouds' and 'Gatherer of the Clouds,'" (The Gaster *Festschrift*) *Journal of the Ancient Near Eastern Society of Columbia University* 5 (1973) 421-426.

[5] Thus, as Hallo notes (*Exaltation*, 51), Inanna "could be compared to the storm, or even the stormgod Iškur. For the notion of the storm or storm cloud as a bird with outspread wings was a commonplace in Sumerian iconography as well as literature." Moreover, these images (especially 11.28-31) are more than mere simile: "They may imply actual or virtual identification."

[6] *Ibid.*, 52.

[7] *Ibid.*, 3, the "Myth of Inanna and Ebih." Ebih apparently represents the revolt of Jebel Hamrim against Naram Sin. In a private communication, Prof. Hallo also suggests the following: "Inanna and Ebih has a very striking use of storm and flood metaphors to describe Inanna's battle tactics. It is, in my opinion, full of word plays, e.g. between flood and quiver (amaru)."

[8] *Ibid.*, 9, 50. See also William W. Hallo and William K. Simpson, *The Ancient Near East: A History* (New York: Harcourt Brace Jovanovich, 1971) 54-60. For further treatment of the role of politics in Sumerian-Semitic syncretism during the Sargonic period, see also J. J. M. Roberts, *The Earliest Semitic Pantheon: A Study of Semitic Deities Attested in Mesopotamia before Ur III* (Baltimore: The Johns Hopkins University Press, 1962) 153-154.

[9] See for example his argument on stanzas vi and x, *Exaltation*, 52, 55-56. For often quite different translations, especially of 11. 74-91, see S. N. Kramer, "Hymnal Prayer of Enheduanna: The Adoration of Inanna in Ur," *ANET*, 581. For detailed comments on the translations of Hallo/van Dijk and Kramer, as well references to numerous other studies, see W. H. Ph. Römer, review of *The Exaltation of Inanna*, by Hallo/van Dijk, in *Ugarit Forschungen* 4 (1972) 173-206.

[10] *Ibid.*, 9.

[11] *Ibid.*, 57.

[12] *Ibid.*, 56-57. (See also n. 9.)

[13] *Ibid.*, 68.

[14] J. J. A. van Dijk, "Une insurrection générale au pays de Larša avant l'avènement de Nūradad," *JCS* 19 (1965) 4. He also suggests that the letter is almost certainly an imitation of an older document. On the "Letter to Assur," see our discussion below in ch. 2.

[15] *Ibid.*, 1.

[16] *Ibid.*, 4; also Hallo, *History*, 92-93, and for more details see the reference therein in n. 68.

[17]Adapted from van Dijk, "Nuradad," 4-5.

[18]Based on the text and French translation of van Dijk, *Ibid.*, 7. The reference to Nur-Adad in 1. 124 is added for clarity.

[19]Note also that the epithet in 1. 118 (sún-gal) corresponds to that in in the Exaltation of Inanna: ù-sun-zi-zi-i ("Impetuous wild cow," 1. 58) and sun-zi-mu ("Oh my divine impetuous wild cow," 1. 91).

[20]Van Dijk, "Nuradad," 16. (Utu/Shamash--Larsa; Ningirsu/Ninurta--Lagash; Inanna/Ishtar--Zabala; Iškur/Adad--Ennegi. These deities will become increasingly familiar in the texts to be examined below, even after their specific political connections are lost.)

[21]It seems clear that Nur-Adad was at least a usurper, if not also from non-royal lineage; *Ibid.*, 4. Van Dijk also cites a change of dynasty in this period indicated in a hymn of Ur-Ninurta (1, n. 1).

[22]Again based on van Dijk's French translation (*Ibid.*, 8).

[23]*Ibid.*, 17; cf. Hallo, *Exaltation*, 78, on igi-mè. The three other texts are CT 42, No. 13, 11. 23ff; No. 22, 11. 6ff; and SBH 105, 11. 16ff. The latter is quoted and translated by van Dijk, 17; for transliteration and translation of the first text, see S. N. Kramer, "Cuneiform Studies and the History of Literature: The Sumerian Sacred Marriage Texts," *Proceedings of the American Philosophical Society* 107 (1963) 503-504.

[24]The expressions are the following: igi-mè, ka-mè, múru-mè, zum- (var.: zíb-)mè, egir-mè, ibi-mè, with the corresponding Akkadian equivalents: *ina pa-an*, *pi-e*, *qá-bal*, *ar-ki*, *ar-ki*, and *pa-an ta-ḫa-zi*.

[25]Kramer, "Cuneiform Studies," 503.

[26]Van Dijk, "Nuradad," 4.

[27]*Ibid.*, 9, 11. 195-224.

[28]The texts were first published in two articles by R. Campbell Thompson: "The Excavations on the Temple of Nabû at Nineveh," *Archaeologia*, 2nd Series, 29 (1929) [London: Society of Antiquaries] 103-148; and "The British Museum Excavations at Nineveh, 1931-32," *Annals of Archaeology and Anthropology* 20 (1933) 71-127.

[29]This task is, fortunately, now nearing completion in a Yale University dissertation by Peter Machinist. (The tentative title is "Studies in Middle Assyrian Literary Activity.") Machinist has graciously provided a draft of his transliteration and translation. Since the final pagination of this dissertation is not indicated on the draft, the prospective reader may refer to the column(s) and line(s) in question. We must emphasize that our citations of Machinist do not necessarily reflect his final draft. For details here and especially with regard to ch. 11 below, the reader is referred to Mr. Machinist's article entitled, "Literature as Politics: The Tukulti-Ninurta Epic and the Bible," forthcoming in *CBQ*, Fall 1976. (My knowledge of this article is limited to a brief oral communication with the author.)

[30]"Three Unpublished Fragments of the Tukulti-Ninurta Epic," *AfO* 18 (1957-1958) 38-51, hereafter cited as "TN Epic."

[31]Erich Ebeling, "Bruchstücke eines politischen Propagandagedichtes aus einer assyrischen Kanzlei," *Mitteilungen der Altorientalischen Gesellschaft* 12, Heft 2 (1938) [42 pp.--the entire issue].

[32]About half of the original remains (Lambert, "TN Epic," 38). For the

summary which follows, see Lambert, 40-41.

[33]Shamash, as the god of justice, is the proper authority for such an appeal regarding a treaty relationship.

[34]Text and translation from Lambert, "TN Epic," 49-51. The still tentative translation by Machinist ("Literary Activity") is essentially the same as that of Lambert, except for some of the more difficult lines. Since Lambert's work is more readily available, it seemed advisable to use his translation. Here are some of the variant translations from Machinist: 1. 5 (Lambert's numbering)--add "controls" in the ellipsis; 1. 8--read "his *mass* is reckoned with the flesh of the gods"; 1. 9--read "he was successfully cast into/or through the funnel of the womb of the gods"; 1. 11--"When the lord of all the lands designated him, in place of himself, as head of the army, he praised (him) with his lips." The language, but probably not the ideology behind the language, of 1. 12 according to Machinist is not as fitting to the typology of exaltation as that of Lambert: "Enlil raised him like a natural father, after his first-born son."

[35]Lambert, "TN Epic," 46.

[36]Note the following: *kīma* in 11. 6-7, 11-12; *itti*, 1. 8; *šanānu*, 1. 14; and *gabarašu*, 1. 15.

[37]Cf. Cassin, *Splendeur*, Ch. VI, especially p. 73.

[38]Rendered by Machinist "as head of the army."

[39]That is, at 1. 12; the cuneiform text is divided into sections between 11. 1 and 2, and 11 and 12.

[40]Lambert, "TN Epic," 43.

[41]Thorkild Jacobsen, *Toward the Image of Tammuz and Other Essays*, ed. by William L. Moran (Cambridge: Harvard, 1970), 30.

[42]Cf. Hallo, *Exaltation*, 66, and see below, ch. 3, (2) a and b. The former may well indicate this process as early as the period of Gudea.

[43]Albert Schott, "Das Werden der babylonisch-assyrischen Positions-Astronomie . . .," *ZDMG* 88 (1934) 316-317. Schott notes that no Assyrian king had a name compounded with Ninurta previously, although it later became quite common. Cf. Ur-Ninurta of Isin, c. 1923-1896 B.C.

[44]Note the occurrence of *šarāhu* in the broken context of VI. 24-25, 36-37. The translation by Machinist ("Literary Activity") appears to have the king glorifying Assur and Assur exalting the king.

[45]Transliterated text and translation based primarily on Ebeling, "Bruchstücke," 7-10; that of Machinist ("Literary Activity") is essentially the same, with some exceptions in 11. 25-26, 32. Cf. also Thompson, "Temple of Nabû," 128-129, 131-132. In the transliteration m=*meš*, k=*ki*.

[46]Conversely, their desertion of Kashtiliash spells his defeat (I.39-47; III.23 and passim), a motif that we shall see again in the annals.

[47]Cf. Horst Klengel, "Tukulti-Ninurta I, König von Assyrien," *Das Altertum* 7 (1961) 70; Hallo, *History*, 117. That "the inspiration and creation of Kar-Tukulti-Ninurta can be included as a particularly important piece of evidence of the dramatic extent to which the monarchic position had been exalted," is the opinion of A. K. Grayson, "The Early Development of Assyrian Monarchy," *Ugarit-Forschungen* 3 (1971) 318.

[48]*Ibid.*, 312 and especially 315-319.

⁴⁹Luigi Cagni, *L'Epopea di Erra* (Studi Semitici 34; Roma: Instituto di Studi del Vicino Oriente, 1969). All references to the epic will use Cagni's numbering.

⁵⁰This reading of the name has been established by J. J. M. Roberts, "Erra—Scorched Earth," *JCS* 24 (1971) 11-12. He suggests that the name derives from an original root *ḥrr, meaning "to scorch, char," and that the agricultural practice of burning fields makes compatible Erra's association with Mami, the goddess of fertility (13 and n. 27; see Tablet I:20). Roberts also concludes that Erra's association with plague is secondary to that with war and famine, 16. For his more recent discussion, see *Pantheon*, 21-29.

⁵¹Clearly related to, if not a personification of, fire; cf. Roberts, "Erra," 24 and n. 13, 33.

⁵²He refers to himself in V. 42 and, in the following lines, describes the occasion of the composition of the work and the benefits that he hopes will flow from it in the future. The fact that the author is named presents another interesting parallel to the Exaltation of Inanna, for in both "the process of *poetic* inspiration" is uniquely described and both poems are commended to future generations in similar ways, according to Hallo, *Exaltation*, 62.

⁵³P. F. Gössmann, *Das Era-Epos* (Würzburg: Augustinius, 1956) 83-84.

⁵⁴*Ibid.*, 84.

⁵⁵*Ibid.*, 61.

⁵⁶*Ibid.*, 86-87.

⁵⁷*Ibid.*, 89.

⁵⁸"More Fragments of the Epic of Era: A Review Article [on Gössmann]," *JNES* 17 (1958) 41 and n. 3.

⁵⁹R. Frankena, "Untersuchungen zum Irra-Epos" [also a review of Gössmann], *Bibliotheca Orientalis* 14 (1957) 2-10.

⁶⁰Review of Gössmann, *AfO* 18 (1957-1958), 395-401.

⁶¹*Ibid.*, 397-398.

⁶²*Ibid.*, 400.

⁶³*Ibid.*, 398, 400.

⁶⁴Cagni, *Erra*, 37-45, with a review of other interpretations. See also René Labat, in *Les religions du Proche-Orient asiatique: Textes babyloniens, ougaritiques, hittites. Le trésor spirituel de l'humanité*, ed. Jean Chevalier (Paris: Fayard/Denoël, 1970) 115.

⁶⁵"Einige Uberlegungen zum Erraepos," *Bibliotheca Orientalis* 30 (1973) 4. The epic was the subject of his own dissertation; see 3, n. to title.

⁶⁶Lambert, review of Gössmann, 400.

⁶⁷The statue is designated by *šukuttu* (presumably a symbolic jewel). "When Marduk leaves or enters his statue the act is described as 'putting off, or on, the lordly turban'" (e.g. I.127f; 142f): *Ibid.*, 399. Cf. also Cassin, *Splendeur*, 49; and Labat, *Religions*, 115-116. The story continues with a puzzling account of the commissioning of Girra and various craftsmen to restore the apparently defiled accoutrements of Marduk in the netherworld. Hruška ("Einige Uberlegungen," 4, n. 7) also notes that "Das 'Verschwinden' der Götterstatue und die 'Veränderung' der

göttlichen Insignien" is a theme shared with the *Kudurru* inscription, though he disagrees with Labat's suggestion of direct influence from the latter.

[68]This alternation, along with the device of extended speeches, has led Lambert (review of Gössmann, 396) to wonder whether the epic presumes a dramatic delivery using a small cast of readers.

[69]These two words play on the meaning of the Sumerian for ^{d}i-šum, fame --slaughter; cf. also "torch" and Išum=flame, 1. 10 (see Lambert, review of Gössmann, 400; Hruška, "Einige Überlegungen," 5, n. 24). Cf. 1. 21: ^{d}en/-gi$_6$/-du-du=*bēlu/muši/muttallik*.

[70]"they" could refer to mankind (so Cagni, 59; cf. 11. 21-23: "O Engidudu [=Išum], lord who goes about in the night, who guides the princes; who constantly guides the young man and woman in safety, who makes [the night] bright as day"). On the other hand, it quite possibly refers to the Sibitti and the great gods who would follow Išum in his role as vanguard.

[71]Supplying *na-a'-du*, as in 1. 4.

[72]Thus Išum is irritated at Erra's disinclination for battle.

[73]So Adam Falkenstein, "Zur ersten Tafel des Erra-Mythos," *ZA* N.F. 19 (1959) 201, with reference to von Soden.

[74]Our position is in general agreement with Falkenstein (*Ibid.*) and contradicts that of Cagni and others (see the convenient listing of interpretations on the Prologue by Cagni, *Erra*, 135-137). See also Labat, *Religions*, 117. Cagni observes that, elsewhere in the epic, Išum does not incite Erra to battle (except at the end of IV; but note also I.13), and that this function is ascribed to the Sibitti, who are somewhat in opposition to Išum as the deity benevolent to mankind (137). Thus the prologue is mostly addressed to Išum and describes the bellicose character or Erra, in contrast to that of Išum, who is irenic (11. 3, 21-22) albeit a warrior also (4-5a, 13), p. 133. One can make only uncomfortable decisions here. Cagni's position requires an abrupt and awkward shift from Erra the impulsive warrior (11. 6-9) to Erra the lethargic shut-in (11. 15-20). This makes Išum's call to arise (1. 13) embarrassingly irrelevant. This problem shows up in another interpretation, which requires that Erra suddenly become "tired of fighting . . . and retire(s) to his bedroom . . .," (Reiner, "More Fragments," 42). On the other hand, our position faces the problem observed above by Cagni. However, we feel that our reading makes for a more consistent Prologue, and that it is quite possible that Išum's later attitude of restraint is a result of the appalling extent of Erra's devastation.

[75]One cannot help but feel that "Erra, the hero of the gods" is an unhappy intrusion; it is at least awkward, although this depends on how one translates the final phrase, *inusu ina subti*. There seem to be two options: (1) as Wolfram von Soden notes [*Akkadisches Handwörterbuch* (Wiesbaden: Harrassowitz, 1957ff., hereafter abbreviated *AHw*)], the expression *nâšu ina šubti* can mean "(vor Angst) weichen" particularly with reference to "Götter(bilder)." It appears to have this meaning in *Enuma eliš* VI. 146, and the action it describes is understood as an ill omen in a divination text (*ú-lu ilu ina šubti-šu inû-uš*--the enemy will fall upon the country) [F. Thureau-Dangin, "Les fêtes d'Akitu d'après un texte divinatoire," *RA* 19 (1922) 143-144]. (2) Although cited along with the above by von Soden, another text may provide an alternative. It reads: *kima bir-qa ib-riq-ma i-nu-uš šub-ti* [A. Jeremias, "Die sogenannten Kedorlaomer-Texte," *MVAG* 21, (1916) 86]. The phrase in question

could easily be read as supplementing the lightning flashes, thus providing a positive action and, indeed, one quite similar to the Erra text (*šubruq*). It is so translated in *CAD* B, 104: "he flashed like a lightning bolt when he moved on (his) seat."

Of course, it is the presence of Erra in the line that makes the latter reading extremely difficult, if not impossible. This is why Erra seems intrusive, and its omission would leave a nicely constructed unit:

Išum ṭabiḫu na'du

  šá ana naše kakkēšu essuti

    qātāšu asma

  ù ana šubruq ulmešu šeruti

    inušu ina šubti

[76]This could be the meaning of *šubti*; see the previous note and especially von Soden's reference to "Götter(*bilder*)" (emphasis provided), which would be most appropriate for the group of texts dealt with in Thureau-Dangin's article (also previous note) since they involve the *akitu* procession. Note also, at the end of the Erra Epic, V.1 (*irmu šubatsu*) and especially V.22 (*irumma [ana] ʾéʾ-mes-lam ir-ta-ʾmi šu-bat-ʾ šu*), both referring to Erra's taking up residence in his dwelling, Emeslam.

[77]Cf. 11. 97-99 quoted below.

[78]Cf. the Tukulti-Ninurta Epic, IV.15 where "'the Weapon' of Aššur or Enlil appears as an independent entity engaging in battle," Lambert, "TN Epic," 49, n. to 1. 15, with reference to the Erra Epic as well as inscriptions of Gudea (on which, see below).

[79]Hruška, "Einige Uberlegungen," 5, n. 26.

[80]Cf. (besides I.11) I.99, 105; III.c.15, 39, 54; V. 13, 46. In IV.15 the reference is to Erra. One should also note here that the attempt to merge Išum, Erra, and Nergal into distinct yet identical deities by Gössman (*Era-Epos*, 69-70) is rightly criticized by Frankena, "Untersuchungen zum Irra-Epos," 5. Moreover, that Išum, unlike other Mesopotamian subordinate deities (or viziers), is not submissive to Erra, but a real partner or comrade, is pointed out by Hruška, "Einige Uberlegungen," 5.

[81]Ll. 40 and 44 (cf. 11. 4, 35 for the latter phrase). Note how *lilliku idaka* is structured to open and close Anu's speech to Erra.

[82]L. 51, *alak šēri šá etluti ki šá isinnumma*: "young men going to war is like a festival." Cf. Tukulti-Ninurta Epic, V.4: *qablu u ippiru isinani*. For another example, see J. J. van Dijk, "Textes Divers du Musée de Bagdad IV," *Sumer* 18 (1962) 24: "Allusion est faite aux jeux cultuels pendant les jours de fête." On the contrast with staying at home, cf. also William W. Hallo, "Antediluvian Cities," *JCS* 23 (1970) 57, and Erica Reiner, "City Bread and Bread Baked in Ashes," *Languages and Areas* (George V. Bobrinskoy vol.; Chicago: University of Chicago Press, 1967) 116-120.

[83]Ll. 96-99 are identical to III. c. 24-27.

[84]The transliterated text is taken primarily from René Labat, *Le poème babylonien de la création* (Paris: Librarie d'Amérique et d'Orient, 1935) 124, 126. Lines 55-56 have been corrected by O. R. Gurney, "Sultantepe Tablets," 26-27, and our readings of these two lines were brought

up to date in accordance with the preliminary collation reflected in the "school edition," published by W. G. Lambert and Simon B. Parker, *Enuma Eliš: The Babylonian Epic of Creation, The Cuneiform Text* (Oxford: Clarendon, 1966) 23. For translations to which we are again indebted, see E. A. Speiser, "The Creation Epic," *ANET*, 66; Labat, *Religions*, 51-52.

[85]Our translation is a weak attempt to capture the music of the line, which is actually based on assonance rather than on alliteration.

[86]The "course" seems to be that of his chariot; cf. II.118.

[87]The line count, as well as the reading, is that of Lambert, *Enuma eliš*, 6. For other versions, the lines are 148-150.

[88]W. G. Lambert, "The Reign of Nebuchadnezzar I: A Turning Point in the History of Ancient Mesopotamian Religion," *The Seed of Wisdom: Essays in Honor of T. J. Meek*, ed. W. S. McCullough (Toronto: University of Toronto Press, 1964) 3-13.

[89]*Exaltation*, 67. Cf. also Ebeling, "Bruchstücke," 2, n. 1.

[90]"The Historical Development of the Mesopotamian Pantheon: A Study in Sophisticated Polytheism," in *Unity and Diversity: Essays in the History, Literature, and Religion of the Ancient Near East*, ed. Hans Goedicke and J. J. M. Roberts (The Johns Hopkins Near Eastern Studies; Baltimore: The Johns Hopkins University Press, 1975) 194.

[91]"Religious Drama in Ancient Mesopotamia," in *Unity and Diversity* [see preceding note], 76.

[92]*Ibid.*, 77.

[93]Cf. Lambert, "Reign of Nebuchadnezzar," 5-10 for the development particularly from the time of Hammurabi. This and the accentuation of the cosmic aspects, were also stressed in a paper read at the 1968 meeting of the American Oriental Society by William W. Hallo entitled "The Typology of Divine Exaltation." Cf. also *Exaltation*, 66, on the survival of texts that have little historical specificity. On the other hand, it is incorrect to assume, as does C. J. Labuschagne [*The Incomparability of Yahweh in the Old Testament* (Leiden: Brill, 1966) 55; cf. 49-54], that the motif of divine exaltation became in general mere hyperbole; this misreads its frequent political correlation.

[94]It is worth noting that such language, and the vanguard motif itself, is not *necessarily* confined to texts involving precise historical circumstances or the typology of exaltation. See the excerpt from the Gilgamesh Epic, cited as the first text in Appendix 1.

CHAPTER 2

THE ASSYRIAN ANNALS

The Assyrian royal inscriptions[1] yield no evidence of anything
resembling the motifs of divine presence discussed above until the reigns
of Tukulti-Ninurta and his immediate predecessors.[2] With Adad-narari I
(c. 1307-1275) we find a formula very close to that which we shall see
with Tukulti-Ninurta:

> With the strong weapons of the god Ashur, my lord;
> with the support of the gods An, Enlil, and Ea, Sin,
> Shamash, Adad, Ishtar, and Nergal, most powerful
> among the gods, the awesome gods, those who go at my
> right hand, I captured by conquest the city of Taidu. . . .[3]

Similar formulae are found with Shalmaneser I: "prince who acts with
the support of the god Ashur and the great gods, his lords . . ."; "with
the support of Ashur and the great gods, my lords, that city [Arinu of
Uratri] I captured . . . ."[4] Significantly, such motifs occur only in
text No. 1, which is the only one from Shalmaneser describing a military campaign; the rest of the texts relate the rebuilding of Ehursagkur-
kurra, the temple of Ishtar, and other buildings.

With Tukulti-Ninurta himself we find a description of the gods accompanying the king in battle three times. It is striking that this motif
is used exclusively for the campaign against Kashtiliash--that is, the
battle that is the subject of the Epic we discussed above.[5] All three
examples of the motif are virtually identical in form, which seems to
indicate that here the motif has achieved the status of a fixed formula.[6]
We shall take Text 5, lines 48-56 as an example:

> 48 i-na tukúl-ti šá ^{d}aš-šur 49 ^{d}enlil
> ù ^{d}šá-maš ilâni^{m} rabûti^{m} 50 bêlê$^{m-ja}$

i-na ri-ṣu-ti 51 šá ^{d}ištar bêlat^{at}
šamê^e irṣiti^{ti} 52 i-na pa-ni um-ma-
ni-ja III 53 il-li-ku it-ti 54 ^{I}kaš-
til-a-šu šar$_4$ ^{mat}kar-du-ni-aš 55 a-na
e-piš tuq-ma-ti 56 as-ni-iq

With the help of the gods Assur, Enlil,
and Shamash, the great gods, my lords
(and) with the aid of the goddess Ishtar, mistress of heaven (and) underworld, (who) march at the fore of my
army, I approached Kashtiliash, king
of Karduniash, to do battle.

The paragraph ends with the defeat of the Babylonians and the humiliating
capture of Kashtiliash. It thus clearly refers to the decisive battle
between the two kings, rather than to the skirmishes that preceded.
Moreover, this motif betrays an obvious similarity to that which opens
the battle scene in Tablet V of the Epic (quoted above). Also, this
paragraph from the annals (and parallels) ends with the proclamation
that through this battle Tukulti-Ninurta "became lord of Sumer and Akkad," again, resembling the Epic.[7] Text 5 then goes on to describe the
construction of the "New Palace" (Elugalumunkurkurra), and the parallel
passages are contained in texts that conclude with the construction of
the cult center Kar-Tukulti-Ninurta, also comparable to the end of the
Epic.[8]

It is very important to emphasize that here we have, for the first
time, the use of a motif of divine presence in both a literary *and* an
annalistic work, in which the literary form and function of the motif is
remarkably similar. This raises an important question: can the similarity be explained by literary influence of one on the other? Unfortunately, our ability to date both epic and annals is scarcely precise
enough to answer this question. Although he does not expressly say so,
Lambert's discussion of Tukulti-Ninurta's literary interests implies a
contemporary date for the composition of the Epic.[9] Similarly, Jacob J.
Finkelstein suggests a date that is at least near the end of the king's
reign.[10] This, of course, must be weighed against the fact, emphasized
by Weidner, that our copies of the Epic come from about a century later.[11]
As for the annals, Weidner concludes that those containing the motif in

question are among the latest from the reign of Tukulti-Ninurta.[12]   In
short, both epic and annals are very nearly contemporaneous, and a decision on literary dependence cannot be decided on the basis of dating.

One may also ask if there are literary features that might indicate
borrowing, but such a question is as complicated as that of dating.   There
is one interesting point to observe, however.   In his work on the annals,
Weidner has noticed that Kashtiliash is consistently referred to as "King
of the land of Karduniash" when the context is that preceding his defeat,
but is subsequently called "King of the Kassites".[13]   When we apply Weidner's observation to the Epic, we find that Kashtiliash is, with only two
exceptions, called "King of the Kassites" throughout, and the name Karduniash is never used.[14]   Thus the Epic does not distinguish between
Kashtiliash as lord of his own land and as deposed king.   This discrep-
ancy would seem to argue against any deliberate borrowing between epic
and annals.

More significant than the use of the royal titles is the literary
form of the vanguard motif.   Although they are quite similar, there are
also clear differences.   The most obvious one is the comparative brevity
of the motif in the annals and, especially, the reduced number of deities
found therein.   There are only four gods named, whereas in the Epic there
are eight.   There is also a marked difference in style: the terse form
in the annals lacks any literary flourishes, while the Epic motif is a
graphic example of the vivid, poetic quality of the entire work, full of
the imagery of fire and flood.   When we add to this the fact that the
motif that we quoted from the annals of Adad-narari appears to be a
forerunner of the motif of Tukulti-Ninurta--both temporally and literar-
ily--we are forced to consider the possibility that the annals represent
a separate literary style from that of the Epic, perhaps even a separate
scribal school.   However, the texts that we discussed in the first part
of this chapter would strongly indicate that the annals have borrowed
from the literary tradition that those texts represent.   The fact that
the motif in the annals most closely approximates that in the Nur-Adad
Letter and especially in the Tukulti-Ninurta Epic would suggest that the
epic literary tradition in particular is the provenance for the use of
the motif in the annals.   It is also significant that the motif first
appears in the annals of Adad-narari I through Tukulti-Ninurta I, for
this reflects the progressive rise of the Assyrian empire that culmi-
nated in Tukulti-Ninurta's conquest of Kashtiliash, celebrated in both

Epic and annals. Thus, A. K. Grayson can conclude that both the quantity and quality of royal epithets in this period "indicate that the position of the ruler of Ashur vis-à-vis his subjects and his gods was exalted at a pace in direct ratio to the expansion of Assyria's political power."[15] The appearance of the motif of divine presence in the annals thus confirms our previous conclusion that such images tend to emerge during particular historical situations as literary heralds of the foundation or renaissance of imperial supremacy.

The motif of the divine vanguard was evidently well-suited to the burgeoning form of the royal annals. Given the close similarity between the vanguard passages in the Tukulti-Ninurta Epic and the annals from that period, it will be instructive to look more closely at the literary use of this motif in the annals of subsequent kings. While the annals can scarcely match the literary art of the epic form, the way in which the motif in question appears to cluster in particular historical periods down to the end of the Assyrian empire will shed further light on the ideological relationship between motifs of divine presence and the fluctuations of political power.

The motif from the annals of Tukulti-Ninurta that we have quoted can be seen to form a literary precedent for a number of closely related expressions that were maintained for six centuries, down through the reign of Assurbanipal. Like many other expressions in the annals, those in question are couched in highly stereotypical language, although idiosyncracies within the annals of a particular king are sometimes evident. The tenacity to literary stereotypes allows us to divide the expressions related to the divine vanguard into four groups, all of which occur in contexts relating the military victories of the kings: (1) general references to divine help (usually *tukultu*); (2) references to the god(s) standing at the side of (*idu*) the king; (3) expressions of the god(s) going before [especially *ina mahri* and *ina pān(i)*] the king; (4) images of the terrifying splendor (*melammu*) and fearsomeness (*puluhtu*) of the gods or of their armament as employed by the king.

(1) With two exceptions,[16] the references to divine help in battle are concentrated in those of Sargon II, Sennacherib, and Assurbanipal. Sargon, for example, is praised in a number of inscriptions as "the king who, with the help of Assur, Nabû and Marduk" conquered regions from Cyprus to Dilmun.[17] The Sargonid annals particularly favor these three deities for this expression.[18] Another, also common for later

kings, is the introductory phrase "(Trusting) in the support of the great gods," followed by a military adventure.[19] The annals of Sennacherib and Assurbanipal also utilize the introductory formula "(Trusting) in the aid of," but prefer to mention only Assur or Assur plus a string of other major deities.[20] A rather peculiar use of this expression in the Assurbanipal inscriptions even has the Assyrian monarch claiming that Gyges of Lydia conquered his own enemies "by the help of Assur and Ishtar, the gods, my lords," after Gyges had obeyed the command received from Assur in a vision to submit to the sovereignty of Assurbanipal.[21] The annals of Sennacherib exhibit a specialized adaptation of the divine help expression in the formula "In my second [etc.] campaign Assur, my lord, encouraged me . . . ," followed by an account of military victory.[22] As the contents of these motifs indicate, there is no explicit reference to the gods as being actually present under this category. Rather, the expressions simply affirm that the king conquered his enemies with divine aid.

(2) Less frequent in occurrence are those images that express actual divine presence "at the side of" the king in battle. In the Letter to Assur, Sargon tells how Assur "sent at my side his terrible weapons" that "despoil the rebellious" from East to West.[23] In the inscriptions of Sennacherib there is one brief reference to "the great gods, who go at my side"[24] which should be compared to a more lengthy example in the introductory paragraph of another text from the same king. The latter passage seems to be an invocation addressed directly to the deities mentioned:

> Assur, Sin, Shamash, Adad, Urta (MASH), and
> Ishtar, the great gods, who stand at the side
> of the king, their favorite . . . to whom
> your (the god's) hands are stretched out. . . .[25]

Comparable texts from the annals of Esarhaddon refer to "Nabû, Sin, Ishtar, Nergal, who go at my side"[26] and "Ishtar, lady of battle and combat, who goes at my side."[27] There are also several examples of this expression in the texts from Assurbanipal.[28]

In summary, our examination of the first two groups of expressions yields some significant data. The expressions themselves are clearly similar in language and literary context to the vanguard motif in the epic and annals of Tukulti-Ninurta I and the other texts we have pre-

sented. Moreover, it is interesting that the occurrence of these particular expressions is almost exclusively in the annals that reflect the
acme of the Assyrian empire--from Sargon II to Assurbanipal. Although
one must beware of arguments from silence, this does indicate that our
findings are not incompatible with the connection we noted between the
use of the vanguard motif in the earlier literary works and the institution and/or renewal of dynastic hegemony.

(3) The third group of expressions deals with images of the god(s)
"going before" the king in battle, and are obviously quite similar to the
previous group. A typical example comes from the inscriptions of Adad-
narari II:

> At the command of Assur, the great lord, my
> lord, and Ishtar, lady of battle and combat,
> who goes before my widespreading armies . . .
> I marched against Hanigalbat.[29]

There are two other occurrences of very similar expressions from Assur-
nasir-pal II (also including other deities),[30] which may be compared to
three occurrences in the inscriptions from Shalmaneser III.[31] Aside
from one possible example from Sargon II,[32] the rest come from the reigns
of Esarhaddon and Assurbanipal. Two occurrences in the latter are comparable to those examined above.[33] The single text from Esarhaddon is
highly reminiscent of the style of the vanguard motif in its epic form:

> šarru šá tal-lak-ta-šu a-bu-bu-um-ma
> ep-še-ta-šú 13 [lab]-bu na-ad-ru
> pa-nu-uš-šú zu(?)-um-ma
> ar-ke-e-šú ti-qú(?)
> qit-ru-ub 14 ta-ḫa-zi-šú dan-nu
> nab-lu muš-taḫ-me-ṭu
> dGira la a-ni-ḫu[34]

> The king whose march is like a flood-storm,
> whose acts are like a raging lion;
> before him is a storm-demon,
> behind him is a cloud-burst;
> the onset of his battle is mighty;
> a consuming flame,
> an unquenchable fire.

Again, the evidence based on statistical occurrence presents an intriguing mirror to the vicissitudes of the Assyrian empire. Following Tukulti-Ninurta I, the image of the gods "going before" the king is not used again in the extant inscriptions until the successive reigns of Adad-narari II, Assur-nasir-pal II, and Shalmaneser III--a period of resurgent Assyrian political power. The occurrences from the texts of Esarhaddon and Assurbanipal seem to reflect a similar historical situation.

(4) Finally, our fourth group of expressions presents a picture that complements our conclusions up to this point. The great frequency of this group is roughly equal to that of the expressions of divine help.[35] Pithy and representative examples are found in the inscriptions of Tiglath-pilesar I: "The splendor of Assur, my Lord, overwhelmed" the enemies; "terror and fear of the splendor of Assur, my lord, overwhelmed them . . . ."[36] Moreover, as in the hymn of praise to Tukulti-Ninurta, the same or comparable expressions can be used of the king himself: "the fiery tempest, whose splendor overwhelms the quarters (of the world) . . . ."[37] This type of expression also occurs quite frequently in the annals of Assur-nasir-pal II, Shalmaneser III, Sargon II, Sennacherib, Esarhaddon, and Assurbanipal[38]--in short, it occurs precisely with the same kings as it did in the other literary groupings.

Thus the evidence from all four groups indicates a definite trend toward their use in the annals of kings whose reigns reflect the renaissance--real or pretended--of Assyrian imperial might. As if to accentuate this, those passages that extend the literary expressions beyond the usual perfunctory length and that more closely approximate the style of the epic form--as does the passage from Esarhaddon quoted above--come predominantly from the last four major kings of the Assyrian empire. Since these texts tend to be comparatively lengthy, and often utilize several of the above groups, we have assembled them in Appendix 1.

Given the original affinity of our motifs with *literary* works--as distinct from annalistic sources--it should come as no surprise that the large majority of passages from Sargon related to the vanguard motif come from his Letter to Assur. William F. Albright has praised the artistic merits of this work along with the Rassam Prism, and has noted literary affinities with the Akkadian epic tradition.[39] A. L. Oppenheim has devoted a lengthy study to the letter, which he feels was not written for deposit nor as the normal report of the king, but to be read in a public ceremony celebrating the return from war.[40] The aesthetic appeal to an audience is indicated by the "overall structure . . . with its slow moving exposition, climax, crisis, divine intervention, and triumphal end."[41] Moreover, there is evidence of borrowing from extinct lyrical works, and "the 'epical' sweep of the battle descriptions" makes us "think of the epical tradition of Assyria, of which only a few fragments have survived."[42] We have seen the relationship to these "fragments" to be most clearly present in the Tukulti-Ninurta Epic, but there are also strong literary and ideological similarities with the Exaltation of Inanna, and the Nur-Adad Letter adds a striking formal parallel.

Before turning to questions concerning the modes of conception of divine presence raised by the preceding discussion, we shall note one further feature of the annals that corresponds to the epic form as we have seen it with Tukulti-Ninurta. In the "hymn of praise" in that epic we noted that, following a description of the divine attributes of the king, the text emphasized the fear this caused on the part of his rivals:

> He who . . . the extremities of the four winds, all
> > kings without exception live in dread of him:
> As when Addu bellows, the mountains tremble,
> As when Ninurta lifts his weapons, the quarters of
> > the world are reduced to continual anguish.

One need not strain to hear an echo of this in the annals:

> Tiglath-pilesar I: "Mighty torch (?), at the
> onset of whose terrible arms the four regions
> (of the world) shook and the habitations (of
> earth) trembled."[43]

> Adad-narari II: "the effulgence of his sur-
> passing glory consumed all of them. The
> lands of the kings were distressed. The
> mountains trembled."[44]

The obsequious reaction of distant lands to the onslaught of the Assyrian king occurs in more prosaic form as well. For example, under Sargon II, even the kings of Cyprus (Ia') "heard from afar, in the midst of the sea, of the deeds which I was performing, . . . their hearts were rent, fear fell upon them, . . ." and they sent tribute.[45] When Sennacherib approached Elam, "fear and terror were poured out over all Elam," and they fled from their land.[46] Later on we shall return to this material in order to enquire

66

about its provenance in hymnic sources: for now we merely note the congruence of the motif in the epic and annalistic works.

It is legitimate at this point to pose a question concerning the texts we have quoted from the annals: in what way do these literary expressions reflect concepts of divine presence? It is clear that the texts nowhere emphasize any sudden appearance of the deities involved, nor is any interest expressed in their visibility as such. Rather, the annals seem to accept the divine presence almost as a matter of course. However, there is unimpeachable evidence to show that more than literary expression of a religious concept is involved. For example, although the "weapon of Assur" is quite frequently mentioned, usually in the context of the expressions noted above, it is not always clear precisely how the author conceived of this image until we make use of several texts that demonstrate that the "weapon of Assur," we well as other images, refer not simply to symbols of divine and royal power but to actual physical objects. Thus, in a typical expression, Shalmaneser III washes the "weapon of Assur" in the Tigris River or in the Sea.[47] More significantly, the same object is set up in the palace built by Tiglath-pilesar II, along with an image of his own majesty.[48]

Can the various expressions of the divine vanguard motif as we have seen them in the annals also be identified with physical objects? The answer, at least in some cases is, clearly, affirmative. This appears particularly to hold true during the reign of Sargon II. One most instructive text, again from the "Letter to Assur," reads as follows:

13   i-na tu-kul-ti-šu-nu rabî-ti šá AN-ŠÁR
     ^dŠamaš ^dNabû ^dMarduk ú-šal-liš-ma a-na
     ki-rib ḫur-ša-a-ni aṣ-di-ra ta-lu-ku
14   a-na ^matZi-kir-te ù ^matAn-di-a šá ^dURI-
     GAL ^dAdad ú-rim-gal-li a-li-kut maḫ-ri-
     ia ú-šat-ri-ṣa ni-ir-šú-un[49]

With the great help of Ashur, Šamaš,
Nabu, (and) Marduk, for the third
time I directed the march into the
mountains. 14 Towards the lands of
Zikirtu and Andia I turned the yoke
of Nergal and Adad, the emblems which
go before me.

There can be little doubt that the "emblems" (*urinnu*) were physical objects representing the presence of Nergal and Adad, just as the "yoke" no doubt represents the storm chariot that we have repeatedly seen in divine warfare. The identification of the emblems with the motifs of divine presence is further illustrated by another text from Sargon referring to a captured city:

> The gods, who go before me, therein
> I caused to dwell and I called its
> [the city's] name Kâr-Urta. My roy-
> al image I set up in its midst.[50]

This text should be compared with another in which the "weapon of Assur" is installed in the captured city and even "appointed as their deity."[51] Actions similar to these are reported for Sennacherib as well.[52]

In sum, a number of texts indicate that the various expressions for the divine vanguard can refer to physical objects. The "emblems," the storm-chariot, and the "weapon of Assur," represent the divine presence in battle, and are closely associated with the physical image of the king himself when they are installed in a defeated city. That a reference to physical objects is not always to be assumed can be seen in the passage quoted above from the Letter to Assur, where six deities are mentioned but only two are equated with "emblems." It is also unlikely that the passages that refer to a large number of deities (there are nine in the Adad-narari I text) actually have physical symbols of all of them in mind.

The installation of such objects, especially as deities to be worshipped, must be seen alongside the corresponding capture and removal of the local gods (i.e. their statues). This is reported continuously throughout the annals in a mechanical way, simply as part of the booty.[53] However, Oppenheim has noted the unusual emphasis on the plundering of the temple and gods of Urartu in the Letter to Assur, and the striking theological justification for this.[54] In general, however, the gods were not summarily destroyed, for a number of texts explain how they were returned to their original abodes upon the submission of their "owners." Thus Sargon II is lauded for returning the gods of Ur, Uruk, Eridu, and Larsa after his victory over Merodachbaladan.[55] Such restorations, of course, were understood as the result of the respective deities relenting from their wrath--the original cause of the defeat of the city. We have already seen this in

68

the Tukulti-Ninurta Epic, and it is portrayed a number of times in the annals of Esarhaddon with respect to Babylon.[56] Thus the cultic exploitation of such objects following a military victory corroborates the importance of the role of similar objects in some of the texts discussed in chapter 1--especially *Enuma eliš*, the Nur-Adad Letter, the Tukulti-Ninurta Epic, and the Erra Epic. Moreover, the fact that these objects at times stand behind the literary descriptions of divine presence, and the fact that their use demonstrates the correlation between divine and political supremacy, adds further confirmation to our previous conclusions.[57]

THE ASSYRIAN ANNALS

[1]Our survey was conducted using Daniel D. Luckenbill, *Ancient Records of Assyria and Babylonia* (2 vols.; Chicago: University of Chicago Press, 1927), hereafter cited as *ARAB*; and A. K. Grayson, *Assyrian Royal Inscriptions* (Vol. 1; Wiesbaden: Harrassowitz, 1972). The latter, abbreviated *ARI*, goes through the reign of Ashur-resha-ishi I, 1133–1116 B.C. Page numbers for both *ARAB* and *ARI* will be cited only where helpful for locating a particular part of a section (§).

[2]A slight exception to this is one phrase that recurs a number of times in the inscriptions from Erishum I (early 19th century), which foreshadows the one discussed below. It reads: "With the god Ashur, my Lord, standing by me, . . .," but its context is consistently that of building operations rather than of battle. See *ARI*, §§62, 69, 91.

[3]*Ibid.*, §393 and n. 118.

[4]*Ibid.*, §526 and 528; cf. §600.

[5]This correspondence between annals and epic has been used as evidence for the exclusion of Assur-banipal from the discussion (Lambert, "TN Epic," 41, n. 5).

[6]For the transliterated text and translation, see E. F. Weidner, *Die Inschriften Tukulti-Ninurtas I und seiner Nachfolger*, *AfO* Beiheft 12 (Graz: privately published, 1959), text No. 5, ll. 48–56, p. 12, which has a duplicate in text No. 15; and No. 16, ll. 56–61, p. 27. For English translation, see *ARI* §716, and *ARAB* I, §145, p. 51 for text No. 5; *ARI*, §774 and *ARAB* I, §166, p. 57 for text No. 16.

[7]Cf. in the Epic, V.30 (quoted above), VI.11, 41.

[8]Cf. in the Epic, VI.19–20, and Lambert's note, "TN Epic," 45, n. 20.

[9]*Ibid.*, 41–42. Cf. Wolfram von Soden, "Das Problem der zeitlichen Einordnung akkadischer Literaturwerke," *MDOG* 85 (1953) 22–23; also H. Klengel, "Tukulti-Ninurta," 69.

[10]J. J. Finkelstein, "Political Propaganda," unpublished manuscript in the Yale Babylonian Collection.

[11]Weidner, *Inschriften Tukulti-Ninurtas*, 45.

[12]*Ibid.*, 11, n. to No. 5, ll. 1–12; and 26, n. to No. 16, ll. 27–30.

[13]*Ibid.*, iii–iv.

[14]The usual expression is *šar*(MAN) *kaš-ši-i* (e.g. I.30, 32); the two exceptions are *šar-ri ma-a-ti ù ni*[*ši͂ᵐ*. . .], I.34, and *bêl* ᵃˡᵘ*Bâb-ili*, II.8.

[15]"Early Development," 315.

[16]Tiglath-pilesar I: "With the help of Assur, my lord, . . ." I fought against the land of Kutmuhi: *ARAB* I, §221, p. 74; Shalmaneser III: "with the aid of Shamash (and) Adad, the gods, his helpers, marched forth in might . . .," *Ibid.*, §685, p. 247.

[17]*ARAB* II, §96, p. 48, with exact parallels in inscriptions 2 and 3, and a close one in 5, of the same group ("Pavement Inscription"). Cf. also §§35, 54, 69, 82, 188.

[18]Perhaps reflecting Sargon's appreciation for Babylonian culture.

[19]For example, *ARAB* II, §183, p. 101. This phrase is very common.

[20]*Ibid.*, §§240 and 352. §253 mentions Assur, Sin, Shamash, Bêl, Nabû, Nergal, Ishtar of Nineveh and Arbela; cf. with Assurbanipal, §§820 and 822.

[21]*Ibid.*, §784, p. 298.

[22]*Ibid.*, §§236, 241, 248, 277; cf. 318.

[23]This "Letter" deserves special attention for a number of reasons, on which see further below. The text of the first phrase quoted is as follows: *kakkê^{pl} -šu iz-zu-ti . . . i-du-u'-a ú-ma-ir-ma*, François Thureau-Dangin, *Une relation de la huitième campagne de Sargon* (Textes cunéiformes du Louvre, III; Paris: Librarie P. Geuthner, 1912), hereafter cited as *TCL* 3; 22, 1. 126.

[24]*ARAB* II, §336, p. 151. This occurs in the context of construction of a canal.

[25]*Ibid.*, §294, p. 139.

[26]*Ibid.*, §§572, 606.

[27]*Ibid.*, §574. The text adds "the Seven, the warrior gods, who overthrow my foes," on which see further above, especially under the discussion of the Erra Epic. On Ishtar, cf. §736.

[28]*Ibid.*, §§771, 803, 805, 900. Note also the references to Ishtar in a text from the temple of Ishtar published by R. Campbell Thompson, "British Museum Excavations," 80-81 and 90-91; *ra-ki-bat ûmê^{pl} rabûti^{pl}*, "riding the mighty storms," 1. 8; *a-li-kat i-di-[ia]*, "marching at my right side," 1. 12; *at-tal-lak ar-ki-ki i-da-a-a-ma tal-li-k[i]*, "[when] I walked behind thee, at my side [also] thou didst go," 1. 22.

[29]*ARAB* I, §373.

[30]*Ibid.*, §§474, 497.

[31]*Ibid.*, §§599, 609, 610.

[32]*ARAB* II, §181.

[33]*Ibid.*, §§794, 1025. Cf. the proper name cited by Thompson as 'Ninurta-alik-pani,' "British Museum Excavations," 104.

[34]From the Zenjirli Inscription; for the transliterated text and translation see Riekele Borger, *Die Inschriften Asarhaddons Königs von Assyrien*, *ArOr*, Beiheft 9 (1956), 97, 11. 12-14, and especially n. to 1. 13, part of which we have adopted in our text. Cf. also *ARAB* II, 576. The problems in 1. 13 are solved differently by B. Landsberger ["Einige unerkannt gebliebene oder verkannte Nomina des Akkadischen," *WZKM* 57 (1961) 2, n. 8], who reads URU-*um-ma* for *zu-um-ma*, yielding: "dessen Handeln tollwütiger Ansturm ([*t*]*i-bu*) ist; liegt eine Stadt vor ihm, so läßt er einen Trümmerhaufen (*ti-l*[*u*]) hinter sich."

[35]On this group in general (particularly *melammu*, "splendour"), cf. Cassin, *Splendeur*, ch. VI passim, and especially 75 and n. 73 on the annalistic sources.

[36]*ARAB* I, §§230 and 223.

[37]*Ibid.*, §218.

[38]In the order mentioned, see *Ibid.*, §§441, 443, 451, 457, 464-466, etc.
(2) *Ibid.*, §§566, 583, 585, 588, 598-9, 609. (3) *ARAB* II, §§22, 63,
80, 208. (4) *Ibid.*, §§239, 240, 309. (5) *Ibid.*, §§519, 540, 544,
549, etc. (6) *Ibid.*, §§771, 800, etc. Also with Šamši-Adad V, *ARAB*
I, §§719, 724; Adad-narari III, §740; Tiglath-pilesar III, §794.

[39]William F. Albright, "The Eighth Campaign of Sargon," *JAOS* 36 (1917)
226.

[40]A. L. Oppenheim, "The City of Assur in 714 B.C.," *JNES* 19 (1960) 143-
145.

[41]*Ibid.*, 143-144.

[42]*Ibid.*, 147. A text from Shalmaneser III reporting his campaign against
Urartu also has an interesting mixture of literary types. W. G. Lambert
["The Sultantepe Tablets, Continued: VIII. Shalmaneser in Ararat," *AnSt*
11 (1961) 144] comments that there are analogies with the epic and annalistic forms as well as the letter to Assur. The text also contains
the vanguard motif in the form of a divine oracle: "'May Ninurta go
before you, may Girru [follow at your rear]'" (150-151).

[43]*ARAB* I, §273.

[44]*Ibid.*, §369.

[45]*ARAB* II, §70, p. 36; cf. §186.

[46]*Ibid.*, §338, p. 151; cf. with Esarhaddon, §524.

[47]*ARAB* I, §§564, 606, 618. Already with Sargon of Akkad, see George A.
Barton, *The Royal Inscriptions of Sumer and Akkad* (Library of Ancient
Semitic Inscriptions, Vol. I; New Haven: Yale University Press, 1929)
105 (and elsewhere).

[48]*ARAB* I, §765, p. 270. Luckenbill (§795, p. 286, n. 1) notes that "weapon" in such an instance is meant "In the sense of symbol; that is, the
cult of Assur." But this does not mean that the "weapon" is not an actual
physical object.

[49]*TCL* 3, 11. 13-14, p. 4. Cf. *ARAB* II, 142, p. 74.

[50]*ARAB* II, 5, §10.

[51]*Ibid.*, 6, §11; cf. §§56-57, 187-188, 203.

[52]*Ibid.*, 138, §289.

[53]References for this are ubiquitous. For example, *ARAB* I, §§368, 402,
443, 561, 717, 815; *ARAB* II, §§59, 246, 518, 804.

[54]Oppenheim, "City of Assur," 136-137. The unusual emphasis and explanation, according to Oppenheim, may be due to one of two reasons: Sargon's act was one of revenge for a similar desecration enacted by
Urartu; or the scribes are attempting to legitimate an act that fla-
grantly violated universal custom.

[55]*ARAB* II, 35, §69.

[56]*Ibid.*, §§642, 649, 659B, etc. Note the frequent reference to Marduk
as king of the gods. Cf. the return of Nanâ from Elam by Assurbanipal
after 1635 years, 311, §812.

[57]The preceding paragraph is confirmed by the recent study of Morton
Cogan, *Imperialism and Religion: Assyria, Judah, and Israel in the
Eighth and Seventh Centuries B.C.E.* (SBL Monograph Series, 19; Missoula:

Scholars, 1974). See especially the first two chapters: "The Assyrian
Empire and Foreign Gods--The Motive of Divine Abandonment," and "Assyrian
Spoliation of Divine Images."

CHAPTER 3

MESOPOTAMIAN ICONOGRAPHY AND THE CULT

(1) Divine Symbols

Aside from the very clear indications in the literary material, the
iconographic representations of divine presence are graphically established by a considerable amount of evidence. The most instructive illustrations come, again, from the later period of Assyrian history.
They have been collected and studied in a number of articles by Friedrich Sarre, Heinrich Schäfer, and others.[1] As these articles have shown,
a number of reliefs from the city of Nineveh depict the use of standards
in battle that are clearly intended to represent divine presence. Eight
of these from the time of Assur-nasirpal and Sargon have been reproduced
by Sarre (see our Fig. 1, in the Illustrations). Sarre notes that the
reliefs picture two standards in use, each on its own chariot, and that
this corresponds to two types of design evident in our Fig. 1. The
first type (b, d, e, f) pictures the god Assur with drawn bow, standing
or riding on a bull, all of which is contained in a circle, with two
tassles suspended from the bottom. The second type (a, c, g) is composed
of two bulls back to back and four bands radiating out to the circle, the
latter related to the iconography of the sun disk. In Fig. 2 one can see
the standard (here, type two) fixed in its chariot with driver and archer.
Again with our literary texts in mind, it is most impressive when Sarre
points out that the first type always precedes the other and

> appears to represent the ʌimperial standard of the
> Assyrians. It is a symbol of the highest god, who
> thereby, as it were, personally takes part in the
> battle and himself employs the weapons against the
> enemies of his people.[2]

That the chariot and its standard were understood as representing divine presence is clear not only from the pictures of battle scenes, but also from a very interesting relief of the Assyrian camp reproduced by Schäfer (Fig. 3). Dominating the various structures that house the soldiers and their equipment is a scene in the top left that portrays a chariot containing, apparently, two standards that seem to be identical to those in Fig. 1. In front of the chariot stand two priests who are offering food, drink, and, probably, incense to the standards. Thus the standards, if not also the chariot, appear to be a medium for the continuous presence of the deity within the camp when the army was on the march, as well as for the incisive moments of actual fighting.

Although the reliefs in Figures 1-3 derive from the later Assyrian period, other evidence indicates that the form and function of the standards and the related chariots can be traced back to quite ancient prototypes. We have already observed in the Nur-Adad Letter--separated by a millennium from the later reliefs--the cultic installation of a golden emblem (šu-nir) for the god Nanna and the reinstatement of the divine statues as part of the religious festivities following the victory of Nur-Adad. Furthermore, this mid-nineteenth century reference to the šu-nir (Akk. *šurinnu*) is already a reflection of much older iconographic traditions and cultic practices. In fact, studies of these objects in art and literature have shown that they reach back to prehistoric times, and that they no doubt originated in the use of graphic symbols to distinguish among the anthropomorphic representations of individual deities.[3] Thus the picture of a plow might signify one deity, that of a bird, another. However, there is a marked fluidity, not only in the referents for each picture, but also in the terms that we use to categorize them. In general, it is possible to speak of a "symbol" as a representation of a deity when he or she is not present or as the means of identifying the anthropomorphic figure; of an "emblem" as a symbol in material form, i.e. understood as a physical object; of a "standard" as an emblem mounted on a portable pole or staff.[4] But the šu-nir, for example, can be any one of these, so that these categorizations are marred by an ineluctable ambiguity.

At any rate, it is clear that the symbols took on a variety of forms and functions. They pictured celestial objects such as stars and moon and "household" objects such as spades or plows, as well as numerous plants, animals, and *Mischwesen*.[5] In written materials, the

symbols often occur with *dingir*, and the fact that they were the objects
of sacrifices further points to their intimate connection with the represented deity.[6] The function, particularly of the "standards," was to
stand "at the entrances to temples where they were believed to be held by
the divine Guardians of the Gate."[7] There is also evidence relating the
proper storage and repair of the standards, as well as their use in apotropaic rites, in the taking of oaths, and in the giving of divine judgment
and oracles.[8]

(2)   Cultic Processions

The most important role for the standards, however, was reserved
for the cultic processions and "divine journeys" that formed the high
point of most religious festivals.[9] In this role, they combined with
vehicles of the gods in the form of chariots and boats that were also
seen as divine and that were the object of sacrifices.[10] Like the standards, these vehicles could be constructed in part from precious metals
and gems, and are often described as "brilliant, blazing, shining," and
the like,[11] thereby alluding to their role as media for divine appearance. Their descriptions are also reminiscent of the divine symbols,
and it is often impossible to tell whether reference is being made to
physical objects in the temple or to mythological vehicles.[12]

The ambiguity between physical and mythical object with reference
to the chariot is vividly illustrated by a very interesting text published
by M. Civil.[13] This is a hymn (a tigi - song of Enlil) consisting of a
sa-gíd-da followed by a sa-gar-ra, and must be seen in the context of
cultic institutions in the Isin dynasty, for one of whose kings (Išme-
dagan) it was composed.[14] The two parts of the hymn, in effect, combine
a "physical description" of Enlil's chariot with a description on "a
symbolic mythical level" that pictures "a procession or festival with
Enlil riding his chariot, surrounded by Ninurta and the Anunnas."[15] The
second section contains several lines that are pertinent to our focus on
the vanguard motif:

> (Enlil) completed his great harnessing, he stepped
>   in [. . .]
> He emb[raced] Ninlil, the Mother, [his] wife.
> Ninurta, the Hero, [. . . in front]
> The Anunnas . . . , after him [. . .]
> The chariot shines like lightning, its bellowing

> [noise] is a pleasure.
>
> [. . .] his donkeys harnessed to the yoke.
>
> Enlil, his mighty chariot, his shining [. . .],
>
> is bright.[16]

It is interesting to see Ninurta in the vanguard once again, this time
in that of the chief god, Enlil, rather than in the Assyrian king. As
the above comment by Civil indicates, however, the situation presumed
by the text is difficult to determine precisely. Is the divine entourage setting out for war with Enlil's mythical chariot, or is this an
oblique reference to a cultic procession involving a physical representation of the vehicle? All we can determine from the fragmented text is
that some kind of "trip" (1. 73), is involved that concludes at a place,
where the king (lugal) is given instructions by Enlil (11. 75-85). The
fulfillment of these instructions involves the participation of Ninurta
in ways that clearly are intended to procure fertility for Išme-Dagan
through the sacred marriage with Inanna.

The ambiguity surrounding the procession in this hymn is overcome
in a number of texts that illustrate the role of the physical symbols in
the cult. In the following pages we shall look at three of the five
major examples of "divine journeys"[17] in which the chief deity of one
city travels to visit that of another in what probably constitutes an
annual or bi-annual festival. On the other hand, according to H. Sauren,
a small minority of literary compositions refer, not to regular festivals,
but to the occasion of temple building or renewal.[18] It has been suggested that such a situation is what lies behind the extremely cryptic lines
in the Gudea Cylinder B that refer to Ningirsu's trip to Eridu, and that
the purpose of Ningirsu's journey is to report to Enki concerning the
building and consecration of the Eninnu temple in Lagash.[19] However,
before going any further, it will be helpful to look at the Gudea Cylinders A and B as a whole, with particular attention to the form and function of motifs of divine presence as well as the role of the divine emblems.

a. The Gudea Cylinders[20]

Despite the length of the Cylinders and the complex cultic instal-
lations and ritual involved, the narrative consists of a very simple
plot: in Cyl. A, Gudea receives a vision of Ningirsu in the form of a
dream in which Ningirsu commands the construction of a new temple for

himself, to be named Eninnu;[21] this Gudea does. In Cyl. B, Gudea expresses his desire to bring Ningirsu into the completed temple; his plea
is accepted, and Ningirsu comes from Eridu.

Despite the simplicity of the plot, the narrative involves a rich
variety of literary images and religious traditions which make for some
stunningly picturesque passages and for some equally complex problems of
interpretation. Not the least of these are a number of references to
Ningirsu's chariot and emblem, or to the emblems of other deities. Near
the beginning of the narrative (Col. IV), Gudea recounts his dream to
Nanshe for her interpretation, describing how Ningirsu (who at this point
he did not recognize) appeared to him:

> In the dream there was a man as gigantic as heaven,
> 15 as gigantic as the earth. 16 According to his
> head he was a god; 17 according to his arms he was
> the "eagle;" 18 according to his lower body he was
> a storm; 19 on his right and left lions were stand-
> ing; 20 he commanded me to build his house; 21 his
> (precise) intent I did not understand.[22]

This passage and its content (highly reminiscent of material in the books
of Daniel and Ezekiel), clearly present a picture of the storm god that
is familiar to us from the numerous examples already discussed in the
epic and annalistic literature. With reference to the divine symbols,
it is interesting to note that the eagle[23] is closely associated with
Ningirsu.[24] Shortly after this passage, Gudea is commanded to construct
a chariot adorned with precious metal and lapis-lazuli, one that will
move like the light (VI.19-20).[25] At the same time, he is to make the
emblem (šu-nir) that Ningirsu loves (1.22). Shortly after the construction of these objects, Gudea has the eagle brought into the old temple
(VII.28-29),[26] and a subsequent passage confirms that this eagle and
the emblem are one and the same: "the eagle, the emblem (šu-nir) of his
king [i.e. Ningirsu] he adorned as a standard (urim)."[27] Thus here we
probably have a clear example of the emblem being made into a portable
standard so that it could be erected in the temple and perhaps also used
in processions.

Other emblems were placed in the temple as well, including "the
holy ship, the emblem of Nanše," "the disc (aš-me) the emblem of Inanna,"[28]
both of which were "placed before" Ningirsu, and "the emblem of the

sun-god, the bison-head"[29] which was placed at one of the gates (A.XIV. 19-27; XXVI.4).[30] Of more immediate interest to us, however, are a number of motifs that again demonstrate the relation between this narrative and the texts already examined in this chapter. One of these involves a procession that is apparently moving along the processional street Girnun ("high-way"),[31] which precedes the ritual involving the brick-mold and sacrifices. This ritual, of course, is performed by Gudea, and his position within the line of march is significant (A.XVIII.14-17):

> The divine king who makes the mountains tremble
> [^{d}lugal.kur.dúb] went before, 15 Igalima prepared
> the way, 16 Ningizzida, his god, 17 held his hand.[32]

In other words, the procession is actually led by the first two gods, with Gudea following behind and Ningizzida at his side.[33] This arrangement is obviously the same as we have repeatedly found in the literary and annalistic texts. Indeed, taken out of context, one could easily assume that this passage refers to the actions of Gudea and his divine vanguard in battle. Moreover, although the text at this point does not say so, we are probably still dealing with the divine standards that, in this case, are carried in front of Gudea, much as they precede the king in the context of battle.

The language of the above passage contained in the divine epithet "king who makes the mountains tremble"[34] is by no means accidental. Indeed, the very construction of the Eninnu temple itself appears to signify the lordship of Ningirsu over all the earth, and the temple as the center of this dominion undoubtedly is heir to very ancient prototypes.[35] Thus the brilliance of Ningirsu's temple will light up all lands, and its name will spread to the horizon, reflecting the fact that Ningirsu is the unrivaled "lord of the world" (en kúr-ra) who subdues all of his enemies (A.IX.16-26).[36] This language is thus remarkably similar to that which we have seen used for the Assyrian king and his exalted divine lord in the epics and annals, where both are often described as warriors without equal who cause the "four corners" of the world to tremble. These expressions of the fearful reaction of the surrounding countries are complemented by an allusion to another familiar motif, that of the awe-inspiring cry of the holy warrior (usually Akk. ragāmu). This is perhaps also implied in B.X.21, which describes Ningirsu as the one "[who speaks?] like the storm," and two other passages refer to the Eninnu temple itself as crying like the eagle (or perhaps even *being* a crying eagle), which causes the heavens to reel.[37] The polymorphous nature of this battle cry (cf. B.V.5 quoted below) is further indication of the variegated possibilities of such imagery, for it combines elements of storm phenomena (thunder) with animal behavior (the roar of the lion, which is often associated with the eagle in both art and literature).[38]

The language that describes the Eninnu temple as a reflection of Ningirsu's world dominion has clear implications for the typology of exaltation. This is bolstered by further evidence from the Cylinders. In fact, the installation of the various emblems may well be an indication of the exaltation of Ningirsu. Landsberger notes that three of the emblems that Gudea has 'mobilized' for the construction of the temple are actually representatives of the three districts (im-ru-a) of Girsu[39] (see on A.XIV.19-27 above). Even more suggestive is Landsberger's equation of the epithet "divine king who makes the mountains tremble" (Lugal kúr dúb) with the eagle (anzu) and with the "exalted emblem of the district of Ningirsu" (šu-nir-mah im-ru-a Ningirsu).[40] The fact that the other emblems are "placed before" Ningirsu could easily demonstrate that the latter, along with his district, is receiving exalted status.

Now we must step back and look once again at the overall schema of the Cylinders with which we began our observations, for our concentration on the above details has necessarily detracted from the dramatic movement of the narrative. As we have seen, Cyl. A ends with the completion of the temple and the various emblems, especially the eagle, which represents the presence of Ningirsu. It is clear from the beginning of Cyl. B, however, that neither the temple nor the emblem can fully contain the divine presence until Ningirsu himself has sanctified them with his advent. This, of course, again raises the hermeneutical problem of how we are to interpret the representational authority of the divine symbols, as well as raising the question of how the author conceived of Ningirsu's advent.[41] The substance of Cyl. B is contained in II.3 where Gudea declares: "I am the shepherd who built the temple; I would cause my king to enter his temple." He then proceeds to "the old temple" where Ningirsu dwelt and offers a prayer to his god (II.10-17):

> O my king, Ningirsu, . . . , O son of Enlil,
> . . . I have built your temple for you; with
> joy may you enter there.

Gudea apparently does not have to wait long for an answer, for Ningirsu
receives his prayer and grants his request:

> The year passed, the months came to an end; a
> new year arrived in heaven; the month of this
> house arrived; three days of this month passed
> by: Ningirsu came from Eridu; light (and)
> .... he spread; he bestowed shining daylight
> on the land of Sumer (III.5-11).

This is clearly the moment for which the whole narrative has prepared, and it is perhaps impossible for us to understand the profound
impact which the author wished to convey. Part of our difficulty again
lies in the fluidity with which the author conceives of divine presence.
Lines III.23-25 state that "On the day in which the good god came, Gudea
had (all that) . . . conveyed to the great storehouse (?)." Although obscure, this--along with the passage quoted above--could imply an annual
harvest festival, which would fit with our general picture of "divine
journeys" as both annual and primarily concerned with fertility.[42] We
must also consider the possibility that these passages may again have in
mind a procession involving the standards. In B.XVI.7-18, Ningirsu enters
his exalted place, and this is connected to "his emblem which goes in
front (of all)," as well as to his chariot. Moreover, in 1. 18 the author
seems to have in mind Ningirsu's *heavenly* throne. Thus we clearly must
not press the material too far in order to force it into our own cognitive
molds. For the author it surely would not have been at all paradoxical
to suggest that the transcendent Ningirsu was present in the form of his
emblem, yet came to the temple himself to take up his dwelling, an advent that had eternal validity, yet was re-enacted regularly.

As we mentioned at the outset of our discussion of the Gudea Cylinders, the references to Ningirsu's coming from or going to Eridu (B.III.
9; VIII.11-13) are naturally interpreted as indications of an annual procession to that city from Lagash. It is difficult to interpret precisely
what relationship between Lagash and Eridu is reflected in such a journey.
Sjöberg has suggested that Ningirsu was originally the son of the god of
Eridu; that his journeys there stem from neo-Sumerian times after he had
become the son of Enlil; and that the journeys were taken with the purpose
of visiting his ancestral home and receiving the fates for the coming
year. But, Sjöberg concludes, the more immediate purpose was to notify

Enki of the construction and consecration of the Eninnu temple.[43]

Sjöberg's speculations are reasonable enough, although they give slight notice to the fact that the emphasis falls not on Ningirsu's journey to Eridu but his coming *to Lagash* to take up residence in the new Eninnu temple--an advent that is surely understood as a definitive move. Moreover, we have noted that Ningirsu was already considered to be dwelling in the "old house" of Eninnu, and thus not in Eridu.

Nevertheless, Sjöberg's suggestion that there is a connection between our text and the accession of Ningirsu to the status of the son of Enlil would imply that we are again dealing with the typology of exaltation. There are other indications--both religious and political--that support this view. Falkenstein has noted that at some point, perhaps as early as old Sumerian times, Ningirsu was elevated from his role as "Hero" alongside Enlil, the supreme god of Nippur, and became the *son* of Enlil, comparable to Ninurta. This status is clearly in evidence in the Gudea Cylinders, where Enlil has given Ningirsu the name "king," the five divine powers (me's), and the tablet of sacrifices, thus placing him "an oberster Stelle des Pantheon von 'Lagaš.'"[44] This latest layer of tradition in the development of the pantheon of Lagash, which Falkenstein calls the "Reichspantheon," reveals:

> a massive external influence, which, along with the
> political and religious events, constituted one
> sphere, which extended out over the borders of the
> city states of Lagaš and its immediate vicinity.[45]

One aspect of the political events can already be seen in the control of Urbaba, Gudea's predecessor and father-in-law, over Ur, which, according to Falkenstein, is demonstrated by the assumption of the priesthood of Nanna by his daughter, Enannepada, thereby repeating an act already performed by her predecessor, Enheduanna.[46] Indeed, this act alone forms the kernel around which the Exaltation of Inanna is built, as we have seen above. Falkenstein also prefers to interpret the significance of Ningirsu's journey to Eridu in the same light: the journey indicates that Lagash had control over Ur and Eridu during the time of Gudea; otherwise such a visit would not have been possible. Further evidence of the ruling power of the Lagash Dynasty is found in the expansive building operations, commercial ventures, and the fame of Gudea even in later times.[47] Indeed, the combination of the extensive divine court personnel, the various symbols of power and of the cult, the statues and stele, the rich sacrifices, and of course the Eninnu temple itself, demonstrate that Ningirsu was seen by his devotees as the possessor of "all the great 'divine powers,'" i.e. the me's.[48] Gudea proved himself the devotee par excellence by the cultic centralization that he brought about with his creation of a "Holy City" in Girsu, thereby not only transferring this term along with the divinities of the ancient Lagash to Girsu, but also welding the majority of sanctuaries in Girsu into a unity with Eninnu.[49]

Thus if the cylinders, along with other texts, reflect the exaltation of Ningirsu, they also reveal the preeminence of Gudea within the second dynasty of Lagash. This position surely lies behind the short birth narrative in A.III.6-9, where Gudea recognizes no mother or father but the goddess Gatumdu.[50] Moreover, Gudea's personal esteem may be indicated in the fact that, within the length of the dynasty, only his two sons ruled in order of primogeniture, Gudea himself succeeding his father-in-law.[51]

b. The Journey of Ninurta

Two other texts, both probably from the Ur III period or shortly thereafter, also present interesting material for the subject of divine presence in cultic processions and in the Sumerian hymn. The first of these concerns a journey of Ninurta to Eridu.[52] Although the first Column is quite fragmentary, it begins with an encomium to the hero Ninurta, predicated by his radiant coming forth from Ekur. After a reference to his going to visit Nammu and Enki, the text relates the many benefits that will accrue from his journey. In Col. II, the journey itself is related, and the visit indeed results in Enki's giving divine power, kingship, and priesthood to Ninurta, who rejoices with An and Enki. Col. III contains a hymn addressed to Ninurta in the second person, praising his divine status alongside An and over the Anunnas, as well as his victory over rebellious lands. Col. IV continues with the second person in further praise of Ninurta, emphasizing the supremacy of his position.

Rather than quoting the text extensively, we shall only point out a number of very interesting features that bear a striking resemblance to texts already discussed above. Again, these concern the means of expression of divine presence and its connection to the typology of exaltation, particularly the language with which the latter is described in the Exaltation of Inanna.

In the beginning Ninurta "comes shining from Ekur" (é-kur-ra è-a)
just as Inanna is described as "resplendent light" (u₄-dalla-è-a).[53] It
is also remarkable that the first half of the latter verse (and the title)
of the Inanna hymn has an almost exact parallel later on in the Ninurta
hymn: Inanna is nin-me-šár-ra ("Lady of all the me's"); Ninurta is en-
me-šár-ra-ke₄ ("Lord of all the me's"),[54] a designation similar to that
applied to Ningirsu in the Gudea Cylinders. As we shall see below, this
fits with the typology of exaltation, but our attention is first diverted
by the description of Ninurta's journey and the results of his visit in
Col. II. Unfortunately, the opening lines are missing, and the first
readable line has simply "lugal," followed by a break. Lines 6-8, however, can be read clearly:

> ᵈnin-urta eriduᵏⁱ-šè gin-[né] gìri mu-na-gá-gá
> kaskal ezem-gim mu-na-dù eden mu-na-[x]
> ᵈNin-urta abzu! eriduᵏⁱ-ga ul-la mi-ni-ib-túm-mu
>
> 6 He prepares the way for Ninurta as [he] goes to Eridu,
> 7 He makes the road festive, he makes the steppe [. . .].
> 8 In joy he bears Ninurta into Abzu, Eridu.[55]

We have already seen this motif of "preparing the way" before the god in
battle, and in the Gudea Cylinders it was used for a cultic procession.
Now we find it within the context of a "divine journey." The question,
of course, is: who is preparing the way? Falkenstein suggests that it
certainly is not Ninurta, nor the "lugal" of line 5, who is probably also
Ninurta. Rather, the figure must be another deity; this is supported by
a comparison with Gudea Cyl. B.VIII.20-22 (*sic*; cf. VIII.14 in *SAHG*) and
the similar role of ᵈlugal-si-sá ("lord who straightens out, prepares
[the way]").[56] We feel that the literature examined throughout Chapters
1 and 2 makes an even better case for Falkenstein's argument. One need
only recall the charge of Erra to his vanguard Išum in the Erra Epic
(I.95-99): "Open the way! . . . go before me." Moreover, the iconographic evidence and the analogy with the Gudea Cylinders examined above
might imply that we are again dealing with a physical standard, both of
the vanguard and of Ninurta.[57] However, this text makes no such indications, and the fact that nowhere do we find mankind taking part in the
story (except as recipients of blessing--Sumer) also argues against this
possibility.[58]

Following Ninurta's entrance into Abzu, our hymn takes on an even more striking resemblance to the Exaltation of Inanna as well as to the Gudea Cylinders. Two stanzas (II.11-18) are worthy of quotation:

11 The hero of An--he presented him with the *me's*
    for life,
12 The lord of all the *me's*--he [restored] the
    me's properly to their place.
13 The lord [. . .], bringing forth the good
    days of Sumer.
14 Ninurta, the son of Enlil,
15 In the royal manner he wore the hat, he bore
    the [. . .]
16 In the lordly manner he bound the shining
    muš, he grasped the [. . .],
17 He has come forth radiantly, he raised his
    head skywards in the Abzu [in Er]idu.
18 The youth who establishes the magnificence
    of the Ekur.[59]

Here the subject of the me's is resumed, and their gift to Ninurta by Enki clearly constitutes a sign of the former's exaltation. After Ninurta has received the me's, he[60] is called "The hero of An," a phrase that is in apposition with en-me-šár-ra at the end of l. 12 (noted above)--and both lines begin with me. This theme receives added emphasis in the following stanza (lines 15-18), where Ninurta receives the signs of kingship and "priesthood" (nam-lugal-še and nam-en-še), probably in the familiar form of vestments,[61] after which he "appears in radiance." Finally, in III.16, Ninurta is depicted on a par with An, just as Inanna was before: "Ninurta, who together with An determines the destiny in the Abzu, in Eridu."[62] To this Falkenstein asks a question which, in the context of what we have learned, must be answered in the negative:

It is more than striking that Ninurta here decides
the fate with An in Eridu. Is it only a matter of
a hyperbolic expression which one need not take
seriously?[63]

In short, we would argue that Ninurta's reception of the me's, the lugal-ship and en-ship, the declaration of his sonship with Enlil, and

his equation with Anu clearly exemplify the typology of exaltation. As
if to accentuate the supremacy of this position, much of Col. IV is imbued with repeated references to Ninurta as "the greatest, the exalted"
(maḫ-àm and maḫ-zu)--in fact, they occur ten times between 11. 7-15.

If we are justified in identifying the exaltation of Ninurta as a
primary theme of this poem, there can be no doubt that the descriptions of
his appearance are intricately tied to it. Immediately following Ninurta's
reception of the me's, the author describes the radiance of his appearance.
This may, in fact, contain an oblique reference to his return journey to
Nippur, for, according to Falkenstein, 1. 13 should best be read: "'he
caused good light to rise for Sumer,' which has a striking parallel in
Gudea Cyl. B.III.10-11, the passage which immediately follows the statement 'Ningirsu comes from Eridu' . . . ,"[64] also with the effect of a
radiating light (see above).

Finally, lest our analysis give the impression of a literary work
composed of an indiscriminate mixture of themes, we must note the artful
scheme of the poet, which is most pronounced in the two stanzas quoted
above. Both are composed of four lines each, with each stanza following
the same pattern:

lines 11-12	15-16
presentation of the me's	presentation of lugal and en attributes
13	17
Ninurta sends light over Sumer	Ninurta appears in radiance
14	18
Ninurta is the son of Enlil	Ninurta is the guarantor of the Ekur

c.   The Journey of Nininsinna

We now turn to the third of our examples of the "divine journey,"
that of Nininsinna to Nippur.[65] Her visit to the Ekur of Enlil is for
the determination of her fate (*Geschick*) for the year, although much of
this portion of the poem is missing. It is clear, however, that her
fortune, as well as that of her devotees, will be bountiful, as Enlil's
promise to her shows: "[May your throne be] firmly secured, the land of
Sumer [have 'rest' through you, on luxuriant pasture]!"[66] The joyous

86

feast that follows her return also witnesses to the procurement of a fruitful year.

Our interest will center on the first part of the poem, especially on the account of the journey itself. The author begins the poem speaking in the first person: "[Nini]nsi'anna the daughter of An, will I ever praise!" (1. 2). The poem then moves immediately into a third person account of Nininsinna's emergence from the cella of her temple into the marketplace of the city, which greets her "like the rising sun" and proceeds along with her (11. 3-5). At this point the author suspends his focus on the action[67] long enough to present a detailed description of the procession itself. Apparently no one is omitted; Nininsinna's husband and child join in with joyous celebration, and the procession is completed by a number of other deities (11. 8-13):

> her benevolent protective spirit of the 'High Palace'
>   goes behind,
> the benevolent Udug of the father Enlil goes at her
>   right,
> the benevolent protective spirit of the lord Nunamnir
>   goes at her left.
> Her emblem goes forth like a heavenly light before her.
> Schumach, the benevolent chamberlain of the 'High
>   Palace,' goes before her,
> purifies for her the street, the market place, purifies
>   for her the city.

Again, we find a rather elaborate description of the entourage of a deity within the context of a cultic procession rather than of a military adventure. Right and left, in front and behind, Nininsinna is surrounded by her protecting deities.[68] Most important, of course, is the mention of her emblem, which precedes her "like a heavenly light." It also raises a problem with which we have had to deal before, in our discussion of the Gudea Cylinders: if the emblem precedes the goddess, how are we to picture the presence of Nininsinna herself? Does the author have in mind her invisible presence, following behind and symbolized by the emblem, or is the goddess in fact represented by a statue? The following lines present even more graphic descriptions of Nininsinna continuing on her way with "proudly uplifted head,"[69] and of her washing herself in the Isin-canal. Moreover, unlike the journey of Ninurta and others,[70] the human king here appears to play a more active role in the story, for he accompanies the goddess on her journey,[71] leads her back to her city (1. 30), and offers sacrifices to her during the feast that ensues (1. 40). Thus Nininsinna's journey is not cast in the form of a purely divine drama, but describes an actual festival-procession. We can only conclude that the most likely interpretation of the text indicates that a statue is presupposed. In fact, a great statue of Nininsinna was constructed by Iddin-Dagan as seen in the eponym of his sixth year,[72] and Nininsinna's use of a ship for part of her journey is quite compatible with the customary procession as we have already seen above.

As for the theme of exaltation, our text itself does not emphasize Nininsinna's supremacy in any way, surely not like that of Ninurta. It is the latter who decided the fates *along with* An; Nininsinna more typically receives hers after humbly entering Ekur and offering sacrifices to Enlil (11. 19-25). Nevertheless, one may ask if this hymn, as well as others, has as its raison d'etre the "exaltation of Nininsinna" along with a political counterpart, fitting the pattern we have already seen above. In this respect, it is interesting that D. O. Edzard has drawn a parallel between this text and the role both of Inanna and of political developments following the Ur III period:

> The rise of the first dynasty of Isin to temporary
> supremacy in Babylon had consequences for the compari-
> son of N[ininsinna] to the highest goddess Inanna.
> N[ininsinna] was named 'the great daughter of An' and
> could even be thought of in terms of Inanna's epithets
> as warrior goddess.[73]

(3)   Summary: Annals, Iconography, and Cult

Alongside the literary texts, the Assyrian annals also utilize motifs of divine presence, and especially the vanguard motif, to describe the intervention of the god(s) on behalf of their royal devotees, usually in military conflict. These motifs seem to have had clear roots, especially in the epic literary tradition, yet soon developed along formal lines of their own. In connection with their historical setting, they are clustered in annals from periods when the Assyrian empire realized its greatest strength.

Secondly, the annals demonstrated that the motifs often referred not only to a *concept* of divine presence but also to actual physical objects that represented it. A survey of the development of divine symbols in Mesopotamian iconography supports and amplifies this point. Moreover, not only were the deities represented by physical objects (such as emblems and statues), but these objects were employed within the context of cultic processions. The use of the vanguard motif in texts describing these processions is often quite similar to its use in the literary and annalistic sources. Finally, the texts that locate these motifs within a cultic setting also betray signs of the typology of exaltation, again revealing a correlation of the divine and the political realms.

MESOPOTAMIAN ICONOGRAPHY AND THE CULT

[1] Friedrich Sarre, "Die altorientalischen Feldzeichen," *Klio* 3 (1903) 333-371; Heinrich Schäfer, "Assyrische und ägyptische Feldzeichen," *Klio* 6 (1906) 393-399; *id.*, "Die ägyptische Königsstandarte in Kadesch om Orontes," *Sitzungsberichte der Preussischen Akademie der Wissenschaften* (Philosophisch-Historische Klasse; 1931), 738-742. These and numerous other studies are considered by O. Eissfeldt, "Lade und Stierbild," *Kleine Schriften* II (Tübingen: Mohr, 1963) 299-301. Since Eissfeldt's study is primarily concerned with the Old Testament, we shall look at it more closely in Part II.

[2] Sarre, "Feldzeichen," 339. Note the elaborate combination of the two types in the standard of Sargon, h in Fig. 1.

[3] The subject was treated in a monograph by F. Douglas van Buren, *Symbols, of the Gods in Mesopotamian Art, AnOr* 23 (1945). This work in many respects formed the basis for the more recent studies in *Reallexikon der Assyriologie* (hereafter, *RLA*), general title "Göttersymbole und -attribute" by the following authors (with respective subtitles): U. Seidl, "Mesopotamien," 483-490; B. Hrouda, "Syrien/Palästina," 490-495; J. Krecher, "Nach sumerischen und akkadischen Texten," 495-598. See also A. L. Oppenheim, *Ancient Mesopotamia* (Chicago: University of Chicago Press, 1964) 197. On the development of symbolic forms see Jacobsen, "Formative Tendencies. . . ," *Tammuz*, 1-15.

[4] An older view repeated by van Buren with reservations as here; *Symbols*, 1-2. Krecher ("Nach sumerischen," 495-496) suggests a strict sense of *Göttersymbol* where the symbol independently represents the deity, and a wider sense where the symbol stands alongside the deity with more or less intrinsic worth, but notes that the latter, especially, involves ambiguity.

[5] The various forms are most conveniently seen in the Table of Contents of van Buren (*Symbols*) with the corresponding numbered Plates. See also Seidl, "Mesopotamien," 485-490.

[6] Cf. van Buren, *Symbols*, 2, and Krecher, "Nach sumerischen," 496.

[7] Van Buren, *Symbols*, 4.

[8] *Ibid.*, 5-9.

[9] A. Salonen, "Prozessionswagen der babylonischen Götter," *StudOr* 13/2 (1946) 3-10; Otto Edzard, "Mesopotamien, Die Mythologie der Sumerer und Akkader," in *Wörterbuch der Mythologie*, Erste Abteilung: Die Alten Kulturvölker, Band I: Götter und Mythen im Vorderen Orient, ed. Hans W. Haussig (Stuttgart: E. Klett, 1965), "Göttereisen," 75-77. This entire work will hereafter be cited as *WM*. H. Sauren, "Besuchsfahrten der Götter in Sumer," *Or* 38 (1969) 214-236; A. W. Sjöberg, "Götter-reisen," *RLA* 3 (1969) 480-483.

[10] Salonen, "Prozessionswagen," 5.

[11] *Ibid.*, 6.

[12] *Ibid.*, 4, n. 1.

[13] M. Civil., "Išme-Dagan and Enlil's Chariot," *JAOS* 88 (1968) 3-14.

[14] *Ibid.*, 3.

[15]*Ibid.*, 4.

[16]*Ibid.*, 6-7, 11. 66-72.

[17]For the other two, see below, n. 58. Aside from these literary compositions, we also have economic records, which list the supplies for festivals of the divine journeys, but yield little beyond time and place; cf.
Sauren, "Besuchsfahrten," 217-219.

[18]*Ibid.*, 216; cf. Sjöberg, "Götterreisen," 482, on Ningirsu's journey to
Eridu (discussed below); Inanna's journey to Eridu; and 483 on Enki's
journey to Nippur.

[19]Sjöberg, "Götterreisen," 482.

[20]The most recent complete translation of the Cylinders is that of Adam
Falkenstein and Wolfram von Soden, *Sumerische und akkadische Hymnen und
Gebete* [hereafter abbreviated *SAHG*] (Die Bibliothek der alten Welt;
Reihe der alten Orient; Zurich: Artemis, 1953) No. 32, 137-182. Unless
otherwise noted, all references to the text of the Cylinders come from
this translation. A thoroughly up-to-date translation awaits the completion of the work on the Gudea inscriptions by A. Falkenstein, begun
in his *Grammatik der Sprache Gudeas von Lagaš*, AnOr 28-29 (1949-1950),
and continued in *Die Inschriften Gudeas von Lagaš*, AnOr 30 (1966), the
latter hereafter abbreviated *IGL*. For an English translation, see George
A. Barton, *The Royal Inscriptions of Sumer and Akkad* (Library of Ancient
Semitic Inscriptions, I; New Haven: Yale University Press, 1929). For
the Cylinders, see 205-255.

[21]The temple is called Eninnu from the Early Dynastic II period, and is
known as the "house of Ningirsu" from Urnanše on. There was also a new
construction under Gudea's predecessor, Urbaba, which is called the "old
house" in the Gudea texts. See Falkenstein, *IGL*, 63, 117, 120. For the
complicated topography of the Lagaš city-state and its cultic complexes,
see especially 17-21, and note that when Falkenstein refers to the city-
state he does so by writing "Lagaš" (i.e., with quotation marks).

[22]The translation is taken from Falkenstein, *IGL*, 95 (cf. *SAHG*, 141) who
suggests that the reference to Ningirsu's "head" means the crown with
horns, the "eagle"-arms refers to constant agitation rather than to
wings, and the flood-storm lower-body refers to his Gargantuan gait.

[23]Benno Landsberger has treated the term anzu ("eagle") to an exhaustive
and highly detailed study in "Nomina," 1-23. Landsberger argues that
the signs must normally be read AN.IM.MI.MUŠEN in place of earlier readings (e.g. Barton's ᵈIM.GIGᵇᵘ), and especially that the first sign not
be seen as the divine determinative (see 14-19 in particular for references to the Gudea Cylinders; 18, No. 4 for the text of A.IV.17-18).
He thus dispenses with the arguments put forward, especially those by
Thorkild Jacobsen, that this group of signs, read as ᵈIm-dugudᵐᵘˢᵉⁿ, is
identical to the personified thunder-cloud on the basis of evidence from
the period of Gudea. Jacobsen (*Tammuz*, 3-4, 16-17, 32) has also worked
out a schematic development of this figure with three stages: (1)
protoliterate period--Imdugud, the lion-headed bird; (2) survival as an
emblem of Ningirsu/Ninurta; (3) later hostility against the older form
results in evil Zû-bird as arch *foe* of Ninurta. Again to the contrary,
Landsberger ("Nomina," 17-18) understands the precursors of the evil
Anzu of the later periods as a phenomenon separate and distinct from the
heraldic eagle of Gudea. Although we have used the translation "eagle,"
we feel that the imagery surrounding the figure is malleable enough to

disallow any firm distinctions given the present evidence. Also, the positions of Landsberger and Jacobsen may not be irreconcilable; note the formation analogous to *anzu* meaning 'shadow, shade' listed by Hallo, *Exaltation*, 76 (s.v. *gizzu*).

[24]Landsberger ("Nomina," 18) expresses grave reservations concerning the interpretations of Falkenstein and Jacobsen which tend to see Ningirsu here as *Mischwesen*, preferring instead the following: "Even this description we may take as a product of inordinate phantasy. Ningirsu is in one person god, gigantic eagle (with regard to the strength of his arms!), and a storm flood which sweeps everything away, 'with regard to that which is under him.'" For examples of pre-Sargonic use of the eagle to represent Ningirsu, see Agnès Spycket, *Les statues de culte dans les textes mesopotamiens des origines a la Ire dynastie de Babylone* (Cahiers de la Revue Biblique, 9; Paris: Gabalda, 1968) 12, n. 2.

[25]The chariot had its own section in the temple: see Falkenstein, *IGL*, 126 (No. 15), and n. 11 for further references in the Cylinders.

[26]So Falkenstein, *Ibid.*, 120, n. 2, with further reference to VII.2 and XVII.22-23--i.e. all of these refer to the *old* temple of Eninnu.

[27]XIII.22-23, here again following Landsberger, "Nomina," 15-16, and Falkenstein, *IGL*, 61. The word for standard here, urim = uri$_3$, is the Sumerian counterpart for the Akkadian *urrinu*, on which see Landsberger, notes 58-59. We have already encountered this term in the Erra Epic (I, 114) and in Sargon's "Letter to Assur" (see above). Landsberger notes that *urrinu* is a homonym for "eagle" and "standard," following Bauer, and suggests that its use in annalistic sources refers to an eagle-standard rather than to a real eagle (see the examples in 15, n. 58). Nevertheless, the homonym cannot be traced back to an original identity between "eagle" and "standard," he goes on to say. Spycket (*Statues*, 100) has noted another passage that demonstrates the identification between emblem and deity. She renders B.XVI.11-12 as follows: šu-nir-bi sag-šù-ga-bi (12 ᵈnin-gir-su zi mu-il-ám--"Son emblème, celui placé au sommet, c'était Ningirsu qui apporte la vie."

[28]Falkenstein, *IGL*, 78. Cf. also William W. Hallo, "Lexical Notes on the Neo-Sumerian Metal Industry," *BiOr* 20 (1963) 141. For photographs and further discussion of such objects of this period of Gudea see the section by Cros in Gaston Cros, L. Heuzey, and F. Thureau-Dangin, *Nouvelles Fouilles de Tello* (Paris: Imprimerie Francaise et Orientale, 1910).

[29]*Ibid.*, 114.

[30]Spycket (*Statues*, 74) discusses a text from Nippur, first half of the second millennium, which presents interesting similarities to these objects. Her text refers to objects according to their metallic components, and includes *an* Ištar [sic], a solar emblem (aš-me), a *statue* of Ištar, and a ᵈLama. Spycket's comments concerning the ambiguity of these objects (e.g. what is the difference between "an Ištar" and a "statue of Ištar"?) is typical of the hermeneutical problem of divine symbols, which we have already discussed.

[31]On this see Falkenstein, *IGL*, 123-124.

[32]For the translation see Landsberger, "Nomina," 17, n. 64, and Falkenstein, *IGL*, 77, 82.

[33]For a similar phrase, note B.II.6-7 which may refer either to the divine guidance which produced Gudea's wisdom (1.5) or to a procession to the new temple: "his gracious Udug went before him, his gracious guardian

deity walked behind him." On the vanguard motif, cf. A.II.19; III.20-21.

[34]On this deity see Falkenstein, *IGL*, 82-83. He is the highest general of Ningirsu's staff, and as such is particularly connected with Ningirsu's staff, and as such is particularly connected with Ningirsu's weaponry, being identical with the šár-ùr weapon, for example.

[35]See *Ibid.*, 185-186.

[36]Cf. XXI.12, 19-25; XXIX.17; B.I.1-10; VII.18-19. However, it has been pointed out to me in a private communication from Prof. William W. Hallo that the title may have to be read as en-kur-ra = engur-ra. This reading was already made, and understood as a reference to "the deep," by Thorkild Jacobsen, "Parerga Sumerologica," *JNES* 2 (1943) 118, n. 6.

[37]A.IX.14 and XI.3, on which see Landsberger, "Nomina," 19, n. 67, and Falkenstein, *IGL*, 62. Note also the interesting passage in Landsberger, 10, n. 46.

[38]Landsberger, "Nomina," 19 (under No. 5) and the reference to Jacobsen. Note the association between eagle and lions in the dream pericope quoted above.

[39]*Ibid.*, 17, n. 64. (under c.). We avoid the more specific terms used by Landsberger: "(Totems) der drei Klans," as our knowledge does not yet permit the sociological implications involved. Falkenstein demonstrates more reserve in his tacit identification of im-ru-a with "estates" (*Länd-ereien*) belonging apparently to the cult; cf. *IGL*, 13, n. 2; 87, 113-114.

[40]Landsberger, "Nomina," 17, n. 64 (under c_1), and Falkenstein, *IGL*, 82.

[41]Cf. Spycket's comment (*Statues*, 57): Gudea "never mentions any order for or enthronement of a divine statue, even though he enumerates in Cylinder B the names of twenty divine beings which he conducted to Ningirsu in his temple. In what form, then, did the god and his retinue present themselves? Human substitutes? Symbols? The absence of these statues in the excavations yields only negative evidence. It is evidently very difficult to disclose that which may partake of the real in a literary composition which is poetic and essentially symbolic."

[42]The passage that comes near the end of Cyl. B in XVI.19-XVIII.8 describes the securing of blessing and fertility, as well as social justice. Cf. also A.XI.5-27; B.XI.16-XII.20; XIV.20-XV.16.

[43]"Götterreisen," 482.

[44]*IGL*, 90-91; cf. 99. Falkenstein suggests that Ningirsu was probably originally the son of Enki and Ninḫursanga. Ningirsu's position at Lagaš thus places him third in the overall hierarchy, i.e. after An and Enlil; cf. 69.

[45]*Ibid.*, 56.

[46]*Ibid.*, 42.

[47]*Ibid.*, 44.

[48]*Ibid.*, 99.

[49]*Ibid.*, 116.

[50]Falkenstein (*Ibid.*, 2-3) suggests that this is to be interpreted as referring to Gudea's birth by a high priestess of Gatumdu, although the specifics of the cultic act are not known to us. Cf. A.XVII.15 and passages in the statue inscriptions.

[51]Falkenstein (*Ibid.*, 6) suggests that Gudea's accession may follow an ancient pattern, and the successors of his sons were in fact also sons-in-law of Urbaba. Is there a connection between this emphasis on son-in-law succession and the fact that, as Falkenstein points out (63-64), Ningirsu was chosen to be the husband of Baba the "first born daughter of An," who thus brought him into the divine circle of his elder generation (Enlil, Enki, Gatumdu, Inanna)?

[52]An annotated translation is provided by A. Falkenstein in *Sumerische Götterlieder*, Teil I [hereafter cited as *SGL* I] (Abhandlungen der Heidelberger Akademie der Wissenschaften, Philosophisch-Historische Klasse, 1. Abteilung; Heidelberg: Universitätsverlag, 1959), No. 2, 80-106. For the dating, see 98, n. to III.2. The text has been edited and translated in English by Daniel Reisman, "Ninurta's Journey to Eridu," *JCS* 24 (1971) 3-10.

[53]I.1-2 and Hallo, *Exaltation*, 1. 1. There is a slightly different reading of I. 1 by Reisman, "Ninurta's Journey," 6. On this phrase, compare also Ninurta II.17: dalla! mu-un-e "[Ninurta] ist dort strahlend erschienen;" *SGL* I, 82, 85.

[54]Line 1 and II.12 respectively. Falkenstein (*SGL* I, 95) also notes the parallel to the title of Inanna. On the problems with II.12, see below, n. 60.

[55]Text and translation from Reisman, "Ninurta's Journey," 4, 6; similarly, Falkenstein, *SGL* I, 84-85. Reisman also fills in 1. 5 as a parallel to 1. 6.

[56]See Falkenstein's note to II.6, *Ibid.*, 93, and the reference cited there. Reisman compares a text where "The offspring of the IMDUGUD" serves as escort ("Ninurta's Journey," 7).

[57]A statue of Ninurta is known from the time of Enlil-bani of Isin (c. 1862-1839), according to Spycket, *Statues*, 76.

[58]In this way the Ninurta hymn is similar to other divine journeys. In the journey of Nanna to Nippur, the story is told as a myth that, apparently, takes place before the creation of man; see Kramer *SM*, 47. There is no mention of a standard or emblem, although a ship (má-gurg) is used for transportation [Falkenstein, *Bibliotheca Orientalis* 5 (1948) 166]. Similarly with the journey of Enki to Nippur, a ship is used with gods for steering- and rear-rudder, but no standard is mentioned, and man plays only an insignificant role as servants at the feast; translation in *SAHG*, 133-137. These texts thus stand in contrast to that concerning Nininsinna, examined below.

[59]Reisman, "Ninurta's Journey," 6; cf. Falkenstein, *SGL* I, 85.

[60]Lines 11-14 present considerable difficulties, which are reflected in the difference between Falkenstein and Reisman. Both agree that Enki is most likely the donor of the me's. However, Falkenstein's translation leaves open the possibility that the epithets in lines 11-12 refer to Ninurta rather than Enki, a tendency that we are following. He also reads the epithet in 1. 11 as ur-sag-aš-an-na-ke$_4$ (Reisman says that "the aš is not written on the tablet," p. 8), "the only hero of heaven," to which he compares 1. 134 of the "Exaltation of Inanna," aša mah-me-en, "you alone are exalted!" (pp. 94-95). Finally, there is a problem in stichometry. Reisman (p. 8) disagrees with Falkenstein's inclusion of 1. 14 along with 1. 13, and sees a new strophe beginning with 1. 14. On the basis of the series of parallel lines from 1. 5 to 1. 20, we would agree with

Falkenstein.

[61]We would thus see this as a continuance of the preceding stanza, contrary to the suggestion that "Ninurta had put on these insignia of his rank already before his entrance into Eridu," made by Falkenstein, *SGL* I, 97.

[62]Reisman, "Ninurta's Journey," 6; see also Falkenstein.

[63]*SGL* I, 99-100.

[64]*Ibid.*, 95-96, including other parralels. However, according to Reisman ("Ninurta's Journey," 4) the possibility of a return is made doubtful by reducing the number of missing lines.

[65]Translation in *SAHG*, 68-70 (Sumerian No. 8).

[66]*Ibid.*, 70.

[67]Note how the author skillfully returns us to the action in 1. 13 by the resumption of the marketplace location, now connected with purifying the path of the goddess.

[68]Very similar language is used to describe the protecting deities (note especially Udug) who precede and follow Gudea on his way to the temple (cf. above).

[69]Cf. the emphasis on a very similar phrase in Ninurta's journey, Falkenstein, *SGL* I, II.17, III.12 (p. 82).

[70]See above, n. 58.

[71]The translation (1. 16) is *geleitete* (in italics), and therefore questionable; also odd is the fact that what the king does is at both sides of the goddess. However, this line is translated "the king placed his feet on both embankments (of the canal)" in *CAD*, K, 191b.

[72]Spycket, *Statues*, 76. Iddin-Dagan's predecessor, Šu-ilišu, built a temple for the return of Nanna from captivity in Elam, but no statue is mentioned (76-77).

[73]*WM*, 78.

CHAPTER 4
NORTHWEST SEMITIC TEXTS

Any discussion of the motifs of divine presence and guidance in the
Old Testament would be inadequate without due regard for the texts discovered at Ras Shamra. Frank M. Cross has stressed this requirement even
more strongly: "any discussion of the language of theophany in early Israel must begin with an examination of the Canaanite lore."[1] The importance of the Ugaritic mythological texts for the study of theophanic
motifs in the Old Testament Psalms and early poetry is beyond dispute.
The descriptions of Baal the "cloud rider" giving forth his voice with
thunder and lightning have clearly influenced many Old Testament passages.
In fact, we have argued elsewhere that the Ugaritic $^c nn$ ("messenger") and
biblical $^c nn$ ("cloud") are both elements of this imagery and that this
parallelism provides some important data for Old Testament interpretation.[2]
The battle between Baal and Sea/River has also obviously left its mark not
only in the Psalms and other texts, but in the Song of the Sea--Exodus 15
--as demonstrated by Cross (see below). These parallels, of course, could
be expanded by innumerable others, but they are so well known and have
been so thoroughly examined that we need not go into them any further at
this point. Instead, we would pose another question. In the Mesopotamian
texts we found that motifs of divine presence--often related to the storm
deity--were used in conjunction with critical *historical* events, often
reflecting the exaltation of a particular deity, and the glorification of
that deity's royal devotee. Can the well-known theophanic motifs in the
Ugaritic literature be understood in the same way?

We feel that *on the basis of available sources*, the answer to this
question can only be a negative one. This is indicated as soon as one
surveys the entire corpus of Ugaritic texts with an eye for the types of
documents in evidence. Aside from the mythological texts, which we shall

look at in more detail below, there are letters, cultic records, diplomatic correspondence, and economic and legal documents. Although these are obviously "historical" records in that they deal with mundane matters, and, as such, are important for a reconstruction of life in an ancient city, they rarely touch on specific *events*, and never in the form of royal annals or historical narrative. At best, we can view the rather ordinary machinations of the current political situation in which Ugarit often found herself squeezed between vying empires, each demanding allegiance and tribute.

Much the same is true for the Northwest Semitic inscriptions in general,[3] despite several exceptions--notably the Moabite Stone.[4] Even the exceptions, however, which may relate specific events involving warfare, rarely utilize motifs of divine presence beyond general reference to divine aid (cf. the first category under our discussion of the Assyrian annals above).[5] There is, to our knowledge, nothing in these inscriptions comparable to the passages in the Assyrian records, where images of divine presence play an important role and are at times clearly related to literary, if not epic, prototypes.

Having noted the lack of annals or historical narrative in the Ugaritic corpus, let us look at a few mythological texts that may be candidates for an historical orientation or that may contain motifs similar to the vanguard motif of our previous discussion.

Patrick D. Miller, Jr., has pointed out that any reference to Baal's deliverance of his earthly people is "markedly absent in the battle myths of Ba^{c}al and El."[6] Yet he insists at several points that the mythology and religion of Canaan must have included this idea even if the texts do not.[7] The only example to which he appeals is ^{c}nt [3] 2, Anat's bloodbath, which he thinks "records the only occasion in the myths in which a god or gods are engaged in battle with human beings."[8] From this he draws the important conclusion that "the pattern of the cosmic battle is sometimes projected onto the realm of human life."[9] However, despite the fact that the text does refer to *lim* and *adm* as Anat's enemies, it does not allow us to determine an historical event as the background.[10] Indeed, the fact that the text may tell of the destruction of all mankind militates against any specific historical situation.

Other texts that are frequently suggested to have historical backgrounds are the Aqht and Krt Legends.[11] The latter in particular has certain characteristics that, at first sight, indicate a possible relationship to the other Near Eastern texts examined in Chapter 1. Thus in A [14].1-2, Krt is commanded by El in a vision to muster his troops by the myriads for an attack against *Udm* in order to obtain a wife. Later, in B [15].3., the divine blessing is promised for Krt's offspring (perhaps even for the youngest) and Krt himself is proclaimed "greatly exalted" (*m^{c}id rm*). The combination of the appearance of the deity in a dream/vision, the dramatic battle, the exaltation of the human protagonist, and the possible establishment of dynastic succession, has much in common with what we have seen in a number of texts from our previous discussion. On the other hand, the proposed battle between Krt and Udm is never actualized, and there are no further references to divine presence or guidance beyond the dream and the later "blessing" in 14.2-3.[12] Because the battle does not occur, there is no opportunity to determine whether or not such motifs--especially the vanguard motif, which would fit the context quite well--were, in fact, used in a way similar to the other Near Eastern texts above.

If the vanguard motif is not used in the Krt legend where we might expect it, there is no doubt that the motif itself was known in Canaanite parlance. In 51 [4].4.1-8 Asherah instructs her minion *Qdš wamrr*, to prepare her elaborately harnessed donkey for her journey to the residence of El, where she is to entreat him to have a house built for Baal. In lines 9-15, *Qdš wamrr* follows her instructions exactly and, after placing his mistress on the saddled donkey,

> qdš . y'uḫdm . šb^{c}r
> 'amrr . kkbkb. lpnm
>
> Qdš was set afire,
> Amrr like a star in front.[13]

There is an obvious similarity between these two lines and the texts we have discussed previously. Asherah's servant precedes her just as we have seen the vanguard preceding other deities. Once again, however, the text does not allow us to decide whether such a motif could function within an historical context in Canaanite literature, as it clearly does in Sumero-Akkadian texts.

Finally, we may look at one more passage that, presumably, could refer to divine activity on earth, and that, it has been suggested, implies the presence of imagery similar to the vanguard motif. 51 [4].7.7-14 occurs after the construction of Baal's house and the banquet that

98

ensues. It follows a lacuna and a number of very broken lines, the
translation becoming clear only with lines 9-12, here following the
translation of Miller:

> Sixty-six cities he seized
>
> Seventy-seven towns
>
> Eighty (took) Ba^{c}al [   ]
>
> Ninety Ba^{c}al of the sum[mit?][14]

In his discussion, Miller describes this as a "triumphal procession of
the victorious god to his palace" to assume kingship.[15] He also thinks
it "quite probable that Ba^{c}al was accompanied by his various military
hosts."[16] It is also clear that Miller sees these hosts as virtually
identical in function to those that form the divine vanguard in Mesopotamian terms (e.g. in *Enuma eliš*).[17] There is no doubt that Baal had
a retinue that *may* have been similar to that of Marduk (and others).
Thus 67 [5].5.6-11 refers to his clouds, wind, thundercloud, rain, messengers, and attendants: the ^{c}nn should probably be included with these.[18]
However, here the description has a distinct emphasis on Baal's procre-
ative powers rather than on his military prowess (note *Pdry* and *Ṭly*).
This would fit with the effect of Baal's downfall--drought and steril-
ity. It thus seems to be at least debatable whether Baal's retinue
was used as weaponry, or whether it simply symbolizes his fructifying
power. At any rate, our point is that the *extant texts* do not portray
this retinue alongside Baal in combat; this is true of 4.7.7-14 (quoted
above).[19] Finally, this text describing Baal's "march" possibly could
be interpreted as referring to historical events, or at least to ter-
restrial "cities" and "towns," but the context is so fragmentary that
such an interpretation would be shaky.

To summarize this section, we would conclude that the motif of the
divine warrior *with his vanguard* in battle is, at best, implicit in the
Ugaritic texts, and that nowhere do we find it employed within the context of historical events. We would also suggest that the very notion
of divine presence and guidance in historical events is not attested
in the available evidence. Thus our major conclusion is that, despite
the salient motifs of theophany[20] in the Ugaritic mythological cycle,
and the extensive correlation which, in many respects, has been properly
made between these and numerous Old Testament passages (particularly in
the hymnic and apocalyptic literature), the Northwest Semitic inscriptions

are of little help for our understanding of how Israel utilized the images of divine presence and guidance within the narration of historical events. Or, to make the point another way, the lack of such literary usage in the Canaanite materials indicates that instructive parallels are to be more fruitfully sought within the texts examined throughout Chapters 1-3.[21] It is, of course, quite possible, and perhaps to be expected, that future discoveries will fill in the gaps that we have discerned. For this reason, any conclusions based on this strange silence are--at best--highly tentative and speculative.

[1]*CMHE*, 147.

[2]"The Pillar of Cloud in the Reed Sea Narrative," *JBL* 90 (1971) 15-30. The identification of Ugaritic ᶜnn is discussed more fully below in ch. 5, (2).

[3]H. Donner and W. Röllig, *Kanaanäische und Aramäische Inschriften* (3 Vols.; Wiesbaden: O. Harrassowitz, 1962-1964).

[4]For the Moabite Stone cf. *Ibid.*, I, 23 for the text; II. 168-179 for translation and commentary; also W. F. Albright in *ANET*, 320-321. This text presents a number of elements familiar to us from our previous discussion: the situation is one of revolt against the overlord Israel; the revolt signals the end of Chemosh's wrath, which has caused the submission of Moab; Chemosh gives the order to attack Israel; after the battle some kind of cultic implements are captured and placed "before Chemosh;" Mesha describes his success as due to the fact that "Chemosh drove him out before me" (*wygrš kmš mpny*--1. 19); in the end Chemosh (his statue?) dwells in one of the captured towns (1. 33; cf. 11. 9-10). Despite the terse and implicit nature of the motif of divine presence in 1. 19 (on which cf. Exod 23.28-31; 33.2; 34.11, etc.), we thus have in this text a notable exception to the lack of literary material in Syria-Palestine comparable to that in Mesopotamia. For an important reconstruction of the historical setting for the composition of this text, see Max Miller, "The Moabite Stone as a Memorial Stela," *PEQ* 106 (1974) 9-18.

[5]Several Aramaic inscriptions also contain exceptions, although these are even less impressive as descriptions of divine presence than is the Moabite Stone. In all three inscriptions, the protection of the god(s) is expressed by the words *qwm ᶜm* plus suffix, "to stand by PN." This is at times combined with some reference to the subject's rise to kingship. Thus in the inscription of Zakir of Hamath, he declares that Baalshamayn "stood by me (*wqm ᶜmy*) and Baalshamayn made me king [over Ha]zrak;" see Donner-Röllig, II, 205, line 3 (text No. 202), and *ANET*, 655. In the following lines Baalshamayn answers Zakir's plea and promises to save him from an enemy coalition that has arisen against him, again using the phrase *qwm ᶜm*. Although there is no account of the battle itself, the latter half of the inscription relates Zakir's cultic construction work, and is thus reminiscent of the annalistic format. The same expression is used in a more general context in a votive inscription of Panammuwa I, [Donner-Röllig, II, 214, 11. 2-3 (text No. 214)], and one from Barrakib [*Ibid.*, 223, 1. 2 (No. 215)]. The latter presents an interesting use of *ṣdq ᶜbh* as the grounds for divine help, as well as the use of *ṣdq* as "loyalty" to the Assyrian over-lord (cf. 11. 1-2, 11, 19). It is also interesting that at the end of this inscription there is an invocation to Rākib-el as *bᶜl byt*, which Donner-Röllig translates "der Herr der Dynastie" *Ibid.*, 224. (For further discussion following Landsberger, see p. 34). This may well reflect the subject of the inscription, which reveals the disorderly succession of Panammuwa II to the throne in opposition to an anti-Assyrian party and with the aid of Tiglath-pilesar (*Ibid.*, 230). This may be why the "rising up" of the god Hadad (here without *ᶜm*) in the beginning (1. 2) and the aid of the gods in general is parallel to the aid of Tiglath-pilesar later on in the inscription. Also germane is the name Rākib-el itself, which

Donner-Röllig have no doubt correctly interpreted as "Streitwagenfahrer des El" (*Ibid.*, 225). In short, although these inscriptions hardly present anything comparable to the rich imagery of the divine vanguard in our earlier discussion, the fact that they provide the closest thing to such imagery and that particularly the last one mentioned is intricately connected to political events, provides at least a faint reflection of the correlation we have repeatedly seen.

[6]*The Divine Warrior in Early Israel* (Harvard Semitic Monographs, 5; Cambridge: Harvard University Press, 1973) 120.

[7]*Ibid.*, 59, 64; on 41, he suggests that Baal's name *aliy* refers "to Ba^{c}al's cosmic battles with the gods and, probably, to his aid in human conflicts."

[8]*Ibid.*, 47. Numbers in brackets are from *CTCA*.

[9]*Ibid.*

[10]Miller himself does not refer to an historical "event," but this seems to be the implication of his conclusions.

[11]That the text has an historical background up through the marriage of Krt, the rest being "domestic history" is the view of John Gray, *The Keret Text in the Literature of Ras Shamra* (Documenta et monumenta Orientis antiqui, V; Leiden: Brill, 1955) 2-3. More specifically, he prefers the terms "social myth" or "social propaganda," and sees the text as rooted in a cultic setting involving the royal wedding and perpetuating the dynasty of Krt (5). Cf. more recently *idem*, "Social Aspects of Canaanite Religions" (Supplement to Vetus Testamentum, Volume de Congrès, Genève, 1965; Leiden: E. J. Brill, 1966) 179 and *passim*.

[12]Thus we would disagree with the interpretation of the text in which one understands "a campaign of 'holy war'" in which Krt is guided by El; see Cross, *CMHE*, 40, 182-183 and cf. Miller, *Divine Warrior*, 58. At least such guidance in battle can only be inferred from the text. The same holds true for Genesis 14, where Cross sees a parallel to the Krt legend in "the succor of Abraham in war by ^{c}El ^{c}Elyōn," *CMHE*, 182-183. But in this passage the narration of the battle is contained in only one verse (15) and there is no mention of divine guidance or aid for Abraham. Only in the Melchizedek episode (vss. 17-24) is reference made to "El Elyon who has delivered your enemies into your hand."

[13]The translation and stichometry are not certain, although this does not significantly affect our argument. It is possible to read *lpnm* with the next line: *lpnm atr.btlt.^{c}nt*, "Ahead went Virgin Anat," as did Marvin H. Pope, "The Scene on the Drinking Mug from Ugarit," *Near Eastern Studies in Honor of William F. Albright*, ed. H. Goedicke (Baltimore: The Johns Hopkins University Press, 1971) 398. This would fit well with Pope's interesting analysis of the literary scene and its ceramic representation. See also Peter J. van Zijl, *Baal*, AOAT 10 (1972) 95-97. We would take *y'uḥdm* as a passive of *'ḥd*, "to seize," and *šb^{c}r* from *b^{c}r*, "to burn."

[14]*Divine Warrior*, 34.

[15]*Ibid.*, 33, 34; cf. Cross, *CMHE*, 93, n. 9.

[16]*Divine Warrior*, 34-35.

[17]*Ibid.*, 19, referring to the *il t^{c}dr b^{c}l*. On Baal's retinue in general, see 18-20. The equation is supported by Anson F. Rainey, "*Ilanu rēṣūtni lillikū!*," AOAT 22 (1973) 139.

[18]See further my "Pillar of Cloud," 21. The possibility of translating

$^c nn$ as "cloud" is now supported by van Zijl (*Baal*, 22, 24) who suggests such a reading for 137 [2].18 and 76.II [10.III].33.

[19]That the texts do not depict the retinue involved in battle is admitted by Miller, *Divine Warrior*, 2, 19, 32. This of course does not mean that there are no similarities between the Ugaritic texts and the Mesopotamian with regard to divine weaponry. Thus, for example, Miller (32) quite rightly points to the similar personification of Baal's and Marduk's weapons.

[20]It seems justifiable, in fact, to raise a semantic issue as to whether the term "theophany" or "epiphany" is appropriate in these texts, since there is no question of divine appearance to human view (except, perhaps, with the vision/dream of Krt). While there can be no question that storm phenomena were understood as divine manifestations, it seems to us that one must distinguish between the Sinai theophany or the pillar of cloud and fire, which were obviously understood to be phenomena visible to human subjects, and the thundering of Baal in the clouds in the mytho- logical texts, which do not function to manifest his power to human sub- jects *in the texts*. Such a distinction, however, may depend on the highly debatable question as to whether an object or viewer is properly a prerequisite for the use of the term "theophany."

[21]Our methodological point has a corollary in recent observations by Wil- liam W. Hallo ["Individual Prayer in Sumerian: The Continuity of a Tradition," *JAOS* 88 (1968 [Speiser volume]) 72] concerning the relevance of Ugaritic poetry for form-critical study of the Psalms. Our conclusions with regard to the relevance of the Ugaritic literature (and, indeed, with regard to the other Near Eastern texts examined above) are largely in agreement with Bertil Albrektson, *History and the Gods* (Lund, Sweden: Gleerup, 1967) especially 115. For a critique of Albrektson's herme-- neutical implications, see W. G. Lambert, "Destiny and Divine Interven- tion in Babylon and Israel," *Oudtestamentische Studiën*, 17 (Leiden: Brill, 1972) 65-72.

SUMMARY

Each of the major documents from Mesopotamia (but not those from Syria-Palestine) indicates the presence of many—if not all—of the following factors: provenance in an historical period experiencing dramatic political developments; a decisive battle where the presence of the god(s), expressed by what we have termed the "vanguard motif," is clearly the victorious force defeating the foe; a resultant emphasis on the supremacy of one monarch, with the corollary "exaltation" of a major deity. In this way, motifs of divine presence are also intimately connected with the human leader. Although, in a much more laconic style, the same motifs function in a similar way in the annals, and their frequency there increases proportionately to the aesthetic literary quality of the annals. The vanguard motif is also frequently accompanied by a motif expressing the fearful reaction of the enemies of the god and/or of the king. Less often explicit in the literary texts, but clearly indicated in the annals, is the use of physical objects as representations of divine presence in battle. These objects, ranging from standards to statues of the deities, play a significant role, both in the historical events themselves, and in the literary works that describe those events. Their loss and subsequent return are often important signs of the religio-political events that form the background of specific texts. Such objects are also used in conjunction with the vanguard motif in the context of cultic processions. Along with the construction of temples, they also may illustrate and embody the cultic celebration of divine exaltation and serve as a means to ensure that divine presence is not ephemeral.

In short, we have found that motifs of divine presence do not occur in random fashion, but are frequently integral elements within a consistent typology which itself mirrors a recurring set of historical circumstances. Our use of the term "typology" in connection with the texts discussed is not intended to be restrictive. By no means can it be assumed that all of these texts belong to one "genre," or that the common elements within them constitute a "form" (*Gattung*). Thus instead of following a rigid form-critical or history of religions approach, we have attempted to correlate various types of data--literary, mythological, epic, annalistic, and cultic. Yet on the basis of this data we have demonstrated that there is a distinct configuration of motifs that reappears at various times and places, under similar historico-political conditions, and that this configuration serves a propagandistic function.

EXCURSUS. PRESENCE AND GUIDANCE

IN PRE-MOSAIC TRADITIONS

Part I of this study is intended to provide the context from which we approach the biblical material in Part II. From this perspective it will be helpful to pause for a moment in order to investigate a question that has been raised by a number of scholars regarding the traditio-historical provenance of the presence/guidance motifs. Although this is certainly not the primary concern of the present study, the traditio-historical issues involve a number of biblical and extra-biblical texts that will have a bearing on our subsequent discussion.

We may begin by posing the question clearly: do the motifs of divine presence and guidance that we shall examine, especially in Exodus, stem from a pre-Mosaic (semi-)nomadic setting that can be uncovered in the history of traditions lying behind the book of Genesis? This question is answered affirmatively by a number of scholars whose work deserves our attention.

Building on the fundamental work of Albrecht Alt and his typology of localized Canaanite deities (in contrast to the "God of the Fathers"),[1] a number of scholars have attempted to search for the patriarchal deity behind the narratives of Genesis.[2] Foremost among these is Martin Buber. In his phenomenological study of divine kingship,[3] Buber attempted to trace a continuous strain throughout Old Testament religion whose provenance lay in the primeval god of the nomadic tribe, *malk*. For Buber, divine presence and guidance seemed to be intuited by the tribe out of its experience during wandering or migration, and inferred from the fortuitous events of the journey:

> As though one possessed ancient trail lore
> one strides ahead without a mistake: there
> is one who leads, ... Innumerable enemy

hordes are put to flight: there is one in the
front rank who wields the sword.[4]

The divine figure here would thus be strikingly similar to the vanguard
motif discussed in Part I. This *malk* figure, or "leader-god," was fun-
damentally different from the localized Canaanite deities, and was carried over into Yahwism, eventually developing into a "king" (*melekh*)
figure.[5] Thus in Genesis 28 we find Yahweh's promise to wander along
with Jacob rather than remain bound to the place Bethel:[6]

> *'nky ᶜmmk wšmrtyk bkl 'šr tlk whšbtyk 'l h'dmh hzz't*

> "I will be with you, and I will protect you wherever
> you go, and will return you to this land" (vs. 15)

In the same manner, Yahweh promises his presence with Moses (Exod 3:12;
4.12, 15) and leads his people out of Egypt in the pillar of cloud and
fire (Exod 13.17ff.,21).[7] Moreover, this image of divine guidance is
incorporated into the cultic institutions of tent and ark at the earliest times.[8]

The thesis developed by Buber and others[9] bears interesting resemblances to the work of F. M. Cross despite the wide methodological gap
that separates them. Also following the typology of Alt's "God of the
Father," Cross propounds that the El who stands behind Israelite patriarchal religion was a "social god" who was related to the human community
through covenant or kinship, who guided their migratory journeyings, and
who fought for them in battle.[10] His evidence for this is based primarily on Amorite personal names, the assumption that the patriarchs
were donkey nomads,[11] and a few passages from Genesis (see below). At
the earliest levels of Israelite religion, this patriarchal El was combined with the Canaanite El who, as well as being a patriarchal figure,
was also the creator and the leader of cosmic armies.[12] The ways of
describing Yahweh's activity are a conflation of this El (Amorite) construct and the figure of Baal (Canaanite) as cosmogonic warrior.[13]

Like Buber, Cross sees Jacob's dream and consequent vow at Bethel
(Gen 28.10-22) as a retouched example of "the old pattern of the patriarchal cults."[14] The basis of this pattern is an act of mutual election
between deity and patriarchal group, which may be expressed in "the explicit language of kinship or covenant," although here it is not.[15]
Along with progeny and land, the deity promises "his direction and

protection," and the human counterpart vows his obedience and promises
"to follow the deity's directives in holy war or in migration (compare
Genesis 12:1)."[16] It is important to note that for Cross this element
of patriarchal religion did not fall into complete desuetude, for belief
in the deity as protector, war leader, and migratory guide was carried
over into Yahwism.[17]

It is clear that two of the major elements in this proposed continuity between patriarchal and Mosaic religion are 1) the themes of
divine presence and guidance, and 2) that Gen 28.10-22 is a major witness to it. As the "God of the Father" promised his presence and guidance for Jacob, Yahweh did so for later Israel. Moreover, the emphasis
on the deity's fighting in historical battles again suggests similarities
to the vanguard motif.

Although absolute certainty in such matters is hardly possible, the
basic phenomenological force of the above arguments is interesting and
highly suggestive. Relatively late evidence from the history of religions provides some support of a general nature at least.[18] Still, one
of the major problems with the proposals of Buber, Cross, and others
has been the lack of relatively early textual evidence outside the Old
Testament.[19] In our judgment, such evidence would have to combine the
use of some form of the vanguard motif with other expressions of the
protective presence of the deity, and perhaps some indications pursuant
to Cross's suggestion of a covenant (though not necessarily treaty)
relationship. Among the treaty texts from Boghazköi,[20] one document
offers a possibility of fulfilling these requirements. The text comes
from about 1350 B.C. and reflects the last stages of what had been the
Mitanni empire, now under the control of the Hittites. The Obverse
describes the political confusion that accompanied the demise of Mitanni
and the threat to the life of its remaining king, Mattiwaza. In desper-
ation, Mattiwaza escapes from his enemies, flees to Suppiluliuma, and
begs for help. The Hittite king accepts his plea, promises to restore
his throne (as a vassal, of course), and sends Mattiwaza off, newly
equipped for battle and accompanied by another loyal vassal.

The description of these events includes a number of expressions
that are of interest in the light of our previous discussion. When
Mattiwaza realizes his plight, he cries out to the gods of Hatti and
Mitanni, who then, he says, "led (him) on a way which was not (dangerous),"[21] and allowed him to reach Suppiluliuma. Responding to

108

Suppiluliuma's pledge of aid, Mattiwaza refers with hope to his future victory over his enemies by saying "when . . . the gods stand as my help . . ." (*šumma ilāni* [*i*]*na rišija* [*sic*; read *riṣija*] *izzizzu*; l. 28). Even more striking is the occurrence of the vanguard motif, which describes the commencement of battle (l. 41).

> ù ilāni^{pl} šá šarri rabî šar māt [^{al}Ḫ]a-at-ti
>
> it-tal-ku a-na pa-[ni-ni]
>
> Then the gods of the great king, the king of the
> land of Ḫatti, went before us.

Finally, returning to our discussion of Genesis 28, the Reverse side of the text, which contains the actual treaty between Mattiwaza and Suppiluliuma, has a very interesting passage that constitutes the treaty blessing:

> 53. . . . um-ma ^mMat-ti-ú-a-za mār
>   šarri um-ma lu-ú mārê^{pl} Ḫar-ri šum-ma ri-ik-šá
>   [*sic*; read, ri-ik-sá]
> 54. ù ma-mi-ta an-na-a-am šá ^dŠamši^{ši m}Šú-ub-bi-lu-
>   li-u-ma šarri rabî šar māt ^{al}Ḫa-at-ti ḳarradi
>   na-ra-am ^dTešup ni-na-za-ar
> 55. ilāni^{pl} šá šú-un-zu-nu ni-iz-ku-ru li-it-tal-ku-
>   na-ši li-ri-bi-šú-na-a-ši li-iz-zu-ru-na-ši
> 56. li-te-mi-ku-na-ši be-li ^mMat-ti-ú-a-za a-na pa-ni
>   líl-li-ik ni-e-nu i-na zi-el-li-lì-šú e-bu-ra
> 57. ma-a-ta lu-ú ni-ku-ul du-um-ka ù nu-uḫ-ta lu-ú
>   ni-mur ^dTešup gú-gal šamê ù irṣiti a-na da-ra-a-ti
> 58. lu-ú ri-iz-zu-ni[22]

Thus (says) Mattiwaza, the king's son, and thus (say) the Ḫurri people: If we keep this treaty (54) and oath with the Sun, Suppiluliuma, the great king, the king of the land of Ḫatti, the hero, the beloved of Tešub, (55) may the gods whose names we invoke go with us, make us great, protect us, (56) (and) do good for us. As lord may Mattiwaza go in front. Under his protection we wish to consume a (57) rich harvest. Goodness and rest we wish to see. May

Tešub, the prince of heaven and earth, forever be
(58) our protector.

The text has a number of interesting features. Obedience to the treaty
with the overlord will result in the accompanying and protective presence of the witnessing deities. Thus the language in 11. 55–56a has
clear similarities to Jacob's vow in Gen 28.20–21, even though in the
latter there is no stipulation of obedience:

> 'm yhyh 'lhym ᶜmmdy wšmrny bddrk hzzh
> 'šr 'nky hwlk wntn-ly lhm l'kl wbgd llbš
> (21) wšbty bšlwm 'l-byt 'by whyh yhwh ly l'lhym

> If God will be with me and protect me in this way
> on which I am going, and provide for me food to
> eat and clothes to wear, and return me in peace
> to the house of my father, than Yahweh shall be
> my god.

Moreover, the Akkadian text again uses the vanguard motif, here to express Mattiwaza's restored status as (vassal-) king of Mitanni.[23]

Of course, there are a number of problems connected with the interpretation of the Mattiwaza text. While the covenant context fits
well with Cross's hypothesis, the picture does not seem to be one of
wandering or migration. Perhaps at best it means that the deities will
accompany the king and his people on their return to their homeland from
wherever the treaty was formally concluded. Otherwise, Mattiwaza and
his people seem to be a settled community with little similarity to the
proposed lifestyle of the patriarchs. However, one should not expect
too much from an isolated textual parallel. Moreover, the striking
affinities between this text and Genesis 28 cannot be dismissed lightly.
In fact, it is intriguing that the Akkadian text has a number of pecu-
liarities that set it off from other treaty texts and that appear to
derive from traditions of Mitanni rather than of Hatti.[24] Also, a
large proportion of the Mitanni population was Hurrian, an ethnic group
that became fairly widespread in the second millennium B.C., whose
customs are generally understood to have influenced the patriarchal
traditions.[25] Thus it is possible that the two texts have preserved an
ancient and analogous religious tradition of divine presence and blessing that figures so largely in the "patriarchal promise" of Genesis.[26]

110

In short, the Mattiwaza text demonstrates that language of divine presence similar to that used in the Genesis passage to which Cross and Buber appeal is, in fact, used elsewhere in the ancient Near East within a covenant setting. The text also contains literary similarities to the material discussed in Part I. Thus although the text may not help us penetrate to a "social god" (Cross) or "leader god" (Buber) who guides tribal groups in migrations and fights their battles, it may provide concrete, albeit very tentative, support for the traditio-historical theories in general.

One other aspect of Gen 28.10-22 that deserves discussion is Yahweh's promise in vs. 15: "I will be with you" ('$\bar{a}n\bar{o}k\hat{\imath}$ $^c imm\bar{a}k$). Is this an expression of divine presence and guidance which, as Buber claims (see above), can be compared to the function of the vanguard motif such as that of the pillar of cloud and fire in Exodus? In our judgment, this question must be answered in the negative, although this by no means implies a negative evaluation of the traditio-historical significance of the motifs in Genesis, nor does it imply traditio-historical priority for the exaltation typology that we shall trace in Part II.

The use of $^c im$ and '$\bar{e}t$ to express divine presence[27] in Genesis is limited to the extent that we can survey all occurrences here. The first is in 21.22, in the story of the agreement with Abraham that Abimelech proposes because "God is with you ($^c mmk$) in all that you do." This has its parallel in 26.28, where Isaac is involved in the same situation, only there it follows upon the divine promise in 26.3, 24 (the latter using 'tk).[28] These passages provide little opportunity to flesh out the meaning of this divine presence, but this can be done with the subsequent uses of the terms $^c m$ and 't, particularly in the Jacob and Joseph narratives which, in fact, constitute the only other occurrences of this expression in Genesis. The context of the expression in 28.15, 20, both in its pericope and in the larger framework of the Jacob stories, indicates that Yahweh's being "with" Jacob does not refer to guidance but simply to protection and general well-being: "keeping" him on his journey, providing food and clothing and a safe return home. This is promised anew in 31.3, when Jacob decides to return to Palestine. In 31.5, Jacob acknowledges that "the god of my father has been with me" (hyh $^c mmdy$, cf. 35.3). The evidence of this seems to be what follows in vss. 6-16--namely, that God arranged matters so that all of Laban's cattle became Jacob's. In other words, the text indicates that it was in the fortuitous turn of events in favor of Jacob that the divine presence was discerned. Thus when Jacob in 32.10 reminds Yahweh of the promise he made in 31.3, he repeats it almost word for word, but using a telling alternative: "I will do you good" (*w'ytybh ʿmmk*, cf. vs. 13). This seems to be a means of expression for Jacob's good fortune, which he relates in 32.11: "with only my staff I crossed this Jordan, and now I have become two companies." This connection between divine presence and human success is even more apparent in the Joseph stories, of which 39.2 is the epitome: "Yahweh was with Joseph, and he became a successful man" (*wyhy yhwh 't-ywsp wyhy 'yš mṣlyḥ*; cf. vss. 3, 21, 23, all using *'t*).[29] A very similar picture can be obtained of David (1 Sam 16.18; 18.12 and especially vs. 14). In short, the *form* of divine presence expressed by Yahweh's being "with" someone clearly is not analogous to phenomena such as the pillar of cloud and fire, and the *function* is not really that of guidance. Of course, Yahweh's presence here, as in Exodus, is a protective one, but this general similarity in function does not provide sufficient warrant for maintaining a strong continuity between patriarchal and Israelite religion.[30]

Finally, we would point out that the expression in Genesis that comes closest to the motif of the divine vanguard that we have examined above also fits the correlation of divine presence and success. In Gen 24.7, Abraham sends his servant to find a wife for Isaac with the encouraging assurance that Yahweh "will send his messenger before you (*yšlḥ ml'kw lpnyk*) to take a wife for my son from there." This whole chapter, which again reminds us of Genesis 28 and the Keret legend, obviously has nothing to do with warfare, and the messenger who goes before Abraham's servant is hardly a divine warrior. (But contrast Exod 23.20, etc. See below.) It is interesting however, that, along with this phrase using *lipnê*, we also have explicit mention of guidance. Thus in vs. 27 the servant praises Yahweh, who has led him on the way (*bddrk nāḥanî yhwh*; cf. vs. 48, *'šr hinḥanî bddrk 'emet*). Yet it is clear that the use of this word *nḥh* does not here connote the same perspective on divine presence that it does in Exodus (see below). This is due not only to the very different situations (there, guidance on the march and in battle;[31] here, the search for a wife) but also to the correlation between the presence of the divine messenger and the success of the servant's journey: Yahweh "will send his messenger with you and prosper your way" (*yšlh ml'kw 'tk whṣlyḥ drkk*, vs. 40).[32]

To summarize: Buber, Cross, and others have presented some highly suggestive theories concerning the traditio-historical provenance of motifs of divine presence and guidance in pre-Mosaic Israel.[33] Such traditions may well stand behind such passages as Gen 28.10-22 and the Mattiwaza text. As we shall see in several instances in Part II, these traditions may have been influential in certain literary formulations that deal with the exodus, conquest, and Davidic empire. However, the primary focus of the present study is not on the traditio-historical *provenance* of the motifs of divine presence and guidance, but on their form and function in the context of certain literary, as well as theological and political, configurations. If it is the case that the traditio-historical provenance of motifs such as the divine vanguard can be traced back to some form of "patriarchal" religion, it is also the case that such motifs are incorporated within a dramatically new setting when we turn to the book of Exodus.

PRESENCE AND GUIDANCE IN PRE-MOSAIC TRADITIONS

[1]"The God of the Fathers," *Essays on Old Testament History and Religion* (Oxford: Basil Blackwell, 1966).

[2]For an extremely negative view of both the methodology and results of such a task, see the recent work by Thomas L. Thompson *The Historicity of the Patriarchal Narratives: The Quest for the Historical Abraham* (BZAW, 133; Berlin: de Gruyter, 1974).

[3]*The Kingship of God*, (New York: Harper & Row, 1967 [original German edition, 1932]).

[4]*Ibid.*, 95.

[5]*Ibid.*, 97.

[6]*Ibid.*, 100.

[7]*Ibid.*, 101.

[8]*Ibid.*, 102, 53, and passim.

[9]Wolf W. G. Baudissin, *Kyrios als Gottesname in Judentum und seine Stelle in der Religionsgeschichte* (Teil 3; Giessen; A. Töpelmann, 1929) 49-- *malik, malk* "originally meant the leader of a tribe." Baudissin (*Ibid.*, n. 5) appears to base his opinion on the reports of J. L. Burckhardt, *Travels in Nubia and Arabia* (1820). His argument, as well as that of Buber and others, reveals the danger of a romantic view of nomadism, which has come under fire more recently. This is even more apparent in the work of Ditlef Nielsen, [*Ras Šamra Mythologie und Biblische Theologie* (Abhandlungen für die Kunde des Morgenlandes, XXI.4; Leipzig: DMG, 1936) 44-45], who identifies *malik* with the Venus god of the south Arabian bedouin, also as a leader of tribes, caravans, and military expeditions. More recently, similar arguments have been made, but apparently based more on Alt than on other studies. Cf. Victor Maag ["Malkût JHWH," *VT Supplement* 7 (Congress Volume; Leiden: Brill, 1960) 139-141], who sees a continuity from Abraham to Jacob to Moses (also with reference to the ark and pillar of cloud) in the "inspirierende, führende, behütende Nomadengott" in contrast to the Canaanite deities. Also R. E. Clements (*God and Temple*, 15), with appeal both to Alt and to Buber. Werner Schmidt [*Königtum Gottes in Ugarit und Israel* (Beihefte zur ZAT, 80; Berlin: A. Töpelmann, 1961) 55-56] accepts the Alt hypothesis while rejecting Buber's as too extreme. Much of this material has been picked up as an important building block for contemporary theology; cf. for example Jürgen Moltmann, *Theology of Hope* (London: SCM, 1967) ch. II passim.

[10]*CMHE*, 6, 42-43, 58-59, 89.

[11]*Ibid.*, 6-11, 43; cf. 143, n. 109. Cross also appeals to the figure of El in the Ugaritic texts, especially in the Keret epic (39-43, 180-183). See our discussion in ch. 4.

[12]*Ibid.*, 89.

[13]*Ibid.*, 163.

[14]*Ibid.*, 270. Cross sees here an Elohistic account based on the Yahwistic pericope relating the promise of the land (vss. 13-16).

[15]*Ibid.* We would tend to agree with Cross that a covenant in a general sense is involved here in the final form of the text. That is, there is

a formal agreement between Yahweh and Jacob, the latter expressing his side formally by making a vow. The formal structure of the vow in vss. 20-21 occurs frequently in the Old Testament, and can be compared to the vow of Keret in the Ugaritic texts. All of this material is discussed by Loren R. Fisher, "Two Projects at Claremont," *Ugarit-Forschungen* 3 (1961) 27-30.

[16]*Ibid.*, 270.

[17]*Ibid.*, 271; also 6, 89-90.

[18]In addition to the evidence cited above in n. 9, there is also some interesting material, unrelated to the Near East, collected by W. W. Malandra, "The Concept of Movement in History of Religions: A Religio-Historical Study of Reindeer in the Spiritual Life of North Eurasian Peoples," *Numen* 14 (1967) 23-69. Malandra describes the contemporary reindeer herders who employ wooden or stone figures to represent a super-human protector. Such figures are "transported on the backs of special 'dedicated' reindeer or on sacred sledges." The role of one such reindeer provides a striking parallel to the use of emblems in Mesopotamian processionals and military marches: "Its main function seems to be to ride in front of the caravan when people are on the move, hallowing the way as they go" (41). In fact, another practice has very intriguing similarities to the events related in 1 Samuel 6: when moving from one dwelling place to another, a white reindeer is used as a guide, but is never saddled or otherwise used during the journey, at the end of which the animal is sacrificed to the spirits it represents (42). It is also interesting that the sacred sleds are often constructed in such a way as to appear like reindeer, and that the sled may carry "a chest or box (for sacred objects) with a cover." Indeed, "even the sled is a living being actively involved in the welfare and protection of man and herd" (42). Malandra emphasizes the fact that the religious life of these people is always a nomadic one involving movement, as witnessed by the various seasonal sacrifices related to change of pasture and migrations (49).

[19]In fact, the picture of wandering, semi-nomadic tribal groups does not seem to present much promise for such written evidence.

[20]Transliterated text and translation in Ernst F. Weidner, *Politische Dokumente aus Kleinasien: Die Staatsverträge in akkadischer Sprache aus dem Archiv von Bogazköi* (Boghazköi-Studien, 8; Leipzig: Hinrichs, 1923) No. 2 (pp. 36-57). For an English translation (without text) see Daniel D. Luckenbill, "Hittite Treaties and Letters," *AJSL* 37 (1921) 171-176. Note that text No. 1 presents a somewhat shorter version, especially of the events leading up to the treaty, and primarily from the viewpoint of the Hittites, whereas text No. 2 contains Mattiwaza's first person account.

[21]Ll. 18-19; *ana girriša la---irteduninni*: the suggestion for the missing word is taken from Weidner, *Politische Documente*, 41, n. 8.

[22]*Ibid.*, 56, 53-58. The more traditional curses run from 11. 25-53a.

[23]L. 56 of the text is translated "Mein Herr Mattiuaza möge vorangehen" by Weidner (*Politische Documente*, 57) who comments that "Mattiuaza soll also ein richtiger 'Herzog' sein," n. 2. Since both Mattiwaza and the Ḫurri are speaking, our translation has followed that of Luckenbill, "Hittite Treaties," 176. The relevance of 11. 53-56 for the Old Testament were first pointed out by Klaus Baltzer [*The Covenant Formulary* (Philadelphia: Fortress, 1971) 70, n. 31] in connection with Deut 31.3. On this, see

below, at the end of ch. 6, for a brief remark; also ch. 10, part 2.

[24]Dennis J. McCarthy, *Treaty and Covenant* (Analecta Biblica 21; Rome: Pontifical Biblical Institute, 1963) 102, 104.

[25]The work of E. A. Speiser is basic. See his "Hurrians," IDB, 2, 664-666, for discussion and further references. More recently, see Harry A. Hoffner, "The Hittites and Hurrians," *Peoples of Old Testament Times*, ed. D. J. Wiseman (Oxford: Clarendon, 1973) especially 224-226. For strenuous objection to the traditional historical and exegetical use of the Nuzi texts in particular, see most recently Thomas L. Thompson, *Historicity*, 197-297 (especially 294-297).

[26]Cf. especially Gen 26.3, 24, and see the discussion of the Genesis material in general below. Along with the expression of divine presence and protection, the Akkadian text quoted above may offer another close parallel to the patriarchal promise in the phrase "make us great" (*liribišunaši*, 1. 55). In fact, it is translated "increase our numbers (widen us)," by Luckenbill, "Hittite Treaties," 176. Cf. the use of *rbh* Hi. in Gen 17.20; 22.17; 26.4, 24; 48.4.

[27]The expressions of divine presence in the following discussion have been studied exhaustively by Horst Dietrich Preuß, "'. . . ich will mit dir sein!'" *ZAW* 80 (1968) 139-173. Preuß's thinking is often indebted to Buber (see above), to whom he frequently refers. He finds the expression of *Mitsein* to have a major locus in the Patriarchal stories, and a second locus in those about David. The former generally reveals "the accompanying, conducting, protecting, and guiding deity" of "nomadic thinking and belief," 153. In the latter (with which he combines the stories about Joseph) the original promises of accompaniment are expanded to formulas of aid, and the motif of wandering now becomes one of history (156). Although we would agree with a great deal of Preuß's study, we feel that he has overemphasized the nomadic setting of the expression in question, particularly in the Jacob stories, and that the notion of guidance is not borne out by the texts (at least, certainly not in the explicit way guidance is portrayed in Exodus; see below).

[28]Regarding the use of this term within the promise, we would see this as perhaps sharing some mutual influence with the use in Exod 3.12. However, the latter cannot be lumped together with the ostensible tribal guide and Yahweh's guidance later in Exodus, but must be studied as part of the prophetic call form--see especially Judg 6.12-13, 16. This became a favorite expression of divine presence for the deuteronomistic school; see below, ch. 10, (2).

[29]Note also vs. 5 and the blessing, with its material benefits. All the verses are from J. The E stratum expresses Yahweh's presence with Joseph primarily through his prowess as an interpretor of dreams, which, of course, are the revelations of his God. Cf. 40.8; 41.16, 25, 28, 32 and especially 38.

[30]Regarding "formulas of good will and blessing," it has been noted that "Such sentences as 'God is with you in all that you do' . . . are simply the recognition of good fortune interpreted as the evidence of divine blessing," G. H. Davies, "Presence," 874.

[31]Actually the closest resemblance to the vanguard imagery in Part I in terms of effect is found in Gen 35.5: "and as they journeyed the terror of God (came) upon the cities surrounding them and they did not pursue the children of Jacob."

[32]This entire verse should be compared with 48.15, which also speaks of divine "leading." However, here the term is r^ch, "to shepherd," a very common metaphor in the ancient Near East for the expression of divine protection and guidance. On $h\d{s}lyh$ see also 24.21, 42, 56.

[33]The scope of our study does not allow space for other motifs and themes. On Yahweh's "appearance" ($nr'h$) see Appendix 2. Note also the use of dreams as a medium for revelation (Gen 15.12; 20.3; 31.11, 24). There are, of course, interesting texts within the Primeval History regarding God's presence. Also, within the patriarchal history, the numerous times in which Yahweh speaks to Abraham and others clearly constitutes a form of divine presence, although we would want to argue that this is often little more than a literary device for the author to introduce his theological message. Of course, the classic theophanies (e.g. to Jacob at Bethel) would have to be covered in a thorough study of Genesis. Indeed, we would be prepared to argue that the way in which these are often connected to the gift of the land may well adumbrate elements of the exaltation typology which we shall discuss below (e.g. in Exodus 15). Also the emphasis on departure as the occasion for expressions of divine presence is one of the most interesting and theologically significant results of the final redactional setting of Jacob's encounter with God in Chs. 28 and 32 (cf. the similar effect in Exodus, Numbers, and Joshua discussed below.) For a standard general discussion of the patriarchal theophanies, see Kuntz, *Self-Revelation*, ch. 4.

PART II

MOTIFS OF DIVINE PRESENCE IN THE OLD TESTAMENT

INTRODUCTION

In Part I, we have discussed a number of major exemplars of ancient Near Eastern texts. We delineated in them a configuration of literary elements and an historical context in which motifs of divine presence were concentrated. We concluded that these motifs, along with other factors, were consistently found in conjunction with the exaltation of a particular deity and of the human leader under the tutelage of that deity.

As we stated in the Introduction to this study, our interest in the Old Testament material is centered primarily in those narratives that tell the story of Israel's journey from Egypt to Canaan, and the final conquest of the land under David. The question before us now is whether this literature shares the typology of exaltation. Do the form and function of motifs of divine presence here resemble those in the Near Eastern texts by expressing this typology? Are they as closely related to the human leaders who dominate the story--Moses, Joshua, and David-- as they are to the protagonists in the Near Eastern literature? If so, what is the role of Israel as a people in this typology? Finally, if the application of this schema to certain biblical texts reveals significant similarities to the Near Eastern material, does it also point to distinctive Israelite forms of the typology?

In our approach, we are quite consciously following the lead set by William W. Hallo, who has suggested that Israel's deliverance at the Reed Sea and her recognition of the supremacy of her God should be explored as another dramatic example of the typology of exaltation.[1] Thus our purpose in Part II is twofold: to test Hallo's thesis concerning the Exodus event, and to see if the typology of exaltation can be used as an interpretive rubric for other Old Testament narratives, especially those dealing with the period from the Exodus to the Conquest, and the Davidic empire. The test of our approach can come only when the results of our conclusions are applied to the Old Testament material. If they serve to illuminate the biblical text, then our method of procedure can be judged successful, at least in part.

[1]*Exaltation*, 67-68.

CHAPTER 5
THE REED SEA AND SINAI

(1) The Song of the Sea

In this chapter we intend to discuss Exodus 15, or "The Song of the Sea," insofar as it relates to our theme of divine presence. In doing so, we will approach it with the assumption that it is part of the earliest corpus of Israelite literature known to us. Although this position is still not without detractors,[1] we feel that recent studies of this material (particularly those made by F. M. Cross and David Noel Freedman),[2] have almost positively established the early date. Moreover, the methods used by Cross and Freedman (lexicography; comparison of poetic meter and style; motifs and epic themes) have been complemented and buttressed recently by the rigid linguistic study of David A. Robertson.[3] In fact, his dating of Exodus 15 as early, and probably from the 12th century, is "the one unequivocal, firmly grounded conclusion" of his work.[4]

There can be little doubt that, despite its brevity, the Song of the Sea is a composition of truly epic dimensions. In a vivid and pulsating style it portrays Yahweh's victory on behalf of his people over the oppressive Pharaoh and his troops and his continuing protection during Israel's journey towards the land destined to be hers from the time of the Fathers. Of course this remarkable poem has been studied in depth by a number of scholars from widely varying methodological principles. Our purpose here, and, in fact, throughout Part II, is not to review that work or even to offer comprehensive interpretations of our own. Our remarks will be limited as much as possible to the pursuit of our theme of divine presence and guidance, and to an attempt to demonstrate the significance of the Near Eastern material that was the subject of the preceding chapters. For what follows we shall rely heavily on the reconstructed translation and strophic analysis of the

Song by Cross,[5] and the reader is urged to refer to that for details.

A cursory reading of the Song will show that its plan is far from chronological. The poet returns a number of times to the actual defeat of the enemy, rather than building up to a dramatic finale (see vss. 1, 4-5, 10, 12). This does not mean, however, that the poem is without structural organization; indeed, studies by Muilenberg and others have discovered its structure.[6] Following the analysis of Cross, the Song is divided into two parts, each of which opens with a short summary of Yahweh's deeds (vss. 1, 13--each is four lines long) followed by longer and more detailed accounts of the same. Each of these sections (the summaries and the expanded narratives) is followed by an antiphon, usually consisting of two lines in 3:3 meter.[7]

Undoubtedly the most striking aspect of this structure for our purposes is that the two parts of the poem provide a most interesting illustration of our topic--divine presence and guidance. Part one (vss. 1b-12) presents the most famous and, for the Old Testament, no doubt the most determinative example of the presence of Yahweh in battle against the historical enemy of Israel. Part two (vss. 13-18) presents a classic example of Yahweh's guidance of Israel in her march to the Promised Land. On the basis of the Near Eastern material that we have examined, this correlation of Yahweh and Israel intimates that we are also confronted with another major aspect of our topic: the typology of exaltation. This indication, we shall argue, is confirmed, above all, by the lines that bracket the entire poem (vss. 1b, 18):

Sing to Yahweh	*šr lyhw*
For he is highly exalted	*k g' g'*
Let Yahweh reign	*yhw ymlk*
Forever and ever	*l^clm w^cd*

With these themes provisionally before us, let us turn to the literary content of the Song to see how it supports our claims. The motif of divine presence in Part 1 is obviously a salient example of the storm deity in battle, a divine figure that we have seen repeatedly in the Near Eastern material. It is important to note that the poet had combined this familiar motif with the particular historical situation of the event as he understood it. Thus both storm *and* sea form the weapons of the divine warrior. As Cross suggests, "it is a storm-tossed sea that is directed against the Egyptians by the breath of the

Deity."[8]

The use of such imagery throughout Part 1 is clearly similar to what we have seen, particularly in the Akkadian material, where the deity employs storm, fire, and flood to overcome his enemies. This combination is dramatically evident in vss. 7-8:

In your great majesty[9]	[] *brb g'nk*
You crushed your foes.	*thrṣ qmk*
You sent forth your fury	*tšlḥ ḥrnk*
It consumed them like stubble.	*y'klm kqš*
At the blast of your nostrils	[] *brḥ 'pk*
The waters were heaped up.	*nᶜrm mm*
The swells mounted up as a hill;	*nṣb km-nd nzlm*
The deeps foamed[10] in the heart of the sea.	*qp' thmt blb-ym*

Along with the motifs of divine presence in battle, we have also suggested that Part 1 of the Song is introduced by an expression of Yahweh's exaltation. Other elements within Part 1 support this thesis. Immediately after the incipit, Yahweh is again exalted by the poet in vs. 2b, using the verb *rwm* (Pō^{c}lēl). Then in vs. 7, as we have seen above, we have a repetition of the root *g'h*, which means "majesty, exaltation." Surely the most telling evidence, however, is not so much in the use of individual words but in the very way in which Yahweh's victory is celebrated and in the theological implications that the poet makes. This is nowhere more clear in Part 1 than in the concluding antiphon, vs. 11:

Who is like you[11] among the gods, Yahweh?
Who is like you, terrible among the holy ones?
Awesome in praises, wonder worker.

m-kmk b'lm yhw
m-kmk n'dr bqdš
nr' thlt ᶜš pl'

It is important to emphasize here what was indicated above--that we do not have a battle between two deities, Yahweh and Sea, but a battle between Yahweh and the *historical* enemy of Israel. This becomes more important when we recognize that, according to Cross, the mythological battle of Canaanite epic was adapted by Israel to express her

historical experience.[12]   In the Near Eastern material in Part I of this
study (especially those texts from the rise of Akkad and the later
Assyrian empire), motifs of divine presence in battle are also used from
an early date--and here they are used within the context of historical
events. The Exaltation of Inanna, the Nur-Adad Letter, the Epic of
Tukulti-Ninurta, and the Assyrian annals are prime examples.[13] Thus
Israel's use of such imagery has much in common with Mesopotamian literary traditions and the way in which these conceive of divine activity in
history.

If the imagery of divine presence in battle in Part 1 of the poem
is, as we believe, strikingly reminiscent of the imagery in the Near
Eastern material, the similarity is even more apparent in Part 2. Just
as Yahweh and his enemy dominate Part 1, Yahweh's people and "the peoples"
dominate Part 2. This is already apparent in the opening summary and its
antiphon (vss. 13 and 14):

You faithfully led	nht $bhsdk$
The people whom you redeemed;	^cm $z-g'lt$
You guided in your might	$nhlt$ b^czk
To your holy encampment.	$'l$ nw $qd\check{s}k$
The peoples heard, they shuddered;	$\check{s}m^c$ ^cmm $yrgzw$
Horror seized the inhabitants of Philistia.	hl $'hz$ $y\check{s}b$ $pl\check{s}t$

As we have already indicated, this pericope sets the theme for Part 2,
in which Yahweh guides his people to the land of Canaan. This is sig-
naled by the occurrence of the key word nhh (here parallel to nhl; see
Appendix 2), which we shall meet again in the prose accounts. The
theme of divine guidance correlated with the terrified reaction of the
surrounding peoples is then expanded in typical fashion by the next
section and its antiphon, which we shall cite in full, again quoting
Cross's version (vss. 15-16):

Yea, they were undone,	$'z$ $nbhl$
The chieftains of Edom	$'lp$ $'dm$
The nobles of Moab	$'l$ $m'b$
Were seized by panic.	$y'hzm$ r^cd
They were melted utterly,	nmg kl

126

The enthroned of Canaan.	$y\check{s}b$ $kn^c n$
16 You brought down on them	tpl $^c lhm$
Terror and dread.	$'mt$ $wph\d{}d$
Be thy great power	$bgdl$ $zr^c k$
They were struck dumb	ydm $k'bn$
like a stone.	
While your people passed over, Yahweh,	$^c d\text{-}y^c br$ $^c mk$ yhw
While your people passed over, whom you have created.	$^c d\text{-}y^c br$ $^c m$ z qnt

This passage has presented a number of problems to interpreters. In fact, in Muilenberg's study of the Song, he complains that these lines are "beset with stylistic and structural difficulties," although he still manages to fit them into his own interpretive schema.[14] From the standpoint of our terminological investigation (see $^c br$ in Appendix 2), it is interesting that Muilenberg should make the following comment:

> a good case could be made out for the contention that different traditional forms are actually associated with the Exodus or Sea motif, on the one hand, and with the desert sojourn and occupation of the land, on the other. More important, perhaps, would be a careful scrutiny of parallel contexts either in the Psalms or in other books of the Old Testament where we encounter a literary, structural, and thematic situation not unlike that which we meet here.[15]

This is precisely what our terminological study enables us to do, and the results for this pericope are significant. One of the cruxes of this passage is the meaning of the antiphon, more specifically of $y^c br$. We would agree with Cross in insisting that the most likely focus is on the crossing of the Jordan, and that the "holy encampment" in the preceding section must refer to Shittim, the traditional axis from which the Conquest radiated.[16] The results of our terminological study point toward such a conclusion, for $^c br$ $lpny$ is a term associated totally with the Jordan-Conquest tradition, where ^{c}br is, of course, also frequent. However, ^{c}br is also used in JE narratives with reference to Israel's "passing through" the lands on her route to Canaan. These narratives stand somewhat in conflict with Exodus 15, for in two instances Israel is denied passage, and in the one with Edom, Israel weakly retreats and is forced to go around the territory (Num 20.14-21 with ^{c}br, passim). On the other hand, in the second instance with Sihon of Heshbon (Num 21.21-32, note ^{c}br in vss. 21-23), Israel defeats her challenger and takes possession of her land. Similar victories occur over "the Canaan- ites" near Arad (Num 21.1-3) and Og of Bashan (21.33-35).[17] Historically it seems that only the mention of Edom and Moab (Exodus 15; Balaam oracles) is more reflective of an early date, whereas the inclusion of Ammon (Num 21.24) harks back to a later time.[18] It is thus possible that Exodus 15.13-16 presents an early witness to these traditions of "passing through," at least to such a connotation of $y^{c}br$, and that these verses refer both to Israel's march through the Trans-Jordanian nations as well as to her crossing over the Jordan.[19]

At any rate, the Song is clearly characterized by hyperbole in comparison to the prose traditions, for in the Song, Israel is depicted as an awesome military force whose very approach terrifies those in her path. This, we believe, is not simply accidental, for the picture in Exod 15.13-16 presents the most graphic parallel to the texts we have examined from the ancient Near East.

In the Near Eastern texts we have repeatedly seen how the approach of the deity and his vanguard and/or of the human king strikes fear in the hearts of his enemies. This was the case not only in the more lit- erary texts, but also--especially--in the annals. As examples, we may cite the following:

> Inanna: Oh my lady, at the sound of you the lands
> bow down.
> Tukulti-Ninurta: He who --- the extremeties of the
> four winds, all kings without exception
> live in dread of him: / As when Addu
> bellows, the mountains tremble, / As
> when Ninurta lifts his weapons, the
> quarters of the world are reduced to
> continual anguish.

> Tiglath-Pilesar I: Mighty torch (?), at the onset
> of whose terrible arms the four regions
> (of the world) shook and the habitations
> (of earth) trembled.

Indeed, we may compare even more specifically vs. 16 ("You brought down
on them terror and dread") to motifs from the Assyrian annals: reaction
of Cyprus to the approach of Sargon II: "their hearts were rent, fear
fell upon them;" of Elam to Sennacherib: "fear and terror were poured
out over all Elam."[20]

The march of Israel through the wilderness and her approach toward
Canaan in Part 2 of Exodus 15 is thus presented in a manner strikingly
similar to the march of the imperial king in Assyrian texts. There is,
however, an important difference. In the Old Testament material, the
march of Israel and the vanguard motif, as we shall see more clearly
below, have been strongly influenced by the theme of guidance (note
already *nhh* in 15.13). In our judgment, the very similar motifs in the
Near Eastern literature never explicitly serve this function, at least
certainly not to the degree that they do in the Old Testament narratives.
This peculiar emphasis is a reflection of the very real concerns of the
wilderness "wanderings," and therefore of intrinsically Israelite tradition. Such concerns, however, are more pronounced in the prose traditions discussed below.

The combination of the motif of Israel's march along with those
of divine presence in battle and the dominating theme of Yahweh's exaltation leads us to suggest a further, and more fundamental, resemblance between the Song and the Near Eastern texts. In the latter we
frequently found that each major literary text examined, as well as the
annals, reflected the institution or renaissance of an empire. We would
assert that Exodus 15 not only uses many very similar literary motifs,
but is also proclaiming a very similar *Tendenz*. Simply put, it declares
that Yahweh's exaltation is also the exaltation of Israel over Egypt and
especially over the peoples of Palestine. Just as Tukulti-Ninurta was
praised as the lord whom all kings dreaded, so it is claimed that Israel is the people before whom all the "enthroned of Canaan" melt in
fear. Indeed, we can press the analogy even further: just as Tukulti-
Ninurta's exaltation was couched in terms of quasi-divine birth, so
Israel's exaltation is expressed in the Song through her special

relationship to Yahweh who has "redeemed," in fact, "acquired" or "created" her.[21] This combination of theological and political exaltation was precisely what we saw in the Exaltation of Inanna, and it is the same correlation that governs Part 2 of the Song of the Sea. Part 2 opens by praising Yahweh's guidance of the people he has acquired; it then describes the supremacy of this people over her Canaanite neighbors and her establishment in Yahweh's newly founded sanctuary. In fact, even the latter (vs. 17), as the final act of the epic drama, has its counterpart in the Tukulti-Ninurta Epic and other texts, where the culminating act inaugurating the empire is the construction of a new (or remodeled) sanctuary. Part 2 ends with the ringing cry announcing Yahweh's exaltation: "Let Yahweh reign forever and ever!" Muilenberg has caught the force of this line in a trenchant way: "Yahweh is now indeed highly exalted, victorious and triumphant as Israel's Leader and King, and he will rule for ever."[22]

(2) The Reed Sea Narrative, Sinai, and the Figure of Moses

Having looked at the poetic account in Exodus 15 of the battle at the Reed Sea and at Israel's victorious march to Canaan, we may now compare it to the prose account. For those familiar with the story, it should be apparent that we are again dealing with the motifs of divine presence and guidance. In fact, the material in these chapters presents the closest literary parallel to the vanguard motif and its function found in the Near Eastern texts.

A brief review of the course of events in the story will prepare us for further observations. Although the question of whether the Reed Sea battle constitutes the end of the Exodus traditions or the beginning of the Wilderness traditions is highly complex and will, no doubt, remain equivocal,[23] 13.17-22 clearly depicts Israel's intended departure from Egypt. In vss. 17-18 (E), God himself guides (nḥh) the people on a way that ostensibly will not confront them with the necessity of fighting and thus cause their retreat back to Egypt.[24] Then, in vss. 21-22 (J), we have a paradigmatic view of Israel's march that both summarizes the event of her departure and sets the scene for the battle of the Reed Sea that follows:

> Now Yahweh continually went before them,
>> By day in a pillar of cloud
>> To guide them on their way,

And by night in a pillar of fire,

   To illumine their march for them,

By day and by night.

The pillar of cloud by day

   And the pillar of fire by night

   Did not depart from before the people.

Not only the highly poetic character of these lines, but also the particular imagery of "going before" (*hlk lpny*), in combination with the
"cloud" and "fire," present remarkable similarities to the vanguard
motif of the Near Eastern texts. Just as here, where it prepares us
for the battle of the Reed Sea, so in the Tukulti-Ninurta Epic the same
type of imagery suddenly appears at the onset of the final battle with
Kashtiliash.[25] Assur leads in the vanguard (*ina maḫra*) with a devouring flame (*išāti*). Enlil is also there with a burning fire, and Adad
uses the familiar flood (*abūbu*) as his weapon. Behind this fearsome
assembly the king marches to battle, just as the author of the biblical
text pictures Israel marching behind the cloud and the fire in which
Yahweh acts as their guide. As we have seen, very similar language is
found in numerous other literary texts and in the Assyrian annals.

The *function* of the cloud and fire in ch. 14 completes the analogy.
In vss. 19b-20 the cloud, which has been the vanguard, now becomes in
effect the rearguard, separating the camps of Egypt and Israel. Then
in the morning, Yahweh looks down from the pillar of cloud and fire and
routs (*hmm*) the Egyptian camp. The sophisticated Egyptian chariotry is
rendered useless when the wheels mire in the mud, and the Egyptians flee
in a panic, wailing their fear of Yahweh, who fights against them (vss.
24-25).

Despite the appearance of a straightforward narrative, for years
commentators have noticed inconsistencies in the text, especially concerning precisely what happened at (or in) the Sea of Reeds.[26] Since
our primary interest is in the role of the motifs of divine presence
and guidance, these problems need not detain us here. There are a few
points, however, that will be important for our later study. If we
accept the traditional source division of chs. 13-14 (here we follow
that of Noth),[27] several interesting nuances emerge in each one. Thus
in J the motif of divine guidance and presence is expressed by the vivid
imagery of the cloud and fire *in which* Yahweh goes before the people

(13.21-22). In E, however, the initial guidance motif is expressed much more simply--without any accompanying phenomena (vss. 17-18), although using the same verb (*nḥh*) as J. This appears to resemble E's version of the battle itself, where the *ml'k* suddenly appears as the vanguard (14.19a) and performs the same function as the cloud in J (vs. 19b; cf. Num 20.16). It is also interesting that E has introduced the theme of the people's complaint (vss. 11-12), which, ironically, defeats the divine purpose already expressed in 13.17. Finally, it is striking that the Priestly source uses no accompanying phenomena for divine presence at all (even the *ml'k*), which, as we shall see below, is not true of subsequent narratives. This may be due to the fact that it is the Priestly account that betrays the clearest links to the plague stories rather than to the wilderness events.

Along with other differences that, it is often suggested, exist between Exodus 14 and 15 (e.g. whether the sea is "divided" or not),[28] the specific literary motifs for divine presence and guidance are significantly at variance. The guidance motif that we traced in 15.13 actually resembles most closely that of E in 13.17-18, for in both it is simply God himself who guides (*nḥh*) his people. However, 15.14-16 uses imagery in a way very similar to the use in the Akkadian sources, as we have seen, and the imagery of Yahweh's fear and terror that overcome the surrounding peoples is much less reserved that the simple use of *nḥh*. The greatest difference lies between the J account and Exodus 15. The former uses not only the vanguard motif (*hlk lpny*), but also the storm phenomena imagery that is predicated to it--the pillar of cloud and fire. None of this imagery is in Exodus 15, although the storm phenomena (which we have seen in 15.5-12) are clearly analogous. Nevertheless, the prose traditions of the Reed Sea event, and especially J, have clearly developed their own set of motifs and expressions (*ᶜnn*, *'š*, *hlk lpny*, *ml'k*), even though they share the key word *nḥh* with Exodus 15.[29]

Thus we have seen that the way in which the cloud and fire are combined with *hlk lpny* to function as the divine vanguard has important parallels in the Near Eastern texts examined in Part I. The distinctiveness of the cloud (*ᶜnn*) in particular, however, demands further attention. Despite persistent difficulties, we would still maintain that there is a connection between Ugaritic and Hebrew *ᶜnn* ("cloud"), as we have argued elsewhere.[30] George E. Mendenhall has recently proposed further similarities with other Near Eastern material. He contends that the Ugaritic $^c nn$ is a substitute for the names of the divine beings "or an aspect of their person."[31] One is tempted to agree with this, although there is only one text that makes such a close connection between deity and $^c nn$.[32] His attempt to demonstrate "the equivalence of the $^c anan$ with the Akkadian $melammu$ as the sun disk,"[33] however, remains highly hypothetical, as Mendenhall himself admits. The comparatively sparse use of $^c nn$ in the Ugaritic texts does not allow us to see it as an active agent in battle (as $melammu$ and Hebrew $^c nn$) nor as a signification of divine kingship. It also does not seem feasible to understand either Ugaritic or Hebrew $^c nn$ as physical descriptions of divine attire, as $melammu$ often is.[34] While Mendenhall is quite right in pointing to the similarity between $melammu$ and Hebrew $^c nn$ as agents of divine warfare, it is also true that the $^c nn$, particularly in connection with the phrase hlk $lpny$, is more similar to the deities themselves as divine vanguard or to their subordinates in the same role. In short, although we would agree with a great deal of Mendenhall's study of $^c nn$ in the Old Testament, we would object to an exaggeration of the equivalence between $^c nn$ and $melammu$, and especially to the broader implications that Mendenhall draws concerning divine sovereignty. In fact, as we shall see throughout this chapter, our position with respect to divine and human sovereignty is precisely the opposite of Mendenhall's.

In summary, it still seems that the most likely background of Ugaritic $^c nn$ is the same storm imagery that is obvious in the Hebrew $^c nn$ as "cloud." Most recently Cross has advanced this interpretation and noted the difficulties it causes for Mendenhall's view.[35] He is careful to add, however, that the equation of the Ugaritic and Hebrew $^c nn$ is also not without problems. Even though it is not at all difficult to see clouds as "messengers," particularly of the storm deity Baal, and likewise to see the Hebrew "cloud" as a form of messenger (note $ml'k$, Exod 14.19a), the identification of the two is not complete. It is also curious that rkb $^c rpt$ is the frequent word used for Baal as the "driver of the clouds" (cf. probably Ps 68.5), an epithet for which $^c nn$ is never used. At any rate, even if the etymology and original background of $^c nn$ in the Old Testament remains relatively obscure, the most telling evidence for its *function* is the material from Mesopotamia that we have presented in Part I.

At this point we must return to Exodus 14 and attempt to see it

in a broader perspective. In our discussion of Exodus 15, we suggested
that the two parts of the poem, with their emphasis on Yahweh the divine
warrior and Yahweh the guide of Israel, presented graphic illustrations
of the major motifs of divine presence and guidance. We also suggested
that the combination of these and other motifs, along with the emphasis,
first on Yahweh and then on Yahweh and his people, could be compared to
the typology of exaltation as we have seen it in the Near Eastern material, particularly in the correlation of divine and national supremacy.
We shall now argue that the same typology of exaltation is evident in
ch. 14 and elsewhere in Exodus, again, often in connection with motifs
of divine presence; however, the prose sources present a different emphasis than does the ancient Song of the Sea. In the prose sources, the
correlation that is most pronounced is that between Yahweh and Moses.
In short, the cumulative effect of a number of passages will show that
we are dealing with the exaltation of Yahweh and of Moses as Yahweh's
representative and leader for Israel.

The correlation of Yahweh and Moses stands in an impressive position in ch. 14. After the dramatic events in which Israel has been
guided by the cloud and fire and saved by Yahweh the divine warrior,
the Yahwist concludes his story with a comment concerning the effect
this had on the people:

> And on that day Yahweh *saved* Israel from the hand
> of Egypt, and Israel *saw* the Egyptians dead on the
> shore of the sea. Then Israel *saw* the great power
> which Yahweh had exercised against Egypt, and the
> people *feared* Yahweh and they believed (*y'mynw*)
> in Yahweh and in Moses his servant (vss. 30-31).

These verses renew a series of expressions in vs. 13, the two units together providing a framework for the battle scene:

> And Moses said to the people: "*Fear* not; take
> your stand and *see* the *salvation* of Yahweh
> which he will work for you today. For just as
> you *see* the Egyptians today, you will never
> *see* them again.

The fact that in vs. 31 the people believe in Yahweh *and* in Moses is
striking. Moreover, this motif is not new to the book but is part of

134

a series of passages that portray the vacillation in the people's trust. The issue is raised already with Moses' call. In 3.16 Moses is commanded to recount to the people that Yahweh the God of the Fathers has appeared (nr'h) to him and commissioned him to bring the people out of their bondage. He is also assured that the people will obey him (wšm^{c}w bqlk, vs. 18). Such promises do not relieve Moses' diffidence, however, and in 4.1 he objects that the people will not believe in him nor obey him (l' y' mynw ly wl' yšm^{c}w bqly) because they will not believe his appeal to a divine appearance (ky y'mrw l'-nr'h 'lyk yhwh). Thus the question of Moses' authority is directly linked to the validity of his witness to a theophany. The signs that are then given to him are to serve as warrants for this claim and are intended to stimulate the people's belief in his leadership (cf. the use of 'mn in vss. 5, 8-9). This, in fact, is accomplished, for, in the end, "the people believed" (wy'mn h^{c}m, vs. 31). The language throughout presents a combination of visual and auditory connotations, for these are "signs" ('ōt) that the people will "heed" (šm^c lql). While all of the above is from the Yahwistic stratum, it is interesting that in the Elohistic view it is the promise of Yahweh's presence that initially counters Moses' fear, using an expression familiar to us from Genesis --"for I will be with you" (ky 'hyh ^{c}mmk, 3.12).[36]

The initial belief in Moses' authority is soon brought into question. After the first encounters with Pharaoh in 5.21, the Israelite foremen complain that Moses' grandiose mission has only worsened their plight (cf. also 6.9, P). The final legitimation of Moses is therefore left suspended throughout the plague narrative. Moreover, when we include the passage (probably Elohistic) in 14.11-12, the final confirmation of Moses' authority is immediately preceded by a serious questioning.

Thus we may conclude that motifs of divine presence, especially in the call of Moses, are intricately connected to his legitimation as the recognized leader of Yahweh's people. The vacillation between his initial commission, the ensuing challenges to his authority, and the people's confirmation of it, is finally resolved in the context of Yahweh's saving presence at the Sea (14.31). Here, as H. Gross has suggested, Moses is "elevated by God himself to a superhuman realm and placed next to God in the act of salvation in Israel."[37] This correlation of divine and human exaltation has a very interesting formal similarity to that in the Tukulti-Ninurta Epic. There too, expressions that are customarily used for the deity are applied to the human figure. Moreover, there can be little doubt that the royal Hymn of Praise in the Epic has its raison d'etre in the battle with Kashtiliash, just as the ascription of trust, belief, or even faith ('mn) to Moses as well as to Yahweh is based on the battle with Pharaoh's forces at the Sea.

With the poetic and prose accounts of the Reed Sea event behind us, we must now turn to the theophany on Mt. Sinai in ch. 19. It goes without saying that in its present form, this material provides a number of different levels of tradition and interpretation, not the least of which is the intrusive nature of the Decalogue. It will not suit our purpose, however, to consider all of the problems that this text presents.[38] As for the theophany itself, we would insist that the imagery used throughout is quite compatible with the ancient motif of the storm deity, and that any resort to volcanic activity to explain the phenomena is unncessary.[39] We would also argue that the cloud (^{c}nn) is a fitting element to this general background, and that the complexity of the evidence does not allow us to specify its occurrence in one text or even in one tradition as original, with others secondary. Indeed, one of our major conclusions is that the cloud serves a number of different, but not mutually exclusive, functions, and it is highly speculative to posit one of them as the provenance for the others. We say this while recognizing that the Near Eastern evidence for the use of such imagery to express the divine vanguard motif is extremely ancient.

Our purpose here is thus not to discuss the theophany as a whole but to focus again on the function of the ^{c}nn, as we did in Exodus 13-14. Of course, the word occurs within the context of the evolving theophany (vs. 16), along with thunder and lightning. Its presence in vs. 9, however, provides more opportunity to question its explicit function:

> And Yahweh said to Moses: "Behold, I am coming
> to you in a thick cloud so that the people may
> hear when I speak with you, and indeed that they
> may believe (y'mynw) in you forever . . . ."

It should be immediately apparent that we are again dealing with the legitimation of Moses as the leader of the people, just as we saw above.

Once more the belief or recognition of the people (expressed by 'mn) is tied to Yahweh's presence or appearance (here bw' and $^c nn$).[40]

A very interesting parallel to 19.9 is provided by 1 Sam 12.18. After the people request a king, Samuel rebukes them for their evil, and, in vss. 16-18, he produces a sign as proof of his and Yahweh's displeasure:

> So Samuel called upon Yahweh, and Yahweh sent
> thunder and rain that day; and all the people
> greatly feared Yahweh and Samuel.

We thus have another combination of storm theophany imagery and legitimation of both Yahweh and his spokesman, Samuel.

It is significant that in Exod 20.20, in what is now the sequel to the Decalogue and theophany, we have another explicit comment, probably again from the Yahwist, concerning the purpose of Yahweh's advent:

> And Moses said to the people, "Do not be afraid,
> for it was in order to test you that God came,
> so that the fear of him might be before you,
> that you might not sin."

Thus, whereas Yahweh himself had declared that his advent would result in the trust of the people in Moses, Moses now explains that its purpose was to instill the fear of Yahweh in the people (who are not to be afraid!).[41]

It is interesting that Exod 19.9 stresses auditory aspects--the people are to hear Yahweh speak to Moses (cf. vs. 19). It is tempting to assign this verse to E and to see here a different orientation concerning divine presence from that of J, who, as in Exod 14.13, 30-31, emphasizes the visual. The latter verses are also similar to 20.18, 20 (note $r'h$, $^c l$-$tyr'w$, $yr'tw$), whereas 20.19 again focuses on dbr and $\check{s}m^c$. Furthermore, 20.20 has a different emphasis from that of 19.9, for the purpose (note again $b^c bwr$) is to test (nsh) Israel and to instill the fear of Yahweh, rather than to legitimate Moses.

However, it is dangerous to claim precision in such matters. Clearly 20.18 shares imagery with 19.19, and 20.18 and 21 both have $m\bar{e}r\bar{a}h\bar{o}q$, which is, reputedly, an Elohistic expression. More importantly, we have already seen a subtle interchange of visual and auditory aspects in Exodus 4, and 19.9 itself clearly includes both in that the cloud is an obvious sign of Yahweh's presence (cf. 19.11b; we shall find the same mixture in Numbers 11-12). Finally, we have also repeatedly seen the correlation between the exaltation of Yahweh and that of Moses and in this sense 19.9 and 20.20 must be seen as complementary rather than as contrasting.

To summarize: we would argue that a primary purpose of the Sinai theophany in Exodus 19 (20.18-21) is the legitimation of Moses as the leader of the people and the recognition of Yahweh as their sovereign. The motifs of divine presence play a major role in this dual exaltation, and present a balanced emphasis on both visual and auditory aspects. This is not an isolated theme, but began, at least, with Moses' call.[42]

It is clear that with Exodus 19 we have left any explicit reference to the other aspect of our study--that of divine guidance. Here the cloud does not go in front of the people on the march, but comes down so that Yahweh may speak with Moses. This other function of the cloud--divine communication and the legitimation of Moses--is central to Exod 33.7-11 and Numbers 11-12, as we shall see below.

In relation to the preceding material, we would see the exaltation theme as a major thread running throughout Exodus 1-20, again, with the primary focus on Moses and Yahweh. This is the context in which the legend of Moses' birth is best understood. The fact that the story is narrated at all, that it concerns Moses, and that it has well-known parallels to the legend of Sargon of Akkad--the protagonist behind the Exaltation of Inanna--is not at all accidental. The birth of Moses is the opening scene in the drama of his exaltation.[43]

Much the same can be said for Exodus 3 and 6 and for the revelation of the divine name "Yahweh." Despite the linguistic and historical problems connected with these texts, it does not seem unreasonable in the light of our previous discussions to see these chapters as the inauguration of Yahweh as the God of Israel, with clear analogies to the theogonic revolutions in the Near Eastern texts above. Such a revolution is clearly indicated in the cogent reconstruction of the origins of the divine name worked out by Cross:

> . . . originally a cultic name of 'El, ...
> the god Yahweh split off from 'El in the radical
> differentiation of his cultus in the Proto-Israelite
> league, ultimately ousting 'El from his place in
> the divine council . . . .[44]

Indeed, Freedman has even suggested that (in Exodus 15) we are presented with a *new* god as well as a new corporate entity in the people.[45] While we still must take seriously the history of traditions that stands behind the identification of Yahweh with the God of the Fathers,[46] Exodus 3 and 6 are primary witnesses to the exaltation of Yahweh. The theme is further developed in the Yahwistic stratum by a series of admonitions addressed to Pharaoh, telling him that soon he too will recognize (yd^c) that Yahweh is the only legitimate sovereign in all the earth.[47] A similar connotation is to be seen in the Priestly reference to the defeat of the Egyptian gods (12.12) and in the combination of Yahweh's "glorification" (kbd) over Pharaoh, who again recognizes (yd^c) Yahweh's superiority (14.4, 17–18).

Although the primary focus of the exaltation theme is, therefore, on Yahweh and Moses, we may draw one final analogy to the Near Eastern material concerning Israel. We have noted--especially in the Tukulti-Ninurta Epic--the close connection between his exaltation and the quasi-divine nature of his birth. It is not unlikely that, despite the obvious influence of the Passover, the designation of Israel as the "first-born son" (bny $bkry$) of Yahweh is to be understood in a similar light.[48]

[1]E.g. Schmidt, *Königtum Gottes*, 65–69; Clements, *God and Temple*, 54.

[2]The most comprehensive expression of Cross's views is found in *CMHE*. See especially chapter 5. For Freedman's most recent contribution, see his "Early Israelite History in the Light of Early Israelite Poetry," in *Unity and Diversity: Essays in the History, Literature, and Religion of the Ancient Near East*, ed. Hans Goedicke and J. J. M. Roberts (The Johns Hopkins Near Eastern Studies; Baltimore: The Johns Hopkins University Press, 1975) 10.

[3]*Linguistic Evidence in Dating Early Hebrew Poetry* (SBL Dissertation Series, 3; Missoula: University of Montana, 1972).

[4]*Ibid.*, 155.

[5]*CMHE*, 126–131. Despite our reliance on Cross, we would insist that our interpretation of the motifs in the Song by no means depends on the acceptance of Cross's reconstruction or on his translation in details. In fact, our conclusions apply equally well to the present Masoretic text.

[6]James Muilenberg, "A Liturgy on the Triumphs of Yahweh," *Studia Biblica et Semitica* (T. C. Vriezen Festschrift; Wageningen: H. Veenman & Zonen, 1966) 233–251. As the title indicates, Muilenberg interprets the Song throughout as a cultic liturgy with the repetitive structure: hymnic confession, epic narrative, hymnic response (for the present pericope, vss. 12–14, 15–16b, 16cd respectively). There is much that is cogent in Muilenberg's study, although we feel that the metrical analysis of Cross is closer to the movement of the text.

[7]Note, however, that the end of each Part is in 2:2.

[8]*CMHE*, 131.

[9]One could easily translate, "In the greatness of your *exaltation*" (g 'nk), the same word as in vs. 1. For a vivid illustration of the use of this term within the context of the manifestation of the storm deity's power, see Job 37.2–5 and note especially the use alongside $r^c m$ and $š$ 'g, both meaning "to thunder, roar," and here precisely analogous to $šagamu$ as we have seen it in numerous Akkadian texts.

[10]In the light of Cross's own defense of this translation (*CMHE*, 128, n. 59), note the lines from the Erra Epic (I.69–70) describing the effect which will happen if Erra "takes to the field": "May the towering mountains hear of it, be afraid and their peaks sink down; / May the surging sea hear of it, be agitated and its produce [fish, etc.] disappear." See Frankena, "Worte der Sibitti," 41, 43; cf. Cagni, *Erra Epic*, 64–65.

[11]On this verse cf. the remark by Labuschagne (*Incomparability*, 97): "We may regard vs. 11 as an elaboration of the main theme, Yahweh's exaltation. His feats of war prove Him to be exalted above other gods and, therefore, incomparable. . . ." On the Song in general, cf. pp. 94–97 and see his Index for other references.

[12]*CMHE*, 143–144 and especially 162–163.

[13]Freedman ("Early Israelite History," 4) also refers to structural and stylistic parallels between Exodus 15 and some of these texts.

[14]"Liturgy," 245.

[15]*Ibid.* The end of the sentence refers the reader to what is evidently Muilenberg's subsequent attempt to follow this procedure. However, his comparison is only made to Psalms 77; 78; 74.11-19.

[16]*CMHE*, 141. Contrast Freedman, "Early Israelite History," 6-7, 9. Not without reason does Freedman equate the "encampment" with Sinai. However, if vss. 14-16 constitute a reaction to what has happened in vs. 13, as seems likely, then vs. 13 most probably refers to Israel's advance toward Canaan, rather than to her experience at Sinai.

[17]Both passages without ^cbr. As for Moab (Exod 15.15), the prose narratives are wholly occupied with the Balaam stories to the extent that it is never said whether Israel was turned away, as with Edom, or whether she defeated Moab in battle, although the substance of the stories clearly points more toward the latter. Cf. Judg 11.15-18.

[18]See Albright, "Catalogue," 10, n. 24; Cross, "Song of Miriam," 239-240; G. M. Landes, "Ammon," IDB, 1, 110a.

[19]Cross (*CMHE*, 124-125) suggests that the reference in the Song to "Chieftains" and "nobles" reflects "the brief premonarchial period in these nations," which is thus "contrary to Epic tradition" in JE. For further examples of ^cbr in this context, see Deut 29.15; Josh 24.17. On the reference to Philistia, see *Ibid.*, 124, n. 39, and Freedman, "Early Israelite History," 9. For the influence of Exodus 15 on the use of ^cbr in the wilderness narrative of Deuteronomy 1-3, see below, ch. 10, (2).

[20]Cf. the text cited above in n. 10 from the Erra Epic. The rest of the passage (11.60-75) refers to kings (*malki*) and countries (*mātāti*), as well as the gods, demons, men and beasts. Freedman ("Early Israelite History," 5) also refers to the Assyrian annals, and suggests that in Exodus 15 the nations may be seen as vassals of Egypt who cowardly eschew support of their overlord against Israel.

[21]Cf. Deut 32.6; Ps 74.2 and Gen 14.19, 22. This may be the original context of Israel as Yahweh's "first-born," on which see further below under Exodus 14.

[22]"Liturgy," 250.

[23]See George W. Coats, "The Traditio-Historical character of the Reed Sea Motif," *VT* 17 (1967) 253-265; Brevard S. Childs, "A Traditio-Historical Study of the Reed Sea Tradition," *VT* 20 (1970) 406-418; more recently, Childs, *The Book of Exodus* (Old Testament Library; Philadelphia: Westminster, 1974) 221-224.

[24]Note the use of *hămušîm*, "in battle array," and its limited occurrences elsewhere in similar contexts (only Num 32.17 [emended]; Josh 1.14; 4.12; Judg 7.11).

[25]For what follows, see ch. 1, (2).

[26]Most recently, see Cross, *CMHE*, 132-137, and, in contrast, Childs, *Exodus*, 243-248.

[27]Martin Noth, *A History of Pentateuchal Traditions*, trans. Bernhard W. Anderson (Englewood Cliffs, N.J.: Prentice-Hall, 1972). See the convenient outline provided by Anderson beginning on p. 261.

[28]See n. 26 above.

[29]Moreover, the position of *nhh* in the prose account where, unlike in Exodus

15, it comes *before* the battle at the Sea, is a strong indication that the battle is seen at least from one aspect as an event after the start of the wilderness march, which, in fact, is the context in which *nḥḥ* occurs in Exod 15.13. As we shall see below, the role of the ᶜ*nn* points to a similar conclusion. For the development of other motifs, see Cross, *CMHE*, 137. He also insists that "the language of the prose sources is secondary to the mythic and poetic imagery descriptive of the storm theophany" (164).

[30] "Pillar of Cloud," especially 19-24. For a recent treatment of the cloud phenomenon in general, with particular emphasis on its use in later Jewish tradition, see J. Luzzaraga, *Las tradiciones de la nube in la Biblia y en el Judaismo primitivo* (Analecta Biblica, 54; Rome: Biblical Institute, 1973).

[31] *Tenth Generation*, 56.

[32] *Ibid.*, text number 4.

[33] *Ibid.*

[34] The basic study, on which Mendenhall has relied, is that of A. L. Oppenheim, "Akkadian *pul(u)ḫ(t)u* and *melammu*," *JAOS* 63 (1943) 31-34. Oppenheim concludes that there are three levels of one and the same concept for *melammu*. Two of these concern physical headgear or masks worn by deity or priest, and the third is a more abstract conceptualization (33). The predominance of the physical aspect has recently been emphasized by William W. Hallo, "The Cultic Setting of Sumerian Poetry," in *Actes de la XVIIᵉ Rencontre Assyriologique Internationale*, Université libre de Bruxelles, 30 juin- 4 juillet 1969, 120. Etudes recueillies par André Finet. Ham-sur-Heure: Comité belge de recherches en Mésopotamie, 1970.

[35] *CMHE*, 165, n. 86. Cf. also Miller, *Divine Warrior*, 190, n. 48 and 195, n. 77. Miller, however, does not discuss the use of ᶜ*nn* in Exodus 13-14.

[36] The relation between the "sign" in this verse and the "signs" in ch. 4 is problematic because of the difficult syntax. It is tempting to take Yahweh's presence itself as the sign, but it is more natural to see 12b as fulfilling this function. Yet the latter presents an odd sign indeed, for it implies that when Moses has completed his mission he will know that Yahweh has been with him! (This, however, is not far from the providential, retrospective view of Joseph.) For a thorough discussion of the problems involved, see Childs, *Exodus*, 56-60.

[37] "Der Glaube an Mose nach Exodus," in *Wort-Gebot-Glaube*, ed. J. J. Stamm and E. Jenni (Eichrodt *Festschrift*; Zürich: Zwingli, 1970) 62.

[38] Note the serious problems with traditional source criticism here discussed by Childs, *Exodus*, especially 348-351.

[39] See my "Pillar of Cloud," 15-17; so also Mendenhall, *Tenth Generation*, 63; Cross, *CMHE*, 167.

[40] We are thus in complete agreement with Childs (*Exodus*, 354): ". . . the focus of the whole theophany here falls on the divine legitimation of Moses before the people (v. 9)."

[41] Cf. on 19.9 Murray Newman [*The People of the Covenant* (New York: Abingdon, 1962) 51], who sees in *leᶜōlām* a reflection of ᶜ*d* ᶜ*wlm* of the Davidic promise and "the establishment of a dynastic office of covenant mediator." Another tradition of the Sinai theophany is reflected in 20.18-20 accord-

ing to Childs, *Exodus*, 353-354; yet here too there is "a legitimation of Moses' office."

[42]Note, even before, the ironic challenge in 2.14.

[43]"The term "exaltation" (and "humiliation") is also applied to the story by Brevard S. Childs, "The Birth of Moses," *JBL* 84 (1965) 115-116. For further discussion of the story itself as a common folk motif, see Donald B. Redford, "The Literary Motif of the Exposed Child," *Numen* 14 (1967) 209-228. Redford (226-227) concludes that the Sargon and Moses stories are the two oldest examples of the particular version they represent, but that it is impossible to decide whether the Moses story is dependent on the Sargon story. However, the Egyptian literature provides only weak examples, at best (219).

[44]*CMHE*, 71. On this (Cross refers to Psalm 82) see below in ch. 11, 2.

[45]"Early Israelite History," 20.

[46]See Cross, *CMHE*, ch. 3, passim.

[47]Note especially 8.18; 9.14, 16, 22. The phrase "there is none like me in all the earth" (*'yn kmny bkl h'rṣ*) in 9.14 has a clear parallel in Exod 15.11. Labuschagne (*Incomparability*, 11) notes that the particular expressions in 8.16 and 9.14 (*'yn k*) are, along with Deut 33.26, the only occurrences in the Pentateuch. Note also that vs. 17 chides Pharaoh for still "exalting" himself. It is interesting that this exaltation language is concentrated in the plague which is a thunder-storm, for that is the phenomena behind much of the imagery discussed above. In fact, this plague has been interpreted as an epiphany of Yahweh by Lipiński, *Royauté de Yahwé*, 220-221.

[48]J. Philip Hyatt [*Exodus* (New Century Bible; London: Oliphants, 1971) 85] notes that "it is only in this section within the entire *OT* that Israel is called the first-born of Yahweh (used of Ephraim in Jer 31:9)." Note also Hos 11.1 (*bny*) and Jer 3.19; 31.20. Hyatt thinks Exod 4.22-23 originally stood before 10.28 or 11.4 and was moved to its present position to cover all ten plagues.

CHAPTER 6

MOSES AND THE DIVINE PRESENCE

(1)   Exodus 33.7-11

In Exod 13.21-22 the motif of divine presence and guidance was con-
densed in a passage that, in effect, constituted a paradigm. As we shall
see below, the same holds true for Num 9.15-23. In each of these passages, the frequentative aspect of the verbs shows that the authors were
describing a customary mode of divine presence and guidance that, presumably, held true for Israel's entire journey through the wilderness.
To this extent Yahweh was seen as being always present with his people.

In Exod 33.7-11 we have another paradigm, frequently assigned to
E.[1] Once again the temporal aspect is frequentative throughout, describing what Moses "used to do" and what customarily happened at the Tent of
Meeting. This is by no means the only resemblance to the other two paradigms, however, for here too the $^c nn$ plays a major role. In what follows
we do not intend to discuss all the problems of this pericope itself,[2]
nor of the history of religions that may illumine it.[3] Instead we shall
look at it, quite briefly, to see how the function of the cloud relates
to the figure of Moses; then we shall investigate how the paradigm unfolds in two actual situations--Numbers 11 and 12.

Even a cursory reading of Exod 33.7-11 indicates that we are dealing with the theme of divine presence, but not with that of guidance.
The cloud here does not function in the latter capacity, but comes down
to the Tent--as we are first told in vs. 7--whenever anyone seeks an
oracle from Yahweh. This particular situation, however, is immediately
passed over, and the rest of the narrative focuses on what happens at
the Tent when Moses goes out to it.[4] The sum of the story is that each
person watches Moses' progress until he enters the Tent, at which point
the cloud descends to the door of the Tent and all the people bow down.[5]
Then "Yahweh would speak to Moses face to face, as one speaks to his

friend, and Moses would return to the camp" (vs. 11a).

We would suggest that, aside from its redactional position,[6] the basic thrust of this passage is in vs. 11, and that it again demonstrates the exalted position of Moses by means of a motif of divine presence.[7] Vs. 11 accentuates the closeness with which Moses associates with Yahweh, who *speaks* to him *face to face*. The fact that Moses is the only individual to whom this honor is ascribed in the Old Testament adds to his distinction.[8] Furthermore, there is again an emphasis on speech and sight, for the people look on (vss. 8b, 10) while Moses converses with Yahweh in the cloud.

   (2) Numbers 11 and 12

To support our interpretation of this passage, we have only to turn to Numbers 11 and 12, where a look at the specific situation involved and the corresponding role of the cloud and Tent will fill out a number of details. We must emphasize that it is only in these two chapters that this particular paradigm involving the cloud is used within the JE narrative.[9] Thus, taken together, these three passages constitute the only use of $^c nn$ in JE other than as a motif of divine guidance (Exodus 13-14) or as a means for the legitimation of Moses (Exodus 19),[10] and, as we shall see, they have much in common with the latter.

Numbers 11 is clearly a conflation of two stories, one dealing with the demand for meat (vss. 4-6 [7-9], 10, 13, 18-23, 31-35), the other with Moses' complaint concerning the heavy burdens of his office (vss. 11-12, 14-17, 24-25, 26-30), with the former story now serving as the occasion for the latter. The second story opens with a poignant speech by Moses concerning the unbearable burden of his leadership. In response, Yahweh proposes the solution of distributing some of Moses' "spirit" (*rwḥ*) to seventy "elders of Israel" who will thus serve as aids to Moses. After this is accomplished, there is a sequel (vss. 26-30) that tells of the extraordinary reach of the "spirit," which even extends to two men in camp. Moses counters the objection that they are not worthy recipients with a classic retort: "would that all the people of Yahweh were prophets!"

At this point a few words about the very problematic literary critical relation between Numbers 11 and Exod 33.7-11 is in order. Generally speaking, it would be odd for the paradigm passage to be from the Elohist, and the specific applications to be from the Yahwist. Of

course, it is possible to see Numbers 11 as the Yahwistic parallel to
Exod 18.13-27 (usually ascribed to E), but one is faced with the embar-
rassing problem that in the latter, there is no mention of "prophets,"
which is one of the ostensible hallmarks of the E source.[11] There are
also a number of very close literary parallels between the two passages,[12]
as well as some important differences.[13] A number of telling correspondences between Numbers 11 and the J stratum elsewhere[14] further complicate
the problem. However, although absolute certainty is not possible, the
emphasis on the prophetic office seems to indicate a date later than that
usually assigned to J, and thus implies association with E.[15]

Now we are prepared to see the way in which Numbers 11 provides a
situational illustration of the paradigm in Exod 33.7-11.[16] As he did
there, Moses goes to the Tent of Meeting (vss. 16, 24) and Yahweh talks
with him (vss. 16, 25) after descending in the cloud (vs. 25).[17] It is
clear that this divine appearance is directly connected with Moses' authority, and the latter is a central concern, only here the conclusion
provides a counterpoint to what we have seen elsewhere. Instead of emphasizing the singularity of Moses' leadership, the story starts with
it as a problem and ends with what we might call a representative demo-
cratization of the prophetic office. Nevertheless, the overall effect
is to depict Moses in a very sympathetic, and, indeed, venerable light:
as the fountainhead of the prophetic spirit.

Turning to Numbers 12 we find a more unified narrative than we did
in ch. 11.[18] Although the relationship between the complaint about
Moses' Cushite wife in vs. 1 and the ensuing story is not clear, the
rest presents a continuous unit. Once again there is a strong resemblance to Exod 33.7-11. Moses, Aaron, and Miriam go to the Tent of
Meeting; Yahweh descends in a pillar of cloud and stands at the door of
the Tent. Vss. 5b-8 then provide an ironic twist. Yahweh does not speak
directly to Moses, but to Aaron and Miriam; yet he declares that he speaks
directly *only* with Moses! The content of Yahweh's speech, couched in
poetic diction, is highly significant:

> Hear now my speech:
>> If there is a prophet among you,
>>> In a vision I make myself known to him,
>>> In a dream I speak with him;
>> Not so with my servant Moses,
>>> Over all my house he is entrusted (*n'mn*).

146

> Mouth to mouth I speak with him,
>
> Plainly and not in riddles,
>
> And the form of Yahweh he beholds.
>
> Why are you not afraid
>
> To speak against my servant Moses?

These verses, of course, hark back to vs. 2, where Aaron[19] and Miriam complain: "is it indeed only with Moses that Yahweh speaks, or does he not speak with us as well?"[20] Thus the issue is, who are the legitimate recipients of revelation? The resolution of this issue provides an interesting contrast to ch. 11. In both chapters the leadership of Moses is the subject; but ch. 11 concludes with the distribution of Moses' prophetic authority among the elders, whereas ch. 12 concludes with the centralization of that authority in Moses. There is also the point in ch. 12 that the authority of the prophet pales in comparison to Moses. In both cases, the text no doubt reflects a deep controversy surrounding the prophetic office for which Moses is seen as the source, although he is one who is "more than a prophet." Thus, the two chapters do not present opposing viewpoints; both affirm the incomparable distinction of Moses over all potential contenders. We thus have in ch. 11 and, especially, in ch. 12 (cf. ch. 16),[21] an outstanding illustration of the theme we traced in Exodus: the exaltation of Moses. Furthermore, this theme is inseparably linked with the question of divine presence and is again found in conjunction with the appearance of Yahweh in the cloud.[22]

A number of phrases in the oracle accentuate the exalted position of Moses and add to our previous findings. Already in vs. 3, immediately after the complaint concerning Moses' authority, we are told that he was in fact the most humble man who ever lived![23] But the most glowing terms are found in the divine speech in vss. 6-8. Once again we see an emphasis on Yahweh's "speaking" as an indication of Moses' pre-eminence--in fact, the root *dbr* occurs six times in vss. 2, 6-8. Here we also learn, as we did in Exod 14.31, that Moses is the "servant" of Yahweh, a term used elsewhere primarily, although not exclusively, for Moses and David, as well as for the prophets.[24] Even more impressive is the fact that Moses is "entrusted over all my house," again using the root *'mn*, which we found repeatedly in Exodus. Here, however, the juxtaposition with *byty* carries the more specific connotation of royal dynastic legitimation and is, like *ᶜbd yhwh*, used primarily with David but also with Samuel (and the latter again in connection with divine revelation and Yahweh's *word*).[25]

Following this, the author stresses the closeness of Yahweh's speaking with the expression "mouth to mouth," corresponding to the "face to face" of Exod 33.11.

As if this characterization of Moses as Yahweh's servant, as the head of his "house" and his intimate interlocutor, is not enough, the description concludes with the remarkable statement that Moses "beholds the form of Yahweh" (*ût^emunat yhwh yabbîṭ*). The connection between divine presence—in both its verbal and visual aspects—and the exaltation of Moses is nowhere more profound than here. The exceptional nature of this statement is all the more impressive in view of the rarity of *t^emūnāh* as a representation of Yahweh. The artistic construction of this "form" is expressly forbidden in the second Commandment (Exod 20.4; Deut 5.8), and the deuteronomistic paranesis on this passage repeatedly emphasizes that Yahweh's *t^emūnāh* was *not* seen at Sinai (Deut 4.12, 15-16, 23, 25). The word occurs only twice elsewhere in the Old Testament.[26]

One additional passage in Exodus deserves brief mention in connection with the foregoing. In 34.29-35,[27] there is the very colorful vignette concerning the effect that Moses' speaking with God on the mountain has on his physical appearance. In fact, the phrase *qrn 'wr pnyw* has been interpreted as referring to the oracular mask or *melammu* that played an important role in the ancient Near Eastern texts in Chapter 2.[28] Thus again we find a very interesting connection between divine presence, Moses' exaltation, and the aspects of talking and seeing. In these seven verses the root *dbr* is used seven times. Moreover, the narrative continually switches from Moses' speaking with Yahweh to his speaking to Israel. As in Exod 14.31, we also have the sequence "they saw . . . they were afraid" (vs. 30; cf. 35), and the use of the frequentative in vs. 34 reminds us of the previous paradigms.[29]

Finally, we may note one other passage that has strong similarities to the foregoing. In Exod 33.11 and Num 11.28 we observed the important position of Joshua as the attendant of Moses. In Deut 31.14-15, 23[30] Joshua's position is advanced to that of being equal to his former master, who now approaches death. It is significant that here once again—in what is probably Elohistic material—the legitimation of Israel's leader is accomplished through the intervention of Yahweh in the cloud at the Tent of Meeting (vs. 15) and that Yahweh's charge to Joshua includes the promise of divine presence—"I will be with you" (vs. 23). Thus, at the end of Moses' life, the editor of Deuteronomy has appropriately introduced

the transmission from Moses' exaltation to that of Joshua. That this became a theme of crucial importance to the Deuteronomistic historian will
be seen below in our discussion of Joshua 1; 3-5.

[1]Beyerlin, *Origins and History*, 23; von Rad, *Theology* I, 235 (and probably from the early, presettlement period); Hyatt, *Exodus*, 49; Manfred Görg, *Das Zelt der Begegnung: Untersuchung zur Gestalt der sakralen Zelttraditionen Altisraels* (BBB, 27; Bonn: Peter Hanstein, 1967) 164-165 (adapted from an earlier literary form); Mendenhall, *Tenth Generation*, 59; Martin Noth [*Exodus* (Old Testament Library; Philadelphia: Westminster, 1962) 254], however, points out the problematic nature of this and the rest of ch. 33 and suggests a "special tradition" deriving from the Wilderness period and taken up by the Yahwist. Jeremias (*Theophanie*, 112) refuses any source identification. On this reluctance, cf. Childs, *Exodus*, 590-91.

[2]This is particularly true for all the questions surrounding the tent itself. For a recent discussion of this in connection with Exod 33.7-11 as well as Numbers 11-12 see Görg, *Zelt der Begegnung*, 138-170.

[3]It is quite possible that the function of the cloud is a result of the role played by the $^c nn$ in the Ugaritic literature, which we discussed above. Görg (*Ibid.*, 170) noted that while the Tent of Meeting most likely came from the desert period, the name itself betrays Canaanite influence and must be seen in relation to the divine assembly as well as to the fact that in some Ugaritic texts the gods are described as dwelling in tents (especially in the Krt and Aqht legends). However, he insists that the appearance of the cloud was not originally a cultic event (as Beyerlin and others) but more likely reflects the actual experience of the people at Sinai (167). Recently, the Tent of Meeting has been discussed in connection with the Ugaritic texts more extensively by Richard J. Clifford, "The Tent of El and the Israelite Tent of Meeting," *CBQ* 33 (1971) 221-227. He has also drawn attention to the connection between El's tent dwelling "in contexts of deities or messengers asking El's decision or taking orders from him" (223). In general, Clifford's view is also that of Miller (*Divine Warrior*, 192-193, n. 60) and Cross (*CMHE*, 185), the latter noting the combination of the tent-dwelling El figure with the storm-deity Baal figure in the picture of Yahweh at Sinai.

Although the connection between the $^c nn$ and El's tent in the Ugaritic texts is never as close as it is with the Tent of Meeting in the Old Testament, it is quite possible that in the latter (as in Exodus 13-14) the cloud is again functioning as a divine messenger and has been influenced by the performance of the same function by Ugaritic $^c nn$. See the more recent study by Richard J. Clifford, *The Cosmic Mountain in Canaan and the Old Testament* (Harvard Semitic Monographs, 4; Cambridge: Harvard University Press, 1972) 125. Here he sees Ugaritic $^c nn$ as a "divinized cloud." In the Old Testament, however, the $^c nn$ has become depersonalized to the point that it is a means of Yahweh's presence and/or guidance rather than a distinct individual being.

[4]The awkwardness is frequently explained by assuming that a more recent tradition has been superimposed on to an older one, cf. Beyerlin, *Origin and History*, 112-113; Görg, *Zelt der Begegnung*, 158-159.

[5]Görg (160-161) suggests that the often cited problems with this picture (e.g. how could all the people see Moses if the Tent was outside the camp?) are not germane to the highly stylized nature of the pericope.

[6]See the following chapter on the redactional position of this passage.

[7]Görg's conclusion (160-164) that an older literary work has been edited throughout to accentuate the importance of Moses complements our interpretation. Cf. also Childs, *Exodus*, 356.

[8]Cf. Deut 34.10 where Yahweh "knows" (yd^c) Moses "face to face." It is interesting that the same expression is used in Deut 5.4, where Yahweh speaks with the *people* face to face (here *pnym bpnym*) at Sinai, which reflects Exod 19.9 but stands somewhat in tension with Exod 20.19. For other individuals: Jacob "sees" God ($r'h$) "face to face," Gen 32.31, and Gideon "sees" ($r'h$) the *ml'k yhwh* "face to face," Judg 6.22. More generally, cf. Ez 20.35.

[9]The Priestly source, of course, uses this paradigm with the cloud (and glory) more frequently, e.g. Exod 16.10; Num 14.10; 16.19; 17.7; 20.6. This too is closely connected with the traditions of Moses' office; cf. Childs, *Exodus*, 262.

[10]Exod 34.5 does not fit as comfortably with any of the three paradigm passages, but we will argue below that it too may best be seen in connection with the legitimation of Moses.

[11]Volkmar Fritz [*Israel in der Wüste* (Marburger theologische Studien, 7; Marburg: Elwert, 1970) 17-18] argues that since Exodus 18 is from E, the "spirit story" in Numbers 11 could hardly be from E also. He resorts to a "special tradition" taken up into J.

[12]Exod 18.18 *ky kbd mmk* and *l' twkl ^c$hw lbdk* // Num 11.14 *ky kbd mmny* and *l' 'wkl 'nky lbdy*; the use of *nś'* in Exod 18.22 and in Num 11.17 (and passim).

[13]Note the different words used for the officials involved, Exod 18.21 // Num 11.16 (on *s̆tr* cf. Exod 5.6-21), not to mention the different settings of each story and the juridical background of Exodus 18.

[14]Cf. vs. 11 *lmh hr^ct l^cbdk* with Exod 5.22 *lmh hr^cth l^cm hzzh*; vss. 11 and 15, *l' mṣty* [sic] *hn b^cynyk* with Exod 33.12-13, *mṣ't hn b^cyny* and *mṣ'ty hn b^cynyk*; vs. 16 the elders, cf. Exod 3.16; 4.29-31; 17.5; and especially 24.1, 9, 14, where there are seventy; Num 16.25. On vss. 17, 25 with *yrd* as predicate, see Appendix 2 where only Gen 28.12 (*ml'kym* subject) and 46.4 are traditionally E (aside from Exod 33.9 of course, and here it may be significant that the narrator avoids picturing Yahweh as himself descending *in* the cloud).

[15]Cf. Görg (*Zelt der Begegnung*, 143) who sees an older source reworked by E.

[16]Of course, it is also quite possible that Exod 33.7-11 did not serve at all as an actual model for Numbers 11-12, but is either the remains of very old traditions, which formed a common basis for both units or even a condensation based on the stories in Numbers. Obviously, the issue remains complex.

[17]Note also that the Tent appears to be outside the camp, and Joshua is described here (vs. 28) almost exactly as in Exod 33.11.

[18]However, the source problems were declared unsolvable by Noth, *History of Pentateuchal Traditions*, 32, n. 120. Görg (*Zelt der Begegnung*, 148) assigns the account of the theophany in vss. 4-10 to E. As with Numbers 11, Fritz (*Israel in der Wüste*, 19) assigns 12.2-5a, 6-8, 9b, 10a$^\alpha$, 11 to a special tradition added to J.

[19]The fact that Miriam is the only one punished has led some commentators to see Aaron as a secondary addition to the story.

[20]The verse ends with "and Yahweh heard," the same phrase as in 11.1.

[21]Ch. 16 provides further illustration. In both P and J the crisis situation arises out of a challenge to the authority of Moses (and Aaron). In P this is explicitly linked to Yahweh's presence and to Moses' exaltation: "You have gone too far! For all the congregation are holy, every one of them, and Yahweh is among them; why then do you exalt yourselves (*ttnśś'w*) above the assembly of Yahweh?" (vs. 3). Moses responds by warning that Yahweh will demonstrate his choice of the one who can draw near to him. Thus the dispute here is one regarding priestly legitimation (cf. vs. 10 and 17.5 [English 16.40]). In J, the challengers accuse Moses of bringing them *out* of the land of promise and of "acting as a prince" (*hstrr*, vs. 12; cf. Exod 2.14). Note how the glory and cloud once again come into play in 16.19; 17.7 (P).

[22]Cf. Childs, (*Exodus*, 356) who compares Numbers 12 to Exod 33.7-11; 19.9, and again refers to the confirmation of Moses' special office.

[23]Cf. Exod 11.3, often assigned to E.

[24]See C. R. North, "Servant of the Lord," *IDB*, 4, 292b.

[25]For Samuel, see 1 Sam 3.19-21. Note also Zadok, 1 Sam 2.35, referring to his priestly dynasty. On David, see 1 Sam 25.28 and especially 2 Sam 7.16 (cf. 1 Kgs 11.38, Jeroboam). The root *'mn* is also ubiquitous in Psalm 89, which provides the most salient example of the typology of exaltation applied to David, and here conceptually much closer to the exaltation of the Assyrian royal figures, as Tukulti-Ninurta. See further below on the Davidic empire.

[26]Only one other time is it used of an individual in a manner similar to Num 11.8, in Ps 17.15. The final occurrence is in Job 4.16, a classic phenomenological description of the perception of divine presence.

[27]On what follows, cf. now Childs, *Exodus*, 356.

[28]J. de Fraine, "Moses' 'cornuta facies' (Ex 34.29-35)," *Bijdragen Tijdschrift voor filosophie en theologie* 20 (1959) 35-36. Cf. also Jack M. Sasson, "Bovine Symbolism in the Exodus Narrative," *VT* 18 (1968) 384-385.

[29]The use of *bw'* and *yṣ'* in this verse indicates that the author may have the Tent of Meeting in mind. The unit was often classified as J, but more recently has been assigned to P by several scholars.

[30]This is the only passage other than Numbers 11 and 12 that employs the motif of the descending cloud in explicit connection with an individual leader. The use of *nr'h* with Yahweh is a *hapax* in Deuteronomy and may indicate a later attenuation of the use of *yrd* in Num 11.25; 12.5; Exod 33.9. Cf. Görg, *Zelt der Begegnung*, 150-151 and n. 39.

CHAPTER 7

ISRAEL AND THE DIVINE PRESENCE:

EXODUS 23-34

Our study of motifs of divine presence and guidance in Exodus would
hardly be complete without some attention to that part of the Sinai Pericope contained in Exodus 23-34.[1] The extreme complexity of these chapters and the limitations of our study make a thorough and definitive
analysis almost impossible. Thus what follows is merely an outline of
the colorful variety of motifs and of their significance within the story
of Israel's stay at the mountain of God.

Exod 23.20-33 presents us with a diffuse, often repetitious, series
of verses which, nevertheless, center around a common theme: the question
of divine presence and guidance on Israel's march from Sinai and *into*
Canaan. The importance of the problem is seen in the fact that there are
four divine pronouncements utilizing a form of the vanguard motif (šlḥ/
hlk lpny) familiar to us--with the ml'k (two times); the terror ('ymh);[2]
and the "hornet" (ṣrʿh),[3] vss. 20, 23, 27, 28. There are clear echoes of
Genesis 28 (Jacob's vow) and Exodus 15,[4] as well as the Moabite Stone.[5]
Surely the most striking element of this passage, however, is the pervasive consciousness of the covenant with Yahweh and the possibility
of disobedience. It is the first indication we have seen of the problem
of sin in connection with divine presence. This, no doubt, is the reason
that vss. 20-33 were placed immediately after the Covenant Code. Divine
presence demands covenant obedience, and divine guidance is not only for
the journey through the Wilderness but for a greater "journey", which
will begin when Israel enters the land. Along with the explicit blessings (vss. 25-26) and the veiled curse (vss. 21b, 33b), the passage
as a whole and in its present position adumbrates the conclusion of the
familiar treaty form.[6] The relationship between the concern for divine
presence and the covenant context here (and elsewhere in chs. 23-34) is

illuminated by a comparison with the Mattiwaza text discussed in the Excursus above. In its entirety, the Mattiwaza text offers an attractive analogy to Exodus, where the concern for divine presence provides a continuity from the Reed Sea deliverance to the departure from Sinai after the conclusion of the covenant. Thus in the Mattiwaza text we have the progression: (1) presence of the Hittite gods in support of Mattiwaza in battle, expressed by the vanguard motif; (2) treaty with the Hittite over-lord; (3) invocation by Mattiwaza and the Hurrians of the continuing presence and protection of the Hittite gods on conclusion of the treaty. On the other hand, it is somewhat frustrating that the *language* of the latter invocation has its closest parallel, not in the Sinai pericope in Exodus, but in Gen 28.10-22 and in Num 10.29-32 (see below, ch. 8). Nevertheless, the Mattiwaza text demonstrates that conclusion of a treaty and concern for continuing divine presence quite properly belong together. Of course, as we shall see below, the construction of the golden calf in ch. 32 to serve as the divine vanguard enormously complicates the relationship between covenant and divine presence.

In Exodus 24 we have, basically, three interspersed units. Vss. 1, 9-11 tell of the ascent of the mountain by Moses, Aaron, Nadab, Abihu, and the seventy elders, who actually see the "God of Israel" without incurring harm and who join in a covenant meal. It is possible that this unusual divine appearance functions to legitimate the leaders involved, just as in those texts concerning Moses that we dealt with previously. This may be the reason for the position of vss. (2)3-7,[7] for the effect of this intrusion is to accentuate the singularity of Moses' intercourse with Yahweh and his role as mediator for the people (cf. above on Exod 33.7-11; Numbers 10-11). Similarly, vss. 12-14 single out Moses and "Joshua his attendant" (cf. 33.11; Num 11.28) in contradistinction to the elders. Finally, vss. 15-18 provide the most extreme emphasis (clearly, from the Priestly view) on Moses' distinctive position.[8] Moses is allowed to enter the cloud, which conceals the divine presence,[9] and he stays on the mountain forty days and nights. In short, the whole chapter is strung on the question of who ascended the mount of God, who was allowed to draw near to his presence, and who were the legitimate recipients of revelation.[10]

After the intervening Priestly material in chs. 25-31, our investigation resumes with ch. 32. As we shall see in more detail, the making of the golden calf is the central event in chs. 23-40. There is no

154

question that it represents an enormous rift in the relationship between Yahweh and his people. For our purposes, the most interesting aspect of this is the way in which the story is built around (or incorporates[11]) the vanguard motif. After the lengthy absence of Moses, the people present their demand to Aaron: "Make us a god[12] who will go before us." The irony of this request is painfully evident to one who knows the previous events in Exodus, where Yahweh himself or his designated agents provided the necessary guidance. On the other hand, the irony is compounded by the expressed reason for the request in the rest of the verse. The people want a god to go in front of them because *Moses'* whereabouts is unknown. This is related to the end of the story (vs. 34) where Moses' role as the guide (*nḥh*) of the people is renewed by Yahweh, along with the promise, "my messenger will go in front of you." Moses' role is thus correlated with that of the divine agent.[13]

Whether the intention of the people is to replace Moses or Yahweh (or both) as their leader, it is clear that the golden calf must be interpreted as a physical representation of divine presence similar in both form and function to those discussed in Part I, and to the ark in Numbers 10 (see below). The use of the vanguard motif is already an indication of this, for we have seen it used with similar cultic objects in literary descriptions of liturgical processions. This also fits with the picture drawn by vss. 5-6, which may well describe an ordinary religious festival rather than a wild orgy.[14] However, as we have seen, more telling evidence comes from archaeology. The credit for the application of this evidence to Exodus 32 goes primarily to Otto Eissfeldt who, in 1940, referred to a considerable number of iconographic studies in support of his suggestion that the golden calf was in fact a standard or emblem used to represent divine presence.[15] Eissfeldt in particular appealed to a number of figures from Mari that depict a victory procession being led by one figure who is carrying a bull emblem mounted on a staff (hence, a standard; see our Illustrations, Fig. 5). More recently, this evidence has been supplemented by the discovery of bull standards at Ugarit, and the connections with Exodus 32 have been confirmed by C. F. A. Schaeffer.[16] In short, we may conclude that the golden calf in Exodus 32 bears a striking resemblance to the divine standards and emblems in the Mesopotamian texts. It was clearly intended to serve as a physical representation-- indeed, a permanent guarantee--of the presence of the God who had appeared on Mt. Sinai, and was also to provide divine guidance to the promised land.

As already indicated, Exodus 32 ends with the provision of both Moses and the divine messenger for the leadership of the people. Although the connection in 32.34 between the divine messenger and the punishment that the people will receive is unclear, the messenger itself does not seem to be a diminution of divine presence, any more than it is in 14.19 or 23.20,23. Such, however, is not the case with 33.1-6. This unit, which has a great deal in common with 23.20-33, shows the first signs outside of ch. 32 of the rift brought about by the golden calf. Once again the vanguard motif is employed to describe divine presence and guidance for Israel's journey into Canaan, but now the messenger is, in some sense, a sign of divine disfavor: "I shall send before you a messenger . . . for I will not go up in your midst, for you are a recalcitrant people, lest I consume you on the way" (vss. 2-3). It has been suggested by Beyerlin that vss. 3b-6 present a view of divine presence "characteristic of the Elohist":

> Yahweh remains on the mount of God; he does not journey
> with them. The people are punished for their apostasy
> by dismissal from Yahweh's dwelling.[17]

Beyerlin's opinion is attractive, and would help explain the deep anxiety over the continuation of Yahweh's presence evident in these verses (and, already, in ch. 32). His interpretation also extends to the unit vss. 12-17, where Beyerlin finds "a burning, existing problem," in affirming "that the God who once revealed himself fully and for the first time on *Sinai* was now present with his people in *Canaan* also."[18] This is a later stratum of J, standing in contrast to an earlier one that dealt with the problem of a human guide through the wilderness (Num 10.29-33; see below).[19] Moreover, the later stratum in vss. 12-17 does not simply concern Yahweh's presence in general, but specifically, his presence in the covenant cult, where Yahweh's *pānîm* is connected with his epiphany over the ark.[20]

Despite the attractiveness of this position and its support by other scholars,[21] there are a number of problems that make it untenable. Although Yahweh's connection with the *region* of Sinai is ancient and tenacious,[22] there is little evidence to show that he was thought to have remained there when Israel departed for Canaan. Already in 33.7-11 we are told that Yahweh regularly appeared at the Tent of Meeting.[23] Indeed, the redactional position of vss. 3-11 provides perhaps the most profound theological import of the pericope, the effect of which is, clearly, to ameliorate the negative implications of the preceding verses.[24] More importantly, the distinction in 33.1-6 is surely more theological than spatial. The sending of the divine messenger here simply means that Yahweh himself is not fully present—and this self-imposed distance is as much gracious as it is punitive, for it prevents the destruction of a sinful people by a wrathful God. An analogy may be drawn to Numbers 14, where Moses at one point reminds Yahweh that he is continually "in the midst of this people" (*bqrb h*ᶜ*m hzzh*, vs. 14; cf. *bqrbk*, Exod 33.3, 5), yet later on, in consequence of the people's rebelliousness, he warns them that "Yahweh is not in your midst" (*'yn yhwh bqrbkm*, vs. 42).[25]

Beyerlin is quite correct, however, in pointing to Israel's anxiety over whether the God who had let them out of Egypt and had revealed himself to them at Sinai would now go with them to Canaan. This is especially true if, as seems likely, Yahweh was originally connected with this region. However, we would disagree with Beyerlin's tendency to see this problem as one developing out of the cult *in Canaan*, and instead would accept the textual evidence that the question of Yahweh's continuing presence was *the* crucial problem of the Wilderness journey, and of the departure from Sinai in particular.[26] This is, demonstrably, the question presented in 33.12-17, where, in our view, the cultic intepretation of Yahweh's "presence" is forced. Although in some contexts the *pānîm* may be a cultic term,[27] this is not the case here. When Yahweh says *pānay yēlēkû* (vs. 14), the meaning is simply "I myself will go (with you)." An interesting parallel is found in 2 Sam 17.11. In opposing Ahithophel's plan of taking a group of soldiers and quickly attacking the fleeing David, Hushai recommends that Absolom wait until the whole army can be gathered, *ûpāneyka hōlᵉkîm bᵉqirbô*--"then you yourself shall go in their midst."[28] Thus Exod 33.14 does not refer to an hypostasis of Yahweh,[29] much less a cultic phenomenon, but uses a common expression for "oneself" in asking Yahweh to accompany his people personally.[30]

Finally, Exod 33.12-17 also provides an intimation of our exaltation theme. After pleading with Yahweh not to send them off to Canaan without his personal presence, Moses gives this poignant reason (vs. 16):

> "how then shall it be known that I have found favor
> in your sight, I and your people? Is it not in your
> going with us that we are distinguished,[31] I and
> your people, from all the people on the face of the

earth?"

The correlation between divine presence and national identity, as well as the legitimation of Moses' leadership, could not be more eloquently expressed.

This is also the context within which the sequel in vss. 18-23 must be seen.[32] Despite the careful restraint with which Moses' experience is drawn, it is clear that his perception of the divine splendor is a mark of his exaltation by Yahweh. The same holds true for the revelation of the divine name in 34.5-7, which is, appropriately, connected with Yahweh's descent in the cloud (ᶜnn). Moreover, Moses' curiously repeated request for Yahweh's accompanying presence in 34.9[33] --and here even despite the people's recalcitrance--is partially answered in vs. 10 with words echoing 33.16 (and Exod 15.11c):[34]

> In front of all your people I will do wonders
> (npl't[35]) which have never been wrought
> (l'-nbr'w) in all the earth and in all the
> nations, and all the people in whose midst you
> are will see the work of Yahweh, for it is a
> fearful thing (nwr') that I will do with you.

Having probed the individual pericopes, we may pause for a retrospective glance at the final redactional position of Exodus 32. This at once reveals the crisis caused by the events therein and the significance for the theme of divine presence. Within chs. 23-34, ch. 32 forms the center of a concentric schema in which covenant faith and divine presence are the major subjects:

> ch. 23 the promise of divine presence (vss. 20-33)
> ch. 24 the people accept the covenant
> ch. 32 the people disobey the covenant
> ch. 33 divine presence is called into question
> ch. 34 the covenant is renewed

This schema also extends to the Priestly material, in that the regulations for the entire cultic institution are promulgated in chs. 25-31, after the acceptance of the covenant in ch. 24, but the cult is actually established only in chs. 35-40--after the broken covenant has been renewed in ch. 34. Since the establishment of Yahweh's presence in the cult is the primary motive of the Priestly legislation in Exodus (25.8 sounds the keynote), this pattern is highly significant. For one thing, it clearly was a message to the Exilic community that, despite the consequences of covenant disobedience and curse, the divine presence would still dwell in their midst.

One final point needs to be made for these chapters in general. It is clear that in most of the pericopes discussed in this section the question of divine presence and guidance arises in connection with Yahweh's command to "go up" to the promised land.[36] These passages have been separated from Numbers 9-10 by a vast amount of Priestly and legal material, with the consequence that Numbers 10 depicts the *actual* close of Israel's sojourn at the mountain, thereby producing an anticlimactic effect in Exodus 23--34. Nevertheless, it is important to see how, in all of this material (including Exod 13.17-22), the motifs of divine presence and guidance are concentrated in narrative sections dealing with departure--the exodus from Egypt and the exodus from Sinai.

[1]Some remarks will be made below concerning the redactional significance
of the Priestly material with regard to the Sinai pericope, but a detailed analysis of the Priestly regulations is beyond the scope of this
study. However, see the following chapter on Numbers 9-10.

[2]Cf. especially Exod 15.16 and Josh 2.9. On the use of *ḥmm* in vs. 27
see below on Judg 4.15 and Exod 14.24.

[3]But note NEB "terror." Elsewhere only Josh 24.12; Deut 7.20.

[4]Cf. *lšmrk bdrk* in vs. 20 with Gen 28.15, 20 (see Excursus 1 on this passage). Note also how vs. 22b resembles Gen 12.3a etc. Along with the
"terror" (above, n. 2) cf. *hmmqwm 'šr hknty* in vs. 20 with Exod 15.17.

[5]Cf. vs. 28 (*grš . . . mlpnyk*) with 1. 19, *wygrš kmš mpny[w]* (Donner-
Röllig, *Inschriften*, I, 33).

[6]Note in particular the connection between the divine messenger and Yahweh's name, vs. 21, which has parallels in the ancient Near Eastern concept of hypostatization, e.g. Astarte's epithet *šm bcl*, "Name of Baal."
On the latter see Cross, *CMHE*, 30, n. 102 and especially S. Dean McBride,
Jr., "The Deuteronomic Name Theology," 130-141, on which Cross's comments
are based.

In general, it is quite possible that Exod 23.20-33 constitutes earlier
literary activity (perhaps E) on which the deuteronomistic theology was
based. Note especially the adaptation of this material in Deut 7.12-26,
and cf. Judg 2.1-5. Cf. Childs (*Exodus*, 460-461), who reckons with a
common oral tradition.

[7]Vs. 2 is often seen as part of the former unit, while vss. 3-8 (ascribed
to E) form the second. However, vs. 2 places us ahead of the action in
vs. 9, and its primary purpose seems to be to negate the role of any of
the participants other than Moses. This may be true of vs. 1bβ ("and
you shall worship from a distance") as well (cf. 20.18, 21).

[8]A most interesting interpretation of this pericope and others in the
Priestly work is contained in the study of Claus Westermann, "Die
Herrlichkeit Gottes in der Priesterschrift," in *Wort-Gebot-Glaube :
Beiträge zur Theologie des Alten Testaments*, pp. 227-249 (Walther
Eichrodt *Festschrift*; Abhandlungen zur Theologie des Alten und Neuen
Testaments, 59; Zürich: Zwingli, 1970). See especially pp. 230-235 on
the function of the *kābôd* in legitimating not only Moses as mediator,
but also the sacred space and time of the encounter.

[9]Thus the cloud here seems to be less closely associated with Yahweh himself than it is elsewhere. Moses' ability to enter the cloud stands in
contrast to 40.35.

[10]Deserving mention here is the extensive work of E. W. Nicholson, *Exodus
and Sinai in History and Tradition* (Growing Points in Theology; Richmond: John Knox, 1973). Nicholson (79) thinks that Exod 24.9-11
"centres exclusively on Yahweh's theophany on the holy mountain. Indeed, what is here recorded is a theophany *par excellence* . . . ," because the representatives of Israel actually saw God. Nicholson also

concludes that the scanty role of Moses here indicates that he and Aaron are later additions to a story that originally mentioned only Nadab, Abihu, and the elders (80-82). Nicholson is also extremely skeptical here, as elsewhere, about any connections with covenant theology at an early date. Cf. also id., "The Interpretation of Exod xxiv 9-11," *VT* 24 (1974) 77-97; id., "The Antiquity of the Tradition in Exodus xxiv 9-11," *VT* 25 (1975) 69-79.

[1]We cannot go into the complicated relation between Exodus 32 and 1 Kgs 12.25-33. It is possible that the vanguard motif has been applied secondarily to the story of Jeroboam's calves to make it more fitting to the Wilderness setting. However, the pervasive emphasis on divine presence and guidance in the Wilderness stories beginning with Exodus 13-14 is enough to indicate the originality of the motif in Exodus 32, and suggests an ancient version of the story--perhaps from the Wilderness period--as well. The iconographic evidence from Mesopotamia and Ugarit would clearly allow for such an early date. For the most recent discussion of the relevant literature on Exodus 32, see Childs, *Exodus*, 557-562.

[2]An alternative reading in the plural may be indicated, reflecting the construction of two calves by Jeroboam.

[3]Cf. Deut 10.11 where Moses is "to proceed on the journey before the people." On the correlation between Moses and the messenger, cf. below on Joshua 1:3-5. Note the ironic emphasis on $h'y\check{s}$, vs. 1; cf. Num 12.3

[4]So Jack M. Sasson, "The Worship of the Golden Calf," AOAT 22 (Orient and Occident--the Gordon *Festschrift*; 1973) 152: "Rather than wild abandoned acts, the scene that unfolds before the calf was probably an orderly ritual that followed practices will [sic] known to the ancient Near East, festivals that consisted of a (ritual) banquet followed by sports, miming, and antiphonal singing to honor the gods." Note also his comparison to 2 Samuel 6 and the ark procession, on which see below, ch. 11.

[5]"Lade und Stierbild," especially 297-302.

[6]"Nouveaux témoignages du culte de El et de Baal a Ras Shamra-Ugarit et ailleurs en Syrie-Palestine," *Syria* 43 (1966) 10-16. The bull standard reproduced in our Fig. 4 is described as fixed to a shaft so that it could be attached to the top of a sceptre or staff (*Ibid.*, 10). Schaeffer also refers to the standard from Mari (11-13).

On the comparison to Exodus 32, cf. also Sasson, "Worship of the Golden Calf," 153, n. 10. A considerably different approach, which also makes use of iconographic evidence, is represented by Lloyd R. Bailey, "The Golden Calf," *HUCA* 42 (1971) 97-115. Bailey consciously follows in the footsteps of J. Lewy and others (112, n. 92) in suggesting that the golden calves of Aaron and Jeroboam are to be connected with the patriarchal cult of the moon god Sin, preserved from traditions located around Harran by the Rachel tribes. This hypothesis is meant to replace the traditional one fostered by Albright, which sees the calves as pedestals for the invisible Yahweh and as replacements for the cherubim.

[7]Beyerlin, *Origins and History*, 23. He assigns vss. 1-3a to J; 3b-6 contain two variants, 3b-4 and 5-6.

[8]*Ibid.*, 101.

[9]*Ibid.* Beyerlin thinks that there are several different layers of tradition

within J. Exod 33.1, 3a, 12a originally formed a complete unit with Num
10.29-33a in which a human guide was sought and provided by Yahweh (the
latter part now lost). The later level refers to Yahweh himself (Exod
33.16-17) or his *pānîm* (33.14-15) or the ark (Num 10.33b) going with the
people, but concerns the problem of Yahweh's presence in *Canaan* and *in
the cult* (98-101, 107).

[20]*Ibid.*, 106-107, 110-111. This also provides the key to the redactional
connection with 33.3b-6.

[21]Clements, *God and Temple*, 26-27; Muilenberg, "Intercession," 168, 181.

[22]Cf. the classic epiphany texts dealt with in ch. 9 and see John Gray,
"The Desert Sojourn of the Hebrews and the Sinai-Horeb Tradition," *VT*
4 (1954) 148-154. The hypothesis of Noth concerning a pilgrimage to
Sinai (1 Kings 19; Numbers 33), followed by Beyerlin (*Origins and History*
102), at best suggests that this was considered a holy place, not that
Yahweh was thought to still dwell there.

[23]Of course, Beyerlin (112-126) considers this passage also as testifying
to the covenant cult *in Canaan*.

[24]So also Childs (*Exodus*, 593), who suggests that the position of the passage indirectly reaffirms God's accompanying presence which had been
demonstrated earlier by the pillar of cloud and fire.

[25]In vs. 14 the divine presence is again connected with the cloud, fire,
and vanguard motif. In vss. 42-44, the divine presence is connected
specifically with the ark. For the author, these were certainly not
incompatible; cf. Num 10.33-36, discussed below.

[26]We would thus disagree most strongly with the view of Noth (*History of
Pentateuchal Traditions*, 204-206), who sees the problems of divine
presence in Exodus 33 as merely secondary accretions (as also Num 10.29-
36).

[27]Beyerlin, *Origins and History*, 103-104. Most of his examples involve
the use of *lipnê yhwh* or the like and are an exaggeration of the literal
meaning. Those concerning "to seek the face of Yhwh" are somewhat more
convincing. Cf. n. 29.

[28]The last word following the LXX, Syriac, and Vulgate. Note RSV "in person."

[29]Cf. Tannit as *panê Baal*, "the presence of Baal," probably related to
Astarte as *šm b^cl*, "Name of Baal;" see Cross, *CMHE*, 29-30; McBride,
"Deuteronomic Name Theology," 135-137.

[30]Cf. the article by A. R. Johnson ["Aspects of the use of the term *pānîm*
in the Old Testament," (*Festschrift* Otto Eissfeldt, ed. J. Fück; Halle:
Niemeyer, 1947) 157-159], who makes many of the same points and also
criticizes the literal reading of expressions like *lpny*. For the possibility of reading vs. 14b as "I will lead you," see Muilenberg, "Intercession," 166, n. j.

[31]On the use of *plh*, cf. Exod 8.18; 9.4; 11.7 and note the use in the
first and third of *yd^c*. This proving of Yahweh's supremacy through
the distinctiveness given to Israel is a picturesque legendary expression of the larger exaltation theme, which runs throughout Exodus 1-15.

[32]Yahweh's *pānîm* in these verses is not to be used to interpret the preceding section, and even here the word means literally "face" rather
than "(cultic) presence."

162

[33]ylk . . . $bqrbnw$; note the similarity to 33.12-17 in the use of the expression '$m-n$' ms'ty hn b^cynyk

[34]The mention of "cutting a covenant" in the first part of the verse is difficult to relate to the rest. For the portion quoted, cf. Deut 7.17-26. Note the use in Exod 15.11c of nr' and pl'.

[35]Note that this word is closely related to plh in 33.16.

[36]Exod 33.1, 12; cf. 32.34 with nhh, "guide." The situation in 23.20-33 is quite similar.

CHAPTER 8

THE DEPARTURE FROM SINAI

(1) Numbers 1.1-10.28

There is another block of material that deserves special attention
because of its emphasis on divine guidance and its use of the ^cnn as well
as other forms of divine presence. The larger unit under consideration
is Numbers 1-10, but our focus will be primarily on chs. 9-10.

We may begin our investigation with a look at 9.15-23. This selection is by no means arbitrary, for an examination of the occurrence of
^cnn as a motif of divine *guidance* shows that in Exodus-Numbers it is
limited to Exodus 13-14 and Num 9.15-23; 10.11-12, 34.[1] As we shall
see later, this in itself is not insignificant.

Num 9.15 presents an abrupt shift from the preceding material, which
deals with Passover regulations. The verse begins with a temporal clause
that appears to refer to the initial construction of the *miškān*. This
seems to presume both 1.1 (but there the *'hl mwᶜd*) and, especially,
Exodus 40, which describes precisely that event. However, it becomes
immediately apparent from the rest of vss. 15-23 that the initial setting
up of the tabernacle is not the subject, but rather the way in which the
tabernacle is connected with the means of divine guidance for the extended
period of Israel's march from Sinai. This is evident simply by the use
of frequentative verbs throughout the passage. In this way vss. 15-23
provide a compact paradigm of the motif of divine presence and guidance,
reminding us once again of Exod 13.21-22 and 33.7-11.

The paradigmatic nature of this passage is almost painfully clear
from the way in which the author answers hypothetical questions. What
if the cloud remained for a very long time over the tabernacle? What
if it was there only overnight? What if it did not descend at evening
and the people had to march all night? The answer to all of these

164

questions is the dogged repetition of the author's point: the people followed the command of Yahweh as it was demonstrated in the movement of the
cloud, no matter how inconsistent that movement might be.

It is obvious that the role of the cloud (and fire)[2] here is an
adaptation of its function in Exod 13.21-22. It is also clear that there
are some important differences. There is no mention of Yahweh himself
throughout the passage, except in the phrase $^c l$ py $yhwh$; Yahweh is certainly not seen here as being *in* the cloud as in J. The vanguard motif
in its strict sense, using hlk $lpny$, is also absent. Instead, the author
conceives of the cloud as "covering" (ksh) or "tabernacling, tenting"
($škn$) or "being taken up" ($n^c lh$)--language that is characteristic of the
Priestly source with such images as the cloud and glory ($kbwd$).[3] The
most important difference, of course, is the incorporation of the cultic
institution of the tabernacle along with the $^c nn$. This connection is
not an original development of P, but stems from much older traditions
(e.g. Exod 33.7-11, see above). What is original is the correlation
between tabernacle and cloud as a means of *guidance*. This correlation
simply reflects the fundamental centrality of the cultic institution in
the Priestly view.

The adaptation of the cloud and guidance motif to the centrality
of the cultic equipment is dramatically presented in the elaborate description of Israel's camp and order of march. The subject is first
broached in 1.50-54, where the Levites are ascribed the honor of carrying the tabernacle and the responsibility of camping immediately around
it. The rest of the tribes then camp around the tabernacle and the
Levites, forming concentric circles. This arrangement is then filled
out in detail in ch. 2, which, in a way, provides a more practical or
earthly paradigm as a counterpart to that in 9.15-23. With meticulous
care, the Priestly author delineates the position of each tribe in the
camp. Actually, there are four "camps" ($mhnh$) composed of three tribes
(mth) each, and each of the "camps" has its own standard ($degel$, or $'ōt$).[4]
Each camp is to follow a strictly defined order when the assembly of
camps is on the march. First to depart are Judah and Reuben, from the
Southern and Eastern sides. After Judah and Reuben, the tent of meeting
sets out along with the camp of the Levites, and only then do Ephraim
and Dan depart from the Western and Northern sides. In a strikingly
simple way, the Priestly author has thus accentuated the conceptual and
literal centrality of the cult within Israel--not only is the tent the

165

center of the entire camp, it also forms the middle position of the line of march. If we combine this graphic picture with that of 9.15-23, we see the great extent to which the earlier vanguard motif of "going in front" has been sacrificed to P's peculiar concept of Israel's cultic life.

If this mechanical organization of the Israelite camp strikes modern readers as humorous pedantry, then they fail to grasp the intense fervor of the Priestly conceptualization. In fact, the potential excitement of this elaborate picture still resonates when the cumbersome machine is put into action in ch. 10. Between ch. 2 and 9.15, numerous cultic regulations are specified and the Passover is observed (9.1-14). Following the paradigm of 9.15-23, Moses is then given further instructions regarding the construction of trumpets to be used on the march and at other occasions. The march itself is described in 10.14-29 in terms almost identical to ch. 2.[5] The few verses that intervene (10.11-13) are far more momentous than their brevity would indicate. At this point all of the Priestly legislation of Sinai has been received and Israel is ready for her departure on the journey to the promised land. The camp has been assigned its order of march and the means of divine presence and guidance has been explained. It is thus a highly dramatic moment that, for the Priestly writer, constituted the emergence of what was truly Israel. In vss. 11-13--still in his laconic style--he describes the climactic event that, for him, must have been exhilirating.

> In the second year, in the second month, on the twentieth day of the month, the cloud was taken up from over the tabernacle of the testimony and the people of Israel set out by stages from the wilderness of Sinai; and the cloud settled down in the wilderness of Paran. They set out for the first time at the command of Yahweh by the authority of Moses.

The juxtaposition of Sinai and Paran here also makes it quite likely that the Priestly author is presenting us with his own commentary on how to interpret the Wilderness March of Yahweh and his people recorded in the classic epiphany texts (see the Excursus following this section). Thus, the march is viewed as primarily that of the *cultic* community.

One issue remains to be considered: the connections between Numbers

1-10 and the Near Eastern material from Part I. We have already pointed
out the use of "standards," which evidently are carried by each of the
four camps. The Priestly source thus provides an interesting parallel
to the use of very similar objects, both in cultic processions and in
the march of armies in the Mesopotamian texts. Although in the latter
it is not always clear whether the standards represented deities, sociological entities, or both, a very similar phenomenon appears to be at
work in Numbers.[6] The use of such standards in both cultic processions
and warfare in the ancient Near East adds weight to the suggestion of
Cross that in these chapters in Numbers, the description of the camp and
march "very likely had its origin in the cultic reenactment of the
Exodus–Conquest."[7] Although there is no indication of the particular
festival here, the connection with Passover (see the end of this chapter),
and resemblances to the cultic procession at Gilgal (see ch. 10) tend
to support such a suggestion. At any rate, the use of these standards
here and the overall picture of Israel's marching ranks presents a more
explicit conception of her march through the wilderness as analogous to
that of a conquering lord, as was the case in Exodus 15.13–16.

Perhaps a more speculative, but still interesting, connection with
the Near Eastern texts concerns P's use of the phrase ^{c}l-py $yhwh$ ("at
the command of Yahweh") in the context of Israel's march throughout
9.15–23 and also in the Priestly itinerary notices elsewhere.[8] This
expression bears a noticeable resemblance to one used frequently in the
Assyrian annals when the king begins a campaign or resumes his march,
stating that he does so "at the command of Assur, my lord."[9] Indeed,
the itinerary itself is well attested in the annals and has more literary exemplars as well.[10] Given our previous discussion of the correlation of deity and king, it is also worth noting that in 9.23 and 10.13
the people move "at the command of Yahweh by the authority of Moses"
(cl-py $yhwh$ byd-$mšh$).

To summarize, the Priestly material in Num 9.15–23 presents us
with another paradigm of divine presence and guidance that utilizes the
image of the cloud. The Priestly author has combined older traditions
(Exod 13.21–22; 33.7–11) in order to demonstrate his view that the
cultic institution of the Tabernacle itself is now the means through
which not only Yahweh's presence, but also his guidance, is made manifest. The spatial as well as the theological centrality of the Tabernacle has resulted in the attenuation of the vanguard motif, but the

use of standards by each of the subsidiary camps, and the fact that the march of Israel moves "at the command of Yahweh," indicate that the Priestly understanding of Israel's march through the wilderness resembles the march of the Assyrian army as we have seen it in the annals.

(2) Numbers 10.29-36

After the description of the order of march that Israel followed at her departure from Sinai (Num 10.14-28), there is a small block of material that rounds off chs. 1-10. Vss. 29-36 have challenged scholars for years with a very complex and difficult set of issues. We cannot go into all of these here but can only sketch the various nuances of divine presence and guidance that these verses present.

The material separates most reasonably into two basic units: vss. 29-32 and 33 (34)-36. The first deals with Moses' request for guidance through the wilderness by Hobab. This unit is most likely from the Yahwist. The language throughout is strikingly similar to a number of passages in Genesis, especially 28.10-22 (see the Excursus above). Thus Moses declares that he and the people are setting out for the land that Yahweh had promised them ('*tw 'ttn lkm*), i.e., the fathers (cf. Gen 28.13b, *lk 'ttnnh*). He then asks Hobab to "go with us" (*leḵā 'ittānû*), suggesting that his doing so will result in "goodness" being done to him because of the "goodness" that Yahweh has done and will do for Israel (*whyh hṭṭwb hhwᶜ 'šr yyṭyb yhwh ᶜmmnw whtbnw lk*). This immediately reminds us of the promise of Yahweh "to be with" Jacob ('*nky ᶜmmk*, Gen 28.15) and to "do good" to him (*w'yṭybh ᶜmmk*, 32.10; cf. 13). Moreover, Moses' plea to Hobab not to "abandon" (ᶜ*zb*) Israel has its counterpart in Yahweh's promise to Jacob not to "abandon" (ᶜ*zb*) him wherever he goes (*bkl 'šr-tlk*, 28.15). Finally, there is a pronounced similarity here to the Mattiwaza treaty discussed above in connection with Genesis 28. There the gods are invoked to "go with" the king and people, to make them great, protect them, and "do good" for them. What is perhaps somewhat surprising is that Num 10.29-33 speaks of a *human* guide and is not at all within a covenant context.[11]

The response to Hobab provides further stylistic analogies to Genesis. He objects that he will not go with Israel but will go to his own land and the place of his birth ('*l 'rṣy w'l-mwldty*), a phrase well known in the stories of the patriarchal journeys (Gen 12.1; 24.4; 31.3; 32.10). These analogies support the traditional ascription of Num 10.29-32 to the

Yahwist, and provide an interesting example of how the same language can be used for both divine and human presence and guidance. As we will show below, the same type of language is picked up again by the Deuteronomist (especially the use of ^{c}m and ^{c}zb) to describe Yahweh's presence and guidance in connection with Moses and Joshua.

The first unit ends in vs. 32 without telling us whether Hobab changed his mind, although other traditions indicate that he did.[12] Instead, the next unit begins abruptly in vs. 33 with another reference to the departure from "the mountain of Yahweh." Since this second unit is probably also from J,[13] even if from a different stratum of tradition, the absence of the above resolution may be explained as an attempt to de-emphasize the apparent contradiction of Hobab *and* the ark as the guide. Another problem within the second unit is presented by the introduction of the cloud in vs. 34. We would see this as an editorial intrusion intended to bring the passage in line with the preceding material in Numbers, especially 9.15-23.[14] It still is significant, however, that the combination of cloud and ark was not seen as incompatible. Indeed, the two are quite complementary, stemming from the fact that the cloud can be an agent of the divine warrior, and the existence of connections between the ark, divine warfare, and the heavenly hosts.

Outside of the Priestly legislation, vs. 33 and 14.44 contain the only mention of the ark in the Tetrateuch, a fact which has given rise to serious scepticism about the historical authenticity of these verses. Moreover, the whole question of the ark itself remains highly debatable, and even a survey of the discussion could fill a volume.[15] Despite the obvious complexities of the issue, we would agree with those scholars who see very old material in Num 10.33, 35-36.[16] Our purpose here will simply be to indicate the bearing of the Near Eastern and biblical material so far examined on the role of the ark in these verses.

In our judgment, both the form and function of the ark in vss. 33, 35-36 have extensive and impressive parallels with the texts discussed in Part I. To begin with, vss. 35-36 leave little doubt that there is a very strong identification between the ark itself and Yahweh. When the ark sets out, Moses cries to Yahweh to arise, and when it comes to rest, he calls Yahweh to return. This close identification between divine presence and a physical representation has clear analogies in Mesopotamian iconographic traditions, as we have already seen in connection with Exodus 32.[17] Here we may point out some additional possibilities in

Egyptian cultic processions. For example, William F. Albright's suggestion that the ark was intricately connected with the *name* "Yahweh of
hosts"[18] may be compared with a text from the Egyptian annals (Papyrus
Harris) in which Rameses III describes the "processional image" of Ptah.
The image is borne along with a shrine on a special barque, and the
shrine has "carrying-poles, overlaid with fine gold, engraved with thy
[the god's] name."[19] This at least suggests a fascinating parallel to
the picture of the ark from the Priestly view (Exod 25.13-15).

The close identification between the ark and Yahweh's presence may
also indicate a key to the conundrum of how the ark was thought to guide
the people. In Egyptian texts, one major type of procession involves
the use of a barque on which was a tabernacle or chapel ("Naos") in which
the deity remained hidden from view. (The "Naos" itself is frequently
boxlike.) Some of these objects had windowlike structures from which the
deity could appear. At any rate, the whole structure represented the
divine presence so profoundly that any movement of the litter itself was
believed to indicate an oracular dictum of the god.[20] It is conceivable
that the guidance of the ark follows a similar procedure. Any movement
was perceived (probably by its bearers)[21] as an indication of the route
of the journey. This would also be quite compatible with the Priestly
theology that connects the movement of the cloud with "the command of
Yahweh."

In short, whether we can specify with any assurance the actual
construction of the ark, it betrays a clear resemblance to those physical representations of divine presence in the Near Eastern texts. We
can also say something more about its function. In vs. 33 we have a
clear example of the vanguard motif: the ark journeys in front of the
people on their march. The fact that the motif here in particular is
adapted to fit the problems of guidance for the wilderness journey does
not detract from its similarity to the motifs in the literary and annalistic texts of Part I. Indeed, vss. 35-36 make it abundantly clear
how compatible the ark is with the militaristic function of the vanguard
motif in the latter, as well as in the Old Testament texts examined above.
When the ark sets out in front of the people, Moses invokes Yahweh to
rise up and scatter his (and therefore Israel's) enemies. Thus, as the
role of the ark in vs. 33 resembles the function of divine standards in
cultic processions in the Near Eastern texts, so in vss. 34-35 it resembles the function of the same objects in warfare. The ark represents

170

the presence of the Holy Warrior at the forefront of the battle.

The fact that, in these three verses, and on the basis of the Near Eastern material, it is possible to detect signs of both cultic procession and military march, is not insignificant. In fact, it provides yet another indication that such texts may reflect a ritual re-enactment of the events of Exodus, Wilderness March, and Conquest.[22] Moreover, the persistent redactional connections between the motifs discussed above and the institution of Passover (see immediately below) may support a cultic setting as well.[23]

One final point to consider is the redactional position of Numbers 9-10. We noticed before that 9.15 appears as a jolting transition from the preceding material. This is accentuated by the temporal clause at the opening and by the following frequentatives. Now it is interesting that the same situation applies to the introduction of the guidance motif in Exodus 13. There the temporal clause (referring to Israel's departure) in 13.17 returns us to the plot of the narrative, and the Yahwistic material in 13.21-22 in particular is comparable to the frequentative force of Num 9.15-23 (note $y\bar{a}m\hat{\imath}\check{s}$).[24] Both passages thus refer to the *customary* form of divine presence and guidance during Israel's wilderness journey.

Alongside these literary observations there is another intriguing correspondence between Numbers 9-10 and Exodus 13. In both, the abrupt introduction of the guidance/presence motif is preceded by legislative and narrative material dealing with the Passover ceremony (Exodus 12-13; Num 9.1-14). The text in these two blocks of material as they now stand thus presents a remarkably similar schema. This similarity is accentuated when we recall that the explicit use of the ^cnn as a means of divine *guidance* is virtually limited to these pericopes.[25] We thus arrive at a striking picture: these themes and motifs converge at two of the most momentous events in the story of Israel's epic beginnings—her departure from the land of Egypt and her departure from the mountain of God. It is not difficult to speculate why this was so. Both departures were faced with radical uncertainties and fears—a fact that the traditions of Israel's "murmurings" make very clear. It was therefore eminently appropriate for the narrator or the redactor to provide a firm assurance of Yahweh's presence and guidance. This was done in a very eloquent way by the employment of motifs that themselves were of ancient origin. In fact, it is not unreasonable to suppose that the ancient traditions

associated with the seasonal "change of pasture" (*Weidewechsel*), traditionally used to explain the origins of the Passover ritual,[26] are still
very much at work in the above passages.

[1]See the terminological study in Appendix 2. $^c nn$ also occurs in Num 14.14 as a motif of guidance, clearly with reference to the traditions in the two major blocks of material, i.e. Exodus 13-14, Numbers 9-10.

[2]Fire is mentioned only in vss. 15-16 and in such a way that it seems to be a nocturnal transformation of the cloud for obvious practical reasons. This secondary aspect of the fire alongside the cloud is evident elsewhere, e.g. Exod 33.7-11, and the various times at which Yahweh appears in the cloud.

[3]For further examples of this point, see my "Pillar of Cloud," 24, n. 45.

[4]Cf. Akk. *diglu*. Note that '$\bar{o}t$ is used in summary positions, vss. 17, 31, 34.

[5]There are some puzzling differences, however. In ch. 2 it was the Tent of Meeting that formed the center of the line of march. In ch. 10 the Tent of Meeting is not mentioned, nor are the Levites specified as a group. Rather, the sons of Gershon and Merari set out with the Tabernacle after the camp of Judah (vs. 17), and the Kohathites set out with the *miqdaš* after the camp of Reuben (vs. 21). The camp of Dan then forms the "rearguard" (*m'sp*), vs. 24.

[6]F. Sarre ("Feldzeichen," 336) considered the standards in Numbers to have been "military idols," just as he saw in the ephod a "Jahve-Bild" used in battle even in Solomonic times. It is certain, however, that the Priestly writer would not think of the standards in such a manner, and we do not have enough evidence to pursue the matter. For the later period, see the discussion of the "banners" at Qumran by Yigael Yadin, *The Scroll of the Sons of Light Against the Sons of Darkness*, trans. Batya Rabin and Chaim Rabin (Oxford: Oxford University, 1962) 38-64. Note also the reference by Miller (*Divine Warrior*, 92) to the Qumran holy war instructions where "the lead banner, which goes before all the army" is inscribed with the expression 'people of God.' Another biblical parallel is found in Exod 17.15-16 with the "banner of Yahweh" (see the usual emendations).

[7]*CMHE*, 321. In his earlier work ["The Priestly Tabernacle," *BA Reader* I, ed. David N. Freedman and G. Ernest Wright (Garden City: Doubleday, 1961) 212-213, 218], Cross followed Gressmann's comparison between the Tabernacle and the Egyptian (and Carthaginian) battle camp.

[8]Exod 17.1; Num 13.13.

[9]E.g., with Sargon (II), *ARAB* II, §§ 5, (p. 3); 31; 66.

[10]*Arab* I, §§ 373, 408-413, 469; II, 558. On the itinerary form, see William W. Hallo, "The Road to Emar," *JCS* 18 (1964) 57-58.

[11]It is also intriguing that Num 10.33 (see below) has the ark acting as vanguard and finding a "resting spot" (*m^{e}nûhāh*), for the Mattiwaza treaty goes on to express the wish for "goodness and rest" (*dumka ù nuhta*). With regard to the covenant context, if it is true that Num 10.29-32 originally connected with part of Exod 33.12-17 (Beyerlin, *Origins and History*, 100), such a context may once have been closer. Still, the pericope is not talking about *divine* presence. At any rate, it is ironic that here, where the covenant context is least felt, the language is so similar to the

Mattiwaza treaty, whereas in Exod 23.20-33, where the covenant context is so strong, the language at best adumbrates the Mattiwaza treaty (the vanguard motif; going "in your midst;" etc.).

[12] Judg 1.16, on which see B. Mazar, "The Sanctuary of Arad and the Family of Hobab the Kenite," *JNES* 24 (1965) 300. It is interesting that Num 10.30 seems to think of a situation in which Hobab is not *now* in his home territory, to which he intends to return. This territory is also here apparently not in the direction Moses wants to go (cf. Exod 18.5, 27).

[13] Note the same phrase "three days journey" in Exod 3.18; 5.3; 8.23; cf. 15.22 and Gen 30.26 (also Num 33.8). "Three days" itself, of course, is a common expression(Gen 40.12-19; Exod 10.22-23; Josh 1.11; 2.16, 22; etc.).

[14] Note that the cloud is "over them," which fits with the imagery of the Numbers passage cited.

[15] See the recent monographs by Johann Maier, *Das altisraelitische Ladeheiligtum*, BZAW 93 (1965); Marten H. Woudstra, *The Ark of the Covenant from Conquest to Kingship* (International Library of Philosophy and Theology, Biblical and Theological Studies, ed. J. Marcellus Kik; Philadelphia: Presbyterian and Reformed Publishing Company, 1965).

[16] For a detailed treatment of the problems involved, and a thorough refutation of the sceptical views of Maier, see Miller, *Divine Warrior*, 145, nn. 234-236.

[17] Such parallels as here presented were cogently argued on the basis of iconographic material by Eissfeldt, "Lade und Stierbild," especially 299-301. Our discussion has added the evidence of literary material.

[18] Review of *L'epithete divine Jahve Seba'ot*, by B. Wambacq, in *JBL* 67 (1948) 378-379. For a more recent discussion, see Miller, *Divine Warrior*, 152-155. The major biblical evidence is 2 Sam 6.2. Cf. also Woudstra, *Ark*, 61-66.

[19] James H. Breasted, *Ancient Records of Egypt* (4 vols.; Ancient Records, Second Series; ed. by William Rainey Harper; Chicago: University of Chicago Press, 1906), vol. IV, § 315; cf. §§ 204, 217, 331, 611, 748, 761, 768, 836, 958L, 988D. The use of such processional vehicles and images in Egypt is, of course, quite prevalent; see the following note.

[20] See especially Hans Bonnet, "Prozession," in (id.) *Reallexikon der Ägyptischen Religionsgeschichte* (Berlin: de Gruyter, 1952) 612b, 610b; also John A. Wilson, "A Divine Oracle through Visible Sign," *ANET*, 448b; Günther Roeder, *Kult, Orakel und Naturverehrung im alten Ägypten* (*Die ägyptische Religion in Texten und Bildern*, III; Zürich: Artemis, 1960) 191-192; Siegfried Morenz, *Egyptian Religion*, trans. Ann E. Keep (Ithaca, New York: Cornel University Press, 1973) 89.

[21] Actually there are at least three possible views concerning the means of this movement: (1) self-propelled (this is the apparent meaning of Num 10.33); (2) carried by bearers (Joshua 3; 2 Sam 6.12-19); (3) borne on a cart pulled by oxen (1 Sam 6.7-9; 2 Sam 6.1-11). We would opt for a combination of (1) and (2) here. Again in comparison to the Egyptian material, note the way in which the Philistines pose their question in 1 Samuel 6, which sounds very much like the request for an oracle. Our suggestions regarding the Egyptian material are, of course, not entirely new; see Maier, *Ladeheiligtum*, 40, n. 2; 52, n. 110; Woudstra, *Ark*, 22-23.

174

[22]Cf. Cross, *CMHE*, 99–105; Miller, *Divine Warrior*, 145–155.

[23]Cf. Cross, *CMHE*, 104.

[24]It is quite possible, of course, that this verb form could be an example of the archaic use of the prefix conjugation for past narrative, but the introductory participle and our interpretation of these verses as referring to the *period* of the wilderness journey point to the frequentative.

[25]The cloud is, of course, a form of guidance also in Exodus 14, but the primary function there is that of representing divine presence in battle. The only other occurrence of the cloud as a means of guidance in the Tetrateuch (Num 14.14) is most likely a reflection of the use in Exodus 13.

[26]The classic study is that of Leonhard Rost, "Weidewechsel und altisrael-itischen Festkalendar," *Zeitschrift des deutschen Palästina-Vereins* 66 (1943) 205–216.

CHAPTER 9

WILDERNESS MARCH AND CONQUEST--

THE "CLASSIC EPIPHANY TEXTS"

In the Introduction to this study we referred to several passages
in the Old Testament as "classic epiphany texts" (Deuteronomy 33; Judges
5; Psalm 68; Habakkuk 3). The reason for such a designation was the
very similar motif of divine appearance contained in each and the fact
that a large number of scholars have followed a comparable classifica-
tion. After studying these passages in the light of the foregoing discussion, we have reached the conclusion that they present quite varying
degrees of resemblance to the typology of exaltation. Thus at the outset of this chapter we must realize that motifs of divine presence and
appearance in the Old Testament are by no means tied exclusively to the
typology of exaltation, but can often have different antecedents. In
our judgment, the epiphany motif in each of the following texts also
presents an alternative literary tradition to the theme of divine presence and guidance in Exod 15.13-18--from the Wilderness March to the
Conquest. In this sense it preserves another description of the departure from Sinai, but here focusing on Yahweh rather than on Israel.
Therefore, we are at a convenient place for a brief survey of all four
texts before turning to Joshua 1; 3-5. We shall take up the individual
passages in the order of increasing conformance to the typology of exaltation.

(1) Habakkuk 3

The first (and longest) of the texts is found in Habakkuk 3, a
passage that betrays distinctive characteristics of early Hebrew poetry.[1]
Although, as William F. Albright has suggested,[2] vss. 3-7 and 8-15 may
well depict two different types of theophanic imagery, both sections
contain motifs that are germane to our investigation. Vs. 3 describes

176

Yahweh's advent from Teman and Mt. Paran, presumably the extreme Southeastern region of Palestine. This advent is accompanied by various
theophanic phenomena that we have seen in the Near Eastern texts:
brightness like the light and flashing rays (vs. 4). Even more directly
related to the vanguard motif is vs. 5: "Before him went pestilence,
/ and plague followed close behind." This motif is clearly similar to
those we have seen before, where the storm deity is surrounded by personified forces of warfare and destruction. Moreover, the reaction that
follows this dramatic appearance of Yahweh is also quite familiar to us.
The nations shudder, the mountains are shattered, the hills sink down.
While the imagery of the following section, vss. 8-15, appears to be
related more to the motif of the thunderstorm deity and his battle with
the sea, the effect is much the same. Yahweh rides upon his chariot of
victory, just as we have seen Marduk doing in *Enuma eliš*. Again the
reaction to his advent is the writhing of the mountains and the surging
of the sea, all accompanied by celestial cataclysm.

The point we wish to make about this passage concerns its mythological orientation. It is clear from the text that, at best, any references to actual historical events are kept to a minimum. There is mention of the geographical region from which Yahweh marched, and a vague
indication that the "land of Midian" was involved. It is also clear
that the poet has in mind a battle in which Yahweh's people are the
benefactors, for his advent ($yṣ'$), vs. 13) is explicitly connected to
this theme. But the basic tenor of the poem is ahistorical. Indeed,
even though the poet nostalgically harks back to Yahweh's deeds of old
(vs. 2), the description of these deeds seems to share the traits of
memory, immediate perception (cf. vs. 16), and anticipation. As such,
ch. 3 adds an eschatological affirmation of Yahweh's approaching vindi-
cation to the yearnings of chs. 1-2. Thus, if this poem speaks of exaltation at all, it refers to Yahweh's future victory over Israel's
enemies.

   (2) Psalm 68

A similar ambiguity beclouds Psalm 68. The composition and structure of this Psalm are obscure and it is almost impossible to tell if
and where there are continuous units.[3] Our primary interest is in vss.
8-9, which provide the counterpart to passages in Habakkuk 3 and
Deuteronomy 33. (The particular structure of this unit, with its close

parallel from Mesopotamian literature, will occupy us later, in our discussion of Judges 5.) Here we shall only make a few observations on
these verses along with implications from elsewhere in the Psalm. The
two most striking differences between vss. 8-9 and the parallels are
in the use of *lpny* ^c*mmk* and *byšymwn*. In place of specific geographical
references we thus have Yahweh's going forth before the people and his
marching through the wilderness. As we have seen in Exodus and Numbers,
this language has much in common with the prose sources of Israel's
victorious march from Egypt to Canaan, which distinguishes it from the
other poetic descriptions.

Despite the difficult and fragmentary nature of the text, there
are implications that other issues familiar to us from the Near Eastern
texts are present here as well. In general, the Psalm is rife with allusions to the divine warrior and his vanguard (especially vss. 18, 22,
34). There are also tantalizing intimations of the exaltation theme,
such as where Yahweh ascends the height, taking captives and tribute
from mankind (vs. 19), and the references to Yahweh's supremacy over
all the "kingdoms of the earth" (vss. 32-33). Finally, vss. 25-28 provide a glimpse of cultic "processions" (*hlykwt*) in which it seems quite
likely that some physical representation of divine presence was used,
as in the Mesopotamian texts. We have seen in the Gudea Cylinders, for
example, that a reference to an emblem of Ningirsu as well as to the
advent of the god himself can be contained in one clearly unified text.
There are also indications from other Old Testament texts (such as Psalm
24) that such processions involved the use of the ark as the representation of Yahweh's presence.[4] In fact, it has been suggested that the
festival procession here is a liturgical reenactment of Yahweh's march
from Sinai to Zion.[5] Moreover, vs. 27 possibly depicts the tribe of
Benjamin "in the lead" or perhaps even ruling over the other participants.[6] Nevertheless, the tenuous nature of the text and the lack of
assured unity do not allow us to go beyond these tentative suggestions.

(3) Deuteronomy 33

The next passage is Deut 33.2-3 (4-5), 26-29. One could easily
extend to the whole passage the characterization that Robertson has
quite rightly applied to vss. 2-3: ". . . one of the most obscure passages in the Old Testament. This makes wholehearted embrace of any
proposal difficult."[7] Despite this cumbersome situation, we would

178

maintain that the pericope as a whole offers a significant number of
literary and conceptual correspondences to the Near Eastern material
that we have discussed before. The problem lies in the extent to which
this pericope conforms to the typology of exaltation, a prospect that
is darkened by the lack of any firm mooring in a specific historical
event.

Our primary focus will be on vss. 2-3, but we shall also incorpor-
ate vss. 4-5 and 26-29 where they are helpful. What follows is a translation by Miller based largely on the evidence from various scholars.[8]

2 *yhwh msyny b'*	Yahweh came from Sinai,
wzrḥ mśᶜyr l[ᶜ]mw/lnw	He dawned from Seir for his people/upon us,
ḥwpyᶜ mhr p'rn	He shone forth from Mount Paran.
w'th-m rbbt qdš	With him were myriads of holy ones,
mymynw 'šd [']lm	At his right hand warriors of the gods,
3 *'p ḥbb ᶜmym*	Yea, the purified ones of the peoples.
kl qdš bydk	All the holy ones are at thy hand,
whmtkw brglk	They bow down at thy feet,
yś'-m dbrtyk	They lift up thy decisions.

The resemblance between the first three lines and their counterpart
in Habakkuk 3 and Psalm 68 is obvious, and we shall have more to say about
this later. Here we must point out the rather startling parallels between this passage and the Near Eastern material. Again we have the advent of the deity described by the imagery of glowing light, and in the
second tricolon Yahweh is accompanied by his heavenly entourage. Especially noteworthy is the second line, which bears obvious similarity to
the vanguard motif elsewhere, as when Marduk or Assur marches to battle
with various divine beings at his right hand, as well as in front and
behind. What is most interesting here is the way in which the third
line appears in apposition to the second. If the interpretation of this
line as a reference to Yahweh's people is correct, then we have the

combination of Yahweh, divine vanguard, and Israel. As Miller says concerning the $^c\bar{e}l\hat{\imath}m$ and the $^c am\hat{\imath}m$, "In this context the two groups represent parts of a single element--the entourage of Yahweh."[9] This combination is strongly reminiscent of the way in which the Assyrian king follows behind the divine vanguard in battle. That is, in this poem, Israel stands in the place where the king would be in the Akkadian texts we have examined previously. Indeed in the light of the exaltation of Tukulti-Ninurta to divine sonship, it is interesting that J. T. Milik refers to Deut 33.3a as a description of Israel as the "first-born" (*premier-ne*) of the nations.[10]

The third tricolon introduces the theme of divine exaltation. Although there is a very viable alternative translation of these lines that would accentuate the motif of the divine vanguard,[11] we find the present translation to be the most likely one. In any case, the repetition of $qd\check{s}$ resumes the subject of the first line of the second tricolon (cf. also *mymyrnw* and *bydk*), the heavenly beings subservient to Yahweh.[12] The implications of this are significant. The description of these heavenly beings doing obeisance to Yahweh and carrying out his decisions clearly proclaims Yahweh's sovereignty over all the heavenly host. Moreover, it is quite possible that "all the holy ones" includes both the divine beings *and* the reference to Israel in the preceding tricolon, thus explicitly associating the "heavenly" and "earthly" armies of Yahweh.[13] Along with the preceding use of the vanguard motif and the correlation with the human devotees of the deity, this emphasis on Yahweh's lordship presents a lucid example, not only of the typology of exaltation, but also of the literary and conceptual context to which it frequently belongs.

In support of this conclusion we may appeal to a number of parallel elements in vss. 26-29. Indeed, the next line (vs. 26) following on the preceding tricolon[14] has the following comparative formulation:

> There is none like the God of Jeshurun
> Who rides the heavens in his strength,
> And in his exaltation,[15] the clouds.

In addition, vs. 29 closes the poem with an ecstatic glorification of Israel in terms directly related to the comparison in vs. 26: "Blessed are you, Israel, who is like you? / A people saved by Yahweh, / The shield of *your* strength / And the sword of *your* exaltation." This use

180

of the comparative and the alternation of expressions for both the exaltation of Yahweh and of Israel resembles especially the "Hymn of
Praise" to Tukulti-Ninurta in the Epic (see ch. 1 [3]).[16]

Finally, we must mention the content and position of vss. 4-5. We
would agree with Miller in recognizing here a later stage in the development of Deuteronomy 33.[17] Vs. 4, especially, interrupts the consistent
imagery of vss. 2-3 and 26-29 and appears to be intended both as an explicit correlation of the theophany of Yahweh with the giving of the law
and as a transition to the "blessings" that follow. Vs. 5, however, may
well be the original continuation of vs. 3. Either way the verses are
significant for our topic:

> Moses commanded us Torah,
>
> A possession of the assembly of Jacob,
>
> And he became king in Jeshurun,
>
> When the heads of the people gathered together,
>
> The assembly[18] of the tribes of Israel.

These verses clearly have as their background the assembly of the Israelite league. For our purposes the crucial element is the third line,
which we have translated literally. The most obvious reading in the context is to assume that "he" means Moses, the subject of the two preceding
lines. Traditionally, of course, it is presumed that Yahweh is the implicit subject, and indeed one could translate "Then there was a king"
although this would not dispel the ambiguity. A definitive decision is
clearly impossible. For our purposes we can only suggest two alternatives: either the line refers to Yahweh's acclamation as king, in which
case we would find another reference to the exaltation typology; or the
line refers to Moses, which we would maintain is yet another aspect of
the typology, i.e. the exaltation of the individual leader (cf. the exaltation of the people, above). This will concern us again below.

One final word about the historical situation that our passage
seems to depict. We noticed that the Habakkuk 3 pericope pictured
Yahweh's march from Southeastern Palestine and his battle with the sea
in predominantly mythological terms with little historical references.
There Yahweh's past deeds have lost their particular historicity in
that they have become a proleptic anticipation of his future act. The
"frame song" in Deuteronomy 33 is very similar in that it refers to the
same geographical region, yet it maintains an historical understanding

of Yahweh's past acts--Israel's victorious march from the wilderness into
the land of Canaan. In fact, vss. 27-29 have been interpreted as referring to "Yahweh's humbling the ancient gods" in connection with the Conquest.[19] The combination of this march with the imagery of divine presence is well expressed by Buber:

> the frame-song [Buber includes vss. 4-5] views an
> historical action, from the exodus up until the
> successful occupation of the land, as a constant
> theophany whose stages it celebrates in the se-
> quence of events.[20]

If the framework of Deuteronomy 33 does in fact reflect an historical period of aggressive invasion of Canaan by Israel, the combination
of this with the imagery of the elevation of Yahweh and of his devotees
again points to the typology of exaltation. Moreover, this march of
Yahweh's from the South with Israel in tow clearly resembles Exod 15.13-
18: the two passages represent alternative literary formulations of
Yahweh's presence and guidance through the wilderness and into the land.

(4) Judges 5

As we have seen, Habakkuk 3, Deuteronomy 33, and Psalm 68 all contain a very similar motif of divine appearance. Although the motif occurs in very different literary contexts in each passage (eschatological
prophecy, collection of hymnic units, framework for a series of blessings), the larger units that contain the passages have a fundamental
point in common: none of the three allows us to penetrate with any
assurance to a particular historical event as the background or stimulus
for the work. On the other hand, the smaller epiphany passages point to
a general period stretching from the Wilderness March to the Conquest.
With Judges 5, not only do we have another parallel to the particular
formulation of divine appearance in the previous passages, but we also
have clear indications of a more specific historical situation behind
the text.

Before pursuing these issues any further, we must look more closely
at the motif of divine appearance in vss. 4-5:

> 4a Yahweh, when you went forth from Seir,
> b   When you marched from Edom's plain,

c The earth trembled,

d   How the heavens dripped![21]

e   How the clouds dripped water!

5a The mountains flowed,[22]

b   At the approach of[23] Yahweh, the One of Sinai,[24]

c   At the approach of Yahweh, the God of Israel.

Because of the comparatively early date of Judges 5,[25] it is tempting to see vss. 4-5 as the most original form of the motif of divine appearance among the parallels in Habakkuk 3, Deuteronomy 33, and Psalm 68. The latter in particular, with its use of *lpny* *ᶜmmk* (vs. 8) betrays the influence of the prose sources in Judges 4 and Exodus 14, etc. However, it is extremely speculative to posit an original literary form from which all others were developed.[26] It is much more likely that all of the parallel passages are dependent on a common store of ancient literary tradition and were shaped by their individual authors to fit a given context.

This brings us to the question of the place of vss. 4-5 in the entire poem. Despite the insistence of several scholars on the integral position of vss. 4-5,[27] it cannot be denied that both in form and content their present place is awkward, a characteristic that mirrors the often noted mosaic structure of the poem as a whole.[28] The explanation that these verses come here because of the primary importance of Yahweh's theophany for victory in holy war[29] does not effectively answer the question of why they were not used at the turning point of the story, i.e. vss. 20-21, where cosmic and natural elements are paramount. One radical proposal has been to see vss. 4-5 as part of a later, Yahwistic addition of psalmodic elements (essentially vss. 1-11) to an earlier epic account (vss. 12-30).[30] This offers an explanation for the confused, eclectic nature of vss. 1-11, but does not jibe at all with the study of early Hebrew poetry.[31] Perhaps a more reasonable literary interpretation is to see in vss. 4-5 a traditional incipit. This would explain its presence at the very beginning of the "song,"[32] would fit with the "fragment" interpretation of Psalm 68, and might reflect Mesopotamian hymnic influence (see below).

If Judg 5.4-5 comes from traditional poetic stock, it is also clear that it has been adapted both to events recounted and to literary elements later in the poem, especially vss. 20-21. It is more reasonable to see this adaptation as part of the original composition rather than as a later gloss. Vs. 4c-e depicts Yahweh's appearance as manifested in a thunderstorm[33] that makes the mountains flow with water (5a). This is quite complementary to the picture in vs. 21, where the Kishon sweeps away the enemy. This, the simplest interpretation of vs. 5a, lacks the serious difficulties often ascribed to it.[34] Moreover, there is an interesting parallel from the Exaltation of Inanna already quoted in ch. 1, (1) which demonstrates the malleability of such imagery:

> When you roar at the earth like Thunder, no vegetation
>   can stand up to you.
> A flood descending from its mountain,
> Oh foremost one, you are the Inanna of Heaven and
>   earth! (11. 10-12)

These lines from the Exaltation of Inanna are by no means the only parallel to the ancient Near Eastern material examined above. Albright long ago noted the general similarity in poetic style between the Tukulti-Ninurta Epic, Rameses II's Battle at Kadesh and Judges 5,[35] and his suggestion has been pursued by other scholars.[36] There is also a striking parallel between vs. 21 and a passage from one of the victory poems of Rameses III describing his defeat of the Libyans: "The stars of the *seshed*-constellation were frightful in pursuit of them."[37]

By far the most important parallels between Judges 5 and the Near Eastern texts, however, concern vss. 4-5. F. Stummer[38] long ago outlined the resemblance between these verses, their counterparts in Psalm 68 and Habakkuk 3, and in Sumerian hymns, especially to Šamaš (ki-^{d}Utu-kám). The latter are constructed according to the schema divine name/temporal determination/place of origin, and depict the going forth (*aṣû*, cf. Hebrew *yṣ'*) of the deity and the reverent fear this causes among the lesser gods and men. Stummer noted that at some point this pattern entered the Israelite cultural milieu from Mesopotamia, but that the sidereal aspects of the schema were repressed.

Stummer's work has been elaborated in much greater detail by E. Lipiński.[39] After an examination of both the Šamaš hymns and hymns to Adad, Lipiński concludes that Judg 5.4-5 is really a combination of the style of the former and the content of the latter, for the Adad hymn emphasizes the reaction of heavens, earth, and mountains, rather than the fear of the gods and men.[40] Excerpts from the two hymns, the first to Šamaš, the second to Adad, will show the cogency of Lipiński's

184

interpretation:

^{d}Šamaš ul-tu šadî^{i} rabî^{i} ina a-ṣi-ka . . .

ilāni^{meš} rabûti^{meš}ana di-ni iz-za-az-zu-ka . . .

a-me-lu-tum niše^{meš} pa-at gim-ri-ši-na ú-paq-qa-ka[41]

Šamaš, when you go forth from the great mountain, . . .

The great gods come to you for judgment, . . .

Mankind, all the people assembled, are turned toward you.

be-lum ina a-ga-gi-šú šá-mu-ú i-ta-na-ar-ra-ru-šu

^{d}Adad ina e-zi-zi-šú er-ṣe-tum i-na-as-su

šá-du-ú ra-bu-tu su-uḫ-ḫu[*sic*]-pu-šú[42]

The Lord, when he is angry, the heavens tremble before
    him,

Adad, when he rises in anger, the earth reels before
    him,

the great mountains sink down before him.

Lipiński also notes resemblances to the Adad hymn imagery in the Tukulti-
Ninurta Epic,[43] in the Amarna letters,[44] and in Ugaritic literature.[45]
Such imagery was, no doubt, widespread, yet the closest parallels to the
biblical texts, including Judg 5.4-5, lie in the hymnic material cited
above. We may thus conclude that the motifs of divine appearance in some
of Israel's earliest poetry--Judges 5, Psalm 68, Deuteronomy 33--reveal
the definite influence of Mesopotamian literary traditions. That this is
by no means limited to Mesopotamian *hymnic* texts will be demonstrated
more fully below.

Concerning the relation to the Mesopotamian hymnic tradition, one
final and tentative suggestion may be offered. William W. Hallo has
noted that "many, if not all of the neo-Sumerian hymns to deities were
perhaps originally commissioned together with statues, and first recited at their dedication."[46] Moreover, beyond such an original situation, the hymn was also recited at the great festivals when the statue
left its throne-dais and paraded in view.[47] Given the clear parallels
between Judg 5.4-5 and the Mesopotamian hymnic tradition, therefore, it
might be fruitful to pursue the possibility that this biblical hymnic
text was somehow connected with a cultic procession, perhaps even involving the ark (cf. Psalm 68). If this were the case, it would tie in

nicely with other biblical texts that speak of Yahweh's (and Israel's) march from Sinai to Canaan.[48]

In summary, we would conclude that Judg 5.4-5 must be read intact, without being pared down to an ostensible original form; that the verses stem from very ancient literary tradition reaching back ultimately to Mesopotamia; and that they were shaped in accordance with the author's view of the actual events involved in Israel's victory (vs. 21), which was apparently achieved in part as a result of a heavy thunderstorm.[49]

Before returning to the historical background of Judges 5 and the significance of Israel's victory, a brief look at Judges 4 is in order. Even a cursory reading of the text, especially with reference to a map, will show the confused and often absurd progress of the narrative.[50] It has been suggested that two stories have been combined, one dealing with Sisera, the other with Jabin,[51] and that the latter story has a parallel in Josh 11.1-9 (10-12).[52]

Our interest centers on the way in which the events of the battle may be inferred from the prose account, and in the particular language used for divine presence. Although it must remain speculative, and the text is still confused, Myers is probably correct in the following hypothesis:

> To meet the Israelites at Tabor, Sisera would have
> to cross the plain (vs. 13) turned into a temporary
> morass by a sudden rise of the Kishon (5:21), which
> ran parallel with the Carmel range from Megiddo to
> the sea.[53]

If this is the case, it would explain why Sisera abandoned his chariot, now mired in the mud (vs. 15b). The resultant picture, in fact, has intriguing similarities, both to the text of Exodus 14 and to various proposed suggestions about what happened at the Reed Sea. In Exod 14.25 it is reported that the Egyptian chariots became bogged down, causing them to flee. It is quite possible that this was also due to a thunderstorm, as many have suggested. It is also interesting that before each of these incidents we are told that Yahweh wreaked havoc (*hmm*) with Israel's foe (Judg 4.15a; Exod 14.24b).[54]

As for expressions of divine presence, Judges 4 uses motifs not found in ch. 5. Immediately after Deborah delivers Yahweh's oracle,

186

Barak insists that the prophetess herself go along with him to battle.[55]
As Myers suggests,

> The accompaniment of the prophetess was designed to
> assure the presence of the Lord and thus lend en-
> couragement to leader and troops.[56]

Even more impressive is the occurrence of the vanguard motif in vs. 14.
At the very moment of battle, Deborah commands Barak to rise up against
the foe, who Yahweh has given into his hand--"for does not Yahweh go
forth in front of you?" The imagery is clearly similar to that which
we have seen in the Near Eastern material in Part 1. Moreover, it is
significant that this motif does not occur in Judges 5.[57] This presents
another correspondence to Exodus 14: there, as here, in a prose account
of events that are also told in poetic form (Exodus 15/Judges 5), the
narrator uses the expression $hlk/y\d{s}'$ $lpny$, an expression not found in
the poetic account.

We must now return to the question of the historical background
of Judges 4-5. Our studies in the Near Eastern material and our literary
analysis of these chapters leads us to disagree with the cultic interpretation espoused by Weiser and Beyerlin.[58] They see Judges 5 in particular as a liturgical composition for the cultic celebration, not simply
of military victory, but also of *renewed* inter-tribal solidarity of Israel as Yahweh's people. Instead, we would understand Judges 5 primarily
under the rubric of a victory song or epic poem, and, with Lipiński,[59]
find no connection with cultic renewal of the covenant or with the Sinai
traditions in the strict sense.[60] This, of course, does not mean that
the poem could not have been sung at cultic occasions, perhaps even involving a procession.

If the evidence for covenant renewal is unconvincing, there is
some merit in seeing behind Judges 4-5 a new *stage* of inter-tribal solidarity. Such has been argued recently by A. D. H. Mayes.[61] In a critique of the amphictyonic hypothesis of Martin Noth, Mayes concludes that
the evidence for the existence of such a tribal union in the premonarchial
period is extremely weak. This is especially true concerning the sup-
posed central sanctuaries, the office of judge, and warfare.[62] However,
Mayes finds a major exception, particularly to the latter category, in
the battle with Sisera. "Here, for the first time, in the period of the
judges, a federation of tribes appears."[63] Mayes thus concludes that,

although there may well have been a consciousness of unity among the tribes before this late stage of the judges period, it did not take the form of an amphictyony or other federation.[64] In place of the amphictyonic hypothesis, he prefers to

> trace the main stages by which the tribes gradually
> came together until they appear as an active unit in
> the time of Saul. The first stage is the battle
> against Sisera which marks the end of the power of
> the city-states to obstruct common action by the
> northern and mid-Palestinian tribes. The second
> stage is the expulsion of the Philistines from
> the mountains in the time of Saul, which opened
> the way for communication between Judah and its
> northern neighbours.[65]

(It is of further interest that the evidence for the second stage under Saul--1 Samuel 14[66]--also presents several interesting connections with divine presence in warfare.[67])

Mayes' analysis adds further support to what we feel is already a proper interpretation on the basis of the text of Judges 4-5. As with much of the Near Eastern evidence adduced previously, we once again have a concentration of motifs of divine presence in conjunction with a crucial military encounter, out of which the victor emerged as a newly established political power. It is reasonable to see as a result of this event a new sense of tribal, if not even national, unity, correlated with an affirmation of the supremacy of Yahweh.[68] This correlation bears a clear resemblance to the typology of exaltation as we have seen it in the Near Eastern sources.

In conclusion, some comparisons between the "classic epiphany texts" and Exod 15.13-17 are in order. Three of the classic texts (in Judges 5, Deuteronomy 33, and Psalm 68) combine a description of Yahweh's advent from the South with allusions to the Conquest of Canaan. This combination is very similar to that in Exodus 15B, which describes Israel's march from the Reed Sea, through the wilderness, and into Canaan. However, there is a significant difference in the language used. In the classic texts, Yahweh's advent or "going forth" is described by bw', zrh, ys', $s^c d$, whereas in Exodus 15 Yahweh's presence is implied more indirectly by *nḥh, nhl*, and *'ymth, pḥd*. Moreover, in the classic texts, Yahweh's action is accompanied by *cosmic* reactions, and, as we have seen, the texts are thus similar to the Mesopotamian hymns to Šamaš. Exodus 15B, on the other hand, focuses on the approach of the *people* Israel, and the reaction is not that of cosmic entities but of the *nations* of Canaan. This we have argued is similar to the picture in the Tukulti-Ninurta Epic and other texts. We would thus suggest that the classic texts and Exodus 15B contain *alternative* literary traditions for the same events, or better, the same era. The analogies to the Šamaš hymns and the Tukulti-Ninurta Epic have further implications. The latter appears to have adapted a hymnic motif from the former type and applied it in an epic context focusing on the human king rather than on the deity and likening the cosmic reactions to those of the king's enemies.[69] The same adaptive process may well be present in Exodus 15B.[70]

Finally, concerning the development of early Old Testament traditions, it is interesting that both Exodus 15 *and* the classic texts are unanimous in seeing the *people* as the central human character within the typology of exaltation. Here there is a profound difference, not only to the Near Eastern material, but also to the prose traditions of the Old Testament, where an individual hero figure plays such a dominant role.

NOTES TO CHAPTER 9

WILDERNESS MARCH AND CONQUEST--

THE "CLASSIC EPIPHANY TEXTS"

[1]Robertson, *Linguistic Evidence*, 33-34.

[2]"The Psalm of Habakkuk," in *Studies in Old Testament Prophecy*, ed. H. H. Rowley (T. H. Robinson *Festschrift*; Society for Old Testament Study; Edinburgh: T. & T. Clark, 1946) 8-9.

[3]See the convenient summary of the debate on this point by Miller, *Divine Warrior*, 102-103. He is in basic agreement with the "fragment" approach of Albright. The chief opponent of this is S. Mowinckel [*Der achtundsechzigste Psalm* (ANVAO II, Hist.-Filos. Klasse, No. 1; Oslo: Dybwad, 1953) 22], who sees the Psalm as a hymnic work unified around the description of a cultic festival--the enthronement festival. Even he admits that the composition is not conventional and consists of "a series of impressionistic images" reflecting the procession of the ark.

[4]Cf. the discussion of Kraus, *Worship in Israel*, 208-218.

[5]Pax, *Epiphaneia*, 100.

[6]Mowinckel (*achtundsechzigste Psalm*, 53), in fact, argues for an original composition of the Psalm during the period of Benjamite hegemony under Saul, which would clearly fit well with the exaltation typology.

[7]*Linguistic Evidence*, 128.

[8]*Divine Warrior*, 75-87.

[9]*Ibid.*, 80.

[10]"Deux documents inédits du désert de Juda," *Biblica* 38 (1957) 254, n. 3.

[11]Milik (*Ibid.*, 252-254) would read the third tricolon as follows: "All the holy ones of God (literally, of him) are close to you,/They surge at your rear (literally, at your feet),/they fall in line behind you." Cf. Miller, *Divine Warrior*, 81 and n. 46.

[12]The shift to the second person form of address is probably accidental; cf. F. M. Cross and D. N. Freedman, "The Blessing of Moses," *JBL* 67 (1948) 200, n. 15.

[13]This suggestion has been made to me in a private communication by Prof. S. Dean McBride, Jr.

[14]This is the usual ordering of the verses in the "frame song." It is quite possible that vs. 5 intervenes, on which see below. For another rather speculative solution, see Miller, *Divine Warrior*, 83-84, and his citation of I. L. Seeligmann.

[15]The suffixes in this tricolon should all be third person. On $g'h$ see our comments above on Exodus 15.

[16]Despite differences in translation, the conclusions of T. H. Gaster ["An Ancient Eulogy on Israel: Deuteronomy 33.3-5, 26-29," *JBL* 66 (1947) 57-59] concerning the point of vss. 3-5, 26-29 fit well with the exaltation typology. He sees this as a eulogy which glorifies Israel as the supreme leader of the nations to which all turn for guidance. However, our translation necessitates a dual glorification, first of Yahweh, then of Israel.

[17]*Divine Warrior*, 82. But see Lipiński, *Royauté de Yahwé*, 215, n. 5.

[18]See Miller, *Divine Warrior*, 218, n. 48.

[19]*Ibid.*, n. 50 on the reconstruction following T. H. Gaster, which we would accept here. On *ygrš lpnk* in vs. 27 note the parallel in the Moabite stone, 1. 19 (see above).

[20]*Kingship of God*, 131, followed by Jeremias, *Theophanie*, 127-128, 130. Cf. also Miller, *Divine Warrior*, 78.

[21]Various commentators have felt *ntp* to be inappropriate. See the discussion of Miller (*Divine Warrior*, 223, n. 74), who retains the MT. The most ingenious and radical suggestion comes from E. Lipiński ["Juges 5, 4-5 et Psaume 68,8-11," *Biblica* 48 (1967) 193], who reads *nātū* from *nwṭ* ("reel, stagger") and takes the *p* as a Northern dialectical conjunction which is attached to 5a, thus omitting 4e as an explanatory gloss for 4d. While Lipiński's exegesis of the entire passage yields a neat structure of 3-3, 2-2-2, 2-2-2 (the latter by omitting the first *yhwh* in 5b), his method is based primarily on a rigid application of form-critical comparisons with Mesopotamian hymnic texts (see below) which we feel is unjustified. Cf. the comments of Alexander Globe, "The Text and Literary Structure of Judges 5,4-5," *Biblica* 55 (1974) 173-174, and 176, n. 2.

[22]For the suggestions using *zll* here, see Miller, *Divine Warrior* 224, n. 75 (Miller himself translates "streamed"). Lipiński ("Juges 5", 197) insists on reading *nzl* but asserts that the original sense is "to fall, descend, be flattened." This too is influenced by his reading of the Mesopotamian texts. On his refusal to admit any sense of "flowing" for *nzl* here (196), see below on the line from the Exaltation of Inanna.

[23]"at the approach of" for *mpny*, literally "from before."

[24]On this epithet and the metrical problems in the verse, see Miller, *Divine Warrior*, 224, n. 76; also Cross, *CMHE* 20, n. 44.

[25]Robertson, *Linguistic Evidence*, 31-32. He concurs with others who date the poem toward the end of the 12th century, second only to Exodus 15; see 154-155. Cf. also Alexander Globe, "The Literary Structure and Unity of the Song of Deborah," *JBL* 93 (1974) 509-511 (apparently unaware of Robertson), and Freedman, "Early Israelite History," 13.

[26]This is the problem with the methodology of Jeremias (see above in the Introduction) and Lipiński ("Juges 5," passim). The latter has quite rightly emphasized the parallels between the biblical material in question and hymnic texts from Mesopotamia. Like Jeremias, however, he insists on a rigid correspondence of formal elements over a wide geographical and historical area. See his use of Mesopotamian parallels to the exclusion of Egyptian examples in his reconstruction of vss. 4-5, *Ibid.*, 186, 189-190.

[27]For example, Jeremias (*Theophanie*, 142-144), followed by Miller, *Divine Warrior*, 91.

[28]Miller, *Divine Warrior*, 87; Freedman, "Early Israelite History," 24, n. 8; 15, n. 63. Cf. G. Gerleman, "The Song of Deborah in the Light of Stylistics," *VT* 1 (1951) 171, 180; K. G. Rendtorff cited in Lipiński, *Royauté de Yahwé*, 81.

[29]Miller, *Divine Warrior*, 91; Lipiński, "Juges 5," 200.

[30]H.-P. Müller, "Der Aufbau des Deboraliedes," *VT* 16 (1966) 446-459.

[31]According to Robertson (*Linguistic Evidence*, 32) the only real resemblance to later standard Hebrew vis-a-vis verbal patterns in the poem is in vs. 28 (and this part of Müller's original epic!). Similar, though less precise, results are found for the use of other syntactical and morphological forms (148-150, 153-155). Note also the strictures on the basis of style in 2nd millennium victory odes suggested by Globe, "Song of Deborah," 499 and 508.

[32]Vs. 4 follows immediately after the singer's introductory exclamation in vs. 3. Note the similarities to Exod 15.1 ("Then Moses and the children of Israel sang this song . . . I will sing") and cf. Judg 5.1 ("And Deborah and Barak . . . sang on that day"); also Deut 33.1.

[33]Here, as elsewhere, it is just as reasonable to interpret the shaking of the earth as the effect of thunder as it is to insist on an earthquake.

[34]Although *nzl* may not have the connotation of "gushing," this does not mean that "to flow" is inappropriate, nor do we need to resort to volcanic phenomena for an explanation. For an example of these alleged difficulties, see Lipiński, "Juges 5," 196. On vs. 5 as referring to the thunderstorm as Yahweh's means of intervention in the battle, cf. Alexander Globe, "Song of Deborah," 504; also "Text and Structure," 174-175.

[35]W. F. Albright, "The Song of Deborah in the Light of Archaeology," *BASOR* 62 (1936) 26-27; cf. also his "Psalm of Habakkuk," 5.

[36]Jacob M. Myers, *The Book of Judges* (*IB*, II; New York: Abingdon, 1953) 718. Myers compares vs. 21 with a line from the battle scene passage of the Tukulti-Ninurta Epic: "'Adad, the hero, drove down a flood against their fighting line'" (726). P. C. Craigie ["The Song of Deborah and the Epic of Tukulti-Ninurta," *JBL* 88 (1969) 253-265] has attempted to show considerably more parallels both in content and literary aspects. Most of these, however, are highly questionable, e.g. the covenant relationship between Israel and Yahweh and Tukulti-Ninurta and his god, or the comparison between the roles of Deborah and Ishtar. Along with the latter, more convincing parallels have most recently been suggested by Globe, "Song of Deborah," 496-499.

[37]John A. Wilson, "The Language of the Historical Texts Commemorating Rameses III" (Medinet Habu Studies, 1928/29; Oriental Institute Communications, 7; Chicago: University of Chicago Press, 1930) 27. Wilson comments: "We have been given, as it were, a prototype of the song of Deborah . . . ," citing vs. 21. On the same Egyptian text, cf. also Myers, *Judges*, 726. For the imagery cf. Rameses III as the "warrior like the shooting-stars in heaven," Breasted, *Ancient Records* IV, §62, p. 36, and "He sends arrow upon arrow like shooting-stars," §91. A number of other motifs from Egyptian texts, especially those recounting the campaigns of Thutmose III at Megiddo and Rameses II at Kadesh, could be included in our study, but it has not proved feasible to do so.

[38]Friedrich Stummer, *Sumerisch-akkadische Parallelen zum Aufbau alttestamentlicher Psalmen* (Paderborn: F. Schöningh, 1922) 40-46.

[39]*Royauté de Yahwé*, especially 187-209; "Juges 5," 186-187.

[40]*Royauté de Yahwé*, 198. It should be noted, however, that the Adad text, which is quoted more fully in *Ibid.*, 198-199 than in "Juges 5," 187, also includes the reaction of the gods, including Šamaš and Sin. Thus Lipiński's "triade" is not as fixed formally as he implies. At any rate, the permutations of these hymnic schemas both in Mesopotamian texts and in the biblical examples do not permit us to reconstruct a text such as Judg 5.4-5 with the certainty that Lipiński assumes.

[41]The text according to Lipiński, *Royauté de Yahwé*, 190-191, 11.2, 10, 14.

[42]*Ibid.*, 198, 11. 10, 12, 14. (This is a bilingual text, hence the omission of the intervening lines.)

[43]*Ibid.*, 199, quoting 1. 6 from the "Hymn of Praise" to Tukulti-Ninurta presented in our ch. 1, (3).

[44]*Ibid.*, the reference to Pharaoh whose voice makes the land tremble, as with Adad's voice. Cf. Cross, *CMHE*, 150-151.

[45]"Juges 5," 191-193. The Ugaritic material, of course, has been treated most extensively by Cross, *CMHE*, ch. 7.

[46]"Cultic Setting," 120.

[47]*Ibid.*, 120-121.

[48]Cf. especially Deut 33.2a (*yhwh mssyny b'*) with the climax of the Gudea Cylinders--"Ningirsu came from Eridu."

[49]So also Globe, "Text and Structure," 176, and see n. 2 on Psalm 68.

[50]The most glaring example is the flight of Sisera on foot reported in vs. 17, which, according to the locations given must have been some forty miles!

[51]Myers, *Judges*, 712-715.

[52]Müller, "Aufbau," 452.

[53]*Judges*, 713. Note however that in vs. 14b Barak descends from Mt. Tabor, which is some fifteen miles to the Northeast of Megiddo. It is also puzzling that the storm is not mentioned explicitly in ch. 4, but this may be due to a deliberate emphasis on Yahweh's role in the battle; cf. with Exodus 14 above.

[54]On this cf. Exod 23.27; 1 Sam 7.10; Ps 18.15.

[55]On this cf. Exod 33.12. Given the fact that the latter concerns Israel's march to Canaan, the contexts are not dissimilar.

[56]*Judges*, 714.

[57]The closest resemblance, of course, is with 5.4a. Although both passages probably have the same thought in mind, i.e. Yahweh's coming from Seir means his fighting in Israel's vanguard, the expressions themselves are not to be equated. For the use of *yṣ'*, see Appendix 2.

[58]For references and further details see above, in the Introduction.

[59]*Royauté de Yahwé*, 254.

[60]*Ibid.* He rightly points out that 5.4 refers to Sinai only as the place

from which Yahweh comes for battle. So already G. A. Smith [*The Early Poetry of Israel* (Schweich Lectures, 1910; London: Oxford, 1912) 83], who remarks that Judg 5.4-5, like other early poems, "describes a Theophany in the usual form of a thunderstorm, not that which took place on Sinai at the giving of the law, but Yahweh marches from His dwelling on the mountains of the south to help His people in this fresh crisis . . . ."

[61]"Israel in the Pre-Monarchy Period," *VT* 23 (1973) 151-170. See now his *Israel in the Period of the Judges* (Studies in Biblical Theology, Second Series, 29; Naperville: Allenson, 1974), ch. 3.

[62]"Pre-Monarchy Period," 157-165.

[63]*Ibid.*, 166. This is only a ten-tribe confederation. The absence of Judah (and Simeon, which was absorbed by Judah) is explained as due to that tribe's political and geographical isolation from the middle and Northern tribes, 168.

[64]*Ibid.*, 167.

[65]*Ibid.*, 170.

[66]*Ibid.*

[67]Note the divine terror referred to in vs. 15 and especially the phrase "and the earth trembled." Several LXX readings for the very confused vs. 18 may indicate the use of the ark and/or ephod as a symbol of divine presence, perhaps even going before (*lpny*) the people. Note also the summary phrase in vs. 23a which is exactly the same as Exod 14.30a, on which see above.

[68]See now the conclusion of Globe ("Song of Deborah," 508-509) that an early date for the poem (he settles on c. 1200, p. 512) means that "we can trace the mixture of national and religious feeling (so characteristic of later Israel) back to the earliest stages of the settlement in Canaan." Note, however, the much more cautious suggestions of Rudolf Smend [*Yahweh War and Tribal Confederation* (New York: Abingdon, 1970), ch. 1], who reckons with an 'amphictyonic will' (borrowed from Buber) expressed in the Song of Deborah, but is reluctant to go much further. Cf. also Freedman, "Early Israelite History," 15.

[69]Cf. also the three examples of a "paean of self-glorification of Inanna" and its use in the Nur-Adad Letter, cited above, p. 35.

[70]Lipiński (*Royauté*, 202-206) has attempted to divide the major biblical texts dealing with epiphany into two typologies, one parallel to the Sumero-akkadian hymns as above, the other of a descriptive, narrative, or epic character. For the latter he appeals to an incantation text concerning the opening of the door of heaven by Šamaš, the passage from the Gilgamesh epic quoted in our Appendix 1, 1., and the Ugaritic text relating Baal's shouting from the window of his palace (*CTCA* 4.7.25-37). The distinction between hymnic and epic literary traditions is cogent, and most of the Akkadian literary texts presented in our ch. 1 add more extensive examples of the latter. While it must be observed that the "Hymn of Praise" to Tukulti-Ninurta reveals a blend of hymnic and epic style, the distinction between the two may be the reason for the pronounced difference in language between certain Old Testament poetic and prose texts. The most obvious example of this difference lies in the use of the vanguard motif in the form of *hlk lpny* or the equivalent by

the prose texts relating the Wilderness March (cf. Akkadian epic and annalistic texts), whereas the poetic texts describing the same march (predominantly of Yahweh himself--Judg 5.4-5; Habakkuk 3--but also including the people--Exodus 15; Deuteronomy 33) do not use this particular literary expression (but cf. Ps. 68.8 [influenced by the prose/epic tradition?] and Hab 3.5 [without human participants]).

CHAPTER 10

THE JORDAN RIVER

The complicated story of the crossing of the Jordan has occupied
scholars for years. The problems are very similar to those we have seen
in Exod 23.20-33; 32; 33, both in the complexity of the material and in
the extensive redactional activity that shaped it. As will become evident, these two groups of traditions also share a number of interesting
literary and theological characteristics which, in turn, involve Exodus
13-14 and the framework of Deuteronomy.

(1) The Early Narrative

Despite the complexity of the text, it seems fairly clear from recent studies that Joshua 1; 3-5 contains older narrative material, which
has been critically expanded by the deuteronomistic editor.[1] The deuteronomistic narrative itself was then surcharged with a number of further
redactional expansions. Essentially, the older narrative contained 1.10-
11; 3.1-4, 9-11, 13-16 (delete vs. 15b).[2] In this account Joshua[3] orders
the "officers of the people" (*šoterê hāʿām*) to have them make provisions
for the crossing of the Jordan, which will take place in three days. In
3.1-4 Joshua and the people move from Shittim to the banks of the Jordan.
After three days the officers go through the camp and instruct the people
about the process to be used in the crossing. The people are to follow
behind the ark borne by the priests,[4] maintaining a very respectful distance.[5] By following the ark they will know the direction in which they
are to go. In vss. 9-11, Joshua describes the imminent sign[6] of the
presence of "El Ḥay in your midst"--the ark will cross over before the
people, and when the feet of its bearers[7] touch the river, the waters
will be cut off. Vss. 14-16 then describe the enaction of the preceding
words and conclude with the people crossing over next to Jericho.

One interesting aspect of this account is the way in which the role of Joshua is almost balanced by that of the "officers" ($\check{s}\bar{o}t^e r\hat{\imath}m$). The initial cultic instructions are given by the latter, and Joshua assumes a commanding role afterwards. Clearly the central focus of the narrative, however, is neither on the officers nor on Joshua, but on the ark.[8] Once again we meet an example of the vanguard motif, when the ark "passes over in front of" the people ($^c\bar{o}b\bar{e}r$ $lipn\hat{e}kem$, vs. 11).[9] As a physical representation of divine presence, it is also understood as a means of guidance: by its progression the people will know "the way" ($hddrk$) to go (3.4). This, clearly, resembles the role of the ark in Num 10.33, 35-36, as well as that of the cloud (^cnn) and the divine messenger ($ml'k$) elsewhere.

Alongside the use of the vanguard motif, the story of the Jordan crossing also has a strong resemblance to the cultic texts we have examined in the Near Eastern material. As in the latter, we have a processional march that is led by a physical representation of the presence of the deity. The analogy supports the hypothesis that Joshua 3-5 is the description of an actual cultic procession that was celebrated repeatedly at Gilgal.[10] There is also a substantial connection with ch. 6, where the ark procession plays a primary role in the ritualistic commencement of Israel's Holy War. Indeed, it is possible to view the ark processional as the unifying factor in chs. 3-6.[11] We shall return to this at the end of this section.

Along with the vanguard motif and the procession of the divine "standard," the narrative also contains an adumbration of the exaltation typology. In the proposed account this is represented only by the rare epithet "Lord of all the land" ($'dwn$ $kl-h'r\underset{.}{s}$; 3.11, 13).[12] The title has been interpreted cogently by Lipinski as a reference to Yahweh as the victor and lord over the gods of the defeated populations of Canaan.[13] Following this lead, Langlamet sees the epithet as the means for a cultic reaffirmation of Israel's legitimate right to the land.[14] This interpretation is supported by the later expansions in 4.24; 5.1 (2.9-11), which are discussed below. In sum, the connection linking the ark as a physical representation of divine presence, the use of vanguard terminology, and the epithet of Yahweh as Lord of the land points once again to the typology of exaltation. Yahweh's lordship over Canaan is to be administered by his people, Israel.

(2) The Deuteronomistic Redaction

If the foregoing and extremely tentative literary analysis produced

197

a straightforward account, this is certainly not the case with the rest
of the material in chs. 1; 3-5. Indeed, to separate strands in the remaining verses with any assurance is extremely difficult. It is likely
that the original story has gone through at least one,[15] and possibly
two,[16] deuteronomistic redactions, along with subsequent editing.[17]
Nevertheless, for the purposes of our topic, the results of this redactional activity can be examined simultaneously.

One of the most noticeable changes in the redactional material is
the emphasis on motifs of divine presence and the way in which this accentuates the exaltation of Yahweh. The role of the ark provides a
salient example. In the proposed earlier account, the ark preceded the
people across the Jordan, guiding them on their way. In the redactional
material this is changed, literally, in midstream. Now the priestly
bearers halt in the middle of the river and wait there until all the
people finish crossing (3.8, 17; 4.10a). This is cearly incompatible
with the earlier account, which contained the admonition to keep the
people far behind the ark so that its function of guidance would not be
impaired.[18] One effect of this change seems to be to emphasize the importance of the ark as a representation of divine presence. This is
especially clear in 4.15-18, where, the moment the priests' feet touch
the western bank, the river dramatically returns to its usual flow.
The miraculous aspect of the event is thus heightened and tied more explicitly to the mysterious power of the ark.[19]

The passage that follows 4.15-18 and now closes the story of the
crossing (vss. 20-24) is remarkable in a number of ways. It makes explicit reference to the crossing[20] of the Reed Sea in Exodus 14, with
which it shares various terminology.[21] The typological relationship
that is drawn between the two events also corresponds to the similarity
between the use of the *Kinderfrage* here and in Exodus 12.25-27; 13.14-15.
Yet for us, the most interesting aspect is the way in which this material
is tied to the exaltation of Yahweh that is implicit in the earlier account. Thus the passage ends with this pregnant purpose clause (vs. 24):

> so that all the peoples of the earth may recognize the
> power of Yahweh, for it is mighty; so that you may fear
> Yahweh your God for all time.

This closing proclamation is highly reminiscent of the end of the Reed
Sea story (Exod 14.31) and the finale to the Sinai experience (20.20),

198

both of which instill the fear of Yahweh in the people.

The reference to the recognition of Yahweh's power by other nations in 4.24 is not the only indication of his exaltation. The terse report in 5.1 serves as a transition between the Jordan crossing and the Conquest, which, properly, begins in ch. 6. In this verse the ruling powers of Canaan melt in fear on hearing the report of Israel's miraculous crossing of the Jordan.[22] The same reaction is told in expanded fashion in 2.9-11, where the exaltation of Yahweh is fervently avowed (vs. 11b):

> for Yahweh your God himself is God in heaven above
> and on earth below.

With this may be compared Deut 2.25, which buttresses Yahweh's first command to Joshua to attack the nations in Israel's path:

> this very day I shall begin to place the dread and
> fear of you before the peoples under the whole
> heaven, who shall hear ($y\check{s}m^c wn$) the report of you
> and tremble ($wrgzw$) and shudder ($wh̲lw$) before you.

Both the imagery in these passages and the fact that they depict the reaction of the inhabitants of Canaan to Israel's approach are strikingly analogous to the picture of Israel's march in Exod 15.13-16. With the above passage, compare especially vs. 14: $\check{s}m^c w \, ^cmmym \, yrgzwn \, / \, h̲yl \, 'h̲z$ $y\check{s}by \, pl\check{s}t$, and note the similarity between Josh 2.9 ($npl h \, 'ymtkm \, ^clynw$) and Exodus 15.16 ($tpl \, ^clyhm \, 'ymth \, wph̲d$).[23] In short, with this bracket to the Jordan crossing in 5.1 we are again dealing with the march of triumphant Israel, and with the exaltation that this brings to her and her God.

The inflation of motifs of divine presence in the deuteronomistic redaction is by no means restricted to the exaltation of Yahweh alone. We have seen that in the prose narratives of the exodus, the exaltation typology vacillated primarily between Yahweh and Moses. The same holds true here for Joshua. In 1.3-9 in particular, motifs of divine presence and guidance abound in Yahweh's encouragement to Israel's new leader.[24] The literary and contextual correspondence between this passage and a number of texts studied above is impressive. In vss. 1-2 we are already dealing with Moses as the familiar $^cbd \, yhwh$ and Joshua as $m\check{s}rt$ $m\check{s}h.$[25] Vss. 3-9 then introduce a number of characteristics akin to Exod 23.20-33. The situations are obviously similar: each text concerns a

major turning point in Israel's long journey. More specifically, each
includes a divine promise that the enemies of Israel will be defeated
(1.5 and 3.10 / Exod 23.28), a description of Israel's future borders
(1.3-4 / 23.31), a pledge of divine presence (1.5, 9 / 23.20, 27-28),
and an exhortation concerning obedience (1.7-8 / 23.21-26).

As we shall see, it is significant that the form of divine presence
in Exodus 23 (the *ml'k*) is not mentioned here. However, it *is*--almost
certainly--a figure that appears in 5.13-15 (not D), "the commander of
the hosts of Yahweh" (*śr-ṣb'-yhwh*).[26] This passage is clearly a trun-
cated example of the call narrative, is very similar to Exod 3.1-6, and
originally related the formal commissioning of Joshua. It is, likewise,
related to Judg 2.1a, where the *ml'k yhwh* goes up from Gilgal to Bochim.
Both texts are thus strategically placed at the moment when Israel is
poised for the Conquest. But, whereas Josh 5.13-15 now is merged with
the stunning victory in ch. 6, Judg 2.1a is joined to vss. 1b-5, which
admonish Israel for covenant transgression in terms very similar to
Exod 23.20-33.[27]

In Josh 1.5-9 the promised divine presence is not that of the *ml'k*
but of Yahweh himself, and this is explicitly compared to Moses (vss.
5b, 9b):

> *k'šr hyyty ᶜm-mšh   hyh ᶜmmk, l' 'rpk wl' 'ᶜzbk*
> *ky ᶜmmk yhwh 'lhyk bkl 'šr tlk*

as I was with Moses so I will be with you; I will
not desert or forsake you, for Yahweh your God is
with you everywhere you go.

The comparison reaches beyond Moses (Exod 3.12), however, for we have
seen this language (especially the use of *ᶜm*) previously. A review of
the divine promise to Jacob--again at a point of departure--shows that
the Deuteronomist is an heir to much older literary convention:

> *hnh 'nky ᶜmmk*
> *wšmrtyk bkl 'šr tlk . . .*
> *ky l' 'ᶜzbk . . .* (Gen 28.15)[28]

Behold I will be with you,
And I will keep you wherever you go . . .
For I will not forsake you . . . .

200

Perhaps the most interesting aspect of Josh 1.3-9 is the way in which the Deuteronomist has both appropriated and enriched the motif of divine guidance. We saw that in Exod 23.20-33 there were indications that covenant obedience played an increasingly important role in keeping Israel "in line." In this sense Israel's keeping[29] the commandments constituted a synergism for the protective guidance of the divine messenger. This intimation of Torah as a form of divine guidance comes to full bloom in Josh 1.3-9. Immediately following the promise of divine presence, Yahweh adds this admonition:

> Only be strong and very steadfast in keeping the
> observance (*lšmr* *l^cśwt*) of all the Torah which
> Moses my servant commanded you. Do not turn to
> the left or to the right, so that you may prosper
> (*tṣlyḥ*) wherever you go. (8) This book of the
> Torah shall not depart (*lō'-yāmûš*) from your
> mouth, and you shall meditate on it day and
> night (*yômām wālay^elāh*), so that you may keep
> the observance of all that is written in it,
> for then you shall make your way prosperous,
> and then you shall succeed (vss. 7-8).

In these sonorous lines "the way," which, throughout Exodus and Numbers was almost always a geographical reference, has now become a metaphor-- "the Way." This is no actual path from which Joshua is not to turn, but the Way of Torah, and it is through his obedience that he will "prosper." In the Patriarchal stories, divine presence (*^cimmkā*, etc.) was almost automatically accompanied by prosperity (*ṣlḥ*, *śkl*).[30] Now obedience is explicitly the condition for the realization of the benefits of that presence.[31] Also, the Deuteronomist is here undoubtedly under the influence of treaty language, as we can see once again from the treaty between Mattiwaza, king of Mittani, and Suppiluliuma, king of Ḫatti, already discussed in the Excursus above:

> Thus (says) Mattiwaza, the king's son, and thus (say)
> the Hurri people: If we keep this treaty and oath
> . . . , may the gods whose names we invoke go with us,
> make us great, protect us, and do good for us. As
> lord may Mattiwaza go in front. Under his protection

we wish to consume a rich harvest.

Moreover, the picture here of Mattiwaza, the vassal king, "going in front" is remarkably similar to that of Joshua who "crosses over before" the people (see below).

For the Deuteronomist, the Torah has, in effect, become the divine guide to supersede those colorful agents from Israel's remote past. This is brought out in a stunning way when we compare the above lines from Joshua to the ancient paradigm of divine guidance found in Exod 13.21-22. There Yahweh goes in front of the people in the pillar of cloud and fire, and, like the Torah, it does not depart ($l\bar{o}'$-$y\bar{a}m\hat{\imath}\check{s}$), but remains day and night ($y\hat{o}m\bar{a}m$. . . $w^{e}lay^{e}l\bar{a}h$). Similarly, in Exod 23.20-21, it is Yahweh's $ml'k$ who goes before the people and to whom they are answerable. In a very creative way, the Deuteronomist has appropriated this language and adapted it to fit his covenant theology. Now it is in following Torah that one will know the way in which to go.[32] Now it is with the statutes that Israel's distinctiveness among the nations is so closely tied, and with which the nearness of Yahweh's presence is associated (Deut 4.5-8; cf. Exod 33.16; Num 14.14). The Deuteronomist could also accept the guidance of the ark under a similar rubric, for in his view, at least, the ark was the receptacle of the tablets of the Torah.[33] Thus, as S. Dean McBride has suggested, although the ark was clearly redefined by the deuteronomistic school, it was, nonetheless, still connected with divine presence. Indeed, the tablets themselves are now "the immediate manifestation of divine indwelling in Israel's midst."[34]

The fact that in 1.3-9, Joshua is the spiritual and political successor to Moses and the recipient of the promise of divine presence, indicates that he is already being exalted in the same way as was his mentor. This is bolstered by several verses from Deuteronomy that employ the vanguard motif and again demonstrate the close correlation between Yahweh and his chosen leader. In 3.28 Yahweh commands Moses to "commission Joshua . . . for he will cross over in front of this people."[35] In 9.3 the people are promised that "Yahweh your God *himself* is about to cross over in front of you—he is a devouring fire."[36] Thus, as Langlamet has observed, here a theophany serves the same function as does the ark in Joshua 3.[37] Finally, in 31.3, after Moses' admission that he can no longer "go out and come in" himself (i.e. function as military leader), both Yahweh and Joshua are combined as subjects of the same imagery: "Yahweh himself is about to cross over in front of you . . . ; Joshua himself is about to cross over in front of you . . . ."[38] This predication of the vanguard motif to Joshua is a splendid illustration of his apotheosis. We would suggest that this correlation of divine and human vanguard is strikingly similar to that used for the Assyrian kings (cf. again Tukulti-Ninurta), and that this adds weight to the argument of those who see a royal background for the "transmission of office" pattern, and Joshua himself as, in part, a royal figure.[39]

Still, the most distinctive elucidation of the theme of exaltation lies in the story of the Jordan crossing itself. In 3.7 and 4.14-- immediately before and after[40] the dramatic event of Israel's entrance into the land--the Deuteronomist has Yahweh pledge and then fulfill a promise to elevate Joshua to the revered position of Moses:

> Then Yahweh said to Joshua: "This very day I will
> begin to exalt you (*gaddelkā*)[41] in the eyes of all
> Israel, that they may know that as I was with Moses,
> I will be with you."

> That very day Yahweh exalted Joshua in the eyes of
> all Israel; and they feared him as they feared Moses,
> all the days of his life.

In short, the story of the crossing of the Jordan in the deuteronomistic redaction ends by making precisely the same point that was made at the close of the story of the Reed Sea--the exaltation of Yahweh and of his chosen representative:

> Then Israel saw the great power which Yahweh had
> wrought against Egypt, and the people feared Yahweh,
> and they believed in Yahweh, and in Moses his ser-
> vant (Exod 14.31).

One final point deserves mention. In our investigation of Exod 13.21-22; 23-34 and Numbers 9-10, we observed that the motifs of divine presence were clustered in these pericopes because each one was concerned with a common overriding issue--Israel's departure on another stage of her journey. We also noticed that the redactional framework for Exodus 13 and Numbers 9 was built around the observance of the Passover. Both

of these points are present in Joshua 1; 3-5. That Israel is now setting out on another exciting and dangerous epoch of her history is indubitable. Moreover, the transitional character of this departure--
the end of the wilderness journey, the beginning of the conquest--is
imaginatively blended with the observance of Passover in 5.10-12. After
crossing the Jordan, on the verge of their perilous entrance into the
land, the people keep the ancient rite that their ancestors had kept on
that dreadful night before the Exodus, the same rite that they observed
before leaving Kadesh in the Wilderness. Then, the next day--"on that
very day"[42]--the manna ceased and they ate of the fruits of the Promised
Land. The cumulative message of the redactor is clear: each departure
of Israel on her way raises the question of divine presence and impels
the people to formally remember that night of deliverance that sealed
their redemption and began their journey.

We are now in a position to summarize our discussion of Joshua 1;
3-5. We noted that a relatively early literary stratum contained a
number of elements bearing on the question of divine presence and guidance. The dramatic role of the ark provides a striking instance of both
of these functions--once again, in connection with the vanguard motif.
This is highly reminiscent of the divine standards as they are used in
cultic processions in the ancient Near Eastern texts examined previously.
Secondly, the early narrative of Joshua 3 contains a strong indication
of the typology of exaltation in the title "Yahweh, Lord of all the land,"
for this epithet, especially in conjunction with the end of the story
in 5.1, implies the sovereignty of Yahweh over Canaan, and thus the legitimation of Israel's rule. This early account therefore has strong similarities to the *Tendenz* of Exodus 15B.

The deuteronomistic redactor of the early narrative material accentuated the miraculous role of the ark as well as the exaltation of Yahweh and Israel vis-à-vis the Canaanite (and perhaps even the world)
nations. His greatest innovation, however, came in his treatment of
the figure of Joshua. Here the language of exaltation (*giddēl*) is
explicit. Yahweh's presence with Joshua results in his exaltation to
the office of Moses. Moreover, the language with which the old epic
literary traditions described Yahweh's theophanic guidance during the
exodus is now shaped to fit the covenant theology--Torah is the guide
for the Way. What is most interesting in this development from the
older narrative of Joshua 3 to the deuteronomistic redaction is the way

in which it resembles the relation between Exodus 15 and 14. In Exodus
15, the exaltation of Yahweh and people was paramount--so in the old
Gilgal narrative; in Exodus 14, the exaltation of Yahweh and his servant
was paramount--so in the deuteronomistic redaction of the Gilgal narrative.

Finally we may also point out that our investigation has produced
a number of factors that tend to support the view of an exodus-conquest
ceremony standing behind the texts. The cultic procession itself, of
course, with its Near Eastern parallels, is the strongest evidence.
Added to this are the analogies to Exodus 14-15 and the connection with
Passover, the latter also being a prominent feature of the departure
from Sinai, as we have seen. Indeed, it is possible to argue that there
are signs of the influence of the Jordan crossing story on that of the
Reed Sea.[43] At any rate, both the Jordan River and Reed Sea narratives
--and events--were eminently worthy opportunities for the development
of the typology of exaltation.

These conclusions point to a further question: to what historical
forces may one attribute the general orientation of both the early and
later strata in Joshua 1; 3-5? It seems clear that the early stratum
may well come from the period of the occupation of the land, and perhaps from the early stages in which Benjamite elements predominated.
The exaltation of Yahweh and, implicitly, of Israel is perfectly fitting in such a context, and has its parallel in the ancient Near Eastern texts.[44] To what, then, may we attribute the different emphases--
especially the exaltation of Joshua--in the deuteronomistic redaction?
The answer is surely to be found in the context of the Josianic reform.
This dramatic movement was clearly as nationalistic as it was religious.[45]
Indeed, most recently Cross has described it as "the resurrection of the
Davidic empire," and has even suggested that "The Deuteronomistic history . . . may be described as a propaganda work of the Josianic refor-
mation and imperial program."[46]

Now it is in precisely such an historical context, i.e. one of
imperial renaissance, that we have seen motifs of divine presence concentrated in the ancient Near Eastern texts, especially in the Assyrian
royal annals. We would suggest that the exaltation of Joshua in chs. 1;
3-5 reflects a very similar period in the history of Judah. Moreover,
the emphasis on Joshua himself is most naturally to be understood as
reflecting the deuteronomistic ideal of Josiah.[47] Recently Dennis J.

McCarthy has observed that Joshua 1-9, seen as a literary whole, has as its basic theme "a theology of legitimate leadership," a theme that is characteristic of the deuteronomistic history in its entirety.[48] We would thus understand the import of Joshua's exaltation as an implicit message to the contemporaries of the deuteronomistic redactor: they are to fear and obey Josiah as their ancestors had Joshua, and indeed, as they had obeyed Moses. It is also intriguing to speculate whether the combination of this appeal, along with the observance of Passover, held a special significance for the Josianic reform (cf. 2 Kgs 23.21-23). At any rate, whether or not we can uncover such an intention in the deuteronomistic redaction, we may conclude that Yahweh's presence with and exaltation of Joshua most likely reflects the Josianic imperial reform, and that this religio-political correlation has strong analogies in the ancient Near Eastern texts discussed in Part I.

[1]The use of the term "deuteronomistic" is not intended to imply an exilic setting, as is often assumed. See our discussion of the Josianic reform at the end of this chapter. For bibliography see the monograph by F. Langlamet, *Gilgal et le récits de las traversée du Jourdain* (*Jos.*, III-IV) (Cahiers de la Revue biblique, 11; Paris, 1969). A more recent study by J. R. Porter ["The Background of Joshua III-V," *SEA* 36 (1971) 5-23] insists that the chapters be read as a unity rather than as a combination of various literary sources and/or traditions (see especially p. 12).

[2]Our proposed narrative by and large follows the JE or the ancient core of ch. 3, according to the survey worked out by Langlamet (*Gilgal*, 30, 37). The only major departure from this consensus is our retention of vss. 2-4, which are usually ascribed to the deuteronomistic level. We feel that the style alone does not necessarily demand this association, and that it is difficult to see why a later redactor would have wanted to emphasize the role of the "officers," who here serve a cultic function (there is thus little resemblance to the "officers" as civil officials nor even to their role in Deuteronomy 20). On their role here and in 1.10-11, see further below. It is also interesting to compare their prominence in Exodus 5, where they play a major role while Moses and Aaron stand off stage. Our narrative, in sum, would combine elements of Langlamet's two early accounts, the "Shittim-Gilgal" and "ark" accounts, as well as his deuteronomistic historian (139). Our analysis is even more closely in agreement with the cultic ceremony account (1.10-11; 3.2-6, 8-11, 13, 14b-15a) posited by Ernst Vogt, "Die Erzählung vom Jordanübergang," *Bib* 46 (1965) 131-134. Yet even here, there are still significant differences (cf. vs. 8 and the continuation in ch. 4).

[3]A number of commentators, of course, omit Joshua from the earliest levels; so Langlamet, *Gilgal*, 139; Maier, *Ladeheiligtum*, 24-25. If this could be verified conclusively, it would make our case below for the accentuation of Joshua in the deuteronomistic redaction even stronger, especially the analogy to Exodus 15 and 14 (emphasis on people; emphasis on individual hero).

[4]Throughout the proposed account, it is assumed that "covenant," "priests," and "Levites" are later additions. Despite the fact that Maier (*Ladeheiligtum*, 25-26) dismisses the ark from the earliest levels of the story, it is interesting that he still finds old material in 3.3-4, and that he posits an original theophany here of "Yahweh, Lord of all the earth," which was later replaced by the ark. Thus we would maintain that, even on the basis of Maier's literary and traditio-historical analysis, our argument below for the implications of the exaltation typology in the early narrative would still stand.

[5]1000 cubits works out to about 3000 feet—over half a mile! (This phrase is probably a later gloss.)

[6]For a discussion of the literary form here (*bzwt td^{c}wn ky X . . . hnh*) see Langlamet, *Gilgal*, 111.

[7]See n. 5 above and ch. 8, n. 21.

[8]Thus we would disagree very strongly with Maier, *Ladeheiligtum*, 24-27 (see further n. 2 above).

[9]Cf. vs. 3 where the people "march behind" (*hlk 'hry*) the ark. In general the expression *cbr lpny* means simply "to go ahead of, to precede." See Gen 33.3; 1 Sam 9.27; 25.19; 2 Kgs 4.31. The situation in Josh 1; 3-5, however, clearly demands the connotation of "to pass or cross over in front of." It is true that there are places where the expression would more logically mean "in the presence of" or "before" (i.e., "in the sight of"). This is certainly the case in 4.13 (*lpny yhwh*), probably referring to the ark (cf. vs. 5). Cf. also 4.11 where, given the picture of the second account (see below), it cannot mean that the ark preceded the people. The connotation "to precede" is more likely for the action of the East Jordanian tribes, 1.14; 4.12. Obviously some of the confusion is due to subsequent redaction. However, it is not unlikely that one account could conceive of more than one "vanguard" preceding the people. (Note, for example, the long retinue in the "Journey of Nininsinna," discussed in ch. 3). This is explicitly the case in Deut 31.3, to be discussed below.

[10]The classic study here, of course, is that of H.-J. Kraus, "Gilgal: Ein beitrag zur Kultusgeschichte Israels," *VT* 1 (1951) 181-199; more recently, *Worship in Israel*, 152-165. Cf. Langlamet's hesitance on this, *Gilgal*, 142-143. The reconstruction is rejected by Maier, *Ladeheiligtum*, 22-23, 33. In support of Kraus, cf. especially Cross, *CMHE*, 99-105.

[11]So J. Alberto Soggin, "Gilgal, Passah, und Landnahme," *VT* Suppl. 15 (1966) 267. Contrast Maier, *Ladeheiligtum*, 35-37.

[12]Elsewhere only Ps 97.5 (note the theophanic context); Mic 4.13 (Zion's supremacy over the nations); Zech 4.14; 6.5.

[13]*Royauté de Yahwé*, 255-256.

[14]*Gilgal*, 113. For an opposing view (i.e. '*rṣ* = the Earth), see Porter, "Joshua III-V," 18-20.

[15]The first redaction may have been quite minimal: 1.1-2, 5-9, 12-16; 3.1 [the addition of Joshua?], 5-6, 10aα. Even here there are vexing difficulties. 1.5-9 is in part redundant and verbose throughout; it has much in common with the language of vss. 17-18; 3.7. The verses regarding the East Jordanian tribes are related to Deut 3.12-20. They are easily removed from any account, and the sequel in 4.12 seems to be tacked on to the (or one) end of the story. The purpose of this first redaction was simply to augment the role of Joshua above that of the "officers," and to provide a fitting setting for the transition from Moses to the new leader; see below.

There are those, however, who see a much more unified narrative. Cf. Jay A. Wilcoxen, "Narrative Structure and Cult Legend: A Study of Joshua 1-6," *Transitions in Biblical Scholarship*, ed. J. Coert Rylaarsdam (Chicago: University of Chicago Press, 1968) 47, 59, and passim; Porter, "Joshua III-V," 12.

[16]The second redaction may have contained roughly the following: 1.3-4 (note the 2nd sing. form of address, which occurs only here; cf. Exod 23.20-33), 17-18; 3.7-8, 17; 4.11 (delete bβ), 14. This account added further paranesis to Yahweh's address and the reply of the East Jordanian tribes to Joshua. The style closely resembles that in 1.5-9. The major shift, however, is an explicit reference to the "exaltation" of Joshua and an altered picture of the ark processional (see below).

[17]The appropriate place of the remaining material is even more hazy. 4.12-13 seems to attempt to ensure that 1.12-16 was carried out and (vs. 13)

to add a more vivid end to the crossing than that supplied in 3.16. An extraneous date formula occurs in 4.19. The major addition, of course, concerns the placing of the stones at the lodging place (4.1-8) or in the river (4.9, and probably the gloss in 3.12). The former seems to continue in 4.10a (the reference in 10b to the command of Moses is inexplicable, and 10bβ conflicts with the preceding). Vss. 15-18 repeat what has already transpired in vs. 11, yet they clearly presuppose the "second redaction" in that they accentuate the role of the ark and the miraculous nature of the event in the description of the *return* of the waters. Vss. 20-24 may belong to 4.1-8, or they may represent a later application of the story (cf. 2.10; 5.1). Both passages, of course, are closely related to the *Kinderfrage* material in Exodus 12. It is difficult to escape the impression that at least 4.13, 19 are related to the Pentateuchal Priestly material (cf. 5.10-12 and comments below). This is also possible for the older core of 3.1.

For all the above, cf. the even more minute analysis of Langlamet, who posits no less than nine literary strata (*Gilgal*, 139). Six layers are projected by Maier, *Ladeheiligtum*, 29 (as also for Joshua 6, 37). At this point, the criticism of Porter ("Joshua III-V," 12) is well taken.

[18]According to the procedure in the redactional account, the ark's important function of guidance would have been rendered impossible after the priests had stopped. This is also one reason why 4.18 cannot be part of the earlier account, for if it were, the people--who were following a half mile behind the ark--would have been engulfed by the waters that returned literally at the heels of the priests!

[19]Cf. Langlamet (*Gilgal*, 90-91), who sees the redactional change as a means of incorporating the etiology of the twelve stones in the middle of the river.

[20]It is noteworthy that ^cbr is not used in Exodus 14. Its use elsewhere for the Reed Sea event may well be influenced by the Joshua story. See Num 33.8; Neh 9.11; Ps 78.13 (Hi.); 136.14 (Hi.); and note the parallelism with *nhr* in 66.6 (reflecting the ancient word pair).

[21]Note especially *bybš*, 4.22, as in Exod 14.22, 29; 15.19; also *hrbh* in 3.17 and Exod 14.21. It is possible that the use of *hwbyš* (2.10; 4.23; 5.1) results from an interpretation of the effect of the East wind (*rwh qdym*) in Exod 14.21 (for the connotation, cf. Ez 19.12). However, it is used in the much more ancient context of the *Chaoskampf*, Ps 74.15; cf. Isa 42.15; 44.27. There is a further strong resemblance between the Jordan being "cut off" (*krt*, 3.13, 16) and the Reed Sea being "divided" (*bq^c*, 14.21).

[22]Langlamet (*Gilgal*, 74, n. 3) goes so far as to suggest that this motif had its provenance among the Gilgal conquest traditions and that Josh 2.24 may well be more ancient than Exod 15.15 (see further below).

[23]For a thorough treatment of these and other parallels between Exodus 15 and Deuteronomy 2-3, see William L. Moran, "The End of the Unholy War and the Anti-Exodus," *Bib* 44 (1963) especially 340-342. For the latter expression cf. Exod 23.27. The parallels are also discussed by Langlamet, *Gilgal*, 67, 72-83. He also cites Deut 28.10; 1 Kgs 8.43, 53 in connection with Josh 4.24 and Deut 2.25. He suggests that Josh 4.24 is the prototype for such expressions, that '*rs* here originally means "country (=Canaan)," not "earth," which was later broadened by the deuteronomistic school to mean the whole earth, reflecting the later period of Israel's history.

[24]Two important studies of this material are Norbert Lohfink, "Die

deuteronomistische Darstellung des Übergangs der Führung Israels von Moses auf Josue," *Scholastik* 37 (1962) 32–44; followed by J. Roy Porter, "The Succession of Joshua," *Proclamation and Presence*, ed. J. I. Durham and J. R. Porter (G. Henton Davies *Festschrift*; Richmond: John Knox, 1970) 102–132.

[25]Cf. Exod 14.31; 33.11; Num 11. 28, all discussed above.

[26]Although dismissing the ark from the early traditions in Joshua 6, Maier (*Ladeheiligtum*, 35) states that the story was originally connected with 5.13–15, which he describes as an "angelophanie." Thus here, as in the Jordan crossing, a motif of divine presence played a crucial role, even if the ark is excluded.

[27]Cf. especially 2.2 with Exod 23.24, 32; 2.3 with Exod 23.29–30, 33. Also cf. vss. 4–5 with Exod 33.4.

[28]This language was also found in the vignette of Moses' request for guidance by Hobab when Israel was ready to begin her march to Canaan (Num 10.29–32, see above, ch. 8).

[29]*šmr* is the key word here; cf. its use in Exod 23.20–21.

[30]Cf. our discussion of this terminology above in the Excursus.

[31]Cf. for example 1 Kgs 8.57–61 and note the exaltation language in vs. 60.

[32]Cf. Exod 32.8 and Judg 2.17; Deut 9.12, 16. Of course, this does not mean that the Deuteronomist has rejected the older traditions. He does not mind repeating them in the context of retelling Israel's journey (Deut 1.30, 33) or her experience at Sinai (4.11; 5.22)--all involving the cloud (cf. 31.15 and the discussion above). However, as we shall see below, the major emphasis in connection with the vanguard motif falls on Yahweh himself or on Joshua.

[33]Maier (*Ladeheiligtum*, 75) sees this as part of D's attempt to limit the monarchical powers of the Davidic kings by an imposition of Sinai covenant theology.

[34]Private communication to the author. Thus the frequent view that the ark was "demythologized" by the Deuteronomist must be revised; cf. Woudstra, *Ark*, 28–29, 33–38, 97–98, 102–103.

[35]*wsw 't-yhwš^c . . . ky-hw' y^cbr lpny h^cm hzzh*. Note that the verse continues with *whw' ynhyl 'wtm 't-h'rṣ ^cšr tr'h*, with which cf. Josh 1.6, *ky 'th tnhyl 't-h^cm hzzh 't-h'rṣ 'šr-nšb^cty . . . .* Both verses also contain the familiar deuteronomistic pair *hzq* and *'mṣ*. The context of Deut 3.28 is Yahweh's refusal to allow Moses to cross over the Jordan. On this and the following texts, see in general Lohfink "Übergangs der Führung," and Porter, "Succession of Joshua."

[36]*yhwh 'lhyk hw'-h^cbr lpnyk 'š 'klh hw'*. For the use of the vanguard motif in the form *hlk lpny* with Yahweh (not an agent) as subject, cf. 1.30, 33 (a reference to Israel's past) and 20.4; 31.6, 8. The Hithpael is used in 23.15. For *hlk lpny* with Moses, cf. Deut 10.11.

[37]*Gilgal*, 142. Langlamet suggests that the liturgical flavor of Deut 9.1–6 combined with the theophanic language provides a good argument for the cultic background of the Jordan crossing.

[38]*yhwh 'lhyk hw' ^cbr lpnyk . . . . yhwš^c hw' ^cbr lpnyk. . . .* Again, as in 3.28, the context includes Yahweh's refusal to allow Moses to cross the Jordan (vs. 2). It is significant that in the preceding passage (31.3)

where this is not the case, there is no mention of Joshua. It is possible that vs. 3b is a later addition. It is intrusive within vss. 1-6 and anticipates vss. 7-8. However, it is clearly in line with 3.28. Moreover, for the author (and/or editor) it is likely that the actions of Yahweh and Joshua in vs. 3 were not understood as contradictory or mutually exclusive; in other words, Joshua could be understood as an agent of Yahweh's presence in battle.

[9]E.g. Porter, "Succession of Joshua," 108 and passim. Cf. Baltzer, *Covenant Formulary*, 68-72. He suggests that Deut 31.3a is an interpolation emphasizing "that Yahweh himself is Israel's 'duke' . . . ."

[0]The position of 4.14 is clearly premature, no doubt due to the extensive redactional process. It would be much more impressive at the end of the chapter. This is, in fact, precisely the case with another reference to Joshua's exaltation, again connected to divine presence, in the last verse of the story of the taking of Jericho in 6.27: "So Yahweh was with Joshua and the report of him (went) throughout the whole land." On the effect of 3.7 and 4.14 on the picture of Joshua, cf. also Langlamet, *Gilgal*, 68. He too sees a pronounced emphasis on Joshua beyond the older material, where the focus was on the ark. Cf. also Wilcoxen, "Narrative Structure," 59, 65.

[1]On the syntax of this expression (using *ḥll*) cf. Deut 2.24-25, 31 and see Langlamet, *Gilgal*, 73, n. 1. In ch. 11 we will argue that the provenance of this use of *giddēl* lies in the Solomonic court.

[2]In the Pentateuch this expression clearly belongs to the Priestly stratum (Gen 7.13; 17.23, 26; Exod 12.17, 41, 51; Lev 23.21, 28, 30; Num 19.16; Deut 32.48). Elsewhere it occurs only in Ez 24.2; 40.1.

[3]We have argued elsewhere ("Pillar of Cloud," 26-27) that the role of the cloud in Exodus 14 has a number of striking analogies to the role of the ark, including the way in which both "stand" (*ᶜmd*) their ground while the people traverse the river and sea. For further details cf. Cross, *CMHE*, 133 and especially 138.

[4]Our conclusions would thus indicate that historical forces are at work in the ancient narrative more so than mythological ones. We would disagree therefore, with the recent study of Porter ("Joshua III-V," passim) who sees the strong influence of the mythical battle against chaos and the renewal of creation and fertility throughout these chapters (even though he too thinks the chapters are more ritual than mythical, p. 14). Clearly the Canaanite myth of the battle against sea/river has influenced the interpretation of the story, as Cross and others have repeatedly shown, but the story can be understood just as well in relation to the *historical* texts discussed in Part I above. Cf. our argument below on 2 Samuel 6.

[5]Cf. the comment by John Bright [*Jeremiah* (Anchor Bible; New York: Doubleday, 1965) xl]: "Indeed, the reform was essentially a facet of nationalism or, if one prefers, nationalism was the political expression of the religion of the people." The recent study of John McKay [*Religion in Judah under the Assyrians* (Studies in Biblical Theology, Second Series, 26; Naperville, Ill.: Allenson, 1973), 43, 72] has tended to confirm this, although McKay wants to emphasize the role of religion in Josiah's reform, and refutes the current view that it was essentially a political revolt against the Assyrians. Cogan (*Imperialism and Religion*, 96) refers to the time of Josiah as a "return of national self-confidence."

[46]*CMHE*, 283, 284.

[47]Following a lead by G. Widengren, J. Soggin ("Gilgal," 276, n. 2) surmises that the picture of Joshua in chs. 3-6 could easily be formed with Josiah in mind. It should also be noted here that, despite a number of basic disagreements with the conclusions of Maier noted at various points above, our view of the implications of the deuteronomistic redaction in particular are quite compatible with his (*Ladeheiligtum*, 39), which sees the story of the Jordan crossing to reflect the propagandistic orientation of the court and temple theology of the later monarchical period.

[48]"The Theology of Leadership in Joshua 1-9," *Bib* 52 (1971) 175. He also notes how the redactional conclusion to the spy story near the end of ch. 6 serves to glorify Joshua; 170-171.

CHAPTER 11

THE DAVIDIC EMPIRE

The major portion of this study has been devoted to those traditions of Exodus, Sinai, and Conquest that dealt with motifs of divine
presence. Now we turn our attention to a number of texts stemming from
the David-Solomonic empire. Actually, the conclusions drawn in Part I
regarding the correlation of motifs of divine presence and the historical rise of empire already pointed in this direction. In what follows,
this indication will be pursued. Although we cannot probe each biblical
text completely, it is our contention that those that reflect this historical period of Israel present the fullest correspondence to the typology of exaltation as it was developed on the basis of the Near Eastern
material.

Before we begin, a word about the nature of the biblical sources
is in order. In what follows, we shall investigate 2 Samuel 5-7 in the
order in which they occur in the present text. By this we do not intend to imply that these three chapters represent an original, continuous narrative. Indeed, it is quite clear that we have before us a number of different sources. In 5.17-25, for example, we have what appear
to be two separate battle reports (probably of incidents that were not
immediately connected), but both are written in annalistic style. In
ch. 6, as has been generally recognized for some time, we have the cul-
mination of the Ark Narrative, which began in 1 Samuel 4-6. Ch. 7 seems
to presuppose the events in ch. 6, yet is premature in relation to ch. 8
(contrast 7.1 with 8.1). In short, chs. 5-7 by no means constitute an
original literary unity.

On the other hand, we would maintain that most, although certainly
not all, of this material fits most reasonably within the historical
context that it claims to relate: the consummation of David's military
and political efforts to establish a stable monarchy. Moreover, both

the internal logic of the biblical sources, as well as the comparative evidence from the ancient Near East, argue for a chronological arrangement of the major events that are basically identical to the present redactional order: military conquest, triumphal procession, request for a temple.[1]

(1) Military Victory and Cultic Procession

The story of the consolidation of the Davidic empire is told in 2 Samuel 5 with David's capture of Jerusalem and his victory over the Philistines. In 5.1-3, David, who has already been annointed king over the house of Judah pursuant to a divine oracle (2.1-4), is now made king over Israel.[2] This is followed by a rapid succession of victories over Israel's enemy, each punctuated by motifs of divine presence and of David's increasing glory. First, in vss. 6-10, there is the capture of Jerusalem, after which "David became greater and greater, for Yahweh the God of hosts was with him."[3] This is immediately followed by the construction of David's palace, with the result that "David recognized that Yahweh had established him as king over Israel, and that he had exalted his kingdom because of his people Israel" (vs. 12).[4]

A second victory occurs when the Philistines attempt to nip David's growing empire in the bud (vss. 17–21). When they assemble near Jerusalem, David again receives a favorable oracle from Yahweh, and the Philistines are defeated. Yahweh's decisive presence in battle is praised by David in language equivalent to the Assyrian annals: "Yahweh has burst through my enemies in front of me like a bursting flood" (vs. 20).[5] An equally impressive parallel occurs in vs. 21: the Philistines abandon their idols[6] on the field of battle, and David and his men carry them away. This is a practice we have seen quite frequently in the Assyrian annals, where the king boasts of the enemy "gods" he has captured.[7]

Finally, despite this defeat, the Philistines muster for one more attack and are decisively defeated (vss. 22-25). This short anecdote is built around an oracle obtained from Yahweh,[8] and it contains a stunning, if mysterious, example of the vanguard motif:

> When you hear the sound of marching ($ṣ^cdh$)[9] in the
> tops of the balsam trees, then look sharp, for Yah-
> weh has gone forth before you ($yṣ' yhwh lpnyk$) to
> strike the camp of the Philistines. (vs. 24)

This oracle has a salient parallel in Judg 4.14 (*hl' yhwh yṣ' lpnyk*; see above), and again in a number of Assyrian texts.[10]

In summary, 2 Samuel 5 establishes David's kingship over all Israel and his military victory over the ancient Philistine menace.[11] The chapter is filled with imagery related to our previous discussion of divine presence, where the Holy Warrior fights in an historical battle in behalf of his devotee. Moreover, ch. 5 also depicts the progressive exaltation of David himself. Thus this material bears a striking resemblance to what we have seen in the Mesopotamian literary texts and in the Assyrian annals.

David's rise to kingship in ch. 5 is appropriately followed by the removal of the ark to Jerusalem in ch. 6. Our purpose here, as above, is not to investigate this material in detail, but simply to point out the significance of the removal of the ark within the context of the foundation of the Davidic empire and the way in which this is related to the Near Eastern texts examined previously.

From the preceding victories over the Philistines in ch. 5, it is already clear, of course, that this act is a political one. To be sure, the return of the ark from Philistine captivity already takes place in 1 Samuel 5-6, but it constitutes a sort of anticlimax to 2 Samuel 6, which, in fact, contains the original conclusion of the "Ark Narrative."[12] Moreover, the strange circumstances under which the ark was returned in 1 Samuel 5-6, and the ignominious defeat of Saul's forces later at Mt. Gilboa (ch. 31), demonstrate that this return was by no means an indication of Israel's military power. The reverse is true for the story in 2 Samuel 6. David's removal of the ark from its caretakers in Kiriath-jearim,[13] and the deposition of it in the newly won "city of David," was clearly a sign of his success against the Philistines. Almost as much as the desire for a temple for Yahweh (ch. 7; see below), this action inaugurated the Davidic empire and proclaimed Yahweh's blessing upon the king.

The removal of the ark to Jerusalem was not only an act reflecting the political and military achievements of David's new empire; it was also an appropriation of the ancient cultic symbol of Yahweh's presence.[14] In fact, despite numerous difficulties involved in the interpretation of both 1 and 2 Samuel 6, it seems clear that, particularly in the latter, we are presented with some form of cultic procession involving the ark and the king. In vss. 12-19 the ark is carried in procession by other (priestly?) participants, while David offers sacrifices and dances before Yahweh, i.e. in front of the ark. After the ark has been set "in its place, inside the tent which David had pitched for it,"[15] he performs several priestly functions; he offers "burnt offerings and peace offerings before Yahweh;" he blesses the people in the name of Yahweh of Hosts (cf. 5.10; 6.2); and he distributes ritual foods to all (cf. 1 Kgs 3.15).

The political role of the ark is even more explicitly connected with divine presence in the context of the processional in Psalm 132, which is essentially a liturgy based on the same historical event recorded in 2 Samuel 6.[16] It is quite likely that the procession in both of these texts was influenced by earlier prototypes. So 2 Sam 6.12-19 occurs in the historical context of Yahweh's Holy War against the Philistines (5.17-25), and the phrase *nose'ê 'ărôn-yhwh* in 6.13 is identical to that used in Josh 3.13-15.[17] Similarly, the summons to the ark in Ps 132.8 (*qûmāh yhwh*) is identical to that in Num 10.35, and the closing reference to the humiliation of David's enemies (vs. 18) again picks up the Holy War language. In short, the motifs of divine presence and guidance from Israel's earlier history are now creatively focused on David's removal of the ark to Jerusalem. That this presence and guidance are directly connected to the exaltation of both David and Yahweh is beyond dispute. As Terence Fretheim has suggested, Psalm 132 reveals a "close relationship . . . between the dwelling place of Yahweh in Zion and the continued existence of the Davidic dynasty."[18] "Thus the continued establishment of the throne of David is directly tied up with the securing of the throne of Yahweh by David."[19]

To summarize: in the battle accounts of 2 Samuel 5 we have seen a close similarity to the motifs of divine presence and the typology of exaltation in the Mesopotamian literary and annalistic texts. Now in ch. 6 (and Psalm 132) we also see a close parallel with those texts that described the cultic procession of physical representations of the deities.[20] Thus it is tempting to compare the journey of the ark of Yahweh to take up its new residence in the tent of David, with the journey of Ningirsu's emblem to Lagash, to take up its new residence in the temple of Eninnu.[21] Still, the most important aspect of 2 Samuel 6 for our purposes is the way in which the *cultic procession* is to be understood in the context of the *historical events* leading up to the Davidic empire. Thus this chapter may well present us with a more elaborate description of the type of ceremony that no doubt lies behind the cryptic

216

comments in the Mesopotamian texts in ch. 1 above. A comparison with
the Nur-Adad text, for example, is most revealing. There the gods, who
had been taken captive by the enemy, are restored "to their place" in
the sanctuary, following Nur-Adad's victory over the oppressors.[22] So,
here in ch. 6 the ark, which had been taken captive by the Philistines
long ago, is deposited "in its place" consequent to David's defeat of
the oppressors. Similarly, the foundation of the Assyrian empire following the defeat of Kashtiliash involved the capture of the statue of
Marduk. Even more dramatically, the exaltation of Marduk to kingship
of the gods in *Enuma eliš* probably had as its most immediate background
the return of Marduk's statue from captivity in Elam. In the light of
this comparative evidence, the correlation of the removal of the ark in
2 Samuel 6 with our conclusions concerning ch. 5 can mean only one thing:
that motifs of divine presence are again found within the context of the
rise of a political empire, and the exaltation of the leader of that
empire and his God.[23]

Before we turn to a closer analysis of the exaltation of king and
deity, two more comments regarding the cultic procession of the ark are
in order. First, the evidence adduced here from the Near Eastern material militates against the interpretation of the "story of the ark" (and
especially 2 Samuel 6) as an historification of myth or even of a cultic
legend.[24] Rather, the evidence points toward political and cultic actions that are perfectly understandable within the context of the momentous historical event in question. The Near Eastern texts of Part I
thus provide solid evidence for the combination of the so-called "cultic"
and "historical" interpretations of 2 Samuel 5-6.[25] The same must be
said for Psalm 132, even though there we are dealing much more with a
liturgy rather than with an historical narrative.[26]

Secondly, the cultic procession of the ark in 1 Kings 8 also clearly
fits within the context of our preceding discussion. Just as David's
first act as king of his newly won empire was to appropriate the ark and
have it brought to Jerusalem, so the first major act of Solomon was the
construction of the temple recorded in 1 Kings 5-8. The lengthy explanation of the process of construction and the various cultic implements
that furnished the temple is climaxed by the dramatic events of ch. 8.
When the ark is deposited in its place in the holy of holies, the cloud
(*ᶜnn*) and glory (*kbwd*) fill the temple, signifying the advent of Yahweh
to his new dwelling. Thus, just as David appropriated the ark as the

sign of Yahweh's presence, so the Solomonic temple appropriated the cloud.
1 Kings 8 thus introduces the first revival of this term within an historical context outside of the Pentateuch.[27]

This event, like those related in 2 Samuel 5-6, is also illuminated
by the Near Eastern texts discussed in Part I,[28] and especially the texts
presenting cultic processions of the divine standard. In fact, all of
1 Kings 5-8 can be compared to the Gudea Cylinders, where the construction of the temple and its implements is described at length, followed
by the dramatic advent of Ningirsu to take up residence in his new dwelling.

(2) Royal and Divine Exaltation

In the preceding pages we have seen how the literary description of
the historical, political, and cultic events involved with the rise of
the Davidic-Solomonic empire bears a striking resemblance to the typology
of exaltation delineated in the ancient Near Eastern texts. In our discussion of 2 Samuel 5, we noticed, in passing, the explicit references
to the exaltation of David by Yahweh. Now we must turn to a closer examination of the exaltation of the king during this historical period,
and then to the exaltation of Yahweh himself.

The major prose text that deserves our attention in this regard
is 2 Samuel 7. Although the first part of this chapter clearly concerns
the mode of Yahweh's presence, the relationship to the typology of exaltation, as we shall see, turns on the figure of the king. Despite persistent difficulties concerning the text and authorship of 2 Samuel 7,
it seems reasonable to assume that this chapter does present an authentic
witness to the actions of David, however embellished the story may be in
its present form. The ark as the physical representation of Yahweh's
presence obviously plays a central role in the story. David's purpose
is clear: he desires to build a temple (*bayit*) for the ark in place of
the tent (*hay^{e}rî^{c}āh*, vs. 2; *hā'ōhel*, 6.17) that houses it. His reason
is a pious one: his own dwelling should not be more elaborate than that
of Yahweh. Yahweh protests that he has never dwelt in a temple but has
always been "going about in tent and tabernacle" (vs. 6). Whatever the
connection between the tent that David pitched for the ark and the Tent
of Meeting in the Pentateuch,[29] the rejection of a temple dwelling for
Yahweh seems final.[30] This is contradicted only by vs. 13, and it seems
reasonable to conclude that this verse is a later addition made to

218

legitimate Solomon's temple.[31]

Now clearly, Nathan's oracle rejecting the suggestion of a temple
is concerned with the nature of divine presence. However, it is a mis-
take to construe this concern as purely theological. The major problem
is not whether or not Yahweh's presence with Israel is in the form of a
permanent or temporary manifestation, often categorized by the terms $y\check{s}b$
and $\check{s}kn$ respectively.[32] Rather, the major problem concerns the underlying presuppositions of a particular cultic institution in relation
to the political legitimation of the Davidic dynasty. From Mesopotamia
to Egypt the rise of empire was correlated with the erection of massive
temple complexes in honor of the patron god(s).[33] We have seen this in
a number of major texts discussed in Part I, where such construction
formed the epilogue or even the climax to military engagements in which
motifs of divine presence were prominent features, just as in 2 Samuel
5.[34] In the light of this comparative evidence, there can be little
doubt that Nathan's oracle represents a fundamental, conservative strand
of Yahwism that rejected the notion of a temple because of its association
with *dynastic* legitimation. In this circle, the institution of the tent
in 2 Samuel 6 would presumably have been acceptable, perhaps because it
was associated with a nonhereditary transmission of office.[35] In this
light, it is significant that the oracle closes by drawing a contrast
between David and the judges of old,[36] a contrast in which the latter
serve as the norm for the acceptable cultic complement to political
leadership. In other words, it may well be more appropriate to speak
of permanent versus temporary *political legitimation* rather than of
divine presence as the crucial concern of Nathan's oracle. At any rate,
one may reasonably conclude, along with Clements, that the oracle served
"as a check upon David's plan to build a temple, with its political as
well as religious implications."[37]

The fact that 2 Sam 7.1-7 is primarily concerned with the problem
of a permanent divine legitimation of the political order--in practical
terms, with dynastic succession--brings us closer to the question of the
exaltation of the king. In vss. 8-11a, Yahweh describes his presence
with David in terms almost synonymous with those used for Joshua (and
Jacob).[38] Yahweh has been with him everywhere he went, cutting down his
enemies before him and making him a name equal to the great men of the
earth (vs. 9). But, interestingly enough, what follows is an indication
of the exaltation, not of David, but of David's *dynasty* (*bayit*). Thus

the second oracle, beginning in vs. 11b,[39] is built around a well-known
wordplay: David will not build a house for Yahweh, but Yahweh will establish a house for David. It is also highly significant that the text
then goes on to refer to David's successor as the *son* of Yahweh (vs. 14).
The full implications of this will have to await our discussion of Psalm
89. For now, it is enough to conclude that this oracle, with its emphasis
on David's dynasty, is best understood as a product of the Solomonic
court.[40] In short, the tendency here is toward the exaltation of Solomon
rather than of David.

This inclination to exalt the figure of the king during the Solomonic era, rather than the Davidic, is further born out by another prose
source, 1 Kgs 1.37. In the preceding chapter we concluded that the
deuteronomistic redactor of Joshua 1; 3-5 had extensively reworked older
material in order to emphasize the exaltation of Yahweh and Joshua. For
Joshua, this was achieved in part by an epigrammatic comparison between
Yahweh's presence with Moses and with the new leader, and by the explicit
use of the word *giddēl*--"to exalt" (3.7; 4.14). An examination of the
use of the verb *giddēl* elsewhere in a context like Josh 3.7; 4.14, shows
that it is reserved almost totally for Solomon.[41] The two occurrences
with Solomon are in 1 Kgs 1.32-48, which relates the precipitous decision of David to have him annointed king in his stead. In response to
this order, Benaiah exclaims:[42]

> Amen! May Yahweh, the god of my lord the king say
> so. As Yahweh was with my lord the king, so may he
> be with Solomon, and may he exalt his throne
> (*wîgaddēl 't-ks'w*) above the throne of my lord King
> David. (vs. 37)

We were dealing with a variant of this formula in Josh 3.7:

> Then Yahweh said to Joshua: "This very day I shall
> begin to exalt you in the eyes of all Israel, so
> that they will know that, as I was with Moses, I
> will be with you."

There is no indication that the saying concerning Solomon is a later
redactional addition to the narrative, as seems to be the case with
Josh 3.7. The implication is thus that in 1 Kgs 1.37 we have an intrinsically royal dynastic formula which was applied retrospectively

by the deuteronomistic redactor to the figure of Joshua.[43] This particular formulation of divine presence and royal exaltation is used only
for Solomon and Joshua, never for David.[44]

On the basis of prose sources in 2 Samuel 7 and 1 Kings 1, therefore,
it already seems clear that the typology of exaltation, inasmuch as it
involves the figure of the king, achieves its acme under the Solomonic
empire. A major witness to the developments in this era is Psalm 89.
It is likely that the Psalm was composed in three stages; the first two
are of interest to us here.[45] The first section (vss. 1-3,[46] 6-19) may
well be the core around which the second (vss. 4-5, 20-38) was built.
Vss. 6-19, especially, are filled with literary and ideological characteristics familiar to us from other biblical texts. Vss. 6-9 proclaim
Yahweh's awesome supremacy over the gods of the heavenly council. Vs.
9 contains an interesting combination of this council and the imagery of
hypostatized attributes, which form the divine vanguard: "Yahweh of
Hosts, who is like you? / Strength and Fidelity (stand) round about you."[47]
The psalmist then describes Yahweh's sovereignty over the sea,[48] the
heavens and the earth; his attributes of strength; and, finally, his
people:[49]

> For thou art the glory of our strength,
> And by thy will our horn is exalted.
> Yahweh is indeed our suzerain,
> The Holy one of Israel is indeed our king.[50]

This section of the poem thus closely resembles the ideology of exaltation found as early as Exodus 15--the exaltation of Yahweh and his people,
those who walk in the light of his "presence" (vs. 16b).[51]

However, when we turn to the rest of the second section of the Psalm
(vss. 20-38), there is a dramatic shift of focus. It is clear that the
mention of *malkēnû* in vs. 19, taken to refer to Israel's earthly king,
has provided the cue for the transition to the exaltation (*rwm*), not of
the people, but of the king himself.[52] The second section is imbued with
the language of exaltation:

> I have made a lad ruler over the warrior,[53]
> I have exalted one chosen from the people (20b)
> and in my name his horn is exalted (25b)[54]
>
> He will call to me, "Thou art my Father . . ."

> And I will make him the first-born,
>
> The highest (ʿelyôn) of the kings of the earth (27-28).
>
> Forever I shall keep my faithfulness to him,
>
> And my covenant shall be confirmed for him,
>
> And I will establish his seed forever,
>
> And his throne like the days of heaven (29-30).

With these lines and other similar texts,[55] we have reached a watershed
in the development of the typology of exaltation. The emphasis is no
longer on Yahweh's *people* exalted above all other nations (Exodus 15).
Even the adumbrations of royal glorification ascribed to Moses pale in
the face of this bold apotheosis of David. The ascription of such language to an individual leader provides the closest correspondence to the
royal ideology of the ancient Near East. The analogy with the "Hymn of
Praise" from the Tukulti-Ninurta Epic is impressive:

> Enlil, like a physical father, exalted him second to
>   his firstborn son.
>
> No one among all kings ever vied with him in battle.[56]

Indeed, even the traditionally conditional covenant theology (cf. vss.
31-33) is not sufficient to temper this unbridled elevation.[57]

It is also significant that, in this section, the focus is entirely
on David. There is no reference to Yahweh's exaltation and no explicit
use of the imagery of divine presence, which we have seen elsewhere.
Indeed, it may be said that both Yahweh's presence and his exaltation
are now mirrored in the chosen king. Despite the exclusive reference
to David, the second section of the Psalm betrays the strong influence
of the Solomonic court theology.[58] Solomon was obviously in the best
position to benefit from an eternal kingship promised to David's lineage, and the methods which he used to succeed to the throne could certainly have stimulated the pressure for divine legitimation.[59]

We may conclude, then, that Psalm 89, along with the prose material
examined previously, describes the exaltation of the king in unmistakable
terms, and that this exaltation received its fullest form during the
reign of Solomon. We must now turn our attention to the exaltation of
Yahweh: to what extent is this theological elevation bound up with the
political developments in the Davidic-Solomonic empire?

Of course, we should preface our investigation of the exaltation of
Yahweh during this period by reviewing the results of previous chapters

on the Old Testament, for it should be clear by now that any elevation of Yahweh's heavenly status was not then without precedent. Indeed, we have seen that Exodus 15, reflecting the earliest levels of Israel's theology, already described the exaltation ($g'h$) of Yahweh: "Who is like you among the gods, O Yahweh?" (vs. 11). Similarly, Deut 33.3 spoke of all the holy ones of heaven doing obeisance to Yahweh. Again, the early narrative of the crossing of the Jordan depicted Yahweh as "lord of all the land" ('dwn kl-$h'rṣ$), thus declaring his sovereignty over the land of Canaan and, implicitly, its gods. In short the exaltation of Yahweh was a process that began long before the Davidic-Solomonic empire, one that received its major impetus, no doubt, from the exodus and conquest.

In his recent study of the Zion tradition, J. J. M. Roberts has traced a similar "development in the conception of Yahweh's universal rule" leading up to the exaltation of Yahweh during the Davidic-Solomonic period.[60] Roberts argues that an earlier view, attested to by Deut 32.8-9, in which the various "national gods" were granted their legitimate regions by the high god Elyon, was dramatically revised in the Davidic era. The revision is reflected in Psalm 82, where the gods or "sons of Elyon" are condemned for misrule, and sovereignty over all the nations is implicitly conferred upon the God of Israel.[61] Thus the earlier tendency to identify Yahweh with El or Elyon, the supreme head of the pantheon in Canaanite mythology, is accentuated in the Davidic period.[62] In a recently published article, Roberts expanded the biblical evidence for the exaltation of Yahweh in a discussion of Psalm 47.[63] The presence in the Psalm of 'foreign gods' and 'foreign princes' points to the nations subject to the Davidic empire; the theological correlate of this is found in the *Sitz im Leben* of the Psalm: "a cultic celebration of Yahweh's imperial accession."[64] In short, Roberts has correctly emphasized that the exaltation of Yahweh is in direct correlation to the rise of the Davidic empire, and he compares this to the exaltation of Inanna and of Marduk, two of our major examples in ch. 1.[65] Roberts' formulation of the comparison deserves direct quotation:

> Just as Marduk's definitive elevation to the head of
> the pantheon took place sometime later than the first
> attempt to exalt him, and under the impact of a more
> recent historical development than that which had

first gained him prominence, so Yahweh's exaltation
really reached its climax only with the rise of the
Davidic-Solomonic empire.[66]

A very similar religio-political configuration in Psalms 2, 46, and
47 has recently been traced by O. Eissfeldt. In Psalm 47, he too finds
that "the predication of Yahweh as king goes hand in hand with the
national-political claims of Israel," and that this must be understood
in the historical context of the Davidic dynasty.[67] Moreover, Eissfeldt
suggests that vs. 6 of this psalm, which refers to Yahweh's ascension
(^{c}lh) amidst the cry of holy war, indicates that the psalm itself is to
be connected with a festival procession of the ark, and should be compared to Psalm 24, 2 Samuel 6, and 1 Kings 8.[68] Such a connection may
be difficult to prove, but it is not at all unlikely in the light of our
previous discussions concerning the interrelationships between cultic
processions and the typology of exaltation.

To summarize: the foundation of the Davidic-Solomonic empire in
many ways represents the clearest correspondence to the typology of exaltation that we discussed in Part I. The victory of David over the
Philistine oppression is described in terms directly related to the vanguard motif, which expresses Yahweh's presence in the conflict. The
return of the sacred ark--itself an ancient representation of divine
presence--to Israelite control, and, in fact, its processional journey
to the new political capitol, Jerusalem, is the cultic correlate to the
military triumph, and both together proclaim the exaltation of Yahweh
and of David, the chosen king. The construction of the temple--first
proposed under David, and fulfilled under Solomon--is the natural consummation of the rise of the Davidic empire. In the royal theology of
the Solomonic era, the typology of exaltation comes to full bloom in the
person of the king, who is elevated above all others as the son of Yahweh,
and whose kingdom is established forever. This near apotheosis of the
royal figure, of course, has its counterpart in the exaltation of Yahweh,
a process that began as early as the Exodus, but culminates in the Davidic
period, when Yahweh fully incorporates the role of Elyon as the highest
deity, and Yahweh's sovereignty extends to the nations surrounding the
Davidic empire.

[1]On the redaction of these chapters, cf. Hans W. Hertzberg, *I & II Samuel, A Commentary* (The Old Testament Library; Philadelphia: Westminster, 1964), 295-296. More recently, see Antony F. Campbell, *The Ark Narrative* (SBL Dissertation Series, 16; Missoula, Montana: Scholars', 1976), 126, 162-163.

[2]According to vss. 1-2 David is approached because of kinship, his military prowess and leadership, and the designation of Yahweh. In vs. 3 it is the elders of Israel who anoint David king and form a treaty with him "before the Lord." (With the last phrase the author could only mistakenly mean the ark, since it was still in Kiriath-jearim.)

[3]*wylk dwd hlwk wgdwl wyhwh 'lhy ṣb'wt ᶜmmw.* On this and the next passage cited, cf. Artur Weiser, "Die Legitimation des Königs Davids," *VT* 16 (1966) 341-342. The phrase "Yahweh was with him" is frequent with David and should be compared to the texts in Genesis primarily centering around Jacob (see the Excursus above). Cf. 1 Sam 16.18; 18.12, 14, 28; 20.13; 2 Sam 7.(3), 9. Weiser (348) calls it "the leitmotif in which the ascendance narrator clothes his own opinion . . . ." On the use of this as a deuteronomistic cliche, see Cross, *CMHE*, 250, n. 130.

[4]Vs. 12: *wydᶜ dwd ky-hkynw yhwh lmlk ᶜl-yśr'l wky niśśē' mmlktw bᶜbwr ᶜmmw yśr'l.* Cf. even earlier in the encounter with Goliath (1 Sam 17.46-47), which is undertaken "that all the earth may know that there is a God in Israel," and that the "assembly" of Israel may know that Yahweh fights for them.

[5]*prṣ yhwh 't-'yby lpny kprṣ mym.* The fact that this involves an etiology of the place name Baal-perazim does not affect the relevance of the description (cf. 6.8). It is remarkable that Yahweh and Baal here are treated as parallel without the slightest hint of disapproval.

[6]The original text probably had *'elōhîm*, cf. LXX and 1 Chr 14.12 (in the latter the gods are burned by the pious David). The picture is clearly that of physical representations of deities precisely as in the Near Eastern texts. Cf. Cogan, *Imperialism and Religion*, 116-117.

[7]See above, p. 68; also *Ibid.*, ch. 2.

[8]Cf. vs. 19; also 1 Sam 23.2, 4, 9-12; 30.7-8; 2 Sam 2.1 and 1 Sam 22.15; 23.6. Weiser ("Legitimation," 335) has correctly observed that this use of the Yahweh oracle is another element in the *religious* (as well as political) legitimation of David.

[9]Cf. the use of this word in Judg 5.4 and Ps 68.8.

[10]Note the divinations in the "Letter to Assur" discussed in ch. 2, and an oracle received by Shalmaneser III before a campaign against Urartu: "Aššur inspired me with confidence and [showed me a dream,] / (He said) 'The People of Assyria have sought the command (?) [. . .] / On a propitious day of the month Iyyar . . . kings (?) . . . May Ninurta go before you, may Girru [follow at your rear].'" See W. G. Lambert, "The Sultantepe Tablets . . . ," *Anatolian Studies* 11 (1961) 150-151. This text as a whole is a curious blend of epic, annalistic, and letter (to the gods) styles (144).

[11]For the historical problems involved in this claim, see Cross, *CMHE*, 262-

263; Freedman, "Early Israelite History," 16.

[12]The basic study is that of Leonhard Rost, *Die Überlieferung von der Thronnachfolge Davids* (BWANT III/6; Stuttgart, 1926) 4-47. Weiser ("Legitimation," 344) assumes that 2 Samuel 6 originally belonged with 1 Samuel 4-7 as a *hieros logos* of the ark sanctuary in Jerusalem (following Rost). Its present position is intentional, providing an important link between David and the sacral league here at the finale of the story of David's rise to power. Maier (*Ladeheiligtum*, 46-47), while also following the cultic legend explanation, doubts the original connection between 1 Samuel 4-7 and 2 Samuel 6, but sees them as now clearly incorporated into the overall story of David. For a survey of other opinions, see Campbell, *Ark Narrative*, 12-54.

[13]The identification of this place with Baalejudah (1 Sam 6.2; cf. 1 Chr 13.5-6) is indicated by 1 Sam 7.1-2 and Ps 132.6. Moreover, it is likely that this town was not politically Israelite until David's victory; cf. Maier, *Ladeheiligtum*, 61. Note also Terence E. Fretheim, "Psalm 132: A Form-Critical Study," *JBL* 86 (1967) 296, n. 32.

[14]For Maier (*Ladeheiligtum*, 60) there is no solid evidence for the existence of the ark before 1 Samuel 4. In the latter, the ark is only the symbol of a political federation of tribes (perhaps containing a document of the federation covenant) which resisted the Philistines. The ark would have ended in oblivion had it not been for the later monarchy. Thus for Maier (72), the ark came to symbolize divine presence only after it had been incorporated into the Temple of Solomon. It is obvious from our preceding discussion that we would disagree with Maier's skepticism about the early history of the ark. However, his repeated emphasis on the story of the ark as serving to legitimate the Davidic dynasty (e.g. 63, 69-70, 73) is supported by our study.

[15]The view of Cross (*CMHE*, 231) and others that the tent of David reflects very old traditions and was (along with the later Solomonic temple) the basis for the Priestly Tabernacle, has recently been strongly supported with archaeological data by Yohanan Aharoni, "The Solomonic Temple, the Tabernacle and the Arad Sanctuary," AOAT 22 (1973) 6. Note that 2 Sam 7.1-7 presumes a close identification between ark and Yahweh (cf. vss. 2b and 5b) and therefore that the ark has always been sheltered in a tent or tabernacle.

[16]See the study of Fretheim, "Psalm 132," for a good, overall discussion.

[17]Note that this differs from the preceding story in vss. 1-11 where the ark is drawn on a cart. The latter is clearly based on 1 Sam 6.7-12 (or a common tradition). However, the mysterious way in which the ark is self-guided here is also comparable to Josh 3.4. On this problem, cf. above, ch. 8, n. 21; also the Excursus, n. 18.

[18]"Psalm 132," 298.

[19]*Ibid.*, 291. For the connections with earlier traditions concerning the ark, see p. 300 and especially n. 48.

[20]For what follows, see now the brief discussion of divine abandonment and cultic statues in Campbell, *Ark Narrative*, 179-191. Much of this is discussed in more detail, of course, in Cogan, *Imperialism and Religion*, and especially in chs. 1 and 2.

[21]Cf. ch. 3, (2)a. Although not using the Near Eastern material discussed in Part I, Woudstra (*Ark*, 42 and passim) refers to the ark as the "emblem" of Yahweh's presence.

²²Cf. above, ch. 1, (2).

²³It should be pointed out here that Campbell's study of the ark narrative has attempted to qualify significantly the connection between religion and politics in 2 Samuel 6 (*Ark Narrative*, especially 202, 205). He argues that the Perez-uzzah incident is used to demonstrate that the legitimation of the new political order under David is conditional to the free grace of Yahweh, and depends on Yahweh's initiative. This fits with the emphasis in the earlier part of the ark narrative (1 Samuel 4) where the political situation was also rejected. Thus "There is here the statement of a distance on the part of Yahweh over against the political order" 205). Campbell's contribution deserves further consideration, and, in fact, is complementary to our understanding of the oracle of rejection by Nathan in 2 Samuel 7 (see below). However, in our judgment the weight of the evidence still points to legitimation as the primary thrust, involving a correlation of theological and political factors which characterizes the typology of exaltation.

²⁴Thus Aage Bentzen ["The Cultic Use of the Story of the Ark in Samuel," *JBL* 67 (1948) 44] interpreted the whole story of the ark in 1 and 2 Samuel as reflecting the myth of Yahweh's battle with the monsters of chaos. For Bentzen, the prose narrative could be seen as the myth, while Psalm 132 was the ritual, associated with a festival inaugurated by David in celebration of his founding of the temple and his dynasty (51). Cf. the less rigid yet still highly debatable remarks by Porter, "2 Samuel vi," 169-171. For more recent discussion, see Campbell, *Ark Narrative*, 51, 84, 87-91, 154-155, 188-189, 253-254.

²⁵The terms are used by Porter ("2 Samuel vi," 163) especially with reference to Mowinckel and Kraus respectively. Cf. the analysis of the ritualistic elements in 2 Samuel 6 (as compared to Exodus 32) by Sasson, "Worship of the Golden Calf," 155-156. Note especially his sound strictures against those who see a "non-Yahwistic ritual" here (in this case, ostensibly 'Jebusite'; 156, n. 21).

²⁶See Fretheim, "Psalm 132," 295-297. Note also Campbell, *Ark Narrative*, 140, 241-243, and Cross, *CMHE*, 94-97.

²⁷The Priestly account of the consecration of the Tabernacle in Exod 40. 33b-38 is very closely related to 1 Kings 8 and is, perhaps, literarily dependent on it.

²⁸There is a particularly intriguing correspondence between the later years of Tukulti-Ninurta and those of Solomon and his successor, Rehoboam. According to Klengel ("Tukulti-Ninurta," 73-75), Tukulti-Ninurta gradually lost the esteem of his early years due to the lack of continued military victories (and the resultant booty) and to the strain caused by his massive building activities. It is also possible that the latter offended religious sensitivities when the new cult city was seen as an insult to the old complex. Moreover, the Assyrians themselves were probably disturbed by the irreverent removal of the statue of Marduk. For these reasons, rebellion was easily fomented by one of Tukulti-Ninurta's own sons, who had his father put to death.

²⁹We would agree with Cross (*CMHE*, 242-243) in seeing some continuity between the two. Cross suggests that the tent of David was in accordance with old traditions reflected also in 2 Sam 7.5-7, and was the successor to the tent at Shiloh (231 and n. 52). Cf. above, n. 15. The reference to the installation of the ark in 2 Sam 6.17 does not

betray signs of deliberate editing, *contra* Görg, *Zelt der Begegnung*, 80. Görg thinks this verse was influenced by a ritual procession of the ark seen in vss. 13, 15, 17-18 (*Ibid.*, 81-82). Later, he suggests that this tent at most could have been only a protective device (84-85). For a link with the story of the ark in 1 Samuel, cf. the use of *yṣg* here in vs. 16 and in 1 Sam 5.2.

It is also intriguing that "*the* tent" is involved in the anointing of Solomon at Gihon. The context gives a strong implication that this was somehow connected with the old *Führerzelt*. Cf. Deut 31.14-15, 23 [see above, ch. 6, (2)].

In 1 Kgs 8.4 the "Tent of Meeting" is explicitly mentioned as identical to the tent erected by David. However, the heavy redactional hand here makes this evidence difficult to use.

[30] The fact that David's request to build a temple is rejected through the word of the prophet which came to him (in a vision?) by night has an interesting parallel in Gudea's visit to Nanše in search of an interpretation of his dream. Falkenstein (*IGL*, 119 and n. 1) has pointed out that a positive interpretation was crucial since it was quite possible for a deity to deny permission to build him a temple.

[31] Cf. Cross, *CMHE*, 242-244; Hertzberg, *Samuel*, 287; Clements, *God and Temple*, 56.

[32] For further arguments against this position, see Clements, *God and Temple*, 58-59, Cross, *CMHE*, 245-246.

[33] Cf. Arvid S. Kapelrud, "Temple Building, A Task for Gods and Kings," *Or* 32 (1963) 56-62.

[34] This is the order of events in the Nur-Adad Letter, the Tukulti-Ninurta Epic, *Enuma eliš*, and many of the Assyrian annals.

[35] Cf. Deut 31.14-15, and our brief discussion above in ch. 6, (2). It is interesting that Nathan is also involved in the *anointing* of Solomon which takes place in connection with "the tent" in 1 Kgs 1.38-40. Nevertheless, there are difficulties involved in harmonizing the role of Nathan here with that in 2 Samuel 7, especially given the bold expression of dynastic succession in 1 Kgs 1.35.

[36] Accepting the standard emendation of *šibṭê* to *šōpᵉṭê*, as in 1 Chr 17.6.

[37] *God and Temple*, 60. This can be compared to Cross (*CMHE*, 243) who concludes that the oracle "testifies to David's acceptance of a limited kingship . . . ." On this, cf. already Fretheim, "Psalm 132," 298, n. 43.

[38] This is particularly the case with the expression *w'hyh ᶜmmk bkl 'šr hlkt*; cf. Joshua 1.9, *ᶜmmk yhwh 'lhyk bkl 'šr tlk*, with Jacob, *hnnh ᶜnky ᶜmmk wšmrtyk bkl 'šr tlk*, Gen 28.15. Of course, the militaristic connotation is lacking with Jacob.

[39] The original form of the oracle of Nathan in vss. 1-7 contained an oath concerning David's progeny, similar to Ps 132.11-12, according to Cross, *CMHE*, 255. There is definitely a new beginning at vs. 8. Cross (254 and n. 155) sees vss. 8-11a as a deuteronomistic linkage, but containing some older material. Vss. 11b-16 thus form the second oracle, the "oracle of the eternal divine decree," with respect to the 'old oracle' of Nathan in vss. 1-7. The oldest core of the second oracle is found in vs. 14 (257-258).

^{40}So also Cross, *CMHE*, 257, 260; Weiser, "Legitimation," 347, 349.

^{41}Other than the texts discussed immediately below, cf. 1 Chr 29.12, a prayer of David in which he acknowledges that it is in Yahweh's power to exalt and to give strength to all; 29.25, a summary accolade on Solomon's accession; 2 Chr 1.1 similar to the latter text; Gen 12.2, *w'gddlh šmk*, referring of course to Abraham--a clear implication of the influence of the Davidic monarchy on the Yahwistic theology. Elsewhere the expression occurs with human subjects in Est 3.1; 5.11; 10.2.

^{42}Benaiah's exclamation is paraphrased in vs. 47, including a reference to Solomon's "name" (*šm*).

^{43}It is interesting that the deuteronomistic prayer of David in 2 Samuel 7.18-29 responds by emphasizing both the exaltation of Yahweh and of his people, both of which are now tied to the confirmation of Yahweh's preceding promise. Thus vs. 22 declares that there is no god like Yahweh, or indeed *except* Yahweh, and vs. 23 follows with the corollary that there is no people like Israel (cf. Deut 4.32-40). This correlation is especially reminiscent of the one in Exodus 15. (Cf. also Deut 33.26a, 29a: *'yn k'l yšrwn* and *'šryk yšr'l my kmwk*; see our discussion above.) Yet this exaltation of Yahweh and people from the past is now inseparably linked to the continuity of the Davidic dynasty: when Yahweh confirms his promise, his name will be magnified forever, and the dynasty of his servant will be established before him (vss. 25-26).

^{44}For approximations of this formulation--and others we have seen before--ascribed to David himself, see above on 2 Sam 7.9. Note especially 1 Sam 20.13, without explicit reference to exaltation.

^{45}The third section, vss. 39-53, has its most likely setting in the Exilic period and is clearly dependent for its language on the second. It should be noted that only the second and third sections have a past orientation.

^{46}Vs. 3 is very corrupt, no doubt due to the insertion of vss. 4-5. At least part of vss. 1-3 have probably been adapted to the Davidic section following. The use of *ḥsd* at least provided an easy transition. Cross (*CMHE*, 257) sees vss. 3-5 and 20-38 as belonging together.

^{47}Read as follows: *yhwh ṣb'wt my-kmwk, ḥªsînah we'ĕmûnāh sᵉbîbôteykā.* Strength and Fidelity represent hypostatizations of divine attributes; cf. vs. 15. For the imagery throughout vss. 6-9, cf. especially Exod 15.11 and Deut 33.26 and our discussion above.

^{48}Vss. 10-11 echo the mythical battle against Sea.

^{49}Vss. 10-11, 12-13, 14-15 (again hypostases as in vs. 9), 16-19 respectively.

^{50}Vss. 18-19. We read the *lamedhs* in vs. 19 as asseveratives; so also Mitchell Dahood, *Psalms II* (The Anchor Bible; Garden City, N.Y.: Doubleday, 1968) 315. Dahood (316) also provides the translation of *māgēn* as "suzerain." Even if the traditional reading were maintained, where *malkēnû* refers to the human king, this older section of the poem places him at best on a par with the people, and certainly not in a central position as in the following unit. In this case, we would argue that the earlier section reflects the incipient development of kingship, perhaps even from the period of Saul's hegemony.

^{51}"Yahweh, in the light of your presence they walk" (*yhwh b'wr-pnyk yhllkwn*). The combination of this with 16a ("Blessed are the people who know the festal shout [$t^e r\hat{u}{}^c \bar{a}h$]), may well indicate that a cultic procession is in mind in which the ark represented Yahweh's "presence."

[52]The process would thus be similar to the introduction of vss. 4-5 following the mention of Yahweh's hsd in vs. 2. Vss. 20-21 also reiterate the use in vs. 4 of bhr and ${}^c bd\dot{y}$. An interesting redactional effect of vss. 4-5 is that vss. 6-19 now become a hymn of praise to Yahweh in response to his covenant with David.

[53]Reading on the basis of Ugaritic lexicography; cf. Dahood, *Psalms II*, 316, and Cross, *CMHE*, 258.

[54]Note the same expression applied to the *people* in vs. 18.

[55]2 Sam 23.1-7 is of further interest. Here we learn of the "utterance of the hero who was raised on high" ($wn'm\ hgbr\ huqam\ {}^c \bar{a}l$); however a better reading is $h\bar{e}q\hat{i}m\ '\bar{e}l$, supported, according to Cross (*CMHE*, 234, n. 65, 66), by 4QSam^a. The meaning, of course, is still the same. Note Cross's translation: "Oracle of him whom '$\bar{E}$l exalted" (235). Other texts could also be discussed in this connection, especially Psalms 2 and 110.

[56]See above, p. 38.

[57]Cf. Cross, *CMHE*, 233, 260. The view of Cross regarding the development in covenant and kingship ideology is anticipated in Fretheim, "Psalm 132," 298, n. 43.

[58]Cf. Cross, *CMHE*, 257-260.

[59]Note also that Solomon's dream in 1 Kings 3, in which Yahweh appears to him, also serves a legitimating function (especially vs. 28). Cf. Porter, "Succession," 128. On this process, compare the role of the Nur-Adad letter in the legitimation of Nur-Adad's son, Sin-iddinam, ch. 1 (2).

[60]"Origin of the Zion Tradition," 340.

[61]*Ibid.*, 340-341.

[62]*Ibid.*, 339-340.

[63]"The Religio-Political Setting of Psalm 47," BASOR 221 (1976), 129-132. I am indebted to the author for giving me a copy of the manuscript.

[64]*Ibid.*, 132.

[65]"Origin of the Zion Tradition," 341-342.

[66]*Ibid.*, 342. Cf. also Porter, "2 Samuel vi," 162-163.

[67]"Jahwes Königsprädizierung als Verklärung national-politischer Ansprüche Israels," *Kleine Schriften*, Fünfter Band (Tübingen: J. C. B. Mohr, 1973), 219.

[68]*Ibid.*

SUMMARY

SUMMARY

In this study we have attempted to discuss only a portion of the
motifs of divine presence in the Old Testament, yet, even within these
limitations, we have found an exceedingly rich and multicolored picture.
The presence of God can be represented by everything from divine messengers to thunderstorms, from fiery theophanies to the silent evidence
of providence. It is thus with considerable justification that G. H.
Davies can propose the following generalization:

> The material of the presence theme is so complex, and
> the media of manifestation so varied, that attempts
> to trace various stages in the development of the
> doctrine have not been successful.[1]

As examples of this variety, we have concluded that motifs of divine
presence are used in the Old Testament in a number of ways, often with
different emphases: they are used (1) in literary contexts now detached
from any particular historical background (Habbakuk 3; Psalm 68; Deuteronomy 33); (2) in folkloristic narratives in connection with an individual's journey (Abraham's servant, Genesis 24; Jacob, Gen 28.10-22); (3)
in archaic poetry in connection with major battles (Exodus 15; Judges 5);
(4) in contexts reflecting a merging of both cultic and historical traditions, especially in connection with Israel's wilderness journey (Numbers 9-10), or the crossing of the Jordan (Joshua 1; 3-5), or the return
of the ark (2 Samuel 6; Psalm 132); (5) in connection with the vicissitudes of political power in Canaan (2 Samuel 5-7); (6) or with the consecration of the cultic establishment of Israel (Exodus 40; 1 Kings 8).
Despite this basic variety, however, it is clear that, certainly
on the redactional level, the motifs at times function as major elements
in a larger, more unified picture. This is dramatically the case in the
material from the book of Exodus, which formed the centre of our discussion.

Indeed, as Moshe Greenberg has suggested,

> It is possible to epitomize the entire story of Exodus
> in the movement of the fiery manifestation of the di-
> vine presence. . . . The book thus recounts the stages
> in the descent of the divine presence to take up its
> abode for the first time among one of the peoples of
> the earth.[2]

This statement by Greenberg leads us to make two observations. First,
we would conclude from the preceding study that it is not only in "the
entire story of Exodus," but also in individual literary and traditio-
historical units that one can trace a certain continuity in the form and
function of motifs of divine presence. This is also true for material
dealing with the Conquest and with the rise of the Davidic Empire. Secondly, the connection between "the divine presence" and "*one* of the
peoples of the earth" points to the very heart of this continuity--the
typology of exaltation.

In Part I the typology of exaltation was discussed within its ancient Near Eastern context. There we concluded that motifs of divine
presence occurred with significant frequency in major literary works or
in annalistic sources in conjunction with the exaltation of a particular
deity as well as the deity's human protégé. Moreover, the particular
literary expression of divine presence was often that of the vanguard
motif, which portrayed the god(s) as being involved in historical battles resulting in the political supremacy of the human ruler and devotee.

In Part II we have repeatedly found a number of striking parallels
to this typology of exaltation in the Old Testament, but also some very
significant differences. The greatest similarity comes where it is perhaps most expected: in the descriptions of the rise of the Davidic-
Solomonic empire. Thus in 2 Samuel 5 we found that Yahweh was "with"
(^{c}im) David, that he exalted his kingdom ($n\acute{s}'$, Piel), that he fought
in front of David as a flood. Moreover, the return of the ark from
Philistine control and its incorporation in the new political capitol
of Jerusalem (2 Samuel 6) closely resembled the role played by cultic
objects in the Near Eastern texts. With Solomon, the typology of exaltation reached its zenith. The construction of the temple, consummated
by the inaugural procession of the ark and the advent of Yahweh in the
cloud and glory, reveal the clearest correlation between divine presence

and imperial splendor. The language of exaltation (*gdl*, Piel; *rwm*,
Hiphil) is now applied to Solomon (1 Kings 1; Psalm 89), whose position
is elevated to that of sonship with Yahweh.

Parallels to the function of motifs of divine presence in the Near
Eastern material were also noticed in connection with the figures of
Moses and Joshua, yet, here in particular, one begins to discern Israel's
own distinctive understanding of this function. The material surrounding
the figure of Joshua (Joshua 1; 3-5) was seen to contain motifs of divine
presence associated with the ark and with Yahweh as the victor over the
land of Canaan. Especially in the deuteronomistic redaction, Yahweh's
presence with Joshua (*ᶜim*), along with the startling events surrounding
the crossing of the river, served to demonstrate Joshua's exaltation
(*gdl*, Piel) in the eyes of Israel. Thus the figure of Joshua reflects
that of his royal counterparts in the later monarchy. But for the
Deuteronomist, Joshua is clearly much more than a royal figure. In
fact, he is a religious leader, and his ultimate legitimation is dependent on observation of Torah, with which Yahweh's presence is now
intimately linked.

Joshua is, in a sense, a mediating figure between Moses and the
Davidic kings, combining characteristics of both the royal potentate
and the religious leader. The same can be said of Moses himself, yet
here the differences from the Near Eastern typology of exaltation are
even more striking. The basic similarity remains, in that motifs of
divine presence are utilized to legitimate an individual leader. Nevertheless, despite the adumbrations of royalty in the picture of Moses, he
remains primarily a religious figure. This is clearly one implication
of the fact that the language of exaltation here is not that used for
the above figures (*gdl*, Piel; *nś'*, Piel; *rwm*, Hiphil), but centers in
the recurring use of the root '*mn*, which carries the connotation of
"belief" or even of "faith." This word occurs in conjunction with motifs
of divine presence in Moses' call (Exodus 3-4), in the Reed Sea deliverance (Exodus 14), at Sinai (Exodus 19), and in the wilderness challenges
to his authority (Numbers 12). Thus, in the end, the basic analogy for
the figure of Moses is not the ancient Near Eastern king, but the priestly
and prophetic mediator of divine presence.

In short, the narrative and later hymnic texts of the Old Testament
discussed above reveal a pronounced tendency to associate motifs of
divine presence with the exaltation of an individual leader. In this

there is a very strong similarity to the way in which analogous motifs within the ancient Near Eastern texts are associated with royal figures. This similarity is most complete with David and Solomon; with Moses, Israel's peculiar understanding of the relationship between divine presence and exaltation is most pronounced; with Joshua, there is a clear mixture of the two types.

Israel's understanding of her religious leader does not provide the only difference from the Near Eastern material. Within the Sinai and Wilderness traditions, there are three others that deserve special mention. First, there is the way in which the vanguard motif has been used to represent Yahweh's presence and *guidance* on Israel's journey from the Reed Sea to the Jordan River. We found that the motif of the god(s) going in front of the king on his march was a prominent one in the Near Eastern texts. This motif, along with others served to express divine presence in historical battles and, in conjunction with oracles, at times indicated that the king marched at the direction of the gods. It is only in the Old Testament material, however, that the theme of *guidance* becomes a prominent feature of the vanguard motif. While this may well be due in part to ancient traditions stemming from Israel's "semi-nomadic" past, it is our conclusion that a greater impetus came from the very situation described in the Sinai material: Israel found herself delivered from Egyptian bondage and entrusted to the care of her God, who alone could lead her to the land of promise. We would thus suggest that the emphasis on the theme of Yahweh's guiding presence is not simply a literary or traditio-historical linking device, but stems from the historical situation of the Wilderness March.

It is also clear that the theme of divine presence and guidance in the Sinai pericope is profoundly disturbed by the catastrophic sin of the golden calf. As we have seen, it is quite reasonable to find in Exodus 32 an attempt to construct a cultic object similar to those in the ancient Near Eastern iconographic traditions—in short, a physical object to represent Yahweh's presence and guidance. The intensity of the impact of this attempt within the Sinai pericope is, of course, greatly multiplied by the deeply rooted aniconic strain within Israelite traditions. Thus the consistent lack of a physical image of *Yahweh himself* provides another major divergence from the Near Eastern material, and one that accentuates the need for the assurance of his presence in the Wilderness traditions.

236

On the other hand, we have seen that Israel did possess a physical object that is often very closely identified with Yahweh's presence-- the ark. The ark is used as the subject of the vanguard motif in connection with Yahweh the Holy Warrior, and this combination has also been adapted to express Israel's peculiar concern with guidance. However, this does not detract from the resemblance between the ark and the use of similar objects in the cultic texts examined in Part I. Indeed, this resemblance adds weight to the view that the stories of Exodus and Conquest in particular were shaped in part within the setting of a cultic celebration of the events themselves. The fact that the vanguard motif --and the typology of exaltation--in the Near Eastern material is shared by both cultic texts and literary and annalistic sources that report the march of the victorious kings, adds a certain cogency to the possibility of an Israelite ark processional that celebrated the march of Yahweh and his chosen people. Moreover, the persistent concentration of the use of the vanguard motif at moments of departure (Exodus, Sinai, Jordan River), and its association, at least redactionally, with Passover, presents an intriguing possibility for the identification of the cultic setting.

Finally, and most importantly, we may return to the statement of Greenberg (quoted above) in order to emphasize a third difference between the Old Testament and the Near Eastern texts. Greenberg noted that the story of Exodus recounted the advent of the divine presence among *one* of the peoples of the earth. This correlation between Yahweh's presence and Israel's nascent corporate identity we have compared a number of times to the typology of exaltation, especially in our discussion of Israel's early poetry. In Exodus 15, above all, the themes of divine presence and guidance are salient. Yahweh's exaltation over all possible contenders through the battle at the Sea is correlated with the supremacy of his people over the nations of Canaan. In Deuteronomy 33 (the "frame song"), Israel is seen in connection with the divine vanguard, and her incomparability is correlated with that of Yahweh. Finally, in Judges 5, Yahweh's advent in the storm sets the scene for the intervention of cosmic forces in the battle of Megiddo, which very likely achieved a major advancement in the unification of the tribes as the "people of Yahweh."

In short, the early poetry of the Old Testament focuses almost totally on the figure of the *people*. Here the presence of the Holy Warrior in battle results in his exaltation over the gods of Canaan,

and the exaltation of his people over the nations. Moreover, we have
observed that it is only with the prose traditions of these events that
the individual leaders come into prominence and are associated with the
typology of exaltation. This, then, is the most distinctive facet within Israel's understanding of divine presence and exaltation. Unlike the
Exaltation of Enheduanna, the Song of Miriam does not proclaim the exaltation of its author--or even of Moses--alongside that of Yahweh. Indeed,
as Labuschagne has said,

> It is remarkable that nowhere else in the ancient Middle
> East was the attribute of incomparability applied to a
> community: we find it only in connection with Israel.[3]

In connection with the prominence of the people in the Old Testament
typology of exaltation, one additional comment is, perhaps, in order.
Despite the clear emphasis on Israel's exalted status vis-à-vis the other
nations, it is also clear throughout the Old Testament that there is a
concurrent strain emphasizing that it was not Israel herself who accomplished her exaltation. One need only look at Deuteronomy 1-11, for
example, to see in classic form the statement that Israel was not only not
the agent of her special status, but was also unworthy of it. Each generation of Israel is called--indeed, commanded--to remember that "we
were Pharaoh *slaves* in Egypt." To be sure, there is even here an interesting analogy to the typology of exaltation in some of the Near Eastern
texts, especially that of the Exaltation of Inanna. In the latter, there
is also a dramatic reversal, which moves from humiliation and oppression
to exaltation, and (as in numerous other texts) the credit for this reversal is ascribed to the deity. But the frequent emphasis in the Old
Testament traditions on Israel's unworthiness, in fact, her stubborn
apostasy, surely bears a theological stamp all its own. As Moses says
in Deut 9.24, "You have been rebellious against Yahweh from the day that
I knew you." Although our study has not focused on this aspect of Israel's self-understanding, it cannot be ignored in any thorough theological interpretation.

Our conclusions concerning the distinctive marks of Israel's understanding of the correlation between divine presence and the typology of
exaltation are not by any means intended to demonstrate the "superiority"
of Israel over her ancient neighbors. Any attempt to do so would be
fraught, not only with very complicated problems of historical methodology,

238

but also with the question as to whether the attempt itself dooms the would-be historian to inevitable failure. Our purpose has been much more modest: to demonstrate the significant correspondence between the form and function of motifs of divine presence in the Old Testament and the ancient Near Eastern texts, but also to take seriously the ways in which the Old Testament reflects Israel's peculiar historical and religious experience. In our judgment, both sides of this discussion must be held in balance if we are to come to grips with Israel's understanding of the presence of God, and of the exaltation which this presence achieved, not only for him, but also for his people and his chosen leaders.

In conclusion, we may suggest some modest proposals concerning the implications that the preceding study holds for further research. For example, despite the clear divergences between the figure of Moses and that of the Near Eastern kings noted above, our study indicates that a careful examination of the final formation of the Yahwistic narrative, at least in Exodus, might be undertaken with the purpose of ascertaining to what extent, if any, the Davidic exaltation has been influential.[4] For a later period, it should come as no surprise that our study has important bearings on the use of major themes in 2 Isaiah. Not only the Exodus typology in general, but also the use of the vanguard motif and the language of exaltation, coupled with the tendencies toward monotheism, again indicate significant correspondence with earlier Old Testament traditions and the ancient Near Eastern texts in Part I.[5]

For New Testament scholars, there are also important implications. Indeed, the explicit references to the exaltation of Christ (cf. Acts 2.32-36; Phil 2.6-11) have led one recent theologian to suggest that the New Testament begins with a "christology of the exaltation."[6] Similarly, one could argue that two of the most important texts for the interpretation of the resurrection were Psalms 2 and 110, both of which could easily be included with our other exemplars for the exaltation typology.[7] More specifically, the portrayal of John the Baptist as the one who prepares the way for the Christ, and the baptism of Jesus, at which he is proclaimed the Son of God, involve both the vanguard motif and the typology of exaltation.[8] Even more so, the transfiguration of Jesus, where Jesus' face shines like the sun, where Moses and Elijah appear with him, and where a voice again proclaims--*out of the cloud*--that Jesus is the Son of God, are clearly heir to major traditions which we have investigated in the Old Testament.[9] Finally, it is not unreasonable to see some of the resurrection appearances as serving the function of legitimating the authority of the apostolic witnesses, a function which would be similar to that of the motifs of divine presence examined in this study.[10]

Along with Old and New Testament studies, there are also suggestions for Church History and Theology. The early and continuing struggles surrounding the correlation of politics and religion, in which the concepts of a "Christian imperial theology" and of an independent secular order vie for the loyalty of the Church, present perennial manifestations of the historical and theological developments with which our investigation has attempted to deal.[11] In short, the typology of exaltation is by no means a phenomenon isolated either in the ancient Near East or in the Old Testament, but constitutes a fundamental tension, intrinsic to any religion that attempts to address itself to the realities of history.

NOTES TO SUMMARY

[1]"Presence of God," *IDB* 3, 875a.

[2]*Understanding Exodus* (Melton Research Center Series, Vol. II, Part I: The Heritage of Biblical Israel; New York: Behrman House, 1969) 16-17.

[3]*Incomparability*, 149.

[4]Basic to this approach, of course, is the study of Hans Walter Wolff, "The Kerygma of the Yahwist," *Interp* 20 (1966) 131-158. For a more recent, and in some ways rather forced, attempt to extend this work, see the article by Walter Brueggemann, "David and his Theologian," *CBQ* 30 (1968) 156-181. Also important is the article by Benjamin Mazar, "The Historical Background of Genesis," *JNES* 28 (1969) 73-83. For more specific correlations, cf. the use of '*mn* and *l^cwlm* in Exod 14.31; 19.9; Num 12.7 and 2 Sam 7.12, 16; Ps 89.28. See above, ch. 5, n. 42, and ch. 6, n. 25.

[5]On the Exodus typology, see Bernhard W. Anderson, "Exodus Typology in Second Isaiah," in *Israel's Prophetic Heritage: Essays in Honor of James Muilenburg*, ed. Bernhard W. Anderson and Walter Harrelson (New York: Harper, 1962) 177-195. For representative examples of several of our motifs and themes, cf. Isa 45.14, 22-25; 52.12-13. For indications of the relation to ancient Near Eastern materials, see Claus Westermann, *Isaiah 40-66* (The Old Testament Library; Philadelphia: Westminster, 1969) 38, 45. Of course, 2 Isaiah presents a fundamental transformation, in that Yahweh's exaltation is declared over against a people defeated and in exile.

[6]Piet Schoonenberg, "Notes of a Systematic Theologian," in *Theology, Exegesis, and Proclamation*, ed. Roland Murphy (Concilium: Religion in the Seventies, 70; New York: Herder and Herder, 1971) 90-97. On the "form of God" in Phil 2.6, cf. Num 12.8 and our discussion in ch. 6. Also worthy of mention is Eph 4.8-11 and its adaptation of Ps 68.18.

[7]See David M. Hay, *Glory at the Right Hand: Psalm 110 in Early Christianity* (Nashville: Abingdon, 1973).

[8]Note Mt 3.3. and parallels, Mt 11.7-15, and Lk 1.76. On the baptism, see Mt 3.16-17 and parallels.

[9]Mt 17.1-9 and parallels. Note also the way in which the cloud is involved in the Ascension, Acts 1.9. Cf. especially Exod 24.15-18 and 34.29-35, and note the parallel between 34.32 and Acts 1.2.

[10]Cf. especially Mt 28.16-20; Acts 1; and 1 Cor 15.1-11. I owe this suggestion to my colleague, Prof. J. Christiaan Beker.

[11]Cf. the recent study by Rosemary Radford Ruether, "Augustine and Christian Political Theology," *Interp* 29 (1975) 252-265. Our study also has clear implications regarding American "civil religion."

APPENDICES

APPENDIX 1

SUPPLEMENTARY CUNEIFORM TEXTS

1. Excerpt from Tablet XI of the Gilgamesh Epic:

96 mim-mu-u še-e-ri i-na na-ma-ri
97 i-lam-ma iš-tu i-šid samê(e) ur-pa-tum ṣa-lim-tum
98 ^{d}Adad ina lib-bi-ša ir-tam-ma-am-ma
99 ^{d}PA u ^{d}LUGAL il-la-ku ina maḫ-ri
100 il-la-ku guzalê^{pl} šaddû(u) u ma-a-tum
101 tar-kul-li ^{d}IRRA(RA).GAL i-na-as-siḫ
102 il-lak ^{d}Ninurta mi-iḫ-ra u-šar-di
103 ^{d}A-nun-na-ki iš-šu-u di-pa-ra-a-ti
104 ina nam-ri-ir-ri-šu-nu u-ḫa-am-ma-ṭu ma-a-tum

With the first glow of dawn,

A black cloud rose up from the horizon:

Inside it Adad thunders resoundingly,

Shullat and Ḫanish go in front,

The throne bearers march over hill and plain.

Erragal tears out the posts,

Ninurta approaches and causes the dikes to flow,

The Annunaki lift up the torches,

Setting the land ablaze with their glare.

The transliterated text is taken from R. Campbell Thompson, *The Epic of Gilgamesh: Text, Transliteration, and Notes* (Oxford: Clarendon, 1930) 62, ll. 96–104. Our translation is indebted in part not only to Thompson, but also to E. A. Speiser, "The Epic of Gilgamesh," *ANET* 94. See also René Labat in *Les religions du Proche-Orient asiatique: Textes babyloniens, ougaritiques, hittites. Le trésor spirituel de l'humanité*, ed. Jean Chevalier (Paris: Fayard/Denoël, 1970) 215.

In light of the context of such language in the texts discussed in

Part I, it is interesting that in Gilgamesh the flood (abūbu) is consistently understood as a battle (qablu, XI.110, 121, 129), and in *Enuma eliš*, Marduk's great weapon in the fight against Tiamat is the flood-storm (abuba kakkašu raba, IV, 49, 75). For the deities involved here cf. I. J. Gelb, "Šullat and Ḥaniš," *ArOr* 18 (1950) 189-198, and W. G. Lambert and A. R. Millard, *Atra-ḥasis: The Babylonian Story of the Flood* (Oxford: Clarendon, 1969) 158, note to 1. 49; also Labat, *Religions*, 215, n. 1.

2. Sargon: along with the passages quoted in ch. 2, the following also are found in the "Letter to Assur" (*TCL* 3, loc.cit.):

(1) pu-luḫ-ti me-lam-me-ia ik-túm-šú-nu-ti
i-na ki-rib mâti-šú-ni im-qut-su-nu ḫat-tu
(p. 12, 1. 69; cf. *ARAB* II, § 149, p. 78).

(2) ᵈAdad gaš-ru mâr ᵈA-nim qar-du ri-gim-šú rabî-tu
eli-šú-nu id-di-ma i-na ur-pat ri-iḫ-ṣi ù aban šame-e
ú-qat-ti ri-e-ḫa (p. 24, 1. 147).

(3) (415)i-na e-mu-qi ṣi-ra-a-te šá ᵈA-šur bêli-ia i-na
li-i-te da-na-ni šá ᵈBel ᵈNabû ilâni^Pl tik-li-ia
(416)i-na an-ni-ki-e-ni šá ᵈŠamaš di-tar-gal ilâni^Pl šá
ṭu-ú-di ip-tu-ma ṣu-lu-lu iš-ku-nu eli um-ma-ni-ia
(417)i-na nir-bi šá ᵈNergal dan-dan ilâni^Pl a-lik i-di-ia
na-ṣir karâši-ia (p. 64, 11. 415-417; cf. *ARAB* II, § 176, p. 99).

(1) [on hearing of Sargon's approach] the fear of my splendor covered them, terror overcame them in their land.

(2) Adad the mighty, the son of Anu, the hero, threw his great voice on them. With a bursting cloud and hail stones he cut off the remainder.

(3) In the exalted might of Assur, my lord, in the power and strength of Bêl and Nabû, the gods my helpers, at the nod of Shamash, the great judge of the gods, who opened the way and spread his protecting shadow over my army, in the greatness of Nergal, the all-powerful among the gods, who goes at my side, guarding my camp. . . . [I marched victoriously to further regions and "returned

in safety to my land"].

3. Sennacherib: depiction of the battle scene from *Enuma eliš* engraved on the copper gates of the *akîtu* temple [text and translation taken from Daniel D. Luckenbill, *The Annals of Sennacherib* (Chicago: University of Chicago Press, 1924) p. 140]:

> 5. abul siparri russâ(a) ša ma-la a-ga-[le^{pl}
> ša] ši-pir ^{d}Nappaḫu
>
> 6. ina nik-lat ramâni-ia ú-še-piš-ma ṣa-
> lam $^⌐d$Aššur ša ana libbi Tiamat]
> ṣal-ti illaku(ku)
>
> 7. ^{w}kaštu ki-i ša na-šú-ú ina ^{w}narkabti ša
> ra-ak-bu a-bu-bu [ša pa-ak⌐-du
>
> 8. ^{d}Amurru ša a-na mu-kil ap-pa-a-ti
> it-ti-šu rak-bu a-⌐na pi⌐-i ša ^{d}Šamaš u
> ^{d}Adad
>
> 9. ina bi-ri ik-bu-nim-ma ṣi-ir abulli
> ša-a-šu e-ṣir ilâni$^{⌐pl⌐}$ pa-ni-šu il-
> laku (ku)
>
> 10. ù arki-šu illaku(ku) ša ru-ku-bu rak-bu
> ša ina šêpâ^{du}-šu illaku(ku) [u] ki-i
> ša ina pâni ^{d}Aššur
>
> 11. si-id-ru u arki ^{d}Aššur si-id-ru Ti-amat
> nab-nit [kir-bi-šu] ša ^{d}Aššur šar ilâni
>
> 12. a-na lìb-bi-šu ṣal-ti il-la-ku a-na ⌐eli
> pi⌐-i ša ^{d}Šamaš u ^{d}Adad ṣi-ir abulli
> ša-a-šu e-ṣir
>
> 5. A gate of burnished copper, with all
> kinds of--, in the workmanship of
> the Smith-god,
>
> 6. by my own artistic ability, I made,
> and the image of Assur, who is
> advancing to battle into the midst
> of Tiamat,
>
> 7. as he raises his bow, riding in a

chariot, bringing on the storm,

8. (and the image of) Amurru, who
rides with him as charioteer (holder
of the reins), (these) I engraved upon
that gate

9. at the command of Shamash and Adad,
as they gave through the oracle.
The gods who went before him

10. and after him, those who rode on
chariots, and those who went on
foot, as they were drawn up in line
before Assur,

11. and as they were drawn up in line
behind Assur. (The image of) Tiamat, (and) the creatures inside her,
into whose midst

12. Assur, king of gods is advancing to
battle,--I engraved upon that gate in
obedience to the command of Shamash and Adad.

4. Esarhaddon: describing a battle against Egypt which he under-
took after receiving a favorable response to his prayer (Borger, *Asarhaddon*, p. 65; cf. *ARAB* II, §§ 561-563, p. 221):

6 lab-biʾ-[iš annadirma]
7 at-tal-bi-iš si-ri-ia-am ḫul-ia-am si-mat
    ˹ṣi]-[ilti âpira]
8 at-muḫ rit-tu-u-a ˢⁱˢqaštu dan-na-tú mul-mul-
    l[u gešru?]
9 šá ᵈAš-šur šar₄ ilâniᵐᵉˢ ú-mal-lu-ú qa-[tûa]
10 kîma arî (Á.MUŠEN) na-ad-ri pe-ta a-gap-pa-a meḫ-ret
    [ummâniia]
11 a-bu-ba-niš al-lak ˢⁱˢšil-ta-ḫi Aššur la p[a-dû]
12 ez-zi-iš šam-riš it-ta-ṣi [. . .]
13 ᵈŠár-ur₄ ᵈŠár-gaz il-la-ku ma[ḫ(?)-riia] (oder:
    ina idi(I[D)-ia]?)
14 [ina] ˹qí-˹bit ᵈAš-šur šar₄ ilâniᵐᵉˢ bêli-iá

ilâni^{meš} ra[bûti^{meš}]

15 [am]-[ḫur]-[šú]-nu-te-ma iš-mu-u su-up-pi-iá x [. . .]

16 ana-ku ^IAš-šur-áḫu-îdina šar₄ mât Aššur a-bu-sat
   ummâniⁿⁱ-ia ERIM x [. . .]

17 ar-ki ilu-ti-šú-nu rabî-tim al-lak ina tukul-ti-
   [šu]-[nu rabîti?]

18 kîma ez-zi ti-ib me-ḫi-i ina bi-ri-šú-nu [azîq]

6 . . . I raged like a lion,

7 I put on my armour, donned the special battle helmet;

8 I grasped in my hand the mighty bow, the powerful dart

9 which Assur, king of the gods, had put into my grasp.

10 Like a raging eagle, with wings outspread, in front
   of [my troops]

11 like a flood I advanced. The unsparing lance of Assur,

12 fiercely, violently was let loose [. . .].

13 Shar-ur and Shar-gaz went before me [or, at my side].

14 At the command of Assur, king of the gods, my lord,
   I addressed the great gods

15 and they heard my prayer [. . .]

16 I, Esarhaddon, king of Assyria, the front of my
   army [. . .]

17 behind their great divinity I advanced. With their
   great aid,

18 like the rage of a stormy wind, I blew into them
   [the enemy].

5. Assurbanipal: (1) The following text is taken from Streck,
Assurbanipal, p. 78, being a section of column IX of the Rassam Cylinder.
There is a striking juxtaposition between recognition of treaty-breaking
and punishment (Streck [n. 3] refers to Deut 29.24 as a parallel). Thus
the recognition comes in the midst of punishment, which is depicted in
graphic detail in the lines preceding 1. 68, and which is renewed in
11. 75ff with the motif of the vanguard (cf. *ARAB* II, § 829, pp. 318-319
[The superscripts e through q refer to Streck's own footnotes.]).

68 niše^{meš} mâtu_{a-ri-bi} ištên^{en} a-na ištên^{en}

69 iš-ta-na^e-'-a-lum a-ḫa-meš

70 um-ma ina eli mi-ni-e ki-i ip-še-e^e-túf an-ni-túf
   limuttu^{tú}

71 im-ḫu-ru ^{mâtu}a-ru^g-bu^h

71 im-ḫu-ru ^{mâtu}a-ru^{g}-bu^{h}

72 um-ma aš-šu a-di-e rabûti^{meš} ša ^{ilu}aššur la ni-iṣ-ṣu-ru

73 ni-iḫ-ṭu-ú ina ṭâbti ^{I} ^{ilu}aššur-bân-aplu

74 šarri na-ram libbi^{bi} ^{ilu}ellil

75 ^{ilu}nin-lil ri-im-tù ^{ilu}ellil me-i-tu^{i}

76 ka-dir-ti i-la-a-ti

77 ša it-ti ^{ilu}a-nim u ^{ilu}ellil šit-lu-ṭa-at man-za-zu

78 ú-na-kip^{k} amêlu nakrûti^{meš}-ia ina karnê^{meš}-ša gaš-ra-a-ti

79 ^{ilu}ištar a-ši-bat ^{alu}arba-ilu^{l}

80 ^{ilu}išâtu^{m} lit-bu-šat me-lam-me na-ša-a^{e}-ta^{n}

81 eli ^{mâtu}a-ri-bi i-za-an-nun nab-li

82 ^{ilu}Gira (Ura) ḳar-du a-nun-tu ku-uṣ-ṣur-ma

83 ú-ra-es^{e}-si-pa^{o} ga-ri-ia

84 ^{ilu}nínib tar-ta-ḫu ḳar-ra-du rabû^{u} mâr ^{ilu}ellil

85 ina uṣ-ṣi-šu zak-ti ú-par-ri-' napištim^{tim} amêlu
      nakrû-ti^{meš}-ia

86 ^{ilu}nusku sukallu^{p} na-'-du mu-ša-pu-u bêlu-u-ti

87 ša ina ḳí-bit ^{ilu}aššur ^{ilu}nin-lil ḳa-rid-tú ^{ilu}be-lit
      [taḫazi]^{q}

88 idâ^{II}-a-a il-lik-ma iṣ-ṣu-ra šarru-u-ti

89 mi-iḫ-rit ummânâte-ia iṣ-bat-ma ú-šam-ḳí-ta ga-ri-ia

68, 69 The people of Aribi asked one another,

70, 71 "Why has such evil happened to Arubu?--

    72 Because we have not kept the great treaties of Assur;

    73 we have transgressed the goodness of Assurbanipal,

    74 the king beloved of Ellil's heart."

    75 Ninlil, beloved of Ellil, the mighty,

    76 the proud one among the goddesses,

    77 who occupies a station of power along with Anu and Ellil,

    78 gored my enemies with her great horns.

    79 Ishtar, who dwells in Arbela,

    80 was clothed with fire, bearing splendor.

    81 Over the land of Aribi fire rained down.

    82 The warrior Girra engaged the battle,

    83 slew my foes.

    84 Ninib, the lance, the great warrior, son of Ellil,

    85 pierced my enemies to the life with his sharp arrow.

86 Nusku, the exalted messenger, who establishes my rule,

87 who at the command of Assur and Ninlil, the valorous
　　　lady [of battle?].

88 goes at my side, guarding my kingship,

89 took the vanguard of my enemies and brought low my foes.

(2)　More typical of the straight annalistic style is a text (K 2656)
describing Assurbanipal's campaign against Elam, which includes three of
the four expressions discussed above, p. 62.　Excerpts are given here
(text from Streck, *Assurbanipal*, No. 7, pp. 194-197; cf. *ARAB* II,　§§
931-932, pp. 360-361):

14 a-na-ku ^ilu^aššur-bân-aplu . . . ina tukulti^ti^ ^ilu^aššur u
　　　^ilu^nergal ilâni^meš^ ti-ik-li-ia

15 ša-ni-a-nu ad-ki ummânâte-ia ṣi-ir ^I^um-man-al-da-si šár
　　　^mâtu^e-lam-ti ak-ba-a a-la-ku . . .

19 ^ilu^aššur šar ilâni^meš^ ^ilu^nergal be-lum ṣi-i-ru ša ina
　　　maḫ-ri-ia il-la-ku ú-ša-zi-zu-in-ni ṣi-ir gar-ri-ia . . .

22 šal-ši-a-nu ^ilu^aššur bêlu ṣi-i-ru ^ilu^nergal kar-rad
　　　ilâni^meš^ ^ilu^i-šum ša kâtâ^II^-šu as-ma* ú-tak-ki-lu-ni-ma
　　　a-na ^mâtu^elamti^ki^ ik-bu-ni a-la-ku.

(14) I, Assurbanipal . . . with the help of Assur and Nergal,
　　　　the gods my helpers,

(15) the second time mustered my troops and ordered them
　　　　to march against Ummanaldasi, king of the land
　　　　of Elam. . . .

(19) Assur, king of the gods, and Nergal, august lord,
　　　　who go before me, supported me against my
　　　　enemy. . . .

(22) A third time Assur, august lord, Nergal, hero of
　　　　the gods, and Išum, whose hand is suited*,
　　　　helped me and ordered me to march to the land
　　　　of Elam.

*On this phrase, cf. its occurrence in the Erra Epic, I.4; see above.

APPENDIX 2

TERMINOLOGY OF DIVINE PRESENCE

IN THE OLD TESTAMENT

One of the most striking aspects of the study of divine presence
in the Old Testament is the way in which the various motifs tend to
cluster in certain literary sections and/or in certain historical periods. What follows is by no means an exhaustive glossary (e.g., terms
such as *kābôd* have not been included), but, with only one exception,
focuses on the verbs *with divine subject* which express divine presence
or appearance. For convenience, the terms are presented in alphabeti-
cal order (x refers to frequency of occurrence; thus "3x" means "three
times"). Our survey was conducted using Solomon Mandelkern, *Veteris
Testamenti Concordantiae* (2 vols; Graz: Akademische Druck- und Verlagsanstalt, 1955 [1937]).

bw' The use of this verb with divine subject is extremely rare
throughout the Pentateuch and the Former Prophets, increasing significantly in a number of Psalms and, especially, in the Latter Prophets.
It is used only 2x in Genesis, both relating dreams.[1] In Exodus its
use is restricted almost totally to the Sinai theophany. In 14.24 the
subject is the *ᶜnn* (and/or *ml'k h'lhym*). Otherwise it is found only
in 19.9; 20.20, 24. The rest of the Pentateuch contains only three
occurrences, one of which is Deut 33.2.[2] In the Former Prophets, we
have the following: Josh 5.14 (*śr ṣb' yhwh*); Judg 6.11 and 13.9 (*ml'k*);[3]
1 Sam 3.10; 4.3. There are several occurrences in the Psalms (24.7, 9;
50.3; 96.13=98.9), most of which can be compared to those in the Latter
Prophets, where the number increases to the extent that citation of all
is not practicable. The fact that a large majority of these occur in
the Qal impf. should occasion no surprise, given the frequent eschatological bent of this material.

252

hlk This verb is, of course, ubiquitous in the Old Testament. Its use along with a divine subject, however, is relatively rare. In several instances, it is used with Yahweh as subject and means "to go away, depart," usually due to Yahweh's anger at a situation.[4] Less well-attested are mythological motifs using the Piel (Ps 104.3) or Hithpael (Job 22.14), which picture Yahweh "going about" in the heavens in connection with clouds (*ᶜbym*) or wind.[5]

We shall first look at *hlk* by itself, then at *hlk lpny*. In the Qal, *hlk* occurs only sporadically throughout the Old Testament. It is used 2x in Genesis,[6] 4x in Exodus. In Exod 33.14-16, the subject is Yahweh's *pnym*, i.e. Yahweh himself, which seems to be followed by 34.9. Except in Num 12.9, there are no other occurrences of the root in the Pentateuch, except for two uses of the Hithpael: Lev 26.12 (Yahweh's presence conditional to obedience); Deut 23.15 (Yahweh's presence during war). In the Former Prophets it occurs only 2x: Judg 6.21 (*ml'k*; cf. with *bw'*) and 2 Sam 7.6 (the final use of the Hithpael). It is also very rare in the Latter Prophets[7] and nonexistent in the Writings.

Turning to *hlk lpny*, we find it exclusively in connection with the Wilderness March (including the Reed Sea event) or with later adaptations of that tradition. We shall simply list the occurrences here: Exod 13.21; 14.19; 23.23; 32.1, 23, 34; Num 14.14; Deut 1.30, 33; 20.4; 31.6, 8. Elsewhere only Isa 45.2; 52.12; 58.8--clear reflections of the vanguard motif.[8]

Returning to *hlk* by itself, we can add that of the roughly 15 occurrences in the Hiphil with divine subject, mostly in the Latter Prophets, most if not all reflect the Wilderness March as well.[9]

zrh This verb occurs only 4x in the Old Testament with divine subject: Deut 33.2; Isa 60.1, 2, 3. Other uses clearly bring out the sidereal nature of the verb.[10]

ypᶜ Hiphil occurs 6x: Deut 33.2; Ps 50.2; 80.2; 94.1; Job 37.15. Job 10.3 appears to be not directly related to the other occurrences in context.

yṣ' in the Qal is very rarely (about 12x) used with God himself as subject, serving more frequently as predicate to divine agents, whether personal (as *ml'k*; *haśśāṭān*) or impersonal (as wrath, justice),[11] even though these are frequently closely associated with Yahweh, since they "go out from" him.

Three of the examples with God as subject are in a highly mythological context: Isa 26.21=Mic 1.3; Hos 6.3. These may be compared to the use in the "classic epiphany texts," where, however, there is a more clear historical reference: Judg 5.4; Ps 68.8; Hab 3.13. It should be observed that in Ps 68.8, $y\d{s}$' is used along with $lpny$ (and thus is similar to the use of hlk $lpny$), and this, in turn, can be compared to the use of the same phrase in a narrative setting: Judg 4.14; 2 Sam 5.24 (note also that Ps 68.8; Judg 5.4; and 2 Sam 5.24 also contain the parallel use of $\d{s}^cd$). The militaristic context in these verses is reflected negatively in Ps 44.10; 60.12=108.12.

Explicit reference to the deliverance from Egypt using $y\d{s}$' (still Qal) is found in Exod 11.4(J) and Ps 81.6.

For the sake of completeness we must make note of the "$h\hat{o}\d{s}\hat{i}$ formula," even though it does not *explicitly* refer to divine presence or even to guidance. The overwhelming majority of occurrences of this term are found in the deuteronomistic and Priestly sources, or in passages that probably reveal mutual influence with the deuteronomistic view (e.g. Jeremiah). In fact, the alignment follows so closely the traditional division of sources that one becomes suspicious of passages that appear to diverge (i.e., traditionally, E and, especially, J). At any rate, the use of $h\hat{o}\d{s}\hat{i}$ with Yahweh (or at times the $ml'k$) as subject and with "out of Egypt" (or the equivalent) is ubiquitous in Exodus, Deuteronomy, and the deuteronomistic material in the Former Prophets, in particular. To our knowledge there are only 8 occurrences of the term in traditionally JE material: E: Exod 3.10, 11, 12; 14.11; 18.1; Num 23.22; J: Gen 15.7; Num 24.8. It is interesting that of these, three of the E occurrences have Moses (and sometimes Aaron) as the subject (3.10, 12; 14.11 [the latter in an accusation!]--compare these to 1 Sam 12.8 (D); and that two others may well stem from more ancient tradition (or, alternatively, are archaisms)--Num 23.22 and 24.8.

yrd with divine subject occurs 21x in the Old Testament, 14x in the Pentateuch and 7x elsewhere. In the Pentateuch, we find it in Gen 11.5, 7; 18.21. These should be compared to Exod 3.8, for all involve some kind of divine judgment (note $\d{s}^cq$ in Gen 18.21 and Exod 3.8). Elsewhere in Genesis we have 28.12 (the $ml'kym$ on the ladder) and 46.4, where Yahweh promises to go down with Jacob to Egypt.[12] The remaining occurrences in Exodus are all connected with the Sinai theophany or subsequent events, and all involve the phenomena of fire or cloud (^cnn): 19.11, 18 ('$\check{s}$), 20; 33.9 $^cmmwdh^cnn$; 34.5 (^cnn). In Numbers yrd occurs 3x in the typical crisis situation of the Wilderness traditions, probably all from the Yahwist, and all involving the ^cnn: 11.17, 25; 12.5.

Other than these occurrences in the Pentateuch, we have the following: 2 Sam 22.10=Ps 18.10; Isa 31.4; 63.19; 64.2; Mic 1.3; Ps 144.5; Neh 9.13. Most of these fit within the context of a storm theophany, and the frequent invocation here for Yahweh to rescue his devotee may be compared, again, with Exod 3.8 (note also that in the latter, Yahweh has first appeared as the $ml'k$ in a "flaming fire").

nhh Outside the Exodus-Sinai traditions, nhh is used in Psalms (about 10x) to invoke or praise divine protection and guidance, often with the connotation of instruction.[13] Other than Gen 24.27, 48[14] and Isa 57.18; 58.11,[15] all the remaining occurrences are historical references to the Exodus-Sinai-Wilderness traditions, and all have divine subjects (except Exod 32.34 [Moses]; Ps 78.72 [David; cf. 77.21]). We shall list those here: Exod 13.17, 21; 15.13; 32.34; Ps 77.21; 78.14, 53, 72; Neh 9.12, 19. (Deut 32.12 may be similar to Psalms and Genesis 24.)

^cbr is used with divine subject 11x in the Old Testament.[16] The most famous of these are, of course, Yahweh's "passing over" Israel in Egypt,[17] and his rather mysterious "passing by" Moses.[18] Yet the most important usage for our purposes is that in combination with $lpny$, again, similar to $hlk\ lpny$ and $y\d{s}'\ lpny$. Although the use of this expression with human subjects elsewhere seems to imply simply "to go ahead of, to precede," rather than "to lead, guide,"[19] we would suggest that the context connotes a dimension of guidance as well. Actually, the use of this expression with Yahweh as subject occurs only twice and in almost identical form, in Deut 9.3, 31.3: $yhwh\ 'lhyk\ hw'\ (ha)^c\bar{o}b\bar{e}r\ lpnyk$. The interesting aspect is the way in which the same expression is used with other subjects within the same context. Thus again in 31.3, it is said that $y^eh\check{o}\check{s}u^{ac}\ hw'\ {}^c\bar{o}b\bar{e}r\ lpnyk$ (also 3.28). It is also stated that the twelve tribal representatives will "cross over before" the ark (Josh 4.5) and that the ark itself (and priests bearing it) will "cross over before" the people (3.6, 11; cf. 4.7, 11). The description of the army ($\d{s}b'$)

"crossing over before Yahweh" (4.13) could refer either to the ark (which stands in the middle of the Jordan until all have passed over) or, more generally, to Yahweh himself. At any rate we can say that $^c br\ lpny$ is a term associated totally with the Jordan-Conquest tradition, and, unlike $hlk\ lpny$, is never used in the *narratives* of the Wilderness March proper.[20] Indeed, it is striking that although $^c br$ is used in the hymnic and later prose accounts of the Reed Sea event,[21] it is never used in Exodus 14, only in 15.[22]

$^c lh$ With regard to our discussion of $y\underset{.}{s}'$, Hi., we may also look briefly at the comparable use of $^c lh$ Hi. This term is used with divine subject much less than $y\underset{.}{s}'$ Hi. and, outside of Exodus, is most heavily concentrated in deuteronomistic and prophetic material. Elsewhere in the Pentateuch it occurs only 4x other than in the citations below.[23] In Exodus we have the following: 3.8, 17; 33.15. It is interesting that the term is used in ch. 32 five times, all without Yahweh as subject: (1) as a complaint by the people [where Moses is subject] (32.1, 23; on this cf. 17.3; Num 16.13; 20.5; 21.5); (2) with the "golden calf" as subject (32.1, 4, 8; cf. 1 Kgs 12.28); and (3) with Moses as subject within a command from Yahweh (32.7; cf. 33.1, 12; Hos 12.14).

Outside the Pentateuch, the term with divine subject occurs as follows: Josh 24.17; Judg 2.1; 6.8, 13; 1 Sam 8.8; 10.18; 12.6; 2 Sam 7.6//1 Chr 17.5; 2 Kgs 17.7, 36; Amos 2.10; 3.1; 9.7; Mic 6.4; Jer 2.6; 11.7; 16.14=23.7; 16.15; 23.8; Isa 63.11; Ps 30.4; 81.11.

$^c nn$ This word occurs 88x in the Old Testament (1x in Aramaic). Of these, only a few present a general meaning without specific mythological or historical reference.[24] The rest may be divided into the following four categories: (1) $^c nn$ in a description of the storm deity or in a mythological motif unrelated to historical events; (2) $^c nn$ as agent of divine guidance during the Wilderness period and at the Reed Sea; (3) $^c nn$ connected with divine communication or consecration; (4) $^c nn$ at the Sinai encounter.

(1) Somewhat surprisingly, there are relatively few occurrences of $^c nn$ in the first category and most of those are late, at least according to final literary context, although they may reflect ancient connotations. The occurrences are: Dan 7.13 (Aramaic); Joel 2.2=Zeph 1.15; Ps 97.2; Job 26.8-9; 37.11, 15; 38.9. Cf. Gen 9.13-16 (vs. 14 has the

only verbal use of the word). Closely related to these texts, and often using the word $^c rpl$ ("dark cloud mass")[25] as well, are several instances in which the "day of Yahweh" figures. All of these (except the Joel-Zephaniah text above) are in Ezekiel: 30.3, 18; 32.7; 34.12 (cf. Job 3.5).

The overwhelming majority of occurrences, however, fall within the remaining categories. Whether the examples are drawn from the Pentateuch or from other material, they all reflect the historical traditions contained in Exodus and Numbers.

(2) $^c nn$ as divine guide at the Reed Sea and during the Wilderness March: Exod 13.21, 22, 14.19, 20, 24; Num 9.15-22; 10.11-12, 34; 14.14; Deut 1.33   Ps 78.14; 105.39; Neh 9.12, 14. Isa 4.5 is a mixture of this usage and those which follow below.

(3) $^c nn$ as an agent of divine consecration or communication. The primary evidence for consecration is Exod 40.34-38; Deut 31.15 (consecration of Joshua as leader); 1 Kgs 8.10, 11=2 Chr 5.14. Related to this is the use in Lev 16.2, 13 (cf. Ez 8.11) and Ez 1.4, 28 (cf. also Gen 9.13-16); 10.3-4.

The use of $^c nn$ in the next examples is distinguished from the preceding by the emphasis on verbal communication; i.e. the $^c nn$ is the means of divine appearance and rendering of judgments: Exod 16.10; 33.9, 10; Num 11.25; 12.5, 10; 17.7. Perhaps related specifically to this usage, and not to the function of guidance, is Ps 99.7 (note $yddbr$--and Samuel!).

(4) $^c nn$ in the Sinai theophany: Exod 19.9, 16; 24.15-18; 34.5. The function here is, of course, closely related to that of consecration and communication.

$pan\hat{i}m$ Especially with a large number of affixes, this word is exceedingly abundant in the Old Testament, and we have not found it feasible to check every occurrence. Our survey seems sufficient to indicate that, by and large, the expression is used in the majority of cases, both for human and divine subjects, as a metaphor for "face" or "presence" in a very general sense. Thus it is used many times, especially in Jeremiah and Ezekiel, in a phrase such as "I will set my face against them," simply as an expression of divine anger.[26] Similarly, the phrase "to seek the face" of Yahweh[27] seems to mean to turn to him in obedience; at least it does not usually seem to mean a seeking

for a divine appearance in any substantial way. We would also see much
the same generality behind two other common phrases: (1) "to entreat
the favor of Yahweh" ($ḥlh$ [Pi.] $'et$-$p^e n\hat{e}$ $yhwh$)[28] is very much of prophetic diction, and here $p^e n\hat{e}$ seems to be almost an untranslatable
euphemism; (2) despite the numerous suggestions for emendation, it is
perhaps best to maintain the traditional reading for "to appear in the
presence of Yahweh" ($l\bar{e}r\bar{a}'\hat{o}t$ $'et$-$p^e n\hat{e}$ $yhwh$).[29] Similar expressions
occur three times without $'t$.[30]

Finally, there is the phrase "face to face," attested six times,
as an expression of intimacy.[31] For Exod 33.14-15, 23, see the discussion in ch. 7. Later references to this (Deut 4.37 and especially Isa
63.9) come much closer to hypostatization.

$ṣ^c d$ This stem is used as a verbal form only 8x. It is used with
a divine subject only 4x: Judg 5.4; Ps 68.8; Hab 3.12; and Isa 63.1
(emended). The noun $ṣ^c dh$, however, clearly refers to Yahweh's action
in 2 Sam 5.24 (note $'z\ yṣ'\ yhwh\ lpnyk$). The connotation of divine intervention in warfare is probably also carried over in the use of the
noun with reference to the king in 2 Sam 22.37=Ps 18.37. Otherwise,
$ṣ^c d$ is used with human subjects to mean simply "walk, wander, tread,"
mostly using the noun.[32]

$r'h$ Niphal The use of this verb is very nearly the reverse of
the use of bw': whereas bw': is most prominent in the Latter Prophets
and rare in the Pentateuch, $nr'h$ is well attested in the Pentateuch and
relatively scarce elsewhere.[33] The predominant use of the term is to
serve as the means for divine communication to an individual. This is
especially true throughout Genesis,[34] in the first part of Exodus,[35]
and in the Former Prophets.[36] This function is also reflected in the
other major concentration of $nr'h$ in the Wilderness traditions, almost always from the Priestly source.[37] Here, however, the communication is one of divine judgment during a crisis situation, and the setting indicates divine appearance to all the people rather than to just
one individual. The final occurrence (Deut 31.15) seems to be clearly
influenced by the Wilderness traditions.

NOTES TO APPENDIX 2
TERMINOLOGY OF DIVINE PRESENCE
IN THE OLD TESTAMENT

[1]20.3; 31.24; both E. On this word, cf. the study of E. Jenni, "'Kommen' im theologischen Sprachgebrauch des AT," in *Wort-Gebot-Glaube*, ed. J. J. Stamm and E. Jenni (Eichrodt *Festschrift*; Zurich: Zwingli, 1970) 251-261.

[2]The other two are Num 22.9 and 20, where the context indicates a dream or vision by night. Both are E; cf. the Genesis occurrences.

[3]Note that in both of the latter *nr'h* is also used (6.2; 13.10, 21).

[4]Num 12.9 (note the cloud in vs. 10); Jer 9.1; Hos 5.14-15 (cf. preceding note). The connection between Yahweh's displeasure and his departure in all of these produces an interesting theological connection with the Wilderness stories (note the explicit reference to the Wilderness in the Jeremiah passage). Also for *hlk* as departure, but without the connotation of displeasure, see Gen 18.33.

[5]For the use of the Hithpael, cf. Gen 3.8; also Zech 1.10f; 6.7 with the patrolling angels, with which cf. Job 1.7; 2.2 of the Satan. The three remaining uses of the Hithpael will be mentioned below.

[6]Along with 18.22 (*ml'kym*) and 33 (above, n. 4) comprise all the occurrences of *hlk* in Genesis.

[7]Other than the references above in note 4, see Ezekiel 1 and 10 passim with the "living creatures" and spirit.

[8]Cf. Hab 3.5 where plague goes in front of Yahweh.

[9]Deut 8.2, 15; 29.4, and Josh 24.3; Amos 2.10 (cf. Deut 29.4); Hos 2.16; Jer 2.6; 31.8, 9; Isa 42.16; 48.21; 63.12, 13. Note also Ps 106.9 and 136.16. The phrase *bmdbr* recurs over and over again in these verses.

[10]Of sun, e.g. Eccl 1.5; Judg 9.33; Job 9.7. Of light, Ps 112.4.

[11]For such agents, see Num 22.32; 17.11; Hos 6.5. Most of these occurrences are in the Latter Prophets.

[12]See our discussion of *ᶜim* in Genesis, above.

[13]Ps 5.9; 23.3; 27.11; 107.30; 139.10, 24; also 31.4; 61.3; 73.24; 143.10, all with *tanḥēnî*. The verb connotes parental guidance in Job 31.18 (human subject). In Proverbs (6.22; 11.3) the *subject* of the verb is instruction (otherwise, only 18.16). *Nḥh* is used with human subjects only 5x, all in the Hiphil with the sense of "to bring to a place, to position, station" (Num 23.7; 1 Sam 22.4; 1 Kgs 10.26; 2 Kgs 18.11). Other than those mentioned below, remaining occurrences are Job 31.18 (human subject); 38.32; Ps 67.5 (atypical of the Psalms examples) and 60.11=108.11 (with a quasi-historical orientation).

[14]See our discussion of these verses in the Excursus.

[15]Although one might expect deliberate allusion to the Exodus events here, the context is more reminiscent of the Psalms occurrences.

[16]Other than those cited below and in notes 17-18, see Num 22.26 (*ml'k*); 1 Kgs 22.24. For the Hiphil, Gen 8.1 and Josh 7.7, the latter no doubt related to the other examples from Deuteronomy and Joshua cited below.

[17]Exod 12.12, 23; this is surely involved in the use of the same verb by Amos, 5.17; 7.8; 8.2.

[18]Exod 33.19, 22; 34.6; as also with Elijah, 1 Kgs 19.11.

[19]Gen 32.17, 33.3, 12, 14; 1 Sam 9.27; 25.19; 2 Kgs 4.31. The Genesis 33 passage provides a clear distinction between *hlk lngd*, which seems to mean either "go beside of" or "in front of," but, in either case, meaning that Esau and his men will set the pace, and *ᶜbr lpny*, which means that Esau will go on ahead and thus allow Jacob to follow at his own pace.

[20]*ᶜbr* by itself, of course, is used a number of times, particularly for the latter stages of the Wilderness March in reference to Israel's "passing through" the nations on her way to Canaan: Num 20.19, 21; 21. 22-23; Deut 29.15; Josh 24.17; Judg 11.20. A notable exception for *ᶜbr lpny* with Yahweh as subject, unrelated to the Jordan crossing, is Mic 2.13, which provides a graphic adaptation of the vanguard motif.

[21]Ps 66.6; 68.13; 136.14; Num 33.8; Neh 9.11.

[22]In fact, it is never explicitly said that Israel *crossed* the Sea; the most explicit reference is in 14.29: *hāleᵏû bayyabāšāh beᵗôk hayyām*

[23]Gen 50.24; Lev 11.45; Num 14.13; Deut 20.1 (with the latter, cf. Ps 81.11 [cf. the use of *yṣ'* in vs. 6] and the general content of the Psalm; elsewhere the term occurs in Psalms only at 30.4, without reference to the Exodus).

[24]Isa 44.22; Hos 6.14; 13.3; Job 7.9. Even here, however, there is a consistent nuance: the cloud serves as a symbol for impermanence. Cf. Lam 3.44 and Jer 4.13, which, however, may be related to the first category below.

[25]*ᶜrpl* is a theophanic word in its own right and is probably related to Ugaritic *ᶜrpt* (see the usual emendation for Ps 68.5). Cf. also *ᶜrp*, "to drip, drop," Deut 33.28; 32.2 (in Ecclesiasticus 43.22 used with *ᶜnn*); and *ᶜārîp*, "cloud," Isa 5.30. For the remaining uses of *ᶜrpl*, see the following (* designates presence of *ᶜnn* also): Exod 20.21; Deut 4.11*; 5.22*; 2 Sam 22.10=Ps 18.10; 1 Kgs 8.12=2 Chr 6.1; Isa 60.2; Jer 13.16; Ex 34.12*; Joel 2.2=Zeph 1.15*; Job 22.13; 38.9*; Ps 97.2*.

[26]Jer 7.15; 15.1; 21.10, etc. Cf. Lev 17.10; 20.3, 5, 6. Note also Yahweh's "hiding" (*str*) his face: Deut 31.17, 18; 32.30; Isa 54.8; Ps 12.2 and passim.

[27]Hos 5.15; Ps 27.8; 105.4.

[28]Exod 32.11; 1 Kgs 13.6; 2 Kgs 13.4; Jer 26.19, etc.

[29]To our knowledge only the following: Exod 34.24; Deut 16.16; 31.11; 1 Sam 1.22.

[30]Exod 23.15; 34.20; Isa 1.12.

[31]Gen 32.31; Exod 33.11; Deut 5.4 (without *bpnym*); 34.10; Judg 6.22; Ez 20.35.

[32]It is possible that a faint echo of the use of this verb in the "classic epiphany texts" may be seen in 2 Sam 6.13, in connection with the bearers of the ark. For the general uses, see e.g. Prv 7.8; 16.9 (note the typical expression of divine guidance for Proverbs here); Job 18.7. Most of the occurrences other than those noted above are in the Writings.

[33]Other than those cited below, only: 2 Sam 22.11 (?); Ps 84.8; 102.17; Isa 60.2; Zech 9.14; Mal 3.2.

[34]See our discussion of Genesis in the Excursus (cf. 12.7; 17.1; 21.14; 26.2, 24; 35.1, 9; 48.3).

[35]I.e. in the call of Moses, Exod 3.2, 16; 4.1, 5; 6.3.

[36]Judg 6.12; 13.10, 21, all to be compared to those in notes 1-2. Note also 1 Sam 3.21 (the call of Samuel; observe the presence of the ark here); 1 Kgs 3.5; 9.2; 11.9 (2 Chr 1.7; 3.1), Yahweh's appearance to Solomon, again comparable to the preceding.

[37]Exod 16.10; 33.23 (J?); Lev 9.4, 6, 23 (at institution of sin offering); 16.2 above the ark; Num 14.10; 14.14 (J; with pillar of cloud and fire); 16.19; 17.7; 20.6.

ILLUSTRATIONS

Fig. 1: Assyrian standards, reproduced from Friedrich Sarre, "Die altorientalischen Feldzeichen, mit besonderer Berücksichtigung eines unveröffentlichten Stückes," *Klio: Beträge zur alten Geschichte* 3 (1903) Fig. 7, p. 8.

Fig. 2: Assyrian standard in war chariot, reproduced from Heinrich Schäfer, "Assyrische und ägyptische Feldzeichen," *Klio: Beiträge zur alten Geschichte* 6 (1906) Abb. 1, p. 393.

Fig. 3: Assyrian standard in camp, reproduced from Schäfer, "Feldzeichen," Abb. 3, p. 396.

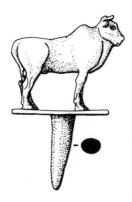

Fig. 4: Bull standard from Ras Shamra, reproduced from C. F. A. Schaeffer, "Nouveaux témoignages du culte de El et de Baal à Ras Shamra-Ugarit et ailleurs en Syrie-Palestine," *Syria* 43 (1966) Fig. 5, p. 9.

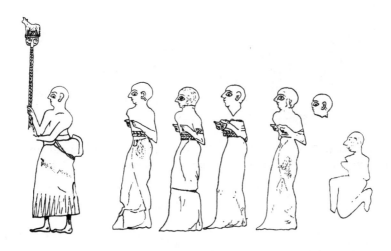

Fig. 5a: Bull standard and procession from Mari, reproduced from Otto Eissfeldt, "Lade und Stierbild," *ZAW* 58 (1940-41) 210; originally published by André Parrot, "Les fouilles de Mari, première campagne (hiver 1933-1934), rapport préliminaire (second article)," *Syria* 16 (1935) Pl. XXVIII, 2.

Fig. 5b: Bull standard from Mari (same as Fig 5a) arranged in a different configuration by Schaeffer, "Nouveaux témoignages," Fig. 9, p. 12.

BIBLIOGRAPHY

BIBLIOGRAPHY

Aharoni, Yohanan, "The Solomonic Temple, the Tabernacle, and the Arad Sanctuary." Alter Orient und Altes Testament 22 (1973) 1-8.

Albrektson, Bertil. *History and the Gods*. Coniectanea Biblica, Old Testament Series 1. Lund, Sweden: C. W. K. Gleerup, 1967.

Albright, William F. "A Catalogue of Early Hebrew Lyric Poems (Psalm LXVIII)." *Hebrew Union College Annual* 23 (1950-1951) 1-39.

_____. "The Eighth Campaign of Sargon," *Journal of the American Oriental Society* 36 (1917) 226-232.

_____. "Jethro, Hobab, and Reuel in Early Hebrew Tradition." *Catholic Biblical Quarterly* 25 (1963) 1-11.

_____. "The Land of Damascus between 1850 and 1750 B.C." *Bulletin of the American Schools of Oriental Research* 83 (1941) 30-36.

_____. "The Psalm of Habakkuk." In *Studies in Old Testament Prophecy*, pp. 1-18. Edited by H. H. Rowley. Edinburgh: T. & T. Clark, 1950.

_____. "Review of *L'épithète divine Jahve S^eba'ôt* by B. Wambacq." *Journal of Biblical Literature* 67 (1948) 378-379.

_____. "The Song of Deborah in the Light of Archaeology." *Bulletin of the American Schools of Oriental Research* 62 (1936) 26-31.

Alt, Albrecht. "The God of the Fathers." In *Essays on Old Testament History and Religion*, pp. 1-77. Translated by R. A. Wilson. Oxford: Basil Blackwell, 1966.

_____. "The Origins of Israelite Law." In *Essays on Old Testament History and Religion*, pp. 79-132. Translated by R. A. Wilson. Oxford: Basil Blackwell, 1966.

Andersen, Francis I. "A Lexicographical Note on Exodus XXXII 18." *Vetus Testamentum* 16 (1966) 108-112.

The Assyrian Dictionary of the Oriental Institute of the University of Chicago. Edited by I. J. Gelb et al. Chicago: Oriental Institute, 1965ff.

Bailey, Lloyd R. "The Golden Calf." *Hebrew Union College Annual* 42 (1971) 97-115.

Baltzer, Klaus. *The Covenant Formulary*. Translated by David E. Green. Philadelphia: Fortress, 1971.

Barr, James. "Theophany and Anthropomorphism in the Old Testament." Congress Volume, *Supplements to Vetus Testamentum*, vol. VII, pp. 31-38. Leiden: E. J. Brill, 1960.

Barton, George A. *The Royal Inscriptions of Sumer and Akkad.* Library
of Ancient Semitic Inscriptions, vol. I. New Haven: Yale
University Press, 1929.

Baudissin, Wolf W. G. "Gott schauen in der alttestamentlichen Religion."
Archiv für Religionswissenschaft 18 (1915) 173-239.

_____. *Kyrios als Gottesname im Judentum und seine Stelle in der
Religionsgeschichte.* 4 Teile. Herausgegeben von Otto Eissfeldt.
Dritter Teil: Der Gottesname Kyrios der Septuaginta und die
Entwicklung des Gottesbegriffs in den Religionen der semitischen
Völker. Giessen: A. Töpelmann, 1929.

Bentzen, Aage. "The Cultic Use of the Story of the Ark in Samuel."
Journal of Biblical Literature 67 (1948) 37-53.

Beyerlin, Walter. *Origins and History of the Oldest Sinaitic Traditions.*
Translated by S. Rudman. Oxford: Basil Blackwell, 1965.

Borger, Riekele. *Die Inschriften Asarhaddons Königs von Assyrien, Archiv
für Orientforschung*, Beiheft 9. Graz, 1956.

Breasted, James Henry. *Ancient Records of Egypt.* 4 vols. Ancient
Records, Second Series. Edited by William Rainey Harper. Chicago: University of Chicago Press, 1906.

Bright, John. *Jeremiah.* Anchor Bible 21. New York: Doubleday, 1965.

Buber, Martin. *The Kingship of God.* Translated by Richard Scheimann.
New York: Harper & Row, 1967; Harper Torchbooks, 1973.

_____. *Moses : The Revelation and the Covenant.* Oxford: East &
West Library, 1946; Harper Torchbooks, 1958.

Buren, F. Douglas van. *Symbols of the Gods in Mesopotamian Art.* Analecta Orientalia 23. Rome: Pontificium Institutum Biblicum,
1945.

Cagni, Luigi. *L'Epopea di Erra.* Studi Semitici 34. Roma: Instituto
di Studi del Vicino Oriente, 1969.

Campbell, Antony F. *The Ark Narrative.* Society of Biblical Literature
Dissertation Series 16. Missoula, Montana: Scholars', 1975.

Cassin, Elena. *La splendeur divine : Introduction à l'étude de la
mentalité mésopotamienne.* Ecole pratique des hautes études,
Sorbonne. *Civilisations et sociêtes* 8. Paris: Mouton, 1968.

Childs, Brevard S. "The Birth of Moses." *Journal of Biblical Literature*
84 (1965) 109-122.

_____. *The Book of Exodus : A Critical, Theological Commentary.* Old
Testament Library. Philadelphia: Westminster, 1974.

_____. "A Traditio-Historical Study of the Reed Sea Tradition."
Vetus Testamentum 20 (1970) 406-418.

Civil, Miguel. "Išme-Dagan and Enlil's Chariot." *Journal of the
American Oriental Society* 88 (1968) 3-14.

Clements, R. E. *God and Temple.* Philadelphia: Fortress, 1965.

Clifford, Richard J. "The Tent of El and the Israelite Tent of Meeting." *Catholic Biblical Quarterly* 33 (1971) 221-227.

Coats, George W. "The Traditio-Historical Character of the Reed Sea

Motif." *Vetus Testamentum* 17 (1967) 253-265.

Cogan, Morton. *Imperialism and Religion: Assyria, Judah, and Israel in the Eighth and Seventh Centuries B. C. E.* Society of Biblical Literature Monograph Series 19. Missoula: Scholars', 1974.

Cooke, G. A. *A Text-Book of North-Semitic Inscriptions.* Oxford: Clarendon, 1903.

Craigie, P. C. "The Song of Deborah and the Epic of Tukulti-Ninurta." *Journal of Biblical Literature* 88 (1969) 253-265.

Cros, Gaston, Heuzey, L., and Thureau-Dangin, F. *Nouvelles fouilles de Tello.* Paris: Imprimerie française et orientale, 1910.

Cross, Frank M., Jr. *Canaanite Myth and Hebrew Epic.* Cambridge: Harvard University Press, 1973.

_____. "The Priestly Tabernacle." In *The Biblical Archaeologist Reader*, pp. 221-228. Edited by David Noel Freedman and G. Ernest Wright. Garden City: Doubleday, 1961.

Cross, Frank M., Jr., and Freedman, David N. "The Blessing of Moses." *Journal of Biblical Literature* 67 (1948) 191-210.

Davies, G. Henton. "Presence of God." In *The Interpreter's Dictionary of the Bible*, vol. 3, pp. 874-875. Edited by George A. Buttrick et al. New York: Abingdon, 1962.

Dijk, J. J. A. van. "Une insurrection générale au pays de Larsa avant l'avènement de Nūradad." *Journal of Cuneiform Studies* 19 (1965) 1-25.

_____. "Textes diverse du musée de Bagdad IV." *Sumer* 18 (1962) 19-32.

Donner, H., and Röllig, W. *Kanaanäische und Aramäische Inschriften.* 3 Bande. Wiesbaden: O. Harrassowitz, 1962-1964.

Ebeling, Erich. "Bruchstücke eines politischen Propagandagedichtes aus einer assyrischen Kanzlei." *Mitteilungen der Altorientalischen Gesellschaft* 12, Heft 2 (1938) 1-42.

Eichrodt, Walther. *Theology of the Old Testament.* 2 Vols. Translated by J. A. Baker. The Old Testament Library. Philadelphia: Westminster, 1967.

Eissfeldt, Otto. "Jahwe Zebaoth." *Miscellanea academica berolinensia*, II, 2, pp. 128-150. Berlin: Akademie Verlag, 1950.

_____. "Lade und Stierbild." In *Kleine Schriften* II, pp. 282-305. Tübingen: Mohr, 1963.

Falkenstein, Adam. *Die Inschriften Gudeas von Lagaš. Analecta Orientalia* 30. Rome: Pontificium Institutum Biblicum, 1966.

_____. *Sumerische Götterlieder*, Teil I. Abhandlungen der Heidelberger Akademie der Wissenschaften, Philosophisch-historische Klasse, 1. Abhandlung. Heidelberg: Universitätsverlag, 1959.

_____. "Untersuchungen zur sumerischen Grammatik." *Zeitschrift für Assyriologie* 48 (N.F. 14; 1944) 69-118.

_____. "Zur ersten Tafel des Erra-Mythos." *Zeitschrift für Assyriologie* (N.F. 19; 1959) 200-208.

Falkenstein, Adam, and von Soden, Wolfram. *Sumerische und akkadische Hymnen und Gebete*. Die Bibliothek der alten Welt, Reihe der alte Orient. Zurich: Artemis, 1953.

Finkelstein, Jacob J. "Mesopotamian Historiography." *Proceedings of the American Philosophical Society* 107 (1963) 461-472.

_____. "Political Propaganda." MS, Yale University Babylonian Collection.

Fisher, Loren. R. "Two Projects at Claremont." *Ugarit-Forschungen* 3 (1971) 25-32.

de Fraine, J. "Moses' 'cornuta facies' (Ex 34,29-35)." *Bijdragen Tijdschrift voor filosophie en theologie* 20 (1959) 28-38.

Frankena, R. "Untersuchungen zum Irra-Epos." Review of *Das Era-Epos*, by P. F. Gössmann. *Bibliotheca Orientalis* 14 (1957) 2-10.

_____. "Weitere kleine Beiträge zur Kenntnis des Irra-Epos." *Bibliotheca Orientalis* 15 (1958) 12-15.

Freedman, David Noel. "Early Israelite History in the Light of Early Israelite Poetry." In *Unity and Diversity: Essays in the History, Literature, and Religion of the Ancient Near East*, pp. 3-35. Edited by Hans Goedicke and J. J. M. Roberts. The Johns Hopkins Near Eastern Studies. Baltimore: The Johns Hopkins University Press, 1975.

Fretheim, Terence E. "Psalm 132: A Form-Critical Study." *Journal of Biblical Literature* 86 (1967) 289-300.

Fritz, Volkmar. *Israel in der Wüste*. Marburger theologische Studien 7. Herausgegeben von Hans Grass und W. G. Kümmel. Marburg: N. G. Elwert, 1970.

Gaster, Theodor H. "An Ancient Eulogy on Israel: Deuteronomy 33.3-5, 26-29." *Journal of Biblical Literature* 66 (1947) 53-62.

Gelb, I. J. *"Šullat and Ḫaniš."* *Archiv Orientální* 18 (1950) 189-198.

Gerleman, G. "The Song of Deborah in the Light of Stylistics." *Vetus Testamentum* 1 (1951) 168-180.

Globe, Alexander. "The Literary Structure and Unity of the Song of Deborah." *Journal of Biblical Literature* 93 (1974) 493-512.

_____. "The Text and Literary Structure of Judges 5, 4-5." *Biblica* 55 (1974) 168-178.

Görg, Manfred. *Das Zelt der Begegnung: Untersuchung zur Gestalt der sakralen Zelttraditionen Altisraels*. Bonner biblische Beiträge 27. Bonn: Peter Hanstein, 1967.

Gössmann, P. F. *Das Era-Epos*. Würzburg: Augustinius, 1956.

Gray, John. "The Desert Sojourn of the Hebrews and the Sinai-Horeb Tradition." *Vetus Testamentum* 4 (1954) 148-154.

_____. *Joshua, Judges, and Ruth*. The Century Bible. London: Nelson, 1967.

_____. *The Keret Text in the Literature of Ras Shamra*. Documenta et monumenta Orientis antiqui, V. 2nd ed. Leiden: Brill, 1964.

Grayson, A. K. *Assyrian Royal Inscriptions*, vol. 1. Records of the Ancient Near East. Edited by Hans Goedicke. Wiesbaden: Otto Harrassowitz, 1972.

_____. "The Early Development of Assyrian Monarchy." *Ugarit-Forschungen* 3 (1971) 311-319.

Greenberg, Moshe. *Understanding Exodus*. Melton Research Center Series. vol. II, part I: The Heritage of Biblical Israel. New York: Behrman House, 1969.

Gulin, E. G. "Die Nachfolge Gottes." *Studia Orientalia* I, pp. 34-50. Helsingforsiae: Societas Orientalis Fennica, 1925.

Gunkel, Hermann. *Die Psalmen*. 5th ed. Göttingen Handkommentar zum Alten Testament. Göttingen: Vandenhoeck & Ruprecht, 1968.

_____. *Schöpfung und Chaos in Urzeit und Endzeit*. Göttingen: Vandenhoeck und Ruprecht, 1895.

Gunkel, Hermann, and Begrich, Joachim. *Einleitung in die Psalmen*. Göttingen: Vandenhoeck & Ruprecht, 1933.

Gurney, O. R. "The Sultantepe Tablets." *Anatolian Studies* 2 (1962) 25-35.

Hallo, William W. "Antediluvian Cities." *Journal of Cuneiform Studies* 23 (1970) 57-67.

_____. "The Cultic Setting of Sumerian Poetry." In *Actes de la XVIe Rencontre assyriologique internationale*, pp. 116-134. Université libre de Bruxelles, 30 juin-4 juillet 1969. Etudes recueillies par André Finet. Ham-sur-Heure: Comité belge de recherches en Mésopotamie, 1970.

_____. "Individual Prayer in Sumerian: The Continuity of a Tradition." *Journal of the American Oriental Society* 88 (1968) 71-89.

_____. "Lexical Notes on the Neo-Sumerian Metal Industry." *Bibliotheca Orientalis* 20 (1963) 136-141.

_____. "Problems in Sumerian Hermeneutics." In *Perspectives in Jewish Learning*. vol. 5, pp. 1-12. Edited by Byron L. Sherwin. Chicago: Spertus College of Judaica, 1973.

_____. "The Road to Emar." *Journal of Cuneiform Studies* 18 (1964) 57-88.

Hallo, William W., and van Dijk, J. J. A. *The Exaltation of Inanna*. Yale Near Eastern Researches 3. New Haven: Yale University Press, 1968.

Hallo, William W., and Simpson, William K. *The Ancient Near East: A History*. New York: Harcourt Brace Jovanovich, 1971.

Hanson, Paul D. *The Dawn of Apocalyptic: The Historical and Sociological Roots of Jewish Apocalyptic Eschatology*. Philadelphia: Fortress, 1975.

_____. "Jewish Apocalyptic Against its Near Eastern Environment." *Revue biblique* 78 (1971) 31-58.

Haussig, Hans W., ed. *Wörterbuch der Mythologie*. 2 vols. Band I: Götter und Mythen im vorderen Orient. Erste Abteilung: Die alten Kulturvölker. Stuttgart: E. Klett, 1965, 1973.

Herdner, André. *Corpus des tablettes en cunéiformes alphabétiques découvertes à Ras Shamra-Ugarit de 1929 a 1939. Mission de Ras Shamra*, Tome X. Paris: Imprimerie nationale, 1963.

Hertzberg, Hans W. *I & II Samuel, A Commentary*. Translated by J. S. Bowden. The Old Testament Library. Philadelphia: Westminster, 1964.

Hoffner, Harry A. "The Hittites and Hurrians." In *Peoples of Old Testament Times*, pp. 197-228. Edited by D. J. Wiseman. Oxford: Clarendon, 1973.

Hrouda, B. "Göttersymbole und -attribute (Syrien/Palastina)." In *Reallexikon der Assyriologie und vorderasiatischen Archaeologie*, vol. 3, pp. 490-495. New York: W. de Gruyter, 1969.

Hruška, Blahoslav. "Einige Uberlegungen zum Erraepos." *Bibliotheca Orientalis* 30 (1973) 3-7.

Hyatt, J. Philip. *Exodus*. New Century Bible. London: Oliphants, 1971.

Jacobsen, Thorkild. "The Battle Between Marduk and Tiamat." *Journal of the American Oriental Society* 88 (1968) 104-108.

_____. "The Myth of Inanna and Bilulu." *Journal of Near Eastern Studies* 12 (1953) 160-188. (Also in *Toward the Image of Tammuz*, pp. 73-103.)

_____. "Parerga Sumerologica." *Journal of Near Eastern Studies* 2 (1943) 117-121.

_____. "Religious Drama in Ancient Mesopotamia." In *Unity and Diversity: Essays in the History, Literature, and Religions of the Ancient Near East*, pp. 65-97. The Johns Hopkins Near Eastern Studies. Edited by Hans Goedicke and J. J. M. Roberts. Baltimore: The Johns Hopkins University Press, 1975.

_____. "Sumerian Mythology: A Review Article." Review of *Sumerian Mythology*, by Samuel N. Kramer. *Journal of Near Eastern Studies* 5 (1946) 128-152. (Also in *Toward the Image of Tammuz*, pp. 104-131.)

_____. *Toward the Image of Tammuz and Other Essays on Mesopotamian History and Culture*. Edited by William L. Moran. Cambridge: Harvard University Press, 1970.

Jeremias, Jörg. *Theophanie: Die Geschichte einer alttestamentlichen Gattung*. Neukirchen-Vluyn: Neukirchener, 1965.

Johnson, A. R. "Aspects of the Use of the Term *pānim* in the Old Testament." In *Festschrift Otto Eissfeldt*, pp. 155-160. Edited by J. Fück. Halle: Max Niemeyer, 1947.

Kapelrud, Arvid S. "Temple Building, a Task for Gods and Kings." *Orientalia* 32 (1963) 56-62.

Klengel, Horst. "Tukulti-Ninurta I, König von Assyrien." *Das Altertum* 7 (1961) 67-77.

Kramer, Samuel N. "Cuneiform Studies and the History of Literature: The Sumerian Sacred Marriage Texts." *Proceedings of the American Philosophical Society* 107 (1963) 485-516.

_____. *Sumerian Mythology*. Philadelphia: American Philosophical Society, 1944.

Kraus, Hans-Joachim. "Gilgal: Ein Beitrag zur Kultusgeschichte Israels." *Vetus Testamentum* 1 (1951) 181-199.

_____. *Psalmen*. 2 vols. *Biblischer Kommentar, Altes Testament* 15. Neukirchen: Buchhandlung des Erziehungsvereins, 1958-1960.

_____. *Worship in Israel*. Translated by Geoffrey Buswell. Richmond: John Knox, 1966.

Krecher, J. "Göttersymbole und -attribute (nach sumerischen und akkadischen Texten)." In *Reallexikon der Assyriologie und vorderasiatischen Archäeologie*, vol. 3, pp. 495-498. New York: W. de Gruyter, 1969.

Kuntz, J. Kenneth. *The Self-Revelation of God*. Philadelphia: Westminster, 1967.

Labat, René. *La poème babylonien de la création*. Paris: Libraire d'Amérique et d'Orient, 1935.

Labat, René et. al. *Les religions du Proche-Orient asiatique : Textes babyloniens, ougaritiques, hittites. Le trésor spirituel de l'humanité*. Edited by Jean Chevalier. Paris: Fayard/Denöel, 1970.

Labuschagne, C. J. *The Incomparability of Yahweh in the Old Testament*. Pretoria Oriental Series 5. Edited by A. van Selms. Leiden: E. J. Brill, 1966.

Lambert, W. G. *Babylonian Wisdom Literature*. Oxford: Clarendon, 1960.

_____. "Destiny and Divine Intervention in Babylon and Israel." *Oudtestamentische Studiën* 17 (1972) 65-72.

_____. "The Fifth Tablet of the Era Epic." *Iraq* 24 (1962) 119-125.

_____. "The Historical Development of the Mesopotamian Pantheon: A Study in Sophisticated Polytheism." In *Unity and Diversity : Essays in the History, Literature, and Religion of the Ancient Near East*, pp. 191-200. The Johns Hopkins Near Eastern Studies. Edited by Hans Goedicke and J. J. M. Roberts. Baltimore: The Johns Hopkins University Press, 1975.

_____. "Literary Style in First Millennium Mesopotamia." *Journal of the American Oriental Society* 88 (1968) 123-132.

_____. "The Reign of Nebuchadnezzar I: A Turning Point in the History of Ancient Mesopotamian Religion." In *The Seed of Wisdom : Essays in Honor of T. J. Meek*, pp. 3-13. Edited by W. S. McCullough. Toronto: University of Toronto Press, 1964.

_____. "Review of *Das Era-Epos* by P. F. Gössmann." *Archiv für Orientforschung* 18 (1957-58) 395-401.

_____. "The Sultantepe Tablets, Continued: VIII. Shalmaneser in Ararat." *Anatolian Studies* 11 (1961) 143-158.

_____. "Three Unpublished Fragments of the Tukulti-Ninurta Epic." *Archiv für Orientforschung* 18 (1957-58) 38-51.

Lambert, W. G., and Millard, A. R. *Atra-Ḫasīs : The Babylonian Story of the Flood*. Oxford: Clarendon, 1969.

Lambert, W. G., and Parker, Simon B. *Enuma eliš : The Babylonian Epic of Creation, The Cuneiform Text*. Oxford: Clarendon, 1966.

Landes, G. J. "Ammon." In *The Interpreter's Dictionary of the Bible*, vol. 1, pp. 108-114. Edited by George A. Buttrick et al. New York: Abingdon, 1962.

278

Landsberger, Benno. "Einige unerkannt gebliebene oder verkannte Nomina des Akkadischen." *Wiener Zeitschrift für die Kunde des Morgenlandes* 57 (1961) 1-23.

Langdon, S. *The Babylonian Epic of Creation.* Oxford: Clarendon, 1923.

Langlamet, F. *Gilgal et les récits de la traversée du Jourdain (Jos., III-IV).* Cahiers de la revue biblique 11. Paris: Gabalda, 1969.

Lewy, Julius. "The Old West Semitic God Hammu." *Hebrew Union College Annual* 18 (1943-44) 429-488.

_____. "Les textes paléo-assyrien et l'Ancient Testament." *Revue de l'histoire des religions* 110 (1934) 29-65.

Lewy, Julius, and Lewy, Hildegard. "The Origin of the Week and the Oldest West Asiatic Calendar". *Hebrew Union College Annual* 17 (1942-43) 1-152.

Lindblom, Johannes. "Theophanies in Holy Places in Hebrew Religion." *Hebrew Union College Annual* 32 (1961) 91-106.

Lipiński, Edouard. "Juges 5,4-5 et Psaume 68,8-11." *Biblica* 48 (1967) 185-206.

_____. *La royauté de Yahwé dans la poésie et le culte de l'ancien Israël.* Brussels: Paleis der academiën, 1965.

Lohfink, Norbert. "Die deuteronomistische Darstellung des Übergangs der Führung Israels von Moses auf Josue." *Scholastik* 37 (1962) 32-44.

Luckenbill, Daniel D. *Ancient Records of Assyria and Babylonia.* 2 vols. Ancient Records. Edited by James H. Breasted. Chicago: University of Chicago Press, 1927.

_____. *The Annals of Sennacherib.* Chicago: University of Chicago Press, 1924.

_____. "Hittite Treaties and Letters." *American Journal of Semitic Languages and Literatures* 37 (1921) 161-211.

Luzarraga, J. *Las tradiciones de la nube en la Biblia y en el Judaismo primitivo.* Analecta Biblica 54. Rome: Biblical Institute, 1973.

Maag, Victor. "Malkut JHWH." *Vetus Testamentum Supplement* 7. Congress Volume, pp. 129-153. Leiden: Brill, 1960.

McBride, S. Dean, Jr. "The Deuteronomic Name Theology." Ph.D. dissertation, Harvard University, 1969.

McCarthy, Dennis J. "The Theology of Leadership in Joshua 1-9." *Biblica* 52 (1971) 165-175.

_____. *Treaty and Covenant: A Study in Form in the Ancient Oriental Documents and in the Old Testament.* Analecta Biblica 21. Rome: Pontifical Biblical Institute, 1963.

Machinist, Peter. "Literature as Politics: The Tukulti-Ninurta Epic and the Bible," forthcoming in *CBQ*, Fall 1976.

_____. "Studies in Middle Assyrian Literary Activity." Ph.D. dissertation, Yale University, 1977 (tentative title and date).

McKay, John. *Religion in Judah under the Assyrians*. Studies in Biblical Theology. Second Series 26. Naperville, Illinois: Allenson, 1973.

Maier, Johann. *Das altisraelitische Ladeheiligtum*. Beihefte zur Zeitschrift für die Altestamentliche Wissenschaft 93. Berlin: A. Töpelmann, 1965.

Malandra, W. W. "The Concept of Movement in History of Religions: A Religio-Historical Study of Reindeer in the Spiritual Life of North Eurasian Peoples." *Numen* 14 (1967) 23-69.

Mandelkern, Solomon. *Veteris Testamenti Concordantiae*. 2 vols. 2nd ed. Berlin: Schocken, 1937; reprint ed., Graz: Akademische Druck- und Verlagsanstalt, 1955.

Mann, Thomas W. "The Pillar of Cloud in the Reed Sea Narrative." *Journal of Biblical Literature* 90 (1971) 15-30.

Matouš, L. "Zur neueren Literatur über das Gilgameš-Epos." *Bibliotheca Orientalis* 21 (1964) 3-10.

Mayes, A. D. H. *Israel in the Period of the Judges*. Studies in Biblical Theology, Second Series 29. Naperville: Allenson, 1974.

_____. "Israel in the Pre-Monarchy Period." *Vetus Testamentum* 23 (1973) 151-170.

Mazar, B. "The Sanctuary of Arad and the Family of Hobab the Kenite." *Journal of Near Eastern Studies* 24 (1965) 297-303.

Mendenhall, George E. *The Tenth Generation: The Origins of the Biblical Tradition*. Baltimore: The Johns Hopkins University Press, 1973.

Milik, J. T. "Deux documents inédits du désert de Juda." *Biblica* 38 (1957) 245-268.

Miller, Max. "The Moabite Stone as Memorial Stela." *Palestine Exploration Quarterly* 106 (1974) 9-18.

Miller, Patrick D. "Apotropaic Imagery in Proverbs 6:20-22." *Journal of Near Eastern Studies* 29 (1970) 129-130.

_____. *The Divine Warrior in Early Israel*. Harvard Semitic Monographs 5. Cambridge: Harvard University Press, 1973.

_____. "El the Warrior." *Harvard Theological Review* 60 (1967) 411-431.

_____. "God and the Gods." *Affirmation* 1 (1973) 37-62.

de Moor, Johannes. *The Seasonal Pattern in the Ugaritic Myth of Ba^{c}lu*. Alter Orient und Altes Testament 16 (1971).

Moran, William L. "The End of the Unholy War and the Anti-Exodus." *Biblica* 44 (1963) 333-342.

Morenz, Siegfried. *Egyptian Religion*. Translated by Ann E. Keep. Ithaca, New York: Cornell University Press, 1973.

Mowinckel, Sigmund. *Der achtundsechzigste Psalm*. Avhandlinger utgitt av det Norske Widenskaps - akademi i Oslo, II. Historische-filosofische Klasse 1. Oslo: Dybwad, 1953.

_____. *Le décalogue*. Paris: Librairie Felix Alcan, 1927.

_____. *The Psalms in Israel's Worship*. 2 vols. Translated by D. R. Ap-Thomas. New York: Abingdon, 1967.

Muilenberg, James. "The Intercession of the Covenant Mediator (Exodus 33:1a, 12-17)." In *Words and Meanings* (D. Winton Thomas volume), pp. 159-181. Edited by Peter Ackroyd and B. Lindars. Cambridge: Cambridge University Press, 1968.

_____. "A Liturgy on the Triumphs of Yahweh." In *Studia Biblica et Semitica* (T. C. Vriezen *Festschrift*), pp. 233-251. Wageningen: H. Veenman & Zonen, 1966.

_____. "The Speech of Theophany." *Harvard Divinity Bulletin* 28 (1964) 33-47.

Muller, Hans-Peter. "Der Aufbau des Deboraliedes." *Vetus Testamentum* 16 (1966) 446-459.

_____. "Die Kultische Darstellung der Theophanie." *Vetus Testamentum* 14 (1964) 183-191.

Myers, Jacob M. *The Book of Judges*. In *The Interpreters' Bible*, vol. II, pp. 675-826. Edited by George A. Buttrick et al. New York: Abingdon, 1953.

Newman, Murray. *The People of the Covenant*. New York: Abingdon, 1962.

Nicholson, E. W. "The Antiquity of the Tradition in Exodus xxiv 9-11." *Vetus Testamentum* 25 (1975) 69-79.

_____. *Exodus and Sinai in History and Tradition*. Growing Points in Theology Series. Richmond: John Knox, 1973.

Nielsen, Ditlef. *Ras Šamra Mythologie und biblische Theologie*. Abhandlungen für die Kunde des Morgenlandes, XXI,4. Leipzig: Deutsche morgenländische Gesellschaft, 1936.

North, C. R. "Servant of the Lord." In *The Interpreter's Dictionary of the Bible*, vol. 4, pp. 292-294. Edited by George A. Buttrick, et al. New York: Abingdon, 1962.

Noth, Martin. *A History of Pentateuchal Traditions*. Translated by Bernhard W. Anderson. Englewood Cliffs, N.J.: Prentice-Hall, 1972.

_____. *Exodus*. Translated by J. S. Bowden. Old Testament Library. Philadelphia: Westminster, 1962.

Oppenheim: A. Leo. *Ancient Mesopotamia: Portrait of a Dead Civilization*. Chicago: University of Chicago Press, 1964.

_____. "Akkadian *pul(u)ḫ(t)u* and *melammu*," *Journal of the American Oriental Society* 63 (1943) 31-34.

_____. "The City of Assur in 714 B. C." *Journal of Ancient Near Eastern Studies* 19 (1960) 133-147.

_____. "Mesopotamian Mythology, II." *Orientalia* 17 (1948) 17-58.

Pannenberg, Wolfhart et al. *Revelation as History*. Translated by David Granskou. New York: Macmillan, 1968.

Parrot, André. "Les fouilles de Mari, première campagne (hiver 1933-1934), rapport préliminaire (second article)." *Syria*, XVI (1935) 117-140.

Pax, E. *Epiphaneia: Ein religionsgeschichtlicher Beitrag zur biblischen*

   Theologie. München: Karl Zink, 1955.

Pope, Marvin H. "The Scene on the Drinking Mug from Ugarit." In *Near Eastern Studies in Honor of William Foxwell Albright*, pp. 393-405. Edited by Hans Goedicke. Baltimore: The Johns Hopkins University Press, 1971.

Pope, Marvin H., and Tigay, Jeffrey H. "A Description of Baal." *Ugarit-Forschungen* 3 (1971) 117-130.

Porter, J. R. "The Background of Joshua III-V." *Svensk exegetisk årsbok* 36 (1971) 5-23.

_____. "The Interpretation of 2 Samuel vi and Psalm cxxxii." *Journal of Theological Studies* (New Series) 5 (1954) 161-173.

_____. *Moses and Monarchy*. Oxford: Basil Blackwell, 1963.

_____. "The Succession of Joshua." In *Proclamation and Presence* (G. Henton Davies volume), pp. 102-132. Edited by J. I. Durham and J. R. Porter. Richmond: John Knox, 1970.

Preuß, Horst Dietrich. "'. . . ich will mit dir sein!'" *Zeitschrift für die Altestamentliche Wissenschaft* 80 (1968) 139-173.

Prichard, James B., ed. *Ancient Near Eastern Texts Relating to the Old Testament*. 3rd ed. with supplement. Princeton: Princeton University Press 1969.

Rad, Gerhard von. *Old Testament Theology*. 2 vols. Translated by D. M. G. Stalker. New York: Harper & Row, 1962, 1965.

_____. "The Form-critical problem of the Hexateuch." In *The Problem of the Hexateuch and Other Essays*, pp. 1-78. Translated by E. W. T. Dicken. New York: McGraw-Hill, 1966.

_____. "The Tent and the Ark." In *The Problem of the Hexateuch and Other Essays*, pp. 103-124. Translated by E. W. T. Dicken. New York: McGraw-Hill, 1966.

Rainey, Anson F. "A Front Line Report from Amurru." *Ugarit-Forschungen* 3 (1971) 131-149.

_____. "ilānu rēşūtni lillikū!" Alter Orient und Altes Testament 22 (1973) 139-142.

Redford, Donald B. "The Literary Motif of the Exposed Child." *Numen* 14 (1967) 209-228.

Reiner, Erica. "City Bread and Bread Baked in Ashes." In *Languages and Areas* (George V. Bobrinskoy volume), pp. 116-120. Chicago: University of Chicago Press, 1967.

_____. "More Fragments of the Epic of Era: A Review Article." Review of *Das Era-Epos*, by P. F. Gössmann. *Journal of Near Eastern Studies* 17 (1958) 41-48.

Reisman, Daniel. "Ninurta's Journey to Eridu." *Journal of Cuneiform Studies* 24 (1971) 3-10.

Roberts, J. J. M. "The Davidic Origin of the Zion Tradition." *Journal of Biblical Literature* 92 (1973) 329-344.

_____. *The Earliest Semitic Pantheon: A Study of the Semitic Deities Attested in Mesopotamia before Ur III*. Baltimore: The Johns Hopkins University Press, 1972.

_____. "Erra--Scorched Earth." *Journal of Cuneiform Studies* 24 (1971) 11-16.

_____. "The Religio-Political Setting of Psalm 47." *Bulletin of the American Schools of Oriental Research* 221 (1976) 129-132.

Robertson, David A. *Linguistic Evidence in Dating Early Hebrew Poetry*. Society of Biblical Literature Dissertation Series 3. Missoula: University of Montana, 1972.

Roeder, Günther. *Die ägyptische Religion in Texten und Bildern.* 4 vols. Vol. 3: *Kult, Orakel, und Naturverehrung im alten Ägypten*. Die Bibliothek der alten Welt. Reihe der alter Orient. Zurich: Artemis, 1960.

Römer, W. H. P. "Einige Beobachtungen zur Göttin Nini(n)sina auf Grund von Quellen der Ur III-Zeit und der altbabylonischen Periode." Alter Orient und Altes Testament 1 (1969) 279-305.

Rost, Leonhard. *Die Überlieferung von der Thronnachfolge Davids*. Beiträge zur Wissenschaft vom Alten und Neuen Testament, III/6. Stuttgart: W. Kohlhammer, 1926.

_____. "Weidewechsel und altisraelitischen Festkalendar." *Zeitschrift des deutschen palästina-Vereins* 66 (1943) 205-216.

Rostovtzeff, M. I. "The Caravan-gods of Palmyra." *The Journal of Roman Studies* 22 (1932) 107-116.

Saggs, H. W. F. *The Greatness that was Babylon*. New York: Hawthorn Books, 1962; Mentor Book, 1968.

Salonen, Armas. "Prozessionswagen der babylonischen Götter." *Studia Orientalia* 13 (1946) 3-10.

Sarre, Friedrich. "Die altorientalischen Feldzeichen, mit besonderer Berucksichtigung eines unveröffentlichten Stückes." *Klio: Beiträge zur alten Geschichte* 3 (1903) 333-371.

Sasson, Jack M. "Bovine Symbolism in the Exodus Narrative." *Vetus Testamentum* 18 (1968) 381-387.

_____. "The Worship of the Golden Calf." Alter Orient und Altes Testament 22 (1973) 151-159.

_____. "Review of *The Tenth Generation* by George E. Mendenhall." *Journal of Biblical Literature* 93 (1974) 294-296.

Sauren, Herbert. "Besuchsfahrten der Götter in Sumer." *Orientalia* 38 (1969) 214-236.

Schaeffer, C. F. A. "Nouveaux témoignages de culte de El et de Baal à Ras Shamra-Ugarit et ailleurs en Syrie-Palestine." *Syria* 43 (1966) 1-19.

Schäfer, Heinrich. "Die ägyptische Königsstandarte in Kadesch am Orontes." *Sitzungsberichte der Preussischen Akademie der Wissenschaften*, Philosophisch-Historische Klasse, 1931, pp. 738-742.

_____. "Assyrische und ägyptische Feldzeichen." *Klio: Beiträge zur alten Geschichte* 6 (1906) 393-399.

Schmitt, Rainer. *Zelt und Lade als Thema alttestamentlicher Wissenschaft. Eine kritische forschungsgeschichtliche Darstellung*. Gütersloh: Gerd Mohn, 1972.

Schmidt, Werner. *Königtum Gottes in Ugarit und Israel.* Beihefte zur
  Zeitschrift für die Alttestamentliche Wissenschaft 80. Berlin:
  A. Töpelmann, 1961.

Schneider, Nikolaus. "Götterschiffe im Ur III-Reich." *Studia Orien-*
  talia 13 (1946) 1-13.

Schnutenhaus, Frank. "Das Kommen und Erscheinen Gottes im Alten Testament." *Zeitschrift für die Altestamentliche Wissenschaft* 76
  (1964) 1-21.

Schott, Albert. "Das Werden der babylonisch-assyrischen Positions-
  Astronomie." *Zeitschrift der deutschen morgenländischen Gesell-*
  schaft 88 (1934) 302-337.

Seeligmann, I. L. "A Psalm from pre-legal Times." *Vetus Testamentum*
  14 (1964) 75-92.

Seidl, U. "Göttersymbole und -attribute (mesopotamien)." In *Reallexi-*
  kon der Assyriologie und vorderasiatischen Archäologie, vol. 3,
  pp. 483-490. New York: W. de Gruyter, 1969.

van Selms, A. "CTA 32: A Prophetic Liturgy." *Ugarit-Forschungen* 3
  (1971) 235-248.

Sjöberg, A. W. "Götterreisen." In *Reallexikon der Assyriologie und*
  vorderasiatischen Archäologie, vol. 3, pp. 480-483. New York:
  W. de Gruyter, 1969.

Smith, G. A. *The Early Poetry of Israel in its Physical and Social*
  Origins. Schweich Lectures, 1910. London: Oxford University,
  1912.

von Soden, Wolfram. *Akkadisches Handwörterbuch.* 2 vols. Wiesbaden:
  Harrassowitz, 1958-1972.

_____. "Etemenanki vor Asarhaddon nach der Erzählung vom Turmbau zu
  Babel und dem Erra-Mythos." *Ugarit-Forschungen* 3 (1971) 253-
  263.

_____. "Das Problem der zeitlichen Einordnung akkadischer Literatur-
  werke." *Mitteilungen der deutschen Orient-Gesellschaft* 85 (1953)
  14-26.

Soggin, J. Alberto. "Gilgal, Passah, und Landnahme." *Vetus Testamentum*
  Supplement 15 (1966) 263-277.

Speiser, E. A. "Hurrians." In *Interpreter's Dictionary of the Bible.*
  vol. 2, pp. 664-666. Edited by George A. Buttrick. New York:
  Abingdon, 1962.

Spycket, Agnès. *Les statues de culte dans les textes mesopotamiens des*
  origines a la Ire dynastie de Babylone. Cahiers de la Revue
  biblique 9. Paris: Gabalda, 1968.

Streck, Karl Maximilian. *Assurbanipal und die letzten assyrischen Könige*
  bis zum Untergange Ninevehs. 3 Teile. Teil II: Texte. Vorderasiatische Bibliothek. Leipzig: J. C. Hinrichs, 1916.

Stummer, Friedrich. *Sumerisch-akkadische Parallelen zum Aufbau alttesta-*
  mentlicher Psalmen. Paderborn: Schöningh, 1922.

Thompson, R. Campbell. "The British Museum Excavations at Nineveh, 1931-
  32." *Annals of Archaeology and Anthropology* 20 (1933) 71-127.

_____. *The Epic of Gilgamesh: Text, Transliteration, and Notes.* Oxford: Clarendon, 1930.

_____. "The Excavations on the Temple of Nabû at Nineveh." *Archaeologia* (2nd Series) 29 (1929) 103-148.

Thompson, Thomas L. *The Historicity of the Patriarchal Narratives: The Quest for the Historical Abraham.* Beiheft zur Zeitschrift für die alttestamentliche Wissenschaft 133. Berlin: W. de Gruyter, 1974.

Thureau-Dangin, François. *Die sumerischen und akkadischen Königsinschriften.* Vorderasiatische Bibliothek, Band 1, Abteilung 1. Leipzig: Hinrichs Buchhandlung, 1907.

_____. "Une relation de la huitième campagne de Sargon." *Textes cunéiformes du Louvre,* III. Paris: Librarie P. Geuthner, 1912.

Vogt, Ernst. "Die Erzählung vom Jordanübergang." *Biblica* 46 (1965) 125-148.

Weidner, Ernst. "Assyrische Epen über die Kassiten-Kampfe." *Archiv für Orientforschung* 20 (1963) 113-116.

_____. *Die Inschriften Tukulti-Ninurtas I und seiner Nachfolger.* Archiv für Orientforschung Beiheft 12. Graz: By the author, 1959.

_____. *Politische Dokumente aus Kleinasien: Die Staatsverträge in akkadischer Sprache aus dem Archiv von Boghazköi.* Boghazköi-Studien 8. Leipzig: Hinrichs, 1923.

Weinfeld, Moshe. "'Rider of the Clouds' and 'Gatherer of the Clouds.'" *Journal of the Ancient Near Eastern Society of Columbia University* 5 (1973) 421-426.

Weiser, Artur. "Das Deboralied: Eine gattungs- und traditionsgeschichtliche Studie." *Zeitschrift für die Alttestamentliche Wissenschaft* 71 (1959) 67-97.

_____. "Die Legitimation des Königs David." *Vetus Testamentum* 16 (1966) 325-354.

_____. "Psalm 77: Ein Beitrag zur Frage nach dem Verhältnis von Kult und Heilsgeschichte." *Theologische Literaturzeitung* 72 (1947) 133-140.

_____. "Zur Frage nach den Beziehungen der Psalmen zum Kult: Die Darstellung der Theophanie in den Psalmen und im Festkult." In *Festschrift Alfred Bertholet,* pp. 513-531. Edited by W. Baumgartner et al. Tübingen: Mohr, 1950.

Westermann, Claus. *The Praise of God in the Psalms.* Translated by Keith R. Crim. Richmond: John Knox, 1965.

Wilcoxen, Jay A. "Narrative Structure and Cult Legend: A Study of Joshua 1-6." In *Transitions in Biblical Scholarship,* pp. 43-70. Edited by J. Coert Rylaarsdam. Chicago: University of Chicago Press, 1968.

Woudstra, Marten H. *The Ark of the Covenant from Conquest to Kingship.* International Library of Philosophy and Theology. Biblical and Theological Studies. Edited by J. Marcellus Kik. Philadelphia: Presbyterian and Reformed Publishing Company, 1965.

Zijl, Peter J. van. *Baal.* Alter Orient und Altes Testament 10 (1972).

285

INDEX

INDEX OF BIBLICAL CITATIONS

INDEX OF AUTHORS

Davies, G. H., 18 n.12; 116 n.30; 233

Dijk, J. J. A. van, 27; 30; 33–35; 57 n.82

Donner, H. (and Röllig, W.), 101 nn.3–5

Ebeling, E., 53 n.31; 54 n.45; 58 n.89

Eichrodt, W., 18 n.11

Eissfeldt, O., 18 n.11; 90 n.1; 155; 175 n.17; 224; 267

Falkenstein, A., 56 nn.73–74; 82; 84–86; 91 nn.20–22; 92 nn.24–28, 31–32; 93 nn.34–35, 37, 39–40, 50; 94 nn.51–52, 54–56, 58–60; 95 nn.61–62, 65; 228 n.30

Finkelstein, J. J., 60

Fisher, L. R., 114 n.15

de Fraine, J., 152 n.28

Frankena, R., 43; 57 n.80; 140 n.10

Freedman, D. N., 123; 139; 140 n.13; 141 nn.16, 19–20; 190 n.12; 191 nn.25, 28; 194 n.68; 225 n.11

Fretheim, T., 216; 226 nn.13, 16; 227 n.26; 228 n.37; 230 n.57

Fritz, V., 151 nn.11, 18

Gaster, T. H., 190 n.16; 191 n.19

Gelb, I. J., 246

Gerleman, G., 191 n.28

Globe, A., 191 nn.21, 25; 192 nn.31, 34, 36; 193 n.49; 194 n.68

Görg, M., 23 n.76; 150 nn.1–5; 151 nn.7, 15, 18; 152 n.30; 227 n.29

Gössmann, P. F., 42–43; 56 nn.68–69; 57 n.80

Gray, J., 102 n.11; 162 n.22

Grayson, A. K., 42; 54 n.47; 62; 70 n.1

Greenberg, M., 234; 237

Gross, H., 135

Gunkel, H., 2–3; 10; 18 n.11

Gurney, O. R., 57 n.84

Hallo, W. W., 27; 30–32; 50–51; 52 n.16; 54 nn.42, 47; 55 n.52; 57 n.82; 58 n.93; 91 n.23; 92 n.28; 93 n.36; 94 n.53; 103 n.21; 120; 142 n.34; 173 n.10; 185

Hanson, P. D., 23 n.73

Hay, D. M., 241 n.7

Hertzberg, H. W., 225 n.1; 228 n.31

Hoffner, H. A., 116 n.25

Hrouda, B., 90 n.3

Hruška, B., 44; 55 n.67; 56 n.69; 57 nn.79–80

Hyatt, J. P., 143 n.48; 150 n.1

Jacobsen, T., 22 n.56; 50; 54 n.41; 91 nn.23–24; 93 n.36

Jenni, E., 259 n.1

Jeremias, A., 56 n.75

Jeremias, J., 6–10; 21 n.43; 150 n.1; 191 nn.20, 26

Johnson, A. R., 162 n.30

Kapelrud, A. S., 228 n.33

Klengel, H., 54 n.47; 227 n.28

Kramer, S. N., 35; 52 n.9; 53 n.23; 94 n.58